VOL. 2 The Christian Family Guide TO MOVIES &VIDEO

VOL. 2 # The
Christian
Family
Guide
TO
MOVIES
&VIDEO

Ted Baehr

with Bruce W. Grimes and

with the help of many others
who contributed articles, excerpts, and reviews

Wolgemuth & Hyatt, Publishers, Inc.
Brentwood, Tennessee

© 1989 by Ted Baehr. Published by Wolgemuth & Hyatt Publishers, Inc., 1749 Mallory Lane, Brentwood, Tennessee 37207. All rights reserved. Published October, 1989. First Edition.
Second Printing August, 1990.

Cover photos:
Eight Men Out, © 1988 Orion Pictures, used by permission
Babbett's Feast, © 1987 Orion Pictures, used by permission
Burke And Wills, © 1987 Hemdale Pictures, used by permission

Library of Congress Cataloging-in-Publication Data

Baehr, Theodore.
    The Christian family's guide to movies and video / Ted Baehr, and Bruce Grimes
        p. cm.
    Includes bibliographical references.
    ISBN 0-943497-62-0 (v. 2) : $9.95
    1. Motion pictures—Moral and ethical aspects. 2. Motion pictures—Religious aspects—Christianity. 3. Motion pictures—Reviews. 4. Television and family. 5. Christian life.
I. Grimes, Bruce W. II. Title.
PN1995.5.B27   1989
791.43'75—dc20   89-22708
                                                          CIP

Printed in the United States of America

2 3 4 5 6 7 8 — 94 93 92 91 90

CONTENTS

ACKNOWLEDGMENTS

We especially want to thank our reviewers: Ted, Lili, Peirce, James and Robbie Baehr, Ralph Barker, Tim Berends, Ed Bez, Kay M. Black, Phil Boatwright, Doug Brewer, Harold Buchholz, Gene Burke, Byron Cherry, Gary DeMar, Evelyn Dokovic, Scott Dugan, Brandy-Brooke Egan, John Evans, Christopher Farrell, Abby Flanders, Bruce Grimes, Nancy Hanger, Rick Hight, Betty Hill, Russ Houck, Beth Humpert, Hannah and Christian Jackson, Joseph L. Kalcso, Ken Kistner, Susan Klaudt, Charlotte Knox, Laura Lindley, F. L. Lindberg, Anne Machell, Clint Manning, Katie Meyer, Dak Ming, Dr. Rick Clifton Moore, Joe Moorecraft, Marlys M. Moxley, Debi Mulligan, Bill Myers, Lauren Neal, Glennis O'Neal, David Outten, Robbie and Lisa Padgett, Benson Poy, John Raines, Stephanie L. Ray, Wendell B. Rhodes, Diane Rich, Rebecca M. Robbins, Patricia Sharp, Troy Schmidt, Bret Senft, Susanne Steward, Billy Tyler, Don Vice, Kathy Wallace, Rebecca Wayt, Richard White, and Marty Zinger.

We want to give special thanks to: Lucille Heimrich, who passed on to us the valiant work of George Heimrich at the Protestant Motion Picture Council. We are blessed to be able to use the Protestant Motion Picture Council's reviews herein.

We also want to thank the following for helping with the book: Papa Baehr (Bob Allen), Greg Clifton, Michael Hyatt, who was patient, Kathy and Charlie Meyer, Frank and Elisabeth Miller, Glynnis O'Neal, for her love, Andre and Helena Pieterse, Eric and Lisa Rice, Steve Schneider, Barry and Lisa Thiessen, Ken Wales, for his guidance, and Richard Walters, without whom our books could not be written.

Also, we want to thank the directors, advisers and friends of Good News Communications, Inc.

PREFACE

ENCORE! ENCORE!

Commend those who do right.

—1 Peter 2:14

Expose "the fruitless deeds of darkness."

—Ephesians 5:11

H ere are a few typical responses to the first volume of *The Christian Family's Guide to Movies and Video.*

Dear Sir: We have found *The Christian Family's Guide to Movies and Video, Volume I* to be so helpful in choosing suitable movies for our family of three boys (ages sixteen, thirteen and eleven), that we would very much like to subscribe to your bi-weekly publication. Your ministry and labor is greatly appreciated as we share your *Guide* and tell other families about it.

☞ ☞ ☞

Dear Good News Friends: I am so grateful for your wonderful ministry. *The Christian Family's Guide to Movies and Video, Volume 1* has helped our family so much. No longer are we caught unaware in the movie theater—we never go until we read about it first in *MovieGuide*. Also, we have been saved from the hassle of arguments from our teenager—if you say it is okay, we will let him go.

Now, my friends are calling me and saying—"What did Ted Baehr say about this movie?" I think they'd better have their own subscriptions. Would you please send one to the names listed below.

Thank you again. I do pray for your whole staff—you have to sit through a lot of muck to help us, and I pray for the Lord to protect you from the 'contamination.'

☞ ☞ ☞

Dear Sir: Where is the next edition of *The Christian Family's Guide to Movies and Video*—we need help!

☞ ☞ ☞

Back by popular demand, the second volume of the *The Christian Family's Guide to Movies and Video* contains reviews of recent movies available at your local video store, on television and on cable. This volume also contains reviews of classic films which were not reviewed in the 1988 edition.

Also, there is a chapter which highlights several excellent movies, such as *Mr. Smith Goes to Washington* and *Chariots of Fire*, which teach important biblical principles. This chapter can be used in conjunction with viewing those films to develop your discernment and enhance your spiritual growth. You will enjoy using that chapter with your family and friends to explain biblical principles through the emotive images of these fine films.

Another chapter examines the moral decay of feature films in the United States partially caused by the influence of independent and foreign films on the major studios. This chapter shows why movies decayed and how the Church could have stopped that decay. This decay is now repeating itself in television, and this chapter will show how the Church can avoid making the same mistake with TV that we made with motion pictures.

The first volume contained: hundreds of informative movie reviews; an excellent history of Westerns; a chapter on asking the right questions to help you and your family evaluate films and television programs from a biblical perspective; a brief, informative analysis of the power of movies; and, a succinct history of the Church's involvement in the movie industry. If you don't have a copy of *Volume I*, you will want to acquire one to help guide you and your family in their movie, television and video choices.

The first two chapters of this volume will review some of the helpful points found in Volume I and provide some new information to help you and yours to take every thought captive for Jesus Christ as we are commended to do in II Corinthians 10:3-6:

> For though we walk in the flesh, we do not war after the flesh: For the weapons of our warfare [are] not carnal, but mighty through God to the pulling down of strong holds; Casting down imaginations, and every high thing that exalteth itself against the knowledge of God, and bringing into captivity every thought to the obedience of Christ.

Father in Heaven, Thank You for making us part of Your Kingdom through the death and resurrection of Your Son, Jesus the Christ. Thank You for entertainment, joy, and imagination. Bless all who read this book. Grant us, as Your people, the discernment, courage, and wisdom to choose good entertainment and rebuke the bad. Help us communicate this discernment to our friends and our families. Help us most of all to lift up Your holy Name, Jesus, through the power of Your Holy Spirit. Thank You for the blessings You have bestowed upon us. Amen.

THE FOUNDATIONS OF DISCERNMENT

1

THE STUFF OF WHICH DREAMS ARE MADE

If there arises among you . . . a dreamer of dreams . . .
—Deuteronomy 13:1

Some while back, I received a copy of a letter which had been sent by a concerned Christian to the FCC commissioner:

I am writing as a *very* concerned citizen, about the decadence occurring now on the "open airwaves" of television.

This past weekend while I was changing channels, I was *stunned* when I ran across a partially nude woman on the screen. Upon further investigation, I discovered that this was not unusual for Saturday night for WATL, Channel 36, in Atlanta. The movie showing was titled *Beach Girls* and had many glimpses of partial nudity; in addition the entire theme of the movie was sexual promiscuity. The following evening the movie shown was *Private Lessons*. . . . The story was about a maid who seduces an adolescent boy and approaches him sexually many times before actually "winning him over". . . . This would be something you would expect from *Playboy* or some other cable channels. . . .

Unfortunately this wasn't cable, it was a broadcast station and it was on at 10:00 P.M. which is hardly too late for teenagers or adolescents. . . .

I believe in the freedoms we enjoy as Americans, but this is taking "freedom" too far. It is tantamount to displaying open *Playboy, Penthouse*, and other pornographic material on stores' shelves so *everyone* can see. . . .

I realize that *Private Lessons* was recently challenged in court and lost. This is a signal to me that the laws need to be changed. . . . I am tired of a few greedy media executives deciding what the country as a whole will watch. Their system of ratings does not account for the thousands of us out here who are so fed-up with their programming. . . .

I am asking you as an employee of the American people, that you would act on our behalf and move to block this kind of programming. I do not want to be afraid of turning my TV on and having to explain to my [young] son why there's a nude woman on the screen, or what those words meant.

I do not think this type of program should be broadcast so every TV set can pick it up. Please on our behalf, move to do something to "stem this tide."

Many other Christians have become very concerned about television, and rightly so. However, few Christians realize that movies lead the entertainment industry in concept, quality, and content. As movies treat a topic, so, shortly thereafter, television follows suit.

Sometimes this imitative process just involves dealing with the concept featured in the movie. Sometimes it involves making a television series from a successful movie, such as *Baby Boom*. Often, it means playing the movie on television; and, with the demise of the broadcast standards divisions of the television networks, the movie may now be broadcast on television without editing out any of the offensive elements.

Part of the reason that television follows the lead of feature films is that the motion picture is the big budget brother of the television program. In fact, movies can be thought of as the entertainment industry's research test products which shape and measure current popular American entertainment tastes. Since the same companies which produce television programs produce movies, they use the market knowledge gleaned from the theatrical release of films in their television programs.

The first volume of *The Christian Family's Guide to Movies and Video* opened with the story of a cross-country flight during which the movie shown featured partial nudity, sex, and violence. The stewardess said that the movie was restricted to adults, but in the closed environment of the plane every child could see it. As I was writing this chapter, the same thing happened again.

Powerful Emotional Images

Not only are movies pervasive in our society, but also movies and television programs are the most powerful tools of communication. They plant emotional images in our minds, direct our purchases, influence our lifestyles, and redirect our hopes and dreams.

Gary Smalley, president of Today's Family, has pointed out that altering someone's actions or attitudes has always been difficult, but in 1942 Walt Disney demonstrated the power of movies to do so. Disney's movie *Bambi* strongly affected the deer hunting industry. As Gary noted:

> The year before the film was released, deer hunting in the United States was a $9.5 million business. But when one particularly touching scene was shown—that of a yearling who sees his mother gunned down by a hunter—there was a dramatic change in men's attitudes. The following season, hunters spent only $4.1 million on tags, permits, and hunting trips![1]

We may applaud this use of the emotive power of film to save wildlife, but we cannot overlook the power of film negatively to affect people and our civilization. This power was dramatically brought to the world's attention by Dr. James Dobson's television interview with Ted Bundy just hours before Bundy was executed in Florida's electric chair. Bundy acknowledged that pornography had played a critical role in leading him to murder as many as twenty-eight young women and children. He also noted that violent criminals are "without exception . . . deeply involved with pornography" and that an "FBI study on serial homicide shows that the most common interest among serial killers is pornography."[2]

Even more disturbing was David Scott's compendium of scientific information entitled *Pornography: It's Effects on Family, Community and Culture* which showed that rapists report a preference for "soft-core" consenting sex depictions before seeking out a victim.[3] R-rated feature films often fall into this category, for example, *Fatal Attraction* and *Skin Deep*.

Dr. Victor Cline's research has shown that the exposure of randomly selected male college students to sexually suggestive theatrical movies increases their aggressive behavior towards women and decreases both male and female sensitivity to rape and the plight of the victim. After viewing this type of material a female rape victim is judged to be less injured, less worthy, and more responsible for her own plight.[4]

Furthermore, Dr. Cline has found that when the viewer is emotionally or sexually aroused, pornographic and violent images are locked into the viewer's brain by the release of the adrenal chemical called epinephrine. These images are almost impossible to erase. So conditioned, the susceptible viewer seeks aggressively to act out these images in his or her own life to fulfill the desire to experience the release which comes with arousal.[5]

The key word in Dr. Cline's findings is *susceptible*. Dr. George Gerbner at the Annenberg Institute at the University of Pennsylvania has found that the majority of people viewing a violent or sexual television program or film seem to be unaffected by what they see. Twenty percent to 30 percent of those viewing the same television program or film become paranoid, depressed, and see themselves as the victim. However, 7 percent to 11 percent of those viewing the program or film are mainlined by what they see in that they want to go out and replicate or mimic the actions of the protagonist in the program. The 1986 *Attorney General's Commission on Pornography: Final Report* detailed the conclusive research which demonstrated that sex and violence in films and on television lead to rape, child abuse, and increased divorce rates in our society.[6]

This breakdown into three groups seems to hold true whether the program in question is an advertisement selling beer, a religious program seeking conversions, or a violent program depicting rape. Most who view it will be unaffected, but a significant percentage will be mainlined in the sense that they will want a beer if they are susceptible to beer, they will convert if they are susceptible to the religious message, or they will want to rape someone if they are susceptible to that message.

The most definitive studies on this mainlining effect of television programs and movies relate to teenage suicide. Studies conducted at Columbia University and the University of California at San Diego demonstrated that movies, television programs, and even news reports on teenage suicide have caused teenage suicides to increase by 7 percent during the week following such programming.[7]

We Can't Ignore Movies

We can't ignore movies or any of the other products of the mass media. If we avoid movies in the theater, they will soon be on broadcast television.

Even those films which we would most like to avoid because they are violent or sexually suggestive have a way of confronting us. Some Christian people who have tried to protect their family have found that their children see films they shouldn't at a friend's house, in school, or somewhere else where parents have little or no control. One friend confided that he had home-schooled his children and thoroughly insulated them, only to discover that they saw an X-rated movie at a friend's house.

Insatiable

As David Puttnam, former president of Columbia Pictures and the producer of *Chariots of Fire*, noted in an interview with Bill Moyers, once people are exposed to the spectacle of blood and sex, they want more and more as they become hardened to the titillation of the last violent or sexual act which they see. Just as a drug addict, whose body becomes less and less responsive to a drug, keeps looking for the initial drug, so those who are addicted to the sex and violence in films seek increasing doses of sex and violence to appease their lust.

Since the days of the bloody sports in the Roman Coliseum, people have demanded increasing decadence with each exposure to the violation of moral taboos. Puttnam urged that someone in Hollywood must cry "Stop!" before we go the way of the Roman Empire, rotting in the juice of our own sin.[8]

When Good Men Do Nothing

Edmund Burke, the English statesman, noted two hundred years ago, "The only thing necessary for the triumph of evil is for good men to do nothing."

The way to stop the proliferation of prurient films and television programs is to follow the biblical mandate and take every thought in the mass media captive for Christ. By supporting the good and rejecting the bad, Christians can make a difference.

Denouncing movies or television programs in general is illogical since movies and television programs are merely tools of communication, just as the telephone is a tool of communication. Like other tools, the movies may be used for good or for evil.

A hammer may be used to build a church, or to hit someone. Either way that it is used, the hammer is not responsible. The *Jesus* film has brought thousands of people to Jesus Christ, while *Rambo* has influenced susceptible men to go out and machine gun innocent people in the United States and England. The medium is not the problem, rather the misuse of the medium by sinful men is the problem.

A telephone may be used to communicate between family members separated by many miles or to communicate pornography to impressionable children and susceptible adults. We are not called to stop using the telephone because someone is using it for pornography, rather we are called to redeem the medium by stopping the evil use of it.

Denial is part of the problem, because it separates the Christian's entertainment choices from his or her moral discernment. By viewing television and movies surreptitiously, Christians insulate themselves from moral judgment. Too often they believe that a violent movie or television program will not affect them, although they know that it will affect others.

Denial short circuits the ability to choose good entertainment and reject bad entertainment, and it is through this process of informed choice that we can make a difference. The movie industry needs money to survive. If we redirect our entertainment expenditures from the bad to the good, the industry will change to making more good movies and fewer bad ones.

While some films present a world view that is opposed to Christianity, others offer insight and beauty. There are many good, entertaining movies being released, such as *Stand and Deliver* and *Chariots of Fire*. Still other movies contain exploitive violence and sex, impossible for Christians to see in good conscience.

People Power

In one of his newsletters, Richard Halverson summed up the problem:

> People power! Let's face it! If people don't buy the product, it goes off the market. . . . If people don't buy, there is no profit. Forbidden fruit and people have the power to close down an undesirable operation. . . . Or prosper it!
>
> Pornography prevails on TV, films, video tapes, magazines because they are profitable. People watch them, read them, buy them. If they didn't, they would be dead.
>
> Pornography prevails because it is profitable. It is profitable because people want it. That is people power![9]

The movie industry is the cash register of the mass media. If Christians would vote for the good and against the bad at the box office, the mass media would turn from its present course toward a course which would include, not exclude, Christians. Christians are the largest group within the United States, but we have been overshadowed in influence by other groups because we have not acted according to Biblical principles in our daily lives.

Once Upon a Time . . .

The philosopher George Santayana said, "Those who cannot remember the past are condemned to repeat it."

Christians often forget that the church exerted a great influence on the entertainment industry from 1933 to 1966, which was explained in the first volume. For thirty-three years, every script was read by representatives of the Roman Catholic Church, the Southern Baptist Church, and by the Protestant Film Office.

Their job was to evaluate a movie in terms of the Motion Picture Code. If the film passed the code, it received the Motion Picture Code seal and was distributed. If it didn't pass, the theaters would not screen it.

The short form of the Motion Picture Code provided:

> The basic dignity and value of human life shall be respected and upheld. Restraint shall be exercised in portraying the taking of life.
>
> Evil, sin, crime and wrong-doing shall not be justified.
>
> Detailed and protracted acts of brutality, cruelty, physical violence, torture, and abuse, shall not be presented.

Indecent or undue exposure of the human body shall not be presented.

Illicit sex relationships shall not be justified. Intimate sex scenes violating common standards of decency shall not be portrayed. Restraint and care shall be exercised in presentations dealing with sex aberrations.

Obscene speech, gestures or movements shall not be presented. Undue profanity shall not be presented.

Religion shall not be demeaned.

Words or symbols contemptuous of racial, religious or national groups, shall not be used so as to incite bigotry or hatred.

Excessive cruelty to animals shall not be portrayed and animals shall not be treated inhumanely.[10]

In 1966, the churches voluntarily withdrew from the entertainment industry. Many media leaders bemoaned the retreat of the churches. One prophesied, "If the salt is removed from the meat, then the meat will rot." Many studio executives felt that the church involvement helped them to reach the large Christian audience in the United States and believed that Christians would avoid films which did not have the Motion Picture Code seal.

Censorship? Or Patron Sovereignty?

Patron sovereignty has traditionally been commended by Hollywood as the right of movie patrons to determine what they want to see, or avoid, by their activity at the box office. When there was talk in the 1930s about government censorship (censorship is prior restraint by the government), the movie industry requested patron sovereignty in the form of the Motion Picture Code. Throughout the life of the code and its successor, the MPAA rating system, the entertainment industry has continued to express its preference for patron sovereignty, rather than government intervention, to curb tendencies in the industry toward obscenity and violence.

When the churches retreated, the Motion Picture Association of America instituted the rating system to take the place of the code. However, this was like letting the fox guard the hen house, and the results were predictable.

Today, scripts are read by feminist, Marxist, and homosexual groups, such as the Alliance of Gay and Lesbian Artists, but not by Christians. These groups award pictures and television programs which communicate their point of view and condemn movies and television programs which disagree with their point of view. For instance, one television network had to spend hundreds of thousands of dollars to re-shoot and re-edit a television movie so that it wouldn't offend the Alliance of Gay and Lesbian Artists.

Whoever Controls the Media Controls the Culture

As a result of the influence of these anti-Biblical groups, movies and television programs have become purveyors of immorality, blasphemy, and rebellion and have influenced too many viewers to mimic the evil they see on the screen. Alan Alda noted in the movie *Sweet Liberty* that to capture an audience a movie must include the destruction of property (as in the car chase), rebellion against authority, and immoral sex. Of course, the audience he had in mind was the teenagers and young adults who flock to movies.

It is interesting to note that Karl Marx had only four goals: abolish property, abolish the family, abolish the nation, and abolish religion and morality. Marx's points concur with Alan Alda's since rebellion against authority serves the goal of abolishing the family and the nation. Since God created property rights ("Thou shalt not steal" and "Thou shalt not covet"), the family, the nation, religion, and morality, it is clear that the movie industry today, divorced from the influence of the church, is proclaiming an anti-Biblical, pro-humanist agenda which appeals to an adolescent audience and undermines the fabric of our civilization.

Already, the United States is considered by many to be the most immoral country in the world. Movies are often re-edited to include more sex and violence when released in the U.S. market. For instance, in Australia the movie *Return to Snowy River* had the hero and heroine get married, whereas when it was released in the United States the hero and heroine went off to live with each other without marriage.

The destructive power of the mass media was highlighted by the 1988 television remake of the movie *Inherit the Wind*, which dramatically retold the story of the famous Scopes "monkey" trial. Having seen the movie many years ago, I had forgotten that the Christians won the trial, but lost the battle in the media. William Jennings Bryan defeated Clarence Darrow in court, but he was defeated by the venomous anti-Christian reporting of H. L. Mencken. As in many cases since then, the Christians won the skirmish, but lost the battle to the manipulators of the mass media.

Christians should never forget the lesson of the Scopes trial: it is futile to win the trial, only to lose the battle to the power of the media. We need to claim His victory and win the war by taking every thought captive for Him.

The lesson of the Scopes trial was summarized by Dennis Peacocke when he said: "Whoever controls the language, controls the culture."

In the Scopes trial, the press controlled the language and communicated a strong anti-Christian bias. Society adopted that bias and moved against the Christians even though the Christians had the law on their side. In the same manner, if those who control the language emphasize rape, pillage, and plunder, the culture will reflect those communications.

Like the Christians involved in the Scopes trial, we often forget that there is a war raging around us. It's not the one in Nicaragua, or Mozambique, or the Persian Gulf, or even in Afghanistan. It's right here in America, and it's being fought by a cunning adversary who is aiming at you, your loved ones, and your future!

This war is not taking place on the usual battlefield. It's being fought inside men's minds. It's a spiritual war for the souls of those who constitute our civilization, and it uses the most effective weapon ever conceived: communications.

Jesus was the master of communications. His parables are as pertinent today as they were two thousand years ago. He knew the power of communications and how ideas shape civilizations. His word toppled one of the most powerful civilizations in history, the Roman Empire, and continues to transform the world today.

Though the tools of communications have changed, the words remain the same. The warfare of ideas and thoughts has exploded through the use of movies and television, revolutionizing our way of thinking. We are fighting against an enemy that is using every possible tactic to control our minds: materialism, secularism, humanism, Marxism—all the isms that conflict with Christianity.

Daily, we are besieged with an onslaught of messages that tear us apart. If not from the morning newspaper, then from the nightly news, or from cable television movies portraying a life of drugs, illicit sex, and violence.

Caring Is the Only Daring

The other side understands what is at stake. Feminist, homosexual, abortion, and communist groups have banded together as Operation Prime Time to lobby the mass media to establish an anti-Christian, antihuman agenda in the entertainment industry. An instructive article in the April 8, 1988, *Wall Street Journal* discussed the success of Norman Lear (People for the American Way/Archie Bunker) in opposing "the religious right" and promoting socialism through the mass media.[11]

An in-depth portrait, which appeared in the April, 1988, *AFA Journal*, noted that Mr. Lear has united the rich, famous, and powerful against Christianity, morality, and freedom. These dilettante revolutionaries pour millions of dollars into campaigns aimed at destroying our free society and Christianity.[12]

We cannot escape as some have tried to do. We must take a stand and resist. We are the body of Christ, and He takes His stand in us (Psalm 82:1). For too long, His body has not responded to the directions of the Head, who is Jesus Christ. Now, He is cleansing and disciplining His body.

Throughout history, God allowed His enemies to discipline His people. His enemies, the idolatrous Babylonians, carried His people into captivity (see Jeremiah). The Lord allowed Satan to scourge the righteous Job, without cause (see Job 1 and 2).

There is a growing attack on the body of Christ. The forces of the adversary are marshaled against His people, but we have been called to stand for Jesus.

Through Him, we are more than conquerors. We must repent of any apostasy and take a stand for Jesus Christ. It is critical that Christians take every thought captive in the mass media for Jesus Christ.

Why?

The question is: Why do surveys show that Christians too often go to bad movies while missing good ones? The answer is sin, peer pressure, curiosity, deceptive advertisements (especially on television), and a lack of guidance.

As an article by the columnist Cal Thomas pointed out, the rating system, based on secular values, doesn't help. In fact, the rating system, devised and determined by the Motion Picture Association of America, has failed to guide individuals in their choice of motion pictures. Often, ratings have kept people from movies which have a Biblical worldview, such as *Eleni,* or are worthwhile viewing but have restrictive ratings for political, economic, or ideological motives, such as *The Killing Fields.*

Ratings are not given for content, but to help the motion picture companies with their advertising needs. The Billy Graham organization asked for a PG-13 rating for their movie *Caught* although it had no overtly offensive elements and witnessed to Jesus Christ. Robert Redford asked for an R rating on *The Milagro Beanfield War* because he was afraid that it was too family oriented.

The elements which Christians would identify as objectionable are not the ones used to classify a movie as an R, PG, or G. In fact, some G movies are worse from a Christian perspective than some R movies. *Labyrinth* is a case in point because it promotes magical thinking which is an anathema to God. Therefore, this book applies Biblical standards to confront every aspect of a motion picture from its premise to its photography.

Some secular reviewers have a pronounced anti-Biblical, antireligious, and anti-Christian bias. Often, a critic's worldview and values are directly opposed to Christianity.

Christians need information from a Biblical perspective to make godly viewing decisions. We need to reclaim the entertainment industry by uniting to support the true, the good, and the beautiful, while opposing the immoral messages of the adversary's entertainment machine. Most of all, we need to know what is good, and what isn't.

Christians prefer wholesome movies and programs, but they have had no one to guide them and their families away from immoral entertainment toward moral, uplifting movies. *The Christian Family's Guide to Movies and Video* meets that need.

Good News

The Christian Family's Guide to Movies and Video reviews movies from a sound Biblical perspective to help you make an informed decision about which movies to see and which to avoid. Of course, some Christians choose not to watch any movies, but over two-thirds of the born-again, evangelical, and/or charismatic Christians watch what non-Christians watch. Helping these individuals choose which movies to see is an important ministry. If Christians redirect their entertainment dollars away from immoral entertainment toward moral movies, producers will take notice and produce movies and programs for us.

The Christian Family's Guide to Movies and Video gives you a detailed review of each movie, both good and bad, so you can discern which ones to see and which to avoid. More importantly, the detailed review lets you know why you would want to see or avoid a movie. Best of all, the detailed review gives you a Biblical perspective toward each movie so you can develop your Biblical worldview and discernment.

By using discernment in your family's choice of movies and entertainment, you will be casting your vote for Hollywood to make better movies, either by your financial support at the box office of good movies, or by your withholding of financial support from immoral and anti-Biblical movies. Already, leaders of two large entertainment companies have recognized the importance of *MovieGuide* and the *Christian Family's Guide to Movies and Video* and have asked us to help them understand what needs to be done to make movies and television programs more acceptable to the Christian audience. They realize that a book like this can awaken Christians to the problem and the solution. If you act on the recommendations in this book, you can make a difference.

Seek the Good, the True, and the Beautiful

A prisoner wrote us a touching letter which underlined both the problem and the solution. Like him, we need to seek guidance to protect ourselves, our families, and our friends from the adversary:

> I'm in prison in New York State. I'm forty years old and my wife, Jennifer, and I have a three-year-old son, Alexander. I am also free in our Lord and born again. . . . Recently, I was elected as an alternate to our prison liaison committee. One task of the liaison committee is to choose the movies we prisoners see. I must confess that for too long I

didn't pay much attention to movies. I felt (back then) that I was being "liberal" and "modern." After all, I used to say, it's "only" a movie. But over the years, I've grown more and more upset by what I see on the screen. This has been especially true since Alexander was born. . . .

I'm writing to request a subscription to your guide. I have two reasons: First, I'd like to read it myself and share it with Jennifer. I'd like to use it so we can choose our family entertainment more wisely. Secondly, I'd like to use it to attempt to influence the men here to alter the type of films we've been seeing.

There are more Christians in prison than you might suspect. And there are good men of other faiths, too. Maybe such men are not in the majority here (or anywhere)—but they exist. One problem all of us face is being unaware of suitable alternatives. Our prison rents videos now. Our movies are not on film—rather, they are projected on a big screen from a video projector. We can rent alternatives, but first someone must know what alternatives exist.

I believe a number of things. First, I believe that good things are contagious. That good movies on positive topics will help us all feel better. That films about loving spouses and loyalty and faith will appeal to us all. Because deep down, who wants to be brainwashed into expecting divorce and violence and lies?

But my second belief is even more certain. I believe that God works powerful good through every little effort we make. If we make the effort to find better films, I trust in the Lord to influence our hearts. . . .

I guess this is an unusual letter for you to receive. After all, those of us in prison have already been "lost" to crime! That's only an illusion. A person's location here or there isn't what determines if he's lost—it's how far we are from Jesus in our hearts that does. . . .

We appreciate this heartfelt plea and the need of prisoners throughout the United States to have guidance in their choice of videos. Movies influence audiences for good or for evil. Therefore, we desperately need to guide individuals, especially those who are prone to violence, away from movies which influence audiences negatively toward wholesome alternatives. We pray that this book will help you and them.

> "I, the LORD, have called You in righteousness,
> And will take hold of your hand;
> I will keep You and give you as a covenant to the people,
> As a light to the Gentiles,
> To open blind eyes,
> To bring out prisoners from the prison,
> Those who sit in darkness from the prison house"
> (Isaiah 42:6–7).

2

THE SLIPPERY SLOPE

The Soviet dissident Alexander Solzhenitsyn said:

> Over a half century ago, while I was still a child, I recall hearing a number of old people offer the following explanation for the great disasters that had befallen Russia: "Men have forgotten God: that is why all this has happened."
>
> Since then, I have spent well-nigh fifty years working on the history of our revolution. In the process, I have read hundreds of books, collected hundreds of personal testimonies and have contributed eight volumes of my own toward the effort of clearing away the rubble left by that upheaval. But, if I were asked today to formulate as concisely as possible the main cause of the ruinous revolution that swallowed up some sixty million of our people, I could not put it more accurately than to repeat: "Men have forgotten God: that is why all this has happened."[1]

Introduction: A Scene from the '50s

Date: 1957.

Place: A drive-in theater, suburbs of Pittsburgh, Pennsylvania.

Burned into my memory is an incident that took place over thirty years ago, when I was about ten years old. My younger brother, who was six or seven, and my second brother, who was two or three, and I witnessed a scene from a movie that has stayed with me for over three decades.

Our family regularly went to the movies, and drive-in movies were very popular then. My brother and I were in the back seat of our father's 1955 Ford, and we viewed the movie through the front windshield.

The first feature was over, and the preview started. I cannot remember what the main attractions were, but the "trailer", the promotional scenes of the next attraction, is indelibly engraved into my mind.

Two police officers were standing in a darkened street with a woman who had gone berserk. They attempted to subdue her by holding her arms, but she broke loose and began tearing her clothes off. She ripped her blouse off, and proceeded to remove her slip.

The first comment from my mother was, "What in the world is this?" Then the second feature for the evening began.

It was during the 1950s that the moral fiber of an entire entertainment industry began to unravel. This chapter will look at the entertainment trade and examine one aspect that has received little attention but which may have been one of the motivating forces influencing what the major studios began producing: the independent production of motion pictures, both domestic and foreign.

Part 1: A Short History Lesson

Controversial, provocative, and overtly lewd films have always existed.[2] Such actresses as Theda Bara, Clara Bow, and Fanny Ward were filmed in suggestive and seminude scenes in the early 1900s. The "roaring twenties" produced such notorious personalities as Fatty Arbuckle and William Desmond Taylor who were involved in a variety of scandals. As one film historian has noted, "sophisticated sex had suddenly become big box office, whether in comedies or played straight. Drinking scenes abounded in pictures, despite the recent adoption of prohibition. Divorce, seduction, the use of drugs were presented in film after film as symbols of the fashionable life."[3]

A direct result of the excesses of the films produced in the teens and twenties was the formation of the Motion Picture Production Code and the establishment of the Motion Picture Producers and Distributors of America organization, later known as the Hays Office.

For many years, the Hays Office, with the assistance of the Protestant, Roman Catholic, and Southern Baptist film offices, worked in concert with the major studios. But a portion of the industry in the United States did not submit to the various reviewing agencies. These independent producers were outside the mainstream of Hollywood. Their movies usually were "drive-in fare" and rarely were exhibited at first-run theaters, many of which were owned by the major studios.[4] Many of these independent producers, who lived primarily in California, Florida, Texas, New York, New Jersey and Chicago, would do their own bookings and project the films themselves. Some had a "carny" (carnival) background and even exhibited their films in tents just outside the city limits to avoid harassment by local authorities.

These producers made films on shoestring budgets and used whatever means to promote their product. While the studios were under the watchful eye of the Hays Office and the church, the independents slipped through the safety net of the morality reviewers. Their productions ranged from the outrageous *(2000 Maniacs)* to the bizarre *(Mondo Hollywood).*

European filmmakers thrived in the late 1950s and 60s, and the resurgence of production there brought a mixed bag to America. On one hand, novel and interesting films (then called "art films"), such as *The 400 Blows, Zorba the Greek, The Seventh Seal,* and *The Umbrellas of Cherbourg* enhanced cinema. Along with these films that were both box office and critical successes, came a wave of controversial and shocking newcomers to the American scene. Names such as Brigitte Bardot, Jeanne Moreau, Fredrico Fellini, Jean-Luc Goddard, and Roger Vadim became part of the American language; and titles such as *And God Created Woman* (1956, released in America in 1958), *491* (1964), *Blowup* (1967), and *I Am Curious—Yellow* (1968) were added to the sexually forthright films being produced by independent American producers. By the late 1960s, the major studios were pushing the outer edge on all fronts (violence, sexual, deviate behavior, etc.). The code, eliminated in 1966 and replaced in 1968 by the already existing self-regulatory body, the Motion Picture Association of America (MPAA), very quickly became the promotional and lobby office of the motion picture industry itself.

With the dawn of the television age in the 1950s, the major American film studios were caught in a vise. On one side was their adherence to the production code, on the other was the erosion of their profits by television, independent productions, and European imports.

The European filmmakers primarily explored aspects of sexuality, often with a flair or chicness. "Violence rarely offended America's censor; Sweden might snip gore from Hammer films, but only an occasional youth picture like *The Wild One* (1953) . . . stirred up some American moralistic wrath by depicting violence. In America, movies were prosecuted and censored principally for sex."[5]

While the European films still met with resistance from the censors and the church, audiences for them were growing and American film producers took this as a signal to create more and more explicit motion pictures. Thus European films played a crucial role in the development of American sexploitation films.

Part 2: Crucial Years: 1959—1972

The years 1959 through 1972 are representative of the decline of value in cinema and share firsts that help mark the beginning and end of a particular downward turn of the industry to the sensibilities of Christians. However, several key milestones prior to 1959 should be noted:

1951:

- Nudity in the Italian film *Bitter Rice*. The thighs of female star Silvana Mangano are clearly seen.
- Nude bathing sequence in *One Summer of Happiness*.
- Perversity of Edwige Feuiller in *The Game of Love*.

1952:

- U.S. Supreme Court decides that Rossellini's film *The Miracle* (where a peasant woman, who is raped, thinks she is carrying the Messiah) was not blasphemous or sacrilegious. The high court reconsiders its judgment of 1915 and decrees that the cinema should benefit from the protection of the freedom of speech of the first and fourteenth amendments.

1953:

- The success of *The Garden of Eden* encourages other independent film producers to make "nudist" films, the precursor of "nudie" films.

1956:

- The Production Code (The Hays Code) undergoes a series of revisions.
- The release of Elia Kazan's film *Baby Doll*, and its stigmatization by Cardinal Spellman.

1957:

- Court of Appeals of New York State rules that the film *The Garden of Eden* is not in violation of obscenity laws, stating that "nudity is not obscene in the eyes of the law."

The decline of morality within the film industry, and media in general, didn't occur in a vacuum. The 1960s and 70s were turbulent years in America as the foundations of American society were assaulted. A war in Vietnam, a peace movement in the United States which helped to create the hippie scene, the rapid introduction of a drug culture, bloody and destructive riots in major cities, assassinated leaders, flower power, and the sexual revolution produced radical change. Billy Graham stated in the introduction to his book *Answers to Life's Problems:*

> Those who grew up in the troubled 1960's in America were told by the media, the rock music culture, their professors at college, and their friends that the values held by their parents and grandparents were old fashioned. They threw off what they regarded as encumbrances in favor of "alternate lifestyles" and "doing your own thing." Tragically, a survey published in *Rolling Stone* magazine revealed that those who bought into the '60's counterculture mentally and believed the lies they were told, are now having trouble communicating to their own children the necessity of values they rejected.[6]

The 1960s produced a decade of questioning, rejecting, and denying Christianity. In the April 8, 1966, issue of *Time* magazine, the black glossy cover questioned in big, bold red letters: "IS GOD DEAD?"

The year 1959 was a watershed for film production with ample amounts of female nudity being displayed. Russ Meyer, an independent producer whose films were not reviewed by the MPAA, could be considered the one individual who single-handedly set off an entire wave of "nudie" filmmaking. His first major release, *The Immoral Mr. Teas*, was produced on a budget of $24,000 and grossed over $1,000,000. A tidal wave was about to happen.

By 1963, at least 150 imitations of *Mr. Teas* were available, and producers were pushing the limits of the local censors as to the amounts of flesh and titillation contained within these films. Made on shoestring budgets and with only a few days to shoot,[7] the independents cranked out the celluloid "nudies" at a dizzying rate. Usually their venue was third-rate and shabby theaters on back streets, with theater owners receiving them gladly as options for Brigitte Bardot or nudist films.[8]

Other film genres were also becoming bolder in their presentations. Biker films, beach party films, juvenile delinquency films, women in prison films, LSD films, and mondo films (named after the film *Mondo Cane*, which started this genre) were becoming more explicit as the straight sexploitation films continued to expose more flesh and in more bizarre manners.

Following Meyer's success hundreds of nudie movies were made in the early sixties. The films were made for specialty houses, formerly known as the "bump and grind" theaters, where burlesque movies,[9] the predecessor of "nudist" movies, had been the common attraction in the 1950s. Both realized that this genre was to be short lived. With the market glutted with dozens of sexploitation titles by the early sixties, producers Herschel Lewis and David Friedman turned to a genre that hadn't yet been exploited: gore.

Their first joint venture was *Scum of the Earth*, released in 1963 and labeled a "roughie."[10] Their second film, *Blood Feast*, which today is considered a cult "classic," was the breakthrough event. As David Friedman stated, "It was like going from silent films to sound. *Blood Feast* was the first to break through to legitimate, commercial theaters"[11] and started a trend.

Lewis recalled:

> With *Blood Feast*, we caught them (the censors) unawares; there was no sex in it. They were all geared for sex; they weren't geared for blood.[12]

What made *Blood Feast* so unique? This film featured a *Playboy* magazine brunette whose brains were scooped from her skull, a blonde whose tongue was pulled out while she was still alive, and other equally gruesome dismemberments.

The mid 1960s saw major changes taking place in the entertainment industry, as well as the entire makeup of American culture. The role of the church was dwindling as an influence in Hollywood, and, as this vacuum widened, the opportunity for self-regulation without the constraints of the Protestant, Baptist, and Catholic film offices looked appealing to the studios.

In 1965, the release by Allied Artists and American International Pictures of *The Pawnbroker,* starring Rod Steiger and directed by veteran Sidney Lumet, was one of the final blows to the Motion Picture Code. It featured female upper frontal nudity in a film released by a major studio and paved the way for the other major studios to become more daring in their films. The death of the code could probably be dated at September 20, 1966, when the Hays Code was replaced by a new code of self-regulation.

This event was the subject of *Mooring's Film and TV Feature Service,* a newsletter published by William H. Mooring. Released September 23, 1966, his "Hollywood in Focus—Ten Points, Not Commandments!" newsletter read:

> Jack Valenti's new, ten-point movie code is no substitute for the original Code of moral and ethical rules (and reasons) based, in the 1930's, upon the Ten Commandments. As forecast here two weeks ago it offers soothing syrup to disturbed public authorities; proposes to label certain movies: "Suggested for Mature Audiences" and then pushes on to parents the sole moral responsibility for showing to children, films no decent society would permit them to see. This form of "classification" does not even face up to an acceptable age of "maturity."
>
> Members of the Motion Picture (Producers) Association of America now subscribing to this code, request but do not attempt to bind other "independent" producers to consider or observe the code. It is not even clear that they are going to see that affiliated companies they themselves have spawned and now control, submit their films for a Code seal of approval. Some of these "affiliates" distribute, here in the USA, many of the most degrading shows, foreign and American, on the market.[13]

A number of films released from the major studios as well as from independent producers during the mid and late sixties are indicative of the end of the code. Such films as *Blowup* (1966), *Who's Afraid of Virginia Woolf* (1966), *Vixen* (1968), *Last Summer* (1969), *Woodstock* (1970), and *Myra Breckenridge* (1970) pushed into new sexual frontiers, while movies such as *Bonnie and Clyde* (1967) and *The Wild Bunch* (1969) exhibited graphic, gory violence. Horror films were beginning to mimic *Blood Feast,* with such titles as *Night of the Living Dead* (1968) and *Mark of the Devil* (1970) reaching new levels of gruesome imagery. Within the next year, two particularly brutal and outrageous films appeared. Ken Russell's *The Devils* and Stanley Kubrick's *A Clockwork Orange* could be considered landmark films in that both were X-rated in the United States, yet they appeared at first-run theaters across the country.

By 1970, the nude scene had become "almost obligatory in any film not bearing the Disney studio imprimatur."[14] More and more actresses and actors, including name stars, were performing in nude scenes, and willing to bare all for the camera.

Independent producers were also pushing hard against all censorship laws. The mid to late sixties saw films such as *Censorship in Denmark, Sex 69,* and *A History of the Blue Movie* from producer Alex DeRenzy. His *Sex 69* was actually filmed at a sex trade show in Copenhagen, and the hard-core pornography exhibited was defended by explaining that he actually took a movie camera and filmed the live sex acts and also filmed the movie screen that was actually showing the various movies. This made his film a documentary, which had fewer restrictions and could pass by the censors easier than a drama.

As DeRenzy said in an interview with *Newsweek* in 1970, "There were certain things that everyone accepted you didn't do—and we did them."[15] The introduction of hard-core scenes was the beginning of the demise of the sexploitation film pioneered by Meyer, Lewis, Friedman and others.

The book *Research #10: Incredibly Strange Movies* notes: The late 1960's were "Golden Years" for sexploitation. Sex films symbolized the new sexual freedom sweeping the country. As the Supreme Court swept away more and more restrictions, the industry flourished.[16]

As pornography came from under the counter and into selected theaters, sexploitation films began to die. San Francisco was the first city to get into hard-core on a citywide, nationally recognized basis in 1969. Within a year, most major U.S. cities were exhibiting hard-core pornography in theaters.

The ultimate blow to censoring or restricting certain film content came with the film *Deep Throat,* released in 1972. Though other films prior to this, such as *Mona* and *Smart Aleck,* were as graphic and obscene, *Deep Throat* set certain legal precedents.

Deep Throat opened in June of 1972 at the New World Theater in New York City. The first week's grosses were $33,033,[17] and within days the movie had patrons lined up in front of the theater. The film received national media coverage, but not all the reviews were favorable. Nora Ephron, writing for *Esquire,* described it as "one of the most unpleasant, disturbing films I have ever seen."

On August 17, 1972, the film was seized by the New York City Police Department, and four months later, on December 19th, the exhibitor of the film was placed on trial. This event triggered even more publicity for the film and vaulted it to grosses in excess of five million dollars. Despite the lawsuits and seizures of prints, *Deep Throat* eventually played in seventy cities and made hard-core pornography legitimate in theaters from coast to coast. It was the death knell for the sexploitation films of the sixties and ushered in an avalanche of hard-core movies into American theaters.

There had been an amazing "growth" curve of sexploitation films in the previous decade. For example, a local, subdistributor in Atlanta, Georgia, Jaco Productions, had a catalog with over four hundred titles, 90 percent of which were sexploitation of one genre or another. However, it was to be a short-lived future for these films. Some producers continued to make sexploitation films, but by 1977, this genre had virtually disappeared. *Deep Throat* had started the floodgate of pornography that has inundated the West for the past two decades.

In 1985, the annual box office at pornographic theaters alone was estimated at $500 million, approximately 10 percent of all box office receipts.[18] Today, the entire pornography industry outgrosses the entire yearly gross of all theatrical *and* home video revenues.

As studio films became bolder and bolder, the effectiveness of the MPAA rating system became watered down, until it meant virtually nothing. When first released in 1968, *The Killing of Sister George* received an X rating. Today's MPAA board would probably give the film a PG-13, if not a PG. The films *Myra Breckenridge* and *Midnight Cowboy* were originally X-rated but are now listed in video catalogues as R. The movie *Medium Cool*, released in 1969 and rated X, today has a PG attached to the video cassette. As the moral standards of not only the industry but its patrons loosened, so did the acceptance of previously unacceptable material find its way into each of the ratings categories.

The review of the 1983 movie *Scarface* in *The Motion Picture Guide* shows how pallid and anemic the rating system has become:

> This film should *not* be seen by children, nor by any intelligent viewer seeking entertainment. For sickies only. De Palma's *Scarface* was originally scheduled to receive an "X" MPAA rating, but producers argued that such a rating would hurt the film at the box office (which it should have), and it got a "hard R" rating instead (which it shouldn't have), and what is a "hard R" rating anyway, other than an "X" rating that has been bullied into something it isn't? So much for the sincerity and credibility of the MPAA rating system.[19]

This is not an isolated example.

Today, some R-rated films are being shot with additional footage added when released on video cassette. Producers know the limit regarding sex and violence, and, in order to preserve their R rating and a successful box office run, producers insert the "rougher" footage after it has been released to the theaters and cable.[20] Also, some producers are making films exclusively for the home video market, appealing to specialized prurient interests.

Part 3: The Present

Where do the movies go from here? All taboos have been violated, either in hard-core pornography or at your local theater, as evidenced in 1988 by the release of *The Last Temptation of Christ*. As audiences become more satiated with and desensitized by their current diet of films and videos, what will audiences require? At what point does a moral decision to avoid such extremes come into play, or will audiences continue to believe that "it doesn't affect me"? Will the double standard continue?

The introduction of home video (about 1984-85), cable networks (1985-86), and the shakeouts in both of these delivery systems[21] (1987-89) has mobilized the networks, which are losing much of their previous share of the market. The major networks, as well as independent television stations, are resorting to more exploitive programming, much as the film industry did twenty to thirty years ago. A fragmented marketplace, with literally hundreds of channels and multiple delivery systems, such as broadcast signals, video cassettes, cable channels, satellite receivers, and laser disks, is resorting to more and more exploitive programs to maintain profits. History is repeating itself in the electronic media.

A few recent examples exemplify this trend. CBS, which in the spring of 1989 was the lowest rated network, introduced a special for teens called "What's Alan Watching?" The opening sequence featured a young boy having his secret fantasy realized: He is able to watch a woman in a TV soap commercial take a shower and see all of her body parts. When shown from the back of the boy's head, his silhouette blocks the view of her anatomy not permitted to be shown. Viewed from the back of the TV and looking at his face, it is obvious what he is seeing.

The same week Phil Kloer, television critic for the *Atlanta Journal*, reviewed the new CBS series "Live-In":

> [It] is pure prurience, aimed squarely at people who think with their hormones rather than their brains. Its high point, if there is such a thing, is a scene in which a teenage girl watches a teenage boy undress through a peephole, then makes double entendres at the dinner table about the smallness of his sexual organ.[22]

The only taboos remaining on network television are full frontal nudity and a few remaining vulgarities and obscenities. The name of God and Christ are commonly used in a pejorative and vain manner, and events over the last year are proof that the networks are going to exploit sex and violence for profits.

Consider these recent examples: A special with host Geraldo Rivera entitled "Devil Worship: Exposing Satan's Underground" vividly described babies being skinned alive and blood-drinking rituals (NBC); In a miniseries called "Favorite Son," a woman clad only in briefs, bra, garters, and stockings, asked her sex partner to "tie me up" during a sadomasochism scene (NBC); In "Thirty Something," Elliot discusses his desire for oral sex (ABC).

The major networks are not the only ones scrambling for a larger market share by promoting sleaze. Independent television stations, which are usually located on the UHF band width from channels 13 through 83, have in recent months pushed more and more suggestive themes, violence, and nudity on the air. A friend, who is a producer at a local UHF station in Atlanta, told me that female upper nudity was becoming more evident on his station, almost always in their movie presentations and that within the next two to three years he wouldn't be surprised if total nudity were the case.

The easy availability of X-rated home videos has opened a whole, new Pandora's box that brings the specter of pornography closer to our homes and our children.

Part 4: The Future

Considering the facts in this chapter, let us forecast for the next twenty-five years.

Fact One: In only thirty-odd years we have come from the first major onslaught of "nudie" films and a pornographic industry that was still underground to where we now have in the United States alone an estimated ten to twelve billion dollar pornography industry. The absolute roughest and rawest films imaginable are available at the local theater. Softcore (and in some instances, hard-core) pornography appear on cable channels. Many video outlets have an "adult" section of soft-core and hard-core pornographic titles.

In one video store on Wilshire Boulevard in Santa Monica, California, the entire second floor is devoted to Triple-X videos. There is even a special section of amateur videos, shot by individuals and couples. In these VHS videos, the amateurs perform sex acts for the video camera, then sell the tape to video distributors for mass duplication and distribution. Hundreds of these types of videos are also listed in the classifieds in video magazines.

Fact Two: Courts, including the U.S. Supreme Court, continue to uphold the broadcaster's right to present almost any type of material. Hard-core pornography isn't suffering much from the courts either. From May 1, 1984 through July 1985, there were obscenity prosecutions in only seven of the ninety-four federal court districts. With such little incentive to prosecute hard-core porn, there is even less to go after the broadcasters.

Fact Three: The major networks have all but eliminated their broadcast standards departments (in-house censors), letting the marketplace determine the viability of content. Also, for years stations adhered to the NAB Code, the television equivalent to the Motion Picture Code. In 1988, the NAB Code was dropped.

Trends to consider: total nudity on broadcast television[23] (it's already available on cable); no ban on the use of any word, however obscene (again, available on cable); "speciality"[24] and "narrowcast" programs appealing to special interest groups[25], such as gays, lesbians, pedophiles, necrophiles, etc.; with the arrival of HDTV (High Definition Television that will have the resolution of a 35MM film) more realistic and vivid portrayals of every conceivable deviance and perversion, available first from mail-order video companies, then eventually being delivered via DBS (Satellite transmission directly to a small, compact receiving dish on everyone's roof); lock-boxes (or lock out devices) for preventing unauthorized use of video equipment and cable channel decoders. Some of these devices are electronic, requiring a secret code to be entered to access certain cable channels. When lock-boxes become a reality, the floodgates will fully open.[26] With twelve-year-old children able to access secret government and industry files via computer (known as "hacking"), are we foolish enough to think that a simple lock device will prevent young people from accessing the cable system?

The Final Report of the Attorney General's Commission on Pornography makes for disturbing reading. It paints a picture of America that is an embarrassment to the rest of the world. Yet, as grim and evil as that text may be in pointing out the major problem with pornography in this country, it may only be the tip of the iceberg if the tide doesn't turn. All indicators point to a closing gap between what we see today in the media and the excesses of hard-core pornography as detailed in the Commission's report. There are no stops, no barriers, no censors, no courts, no church to prevent this downward spiral. It will take individuals with vision and concern for America's moral health to regain the territory.

We are raising the second generation in the history of the world brought up with television. How does this mesh with the intensification of problems the West has created and endured and not sufficiently dealt with: drug use, divorce, increasing crime rates, loss of religious faith, declining institutional effectiveness (declining student test scores, as example), widespread alienation and depression, an increase of youth suicide, and a sexual revolution characterized by teen pregnancy, rampant diseases, and AIDS?

Only by recapturing the media from a Biblical perspective can this most powerful tool be used to rebuild our crumbling institutions, from the family, the center of civilization, to the governments we create to order our society.

3

DEVELOPING DISCERNMENT: ASKING THE RIGHT QUESTIONS

"They shall teach My people the difference between the holy and the unholy and cause them to discern between the unclean and the clean."

—Ezekiel 44:23

Volume 1 of *The Christian Family's Guide to Movies and Video* had a chapter on "Asking the Right Questions" about movies and television programs to help you discern the wheat from the chaff. Here is a synopsis of it to give you guidance.

Most of us tend to reduce the issues to immoral sex and violence, even though sex and violence are only important parts of the problem. The false gods and doctrines, which beckon us with deadly appeal, are often more dangerous. Too many Christians demand saccharine movies and other communications, which fail to capture an audience because they lie about the truth of man's corruption and fail God's Word because He is the Truth. On the contrary, from a Biblical perspective we must present and demand that others present the truth about reality: Evil is real; sin is real; our salvation from sin and death was bought and paid for by the real death of Jesus on the real cross. Any avoidance in any communication of the reality of sin, death, and evil ultimately discounts the reality of the gospel and cheapens the sacrifice which Jesus made for each of us.

At the same time, we must renounce the false dualism found in many movies which portrays the adversary and evil as stronger than they are, as is the case with some horror movies. These movies and many other contemporary films focus solely on evil, to such a degree that evil becomes the norm and any victory over evil is merely a temporary respite in a war which evil has won. Of course, this is the other extreme from denying the reality of evil, but it achieves the same effect, which is to diminish the importance of the death and resurrection of Jesus Christ and the sovereignty of God Almighty.

Asking the right questions about the mass media requires a solid knowledge of Scripture and a working knowledge of how movies and most television programs communicate. To go forward in the victory which Jesus has won for us and take every thought captive for Him, we must study His Word.[1]

Let us look briefly at those elements which make a motion picture work as a powerful, dramatic communication. This analysis will be framed as a series of questions to guide you in asking the right questions about the movies you, your children, or friends see, or are going to see. These questions will help you look beneath the surface of the movie to see whether you and God's Word written agree with the messages the movie is communicating.

1. What is the premise of the movie?

If you know what the premise of a movie is, then you understand the message the movie is communicating to the audience. The premise drives the story of the movie to its conclusion. Whether or not the audience is conscious of the premise, it implants the message of the audience.

The premise of a movie is an active statement of the story which the movie is telling. The story line logically proves the premise. If the premise is "good triumphs over evil," then the story line of the movie has to tell step by step in a logical manner how the good hero triumphed over the evil villain, or the movie will fail.

If the story line misses a step, or goes off on another premise, the movie will be confused and will fail to hold the attention of the audience. If the good guy really isn't good, or the bad guy really isn't bad, then the story will fail because the premise will not be able to be proved in the telling of the story.

Without a clear-cut premise, no idea is strong enough to carry a story through to a logical conclusion.[2] If there is no clear-cut premise, the characters will not live.

A badly worded or false premise will force the moviemaker[3] to fill space with irrelevant material. A movie with more than one premise is confused because it is trying to go in more than one direction at once. A premise that says too much is ambiguous, and, therefore, says nothing. A premise that does not take a position is ambivalent and, therefore, says nothing. No one premise expresses the totality of universal truth, and every premise is limiting. For example, poverty does not always lead to crime, but if the filmmaker has chosen the premise that poverty leads to crime, it does in that case, and he or she must prove it.

Here are some sample premises: God triumphs over self-centeredness (example: *Mass Appeal*); great vision brings success (*The Glen Miller Story*); God's call triumphs over bondage (*Trip to Bountiful*); ruthless ambition destroys itself (*Macbeth*).

In every movie, the premise can be found by analyzing the story. In the *Star Wars* trilogy, a good young man fights the evil Empire and wins. Good triumphs over evil is clearly the premise. Every film or television program with the premise, "good triumphs over evil," tells a different story by proving that premise in a different way. However, it is the process of proving the premise that satisfies the expectations of the audience.

2. Does the premise agree with, or conflict with, a Biblical worldview?

Once you find the premise, you need to evaluate whether or not the premise is consistent with a Biblical worldview. For example, the premise of *Labyrinth* is a strong will defeats evil, which does not square with the Christian worldview that only Jesus Christ has defeated evil and we share in His victory only through faith, which is a gift from God.

If the premise of the movie does not square with a Biblical worldview, then you need to question the message which the movie is leaving in the memory of the audience. The premise of *Impure Thoughts*, good works take us to heaven, stands in contrast to the premise of the gospel even though the movie appears to be overtly Christian in its trappings, setting, and moral statements. If good works saved us, as *Impure Thoughts* suggests, then there would have been no need for Jesus to suffer and die on the cross. As Biblical Christians, we know that we are saved by God's grace, and faith in Him is a gift from God.

It is important to understand what the premise of the movie is, so that you know how the movie is motivating and programming its audience. If the premise is known, then you can decide whether you, your children, or your friends should see it. If you have seen the movie, then knowing the premise will help you to counter any anti-Christian message which the movie might be communicating and help you to counsel and advise others.

3. How is the premise solved?

It is quite possible that the premise can agree with the Biblical worldview, but the way that premise is solved may be anti-Christian, immoral, or evil. If that is the situation, then the movie is not acceptable viewing for Christians.

In *The Dirt Bike Kid*, good triumphs over evil, but only by means of a magic bicycle. Therefore, although the premise (good triumphs over evil) agrees with the Biblical worldview, the method by which the premise is solved (magic) is anti-Biblical (God condemns magic throughout the Bible), so the movie is suspect for anyone who does not understand that all magic is evil. If the magic were a literary device to point away from the manipulation of the supernatural for personal gain toward Jesus and God's grace, as in *The Chronicles of Narnia*, then there would be a redemptive aspect to the story to make the movie acceptable.

Therefore, it is very important not only to find out what the premise is, but also to see how the premise is solved. The premise can be Biblical, while the solution is immoral or demonic.

4. What are the moral statements in the movie and do the moral statements agree or conflict with a Biblical worldview?

Besides having a premise which drives the story to its logical conclusion, many movies make one or more moral statement(s). *Echo Park* has the premise that "love triumphs over alienation" and the implicit moral statement that "the wages of sin are death." The French film *Three Men and a Cradle* (not the American remake) has the premise that "love triumphs over selfishness and the moral statements that love is a decision, hedonism is empty, and caring for others is the true meaning of life.

Sometimes the premise of a movie is anti-Christian, while the moral agrees with a Biblical worldview. For instance, we noted that the premise of *Labyrinth*, a strong will defeats evil, is contrary to the Biblical worldview; however, the major moral statement of *Labyrinth*, that possessions are worthless when compared to the value of the life of another human being, agrees totally with God's Word written.

5. Who is the hero and what kind of a role model is he?

It is not safe to assume that the heroes of today's movies are the positive role models we want for our impressionable children, family, and society. Even where the premise is positive and the morals reflect a Christian worldview, we must ask the question Is the hero compatible with the Biblical role model?

Christians cannot answer this question by listening to the complaints of secular reviewers. Instead, we need to look carefully at the character traits of the hero to see whether he or she is in fact a worthy role model.

Comparing Sylvester Stallone's three heroes, Rocky, Rambo, and Cobra, illustrates the different messages which a hero can communicate through his or her character traits in movies with basically similar premises.

Rocky is an ironic hero who loves his family, prays, and tries to do the right thing although he is reduced to using brute force to prove his worth in our complex modern society. Rocky's use of force is mitigated by the fact that he prays before each fight, demonstrating his reliance on God and not on his own prowess.

Rambo is a haunted man who strikes out at the country which abandoned him to die and tries to rescue his buddies who have suffered a similar fate. Rambo has lost faith in everyone and ends up by asking why the rug of faith was pulled out from under him by the country he loved.

Cobra is a killing machine who sets himself up as judge and jury. He is the ultimate humanist who exhibits the solipsistic heresy of titanism.

As Stallone's three heroes point out, in spite of similar premises, the hero's characteristics determine what message he or she may communicate to the viewer. Movies today are riddled with characteristics which tempt the viewer to repudiate the Truth.

To understand who the hero is, we must analyze the hero's bone structure, which for any character is the combination of all the characteristics that make up the character. We need to look at the physical characteristics, background, psychological characteristics, and religious characteristics.

6. Who is the villain?

The Motion Picture Code, no longer in force, provided that ministers of any faith should not be portrayed as villains or in a comic role, because the framers of the code felt that religion should not be ridiculed or demeaned in the minds of the viewers.

In *Poltergeist II*, the villain is a preacher. There is no swearing and no nudity in *Poltergeist II*, but it is an evil film which attacks Christianity and lifts up witchcraft and spiritism. It is a perfect example of a demonic movie.

Today, all too often, the villain is a minister or even a layman or woman of faith. This is unacceptable, because it undermines faith itself. As Christians, we need to analyze the character of the villain as well as each of the other characters in a movie to determine whether he, she, or them are being used to attack a religious, Biblical worldview. If they are being so used, then we need to protest and even boycott the movie in question.

7. How are religion, Christians, and the church portrayed?

It is also important to be aware of how religion, the church, and believers are characterized. All too often in contemporary movies, religion, individual believers, and the church are portrayed as evil, weak, insincere, obsequious, rotten, or foolish.

Although it had nothing to do with the premise, a series of morning prayer meetings were inserted into *Head Office*, which caricatured Christians as neo-Nazis who prayed with German accents for world conquest. In *Hannah and Her Sisters*, Christianity, Roman Catholicism, and even Hinduism is mocked.

We may think that mocking a false religion is okay, but the truth is that mocking false doctrines is a sign of hubris and not of a godly desire to lift up the Truth, who is Jesus the Christ. As history has constantly proven, mockery is certain to backfire.

The director of the Jewish Defense League, Irv Rueven, joined the ten thousand who picketed *The Last Temptation of Christ* in front of Universal Studios. Irv pointed out that any attack on religion must be stopped before it leads to persecution. He notes that Jesus was Jewish, and this attack on Jesus is repugnant to Jews.

Irv notes that blasphemy is unacceptable speech. Many states have laws against blasphemy. The courts have consistently upheld blasphemy laws and other laws which preserve the peace by preventing bigotry.

The Last Temptation of Christ was the most direct assault on Christianity, but what about films such as *Phantasm II*, which mocked ministers, and *Midnight Run* where Jesus' Name is taken in vain continually?

Christians have put up with this for a long time. Don't you think it is about time we take a stand regarding these movies and say to Hollywood, "We are not going to put up with this anymore"? The way to take a stand is to vote at the box office by going to good movies and avoiding bad movies.

Let's act as the body of Christ. Not just with regard to movies which are the cash register which supports the entertainment industry, but also in television, radio, newspapers, and magazines. Every medium of communication must be brought under the Headship of Jesus Christ.

8. How is the world portrayed?

The environment in which the action of a movie takes place has an immense impact on the audience. Because every communication excludes what it does not include, its omissions create powerful secondary messages in the mind of the audience.

In an Annenberg School of Communications study on "Television and Viewer Attitudes About Work,"[4] it was found that in the environment as portrayed on television, blacks and other minorities were generally excluded from prestige professions. These omissions had a profound affect on specific demographic groups; some groups were demoralized by the exclusion, and others affirmed.

The State University of New York found that the background environment of a television program has a tremendous impact on the worldview of children. One little girl said she wanted to be a doctor when she grew up. When asked why, she did not answer that she felt called to heal others; rather, she wanted a big house with a pool, a yacht, and to travel. Her image of doctors was conditioned by the environment in which they are placed on television, not by the reality of medical practice.

It is important that we are aware of how the movie is portraying the world so that we can counter any misconceptions which the film might create. Movies, television, and the electronic audio media are more prone to willful distortion of the real world than other media because such distortion is easy to effect and the tampered product appears to be the truth. Editing, close-ups, shadow shots, reverse shots, and other conscious camera techniques can distort the meaning of a scene.

Since a camera excludes everything beyond its field of view, television journalism is technically biased in its reporting, yet the viewer interprets what he or she sees as the truth. During my junior year at Dartmouth College, there was a small student take-over of the administration building to protest the war in Vietnam. In the middle of the night, the National Guard was evacuating the administration building. The landscape was empty except for a few observers, a handful of guardsmen, thirty students who occupied the building, and the television news. However, the next day on the television news, the operation looked like a major military maneuver. Frightened parents from all over the country called the college. The TV news team had shot the scene so tight in the midst of the small crowd that the event looked larger and more important than it actually was. The camera had been used to distort the real environment where the protest had taken place.

9. How is reality portrayed?

Closely related to how the world is portrayed is the question of how reality is portrayed. This question about how reality is presented in the movie is the classic ontological question, that is, how is the very nature of being, or reality, presented in the movie.

Any non-Christian ontology, or view of the nature of being, denies the gospel. For instance, classical Buddhism considers reality to be an illusion and the ultimate reality to be nonbeing, which means that there is no evil and no need for redemption.

A nominalist premise, such as the one found in the movie *Labyrinth*, causes the viewer to see the world from a perspective which is contrary to the Truth. Evil is real and denying its reality denies the need for Jesus' death on the cross to save us from our sins and from sin itself.

A Universalist worldview, such as that found in *A Passage to India* and *Enemy Mine*, suggests that Jesus is not the only way to salvation. If that were the case, then it was futile for Him to suffer a vicious death on the cross. The Universalist worldview makes a mockery of the reality of His suffering, death, and resurrection.

We need to take stock of how reality is portrayed in movies, and compare that with the Biblical perspective which will enable us to discern ontologies which conflict with His Word written. Nothing less than our faith is at stake.

10. How is evil portrayed?

Heretical doctrine can often be traced to an incorrect view of evil, as is the case with humanism which sees man as basically good and minimizes evil and sin, or new age religions like TM and EST which see evil as simply an illusion, or occultism and Satanism which view evil as strong as, if not stronger than, the ultimate good, God.

Sweet Liberty is a typical humanist movie: neither God nor evil is a factor; everything is okay, in the right context; and man's actions don't have consequences. *Big Trouble in Little China* portrays evil as having power, while good can only succeed by participating in the magic whereby the evil draws its strength. The *Star Wars* movies show evil as being simply the other side of good, with the Force, the god of *Star Wars*, being ambiguous and ambivalent.

Many movies blur the line between good and evil. Therefore, lest we be led astray by false worldviews, we must discern the manner in which evil is portrayed in a movie and counter any anti-Christian messages which may be aimed at our subconscious.

11. How is government portrayed?

This question belongs as a subset of the question, "How is the world portrayed?" However, because so many movies attack republican-democratic governments and promote socialism/communism, it behooves us to pay close attention to the way a movie portrays government. Furthermore, to really analyze what worldview is being foisted upon us by a motion picture, we should also ask, "How is private enterprise portrayed in the movie?"

Attack on legitimate governments found in some movies, such as *Salvador*, is contrary to the Biblical mandate which calls us to support the government (Romans 13:1), except in the very rare circumstances where the government has commanded Christians to act contrary to His gospel; even then, we must suffer the consequences of our disobedience unless God intervenes supernaturally as He did with Peter, and with Paul and Silas.

Salvador is a particularly coarse example of a moviemaker's attack on a legitimate democratic government aimed at promoting the goals of communist revolutionaries. The movie is so constructed that every questionable occurrence in Latin America is attributed to the government and conservative groups. The rebels, on the other hand, are a nice bunch of young people with no weapons except their good cause. The hero makes it clear that he hates all authority, especially American.

Remo Williams: The Adventure Begins is the ultimate fascist fantasy— mystical, humanistic violence used to defend the Big Brother state from unscrupulous free enterprise capitalists. The savior in this movie is an ancient Korean martial arts master who can walk on water. Unfortunately, this savior is dedicated to serving Big Brother and death. The values in this movie are inside out. Since many people become infected by the virus of the corrupt mystic statism in such movies, we need to be aware of these deceptions and prepared to rebuke them.

12. How is love portrayed?

Love is at the heart of the gospel. Not only does God manifest perfect love, for "God is love" (1 John 4:16, NIV), and God loves us beyond the scope of our imagination, "for God so loved the world that He gave His only begotten Son, that whoever believes in Him should not perish but have everlasting life" (John 3:16, NKJV), but God also calls and woos us to love Him with all our heart and all our soul and with all our strength (Deuteronomy 6:5), for "whoever lives in love, lives in God, and God in him" (1 John 4:16, NIV).

The beauty of God's love is wonderful, and yet many movies reduce love to one-night sexual relationships, tedious ordeals, eternal battles, or homosexual coupling. This desecration of love should be an anathema to His people. That is not to say that we should romanticize love; rather, it is to say that love is a decision which must be honored because it is the greatest gift we have from God, which marks us as His children, made in His image and likeness. In effect, we make the decision to love, which is a sacred commitment, and, by making the decision, we find that the object of our love is lovable and that love is both a gift from God and an attribute of the person He created us to be.

The number of movies which demean love, thereby striking at the heart of the gospel, is legion. *Skin Deep* starts out with the hero sleeping with one woman after another. The Disney movie *Ruthless People* has the husband trying to murder his wife, while the wife is trying to blackmail the husband. *Desert Hearts* has a woman who is getting a divorce find out that lesbian love is better than heterosexual love. *Accidental Tourist* supports the premise that self-indulgence is more important than love.

Many horror movies capture an audience by luring them with the thought of forbidden love, such as necrophilia, fornication with the dead, and bestiality (fornication with animals).

13. How is the family portrayed?

Closely related to how love is portrayed is how the family is portrayed in motion pictures. Unfortunately, the family is under attack. Whether today's films are lifting up homosexuality, as was the case with *The Kiss of the Spider Woman* and *Desert Hearts*, or promoting free love, as in *Down and Out in Beverly Hills* and *Hannah and Her Sisters*, or tearing down marriage, as in *Heartburn* and *The Color Purple*, they are attacking the basic building block of our society, the family, and the Will of God.

The Bible is very clear about the importance of the family, so much so that when a man and a woman are married they become one flesh (Genesis 2:24); a husband and a wife must not separate, except for the most extraordinary circumstances (Mark 10:1–12 and 1 Corinthians 7); children are a reward from the Lord (Psalm 127); children are commanded to honor their father and their mother (Exodus 20:12); and God gives blessing and inheritance not just to the individual who honors Him, but also to that person's family from generation to generation (Numbers 36).

Today in the United States, 50 percent of all marriages end in divorce. As Dr. Paul Mauger, director of the Psychological Studies Institute, has noted: "The family is the basic building block of society; therefore, a society which does not support the family will not survive." Christians must protest antifamily, anti-Christian odes to selfishness and adultery because they eat away at our culture and they mock God's Word written.

In spite of the spate of antifamily movies, there are some refreshing films which promote the family. *Eleni* is one of the best, the story of a mother who loved her children so much she died to save them from the communists during the Greek Civil War.

14. Who are the stars, the director, and the other important production people and what are their worldviews?

Not only does the bone structure of the characters effect the nature of a movie as communication, but also the creative people behind the production influence the communication. Many excellent communicators make it a point of proclaiming false gods, including sex, money, and even the forces of darkness in their movies.

Oliver Stone who wrote and directed *Salvador* inserts a sexual and a political bias into his movies. Jane Fonda interjects a political agenda into most of her movies. Ed Asner has a procommunist, prohumanist perspective. The great director, John Huston, refused to live in the United States because of his anti-American feelings. Charlton Heston has taken a very clear stand for traditional American republican democracy which is reflected in the roles which he plays. Paul Newman is very active in humanist/socialist liberal causes.

If you follow the careers of any of the stars, directors and the other important motion picture production and distribution personnel, you will quickly discern in most cases a pattern to their communications. We should note the biases of key people of the media elite to understand how those preferences influence their communications.

Those individuals involved with the *The Last Temptation of Christ* are an interesting example of personal bias. Martin Scorsese, who directed this blasphemy, was kicked out of a Catholic seminary for his illicit relationship with a young woman. Paul Schrader, who wrote the script, has a history of rebelling against the evangelical church in which he grew up. Are these men trying to take revenge on their idea of God?

Of course, there are many talented individuals who have been able to separate their work from their personal preferences and prejudices. Horton Foote, who wrote the scripts for *To Kill a Mockingbird, Tender Mercies,* and *Trip to Bountiful,* is a great screen writer and many of his movies have a solid, Biblical Christian worldview. However, Horton himself is not a Christian; rather, he is a Christian Scientist, whose theology is distinctly different from Biblical Christianity.

Horton states with conviction: "I don't think that a real artist is a proselytizer. An artist tries to be honest and truthful. My characters are involved with the problems of faith and how to proceed in life. However, I don't think that many films are based on life—they are proselytizing."[5]

15. Is there any redeeming value?

It is very rare that a film can have a redemptive element which will transcend the negative elements. Some children's films, such as *The Dirt Bike Kid,* do transcend their negative parts because those parts are treated lightly, with deference and a lack of conviction as storytelling devices, while the redemptive element of love, or courage, or integrity is emphasized. If a motion picture does transcend its parts because of some redemptive element, then we need to be aware of the good and the bad in the movie so that we can discuss it honestly and rebut any negative elements which may be detrimental to our Christian worldview.

16. Would you be embarrassed to sit through the movie with your parents or your children—or Jesus?

Probably the most important question to ask ourselves is, "Would we be embarrassed to sit through the movie with our parents and/or our children and/or Jesus, the Christ?" When we are alone, or with a friend, we can deceive ourselves regarding the true nature of a motion picture (or a television program); however, if we shift our perspective, then the faults of the film will stand out clearly. If we ignore the faults in a movie we are watching, then we will slowly be conditioned to condone, if not accept, a non-Christian point of view.

☞ ☞ ☞

A Biblical Worldview

After the first volume of *The Christian Family's Guide to Movies and Video* was published, a reader, Dr. Rick Clifton Moore, sent a written critique of some of the movies he had seen. His analyses of these popular movies is instructive. I include one of them so you can see how looking at films and television programs from a Biblical perspective can make a difference:

As I left [the theater], it was difficult to judge the afternoon's experience as anything but positive. Even if the film [*Short Circuit 2*] will never be considered a classic, the audience seemed to think it well worth the price of admission. . . . Moreover, the entertainment fare was relatively free of gratuitous sex and violence. With the exception of some unneeded profanity in the script, there was little with which to disagree.

Yet, as a Christian, I left the theater with a slight sense of malaise. Though the afternoon seemed to offer "good clean fun" to a largely family-oriented audience, I could not help but feel there was a problem. What bothered me was a subtle message left by the film that there was no difference between man and machine, or even man and animal.

At the risk of being seen as a wet blanket, I offer the following observations.

Motion pictures shape us and mold us. They affect the way we think, the way we act, the way we dress, the way we talk.

This much is nearly taken for granted anymore. We have seen John Travolta lead a nation into a disco craze (albeit short lived). We have seen torn sweatshirts become a fashion boon after Jennifer Beals' modeling in *Flashdance*. Certainly, we all heard far too many "E.T. phone home" jokes.

On a more negative note, most Americans have come to the realization that you are what you watch, regardless of what their film diet might actually be. They have heard enough social scientists discuss the problems of the medium that they can offer a conditioned response that there is a rusted side to the silver screen.

Yet, at the same time, most of us do not take into account the subtle and insidious means by which the moving image can transform us. The "instant" and rather harmless ways in which we are moved by the movies are quite manifest and easily discernible. The more latent forms of such change are often difficult to grasp.

The point is, motion pictures (in conjunction with an entourage of other cultural products) affect us over time, with subdued, repeated images which by no means stun us into immediate change.

Instead, they slowly and deftly mold the way we think, reifying thoughts that may have already been in agreement with them, and gradually seducing us in areas where we might have been at variance. This should be an area of urgent concern for the Church. Like the wider population, Christians have long realized that movies, though entertainment, have wider effects than immediate laughter or tears. Yet, following the norm of the larger culture in which it is situated, the church has often resigned itself to evaluating films largely on the basis of quantifiable visual factors such as sexual material and acts of violence. While it is important to keep an eye on such content, it is equally important to note the ways in which such subjects are presented as well as some of the other subtle messages which are less easily quantifiable.

. . . there was little in *Short Circuit 2* which resembles the material that traditionally incites the rage of Christians. . . . It is doubtful that many would see anything negative. . . .

Yet, the negative effects of *Short Circuit 2* come with other films which might reinforce its subtle message which blurs the lines between humanity and inhumanity. More than a film about a robot out to have a good time, *Short Circuit 2* is a statement about a particular way of seeing the world. Our discernment must not be limited to this individual film, but to others which in collaboration might add to its confusing image. . . .

Short Circuit tells the story of Johnny Five in relation to his creators, Newton Crosby and Ben Javeri, two engineers who work for NOVA, an Oregon high tech firm involved in defense contracts. Most highly honored among their productions is a line of robots which are programmed to do military dirty work. One of these robots, "Number Five," is struck by lightning while being recharged, and through a series of mishaps is carried out with the trash of the defense plant. Once outside the gates, he runs free.

Number Five soon finds himself at the home of a young woman named Stephanie, an animal lover who mistakes him for an alien from another planet. After getting over her initial fear of him, Stephanie begins treating Five like one of her homeless animals, inviting him into the house. There, he begins taking in "input", voraciously consuming any information he can find. Apparently, as a result of his freak accident, Number Five has developed his own brain. He now wants to fill it.

Yet, the manufacturers of the robot are not about to lose their multi-million dollar investment. They soon locate the errant automaton and try to bring it back to the factory. Meanwhile, Number Five has convinced Stephanie that, though not an alien, he is alive, a thinking being just like her. Seeing him as just another animal, she decides to protect him, harboring him from his creators.

After several unsuccessful attempts to retrieve the robot, the high tech firm decides to send out Crosby and Javeri, hoping they can overcome the *Short Circuit* which caused the problems. Stephanie, however, soon persuades the two scientists that Five is alive, and they join her in her efforts to protect him. An obligatory meeting occurs in which the other robots are programmed to destroy Number Five. Escaping this danger, Crosby, Stephanie and Number Five retreat to Montana, presumably to live happily ever after.

In many ways, this seems a typical Hollywood ending. Man and woman, riding off into the sunset (to Montana, no less!). Yet, with them they do not take the man's horse, they take a being that has convinced them that he is on par with themselves. The most disturbing thing about *Short Circuit* is the subtle way in which this third character is developed and presented. Number Five, who begins as a mere assemblage of steel and wire, soon develops a full-blown personality. The transition is not merely from material object to living being, but from material object to human being, or at least material object on par with human being.

The point is, little distinction is made in the film between animal and human. Stephanie's point of view (that humans are merely one more animal in the kingdom) is in the end shown to be most reasonable. In explaining her beliefs about Number Five to Crosby, for example, she states, "Number Five is alive. I mean, he is really alive like you and me."

As the film presents the case, Five is a machine that thinks. Humans are also machines that think. What differences could exist between them?

Short Circuit . . . [begins] with a rather archetypal event. That event is the "creation" of Johnny Five. When he is tethered to an adaptor for refueling, he is struck by lightning, suddenly giving him life.

The similarities with various theories of origins are obvious. A pool of non-living matter is altered by high amounts of energy to become living. This is the scenario by which many explain the origin of living matter on our planet, when lightning struck the "primordial soup" causing organic molecules to develop from inorganic. Certainly, this is not the image we receive consciously when we view this scene, but the message is there and reflects a primary sensation in our contemporary culture.

In addition, evolutionary theory can be seen to be subtly reinforced in the very title. . . . What occurs when lightning strikes the robot is a short circuit. . . .

In the case of Number Five . . . the result of the malfunction is a better, more complex machine than before the accident. The parallels here are clear. Evolutionary theorist explains that higher organisms evolved from lower organisms by virtue of the fact that lower organisms experienced mutations.

The difficulty this poses for the layman is that we note "mutations" all around us and none of them seems to be beneficial. In fact, most seem to be fatal. We have difficulty understanding how a mutation can produce a complex sense such as sight, or a brain. It is little wonder that one of the books Johnny Five reads at a local bookstore is *The Origin of the Species*. There are clear difficulties involved when we take for granted that all forms of life sprang from an early catastrophic occurrence.

The reader might argue that I am making a mountain out of a molehill here . . . Yet, there comes a point when we must look even at entertainment as a reflection and a projection of the broader culture in which we live. I am suggesting that the problematic element of . . . [this film] is also a problematic element of our society as a whole. We cannot look at one out of the context of the other.

One need only look at a recent edition of any newspaper to see that this is the case. These films indicate a struggle within our culture to discern between human and non-human, and an inability to make discriminating choices based on such discernment.

In the daily news, we note the same challenge. We spend millions of dollars protecting certain species of wildlife or protesting mistreatment of lab animals (not unworthy objectives in themselves). Yet, at the same time we stand quietly by while in our country millions of fetuses (baby humans) are aborted over the years. Beyond a doubt, the church needs to be concerned with clarifying the distinction between human and animal.

It is this need which sparks the necessity of looking more closely at [such] films. . . . The trouble arises not only from the imagery itself, but the logical conclusions of it. . . . When humankind comes to the realization that it has gradually arisen from all the other creatures on earth, where do reason and morality come into play?

If audiences are better trained to be critical viewers, they can gain from messages that challenge them. It is possible in this instance for example, that many who never considered God's creation of us and our own humanity to contemplate these subjects further. Or, it may cause some to question previous orientations which they have taken in these areas. Many today take a theistic approach to Darwin's theories on human origins, believing that human evolution occurred just as the textbooks explain it. They merely posit that God was in control. The materials discussed here suggest some of the difficulties of such a stand and call us to reconsider. If, in fact, God created humans by a gradual process of evolution (from one-celled organism to primate) when did God's creation become "man"? . . . I am not suggesting that [. . . this film is] inherently dangerous and should be avoided at all cost. . . . On the other hand, I am suggesting that Christians begin looking very closely at what they and their children are watching and reading. This essay should predominantly lead the reader to further consider the subtle ways in which seemingly innocuous material molds our thinking. This realization could lead to any number of actions. First, Christians can discuss with other Christians the films they have seen. Often, it is difficult to determine subtle messages in films without explaining elements of the motion picture to others. This is especially important for Christian parents to consider. Stimulating children to interact with their cinematic experience rather than simply absorbing it is crucial. Secondly, Christians can support films which promote messages with which they agree. Hollywood's greatest incentive is to make a profit. When we tell friends about a worthwhile film and they go to see it, it increases the probability that studios will produce similar films in the future. Finally, filmmakers who claim to follow Christ can strive to carefully examine their products to examine what they are actually saying.[6]

If nothing else, this essay should demonstrate that films often "teach" us more than we would ever think they do. With that in mind, both student and teacher should pay much more careful attention. We thank Rick for that excellent critique and hope that you will contact us with similar comments.

4

PARABLES

The disciples came to Him and asked, "Why do you speak to the people in parables?"

He replied, "The knowledge of the secrets of the kingdom of heaven has been given to you, but not to them. Blessed are your eyes because they see, and your ears because they hear."

Jesus spoke all these things to the crowd in parables; He did not say anything to them without using a parable. So was fulfilled what was spoken through the prophet:

"I will open my mouth in parables, I will utter things hidden since the creation of the world."

—Matthew 13:10-11, 16, 34-35 (NIV)

Jesus used parables to communicate God's will to the disciples and the multitudes who gathered around Him. For good or evil, movies are powerful visual parables that communicate either Biblical principles or ungodly thoughts and desires.

At this point in history, movies and television are the most powerful tools of communication. Campus Crusade has used the *Jesus* film to introduce thousands of people throughout the world to Jesus Christ. Movies like *Chariots of Fire, Ben Hur, The Ten Commandments,* and *Jesus of Nazareth* have brought people to Christ and into the ministry. When *A Man Called Peter* played in theaters throughout the United States, many young men went into the ministry. Clearly, movies change lives.

The power of film was brought home to me with great clarity when

I was teaching Christians in India how to communicate the gospel through the media. One of the instructors, as part of a class on film appreciation, showed Sergei Eisenstein's *Battleship Potemkin*, commenting that it was an innocuous film. In fact, *Battleship Potemkin* is a well-executed piece of communist propaganda which states its premise clearly: rebellion brings eternal glory. The church and the state are mocked, and the solution to man's problems, however trivial, is revolution. When asked what was the predominant feeling they had after seeing the movie, the Indian students all said that they wanted to join the revolution. It took much discussion before they revised their point of view to see this emotive movie through the Bible, and thus to see that Jesus, not revolution, is the answer.

Christians need to develop Biblical discernment with respect to the mass media. We need to look at the world through the Bible, and not look at the Bible through the world. This chapter will help you to develop that discernment and acquire a Biblical perspective toward the world of entertainment and to help you defend yourself and your family against the lies and other wiles of the adversary.

We will look at a few films as parables—storytelling tools which you can use to communicate Biblical principles to your family, friends, and Sunday school classes. These movies are entertaining feature films that people enjoy watching. Most are classics that have stood the test of time. These examples are models upon which you can expand. These movies are available from your local video store, or from *MovieGuide* (see page 415 for our address).

The movies are organized to be used in the sequence they are presented in the book. In the first few examples, frequent Biblical references are made to help you see the Biblical principles in the films. Thereafter, the Biblical references are less frequent, so your answers to the "Questions for Discussion" will help you to discern the Biblical principles suggested in each example.

Several Christian writers have generously contributed to this chapter by picking their favorite films and analyzing their Biblical impact. (I would especially like to acknowledge Gary DeMar, Bruce Grimes, Beth Humpert, David Outten, and Benson Poy.) Reviews of each of these films appear in the second section of this book. We thank each contributor and would like to receive any feedback that you might have.

It's a Wonderful Life
Analysis by David Outten

A perennial Christmas season favorite, *It's a Wonderful Life*, has its flaws, such as implying that angels are dead men who, once in heaven, earn promotions by helping out those still alive on earth. However, with this flaw explained, there is much to recommend in the film.

It is a rare film that takes prayer seriously, and, in this one, God answers prayer. As the film opens on Christmas Eve, we hear the voices of the people of the town of Bedford Falls praying to God, petitioning the Lord for help in their lives and in the life of George Bailey. Thus, the film immediately establishes that most people pray and God hears those prayers. As in real life, God does not always answer prayer in a manner expected by the person who prayed, but often the way He answers teaches a valuable lesson. This is certainly the case with George Bailey, played by James Stewart.

In the story, George Bailey gives up his dreams of becoming an architect and traveling the world in order to see a savings and loan association that his father started continue to offer affordable loans in a small American town. George believes that people sometimes need a little help to get started, and his confidence in each borrower has proved correct many times. Again and again George Bailey puts aside his own desires to help others and to stand for what he believes is right.

In fact, as a young boy, George saves his younger brother from drowning when his brother falls through a hole in a frozen lake. As a result, he partially loses his hearing.

George manifests several Biblical virtues: sacrificing himself for others, giving to those who asked as Jesus commanded, standing up for the rights of the townspeople against the selfish Mr. Potter who wants to control everything and everyone in Bedford Falls.

However, although George has put the welfare of others before his own, he has not put God first in his life. The climax comes when eight thousand dollars of the savings and loan's money is lost by George's uncle, and George finds his world falling apart. Faced with jail and disgrace, he considers taking his life so that his insurance policy will cover the missing funds.

At this point, George calls out to God for help. As he sits at a bar, he whispers into his hands: "Dear Father in Heaven, I'm not a praying man, but . . . show me the way. I'm at the end of my rope. Show me the way, God."

George stops trying to do the right thing in his own power, and, for the first time, he acknowledges his powerlessness by seeking God.

Help comes in the form of an unorthodox angel named Clarence. Feeling hopeless, helpless, and worthless, George tells Clarence he wishes he had never been born.

To help George see his situation in perspective, Clarence lets him see what his town would be like if he had never been born. This supernatural plot device is an effective means of revealing to George God's purpose for his life. George learns that his home town and the lives of the people whom he loves would have been a disaster without him, for he gave sacrificially to all who needed help.

One of the strengths of the film is that George Bailey is not portrayed as so good that he appears unrealistic. He is sometimes mischievous. He is sorely tempted to satisfy his longings; struggles when under pressure; is capable of unkind treatment of his wife, his children, and a schoolteacher. However, when George is faced with a choice to do what he wants or what he believes is right, George choses what is right.

Frank Capra's *It's a Wonderful Life* inspires its audience to be unselfish. Capra helps his audience to see that doing what is right in your work and to others really does affect the world around you.

Questions for Discussion:

1. Why is it so important that the people of Bedford Falls are praying as the movie opens?
2. Does God hear their prayers?
3. What does the Bible teach us about prayer?
4. How is prayer treated in the media, in schools, and in our society today?
5. How do you think George wanted his prayer answered?
6. How did God answer George's prayer? Why?
7. How did George sacrifice himself for others?
8. Why is humility important?
9. How does George help others?
10. How does George stand up for what is right?
11. How does God want us to stand for what is right?
12. Why is it important to put God first?
13. How does George put God first?
14. Why is it important that God created each of us for a specific purpose?
15. For what purpose did God create George Bailey?
16. Why is it important that George is not perfect?
17. What does *It's a Wonderful Life* teach about how we should then live?
18. How was George Bailey the salt of the earth?
19. How does being salt make this a wonderful life?
20. In what way does this film show that life is wonderful?
21. What is the premise of *It's a Wonderful Life?* Do you agree with it?

Mr. Smith Goes to Washington
Analysis by David Outten

Another Capra film for use in a discussion of Biblical principles is *Mr. Smith Goes to Washington.* James Stewart plays Jefferson Smith, a young patriot sent to Congress to finish out the term of a senator who died a few months before his term was to expire.

Smith is a wide-eyed innocent completely unfamiliar with how the Senate works. The other senator from his state is a man Smith has always admired but who is actually involved in graft and is a pawn of a big party boss back home.

The party bosses expect Smith to march to the orders of the elder senator and to enjoy a few months of sightseeing in Washington, but, the honest guy winds up bucking the bosses. It's truth and justice against lies and the power of money and politics. It's David versus Goliath, and it's a joy to watch.

Christians watching this film will appreciate that Smith reads to the Senate from the Bible. Also, when the going gets tough, there is a scene where Smith's secretary asks for prayer on Smith's behalf. This film also illustrates the fact that scoundrels may appear to have the upper hand at any given moment, but nothing will ever revoke the principles upon which God established the universe.

Mr. Smith Goes to Washington makes clear the need for men of integrity in a system rife with graft. Christians should be encouraged by this film to be salt in the political arena. As God said: "Righteousness exalts a nation, But sin is a reproach to any people" (Proverbs 14:34).

Questions for Discussion:

1. Why is it important that Mr. Smith read to the Senate from the Bible?
2. Why is it important that the secretary asks for prayer on Smith's behalf?
3. Why is it that scoundrels will never triumph?
4. Who has triumphed?
5. What difference does that triumph make to you?
6. Why should God's people be involved in government?
7. Discuss those stories in the Bible which show that a righteous man does make a difference.
8. What is the premise of *Mr. Smith Goes to Washington*? Do you agree with it?

Chariots of Fire
Analysis by David Outten

A more recent film that can be used effectively for Biblical instruction is *Chariots of Fire*.

This is the true story of two Olympic gold medal winners in the 1924 Paris Olympics. One is a young Jewish man, Harold Abrahams, who is extremely sensitive to rejection by his peers at an elite Cambridge University college. He approaches the Olympics in an attempt to prove to the world that he is every bit as good as, if not better than, his peers, in complete disobedience to the law God gave the people of Israel and those who are called by His Name.

The second man is Eric Liddell, a Scottish Christian who runs for the glory of Jesus and who believes that Christ is his trainer. Liddell sees his running ability as a gift from God to be nurtured and used for God's glory. Liddell's goal in life is to become a missionary.

The contrast in attitude between the two runners is striking. Both work hard to develop their skill, but while Liddell finds joy in running, Abrahams finds a selfish pride. When Liddell beats Abrahams in a race, Abrahams is almost destroyed.

The climax of the film occurs at the Olympics where Liddell decides not to run in his best race for which he has prepared so hard because the heats leading up to the final race are scheduled on Sunday. It is gratifying to see a film where a faithful decision to obey God is portrayed as honorable.

Abrahams wins his Olympic gold medal, but finds his victory to be empty and winds up in a bar to "celebrate." Liddell, given a chance to run in a longer race, wins the gold and has twice the pleasure of a victory. Because of his willingness to give up his chance at victory in his best event, he has brought twice the glory to God.

A note at the end of the film says Liddell died as a missionary in a Japanese internment camp near the end of World War II.

One of the lessons of this film is that God gives each person special gifts and abilities, and great joy comes in using one's gifts for the glory of God, rather than for the glorification of oneself. Another lesson is that faithfulness to God's principles, even when it appears foolish to the world, will bring its own reward from God: "The wicked man does deceptive work, But to him who sows righteousness will be a sure reward" (Proverbs 11:18).

Questions for Discussion:

1. What is wrong with Harold's attitude?
2. Why is it important to do all to the glory of God?
3. In what way is Christ our Teacher?
4. God gives gifts, talents, and motivations. What is the difference among these? Discuss which gifts, talents, and motivations He has given you.
5. How does envy rot the bones?
6. Should Liddell have refused to run on Sunday? What difference did it make?
7. How do films and television programs usually portray adherence to God's law? Cite examples.
8. How did Liddell's running bring glory to God?
9. What insight did Eric's decision not to run on Sunday give you about his character?
10. Why should we retain the place in life that God has assigned to us?
11. Does God ever call us to a new place in life? How do we know? Give examples from the Bible.
12. What kind of reward does faithfulness to God's Word entail?

13. How was this movie an answer to Eric Liddell's prayer?
14. What is the premise of *Chariots of Fire?* Do you agree with it?

Sergeant York
Analysis by Beth Humpert and Benson Poy

Sergeant York (1941) is based on the diary of Alvin York, the most decorated soldier in World War I. The story begins in the mountains of East Tennessee before the war.

Mrs. York expresses concern to the local pastor about her wayward son, Alvin, who works hard during the day but gets drunk at night. The pastor (Walter Brennan) confronts Alvin (Gary Cooper), as he plows a cornfield, "It 'pears to me it's planned a fellow's gotta have his roots in something outside himself." Alvin's immediate response is, "Ain't no use in a fellow goin' out lookin' for religion. It's just gotta come to a fellow." The pastor's reply proves to be prophetic, "It'll come. Maybe slow like the way daylight comes and maybe in a flash like a bolt of lighting, when you ain't even expecting it."

The Biblical principles here are instructive. Our roots support us and nourish us. We are either rooted in the world or in God, and the parable of the sower underlines this Biblical principle. If we are rooted in the world, we will manifest the ways of the world; whereas if we are rooted in God, we will manifest His Will. Also, it is God who saves us, not we ourselves.

Complications develop as Alvin despairs because of his failed efforts to buy bottom land in order to win a young lady's affections. After drinking all evening, Alvin rides his mule through the rain, as he contemplates killing his rival, Zed. Unexpectedly, lightning knocks him off his mount. His gun is destroyed, but Alvin and his mule survive. As Alvin realizes he could have been killed, he looks toward the sky and is suddenly sober.

Alvin leads his mule through the storm until he sees the country church. He attempts to walk past, but is drawn inside. As he enters, Pastor Pyle leads the congregation in singing "Give Me That Old-Time Religion." Alvin begins to sing along, "It's good enough for me." He slowly walks to the front of the church, kneels down, and shakes the pastor's hand while his family and friends surround him.

Alvin's behavior changes drastically after his conversion. The next scene shows results of his new life when he asks forgiveness from the man he had planned to murder, "I'm askin' your forgiveness for flarin' up at you. It were Satan speakin' outa me." The rest of the film shows Alvin's growth as a Christian and the manner in which he deals with conflicts of faith, especially related to pacifism and war.

Alvin is a hero, yet he is touchable. The viewer gets to see Alvin's humanity played out both before and after his conversion to Christ.

Initially he is a drunkard and a troublemaker, yet he is lovable because of his good intentions.

After his conversion Alvin is the same good-hearted fellow but is able to respond differently in situations which would have defeated him before. He also has a new source of practical wisdom, the Bible. He is deeply troubled about fighting in the war because he cannot reconcile the Bible's teaching against killing with participating in a war to protect his country. Before making his final decision about filing for conscientious objector status, Alvin spends time reading the Bible and being alone with God on the mountain. There it becomes clear what God wants him to do: "All Scripture is given by inspiration of God, and is profitable for doctrine, for reproof, for correction, for instruction in righteousness, that the man of God may be complete, thoroughly equipped for every good work" (2 Timothy 3:16–17).

Questions for Discussion:

1. Why did the pastor say that every one has to have his roots in something outside himself?
2. Where are your roots?
3. Was Alvin right when he said that you can't go out looking for religion, but "it's just gotta come to a fellow"?
4. How did God get Alvin's attention? How did He get your attention?
5. How does Alvin's behavior change drastically after conversion?
6. Why is forgiveness so important?
7. Why is it so important that the pastor be a part of the community?
8. What does Alvin find by studying the Scriptures?
9. Why is Alvin's Bible study so important?

A Man for All Seasons
Analysis by Beth Humpert

A Man for All Seasons (1966) is a film in which the protagonist is a man of faith, conviction, and courage. Directed by Fred Zinneman, it was written by Robert Bolt from his own play. The film relates the events that led to the martyrdom of Thomas More (Paul Scofield), who was canonized as a saint in the Roman Catholic Church in 1935.

The main conflict of the story concerns King Henry VIII's decision to marry Anne Boleyn and the pressure he puts on his officials, including More, to accept and approve his divorce from the queen and his remarriage to Anne. In good conscience, Thomas cannot and does not accept the king's plans, for those plans disagree with God's will.

More's faith affects his morals and guides his decisions, at the cost of his political career and eventually his life. In this respect, he follows in the footsteps of the apostles who did not rebel against authority, but accepted the human consequences (even unto death) of their decisions to obey God when God's law conflicted with man's.

The screenwriter reveals More's incarnational character through his relationships as well as by his decisions. More is a lawyer and judge who is known for his fairness in the courts. He shows kindness and generosity to the boatmen who ferry him from the court to his country home. However, More has little sympathy for those who forfeit personal integrity for advancement in government.

A man of faith, he prays with his wife and daughter before he leaves home to see the chancellor. His prayer is unpretentious, simple, and even humorous.

More displays Christlike virtues in his personal and business relationships. His wife and daughter treat him with love and respect, and his friend Norfolk admires him, although he does not always understand More's personal convictions. The king regards More as a man who will tell the truth, but Henry refuses to be dissuaded from marrying Anne, and he does not let Sir Thomas stand in his way.

Though More is a strong character, he is also vulnerable. Through the persistence of his enemies at court, More is put in prison where, over a period of time, he grows weaker physically. In the scene where More says goodbye to his family, he breaks down and weeps. In his time of fear and pain, More proves he is made of the same flesh as anyone else; but even though he knows death awaits him, Sir Thomas remains true to his faith so that in the end: "When this corruptible has put on incorruption, and this mortal has put on immortality, then shall be brought to pass the saying that is written: 'Death is swallowed up in victory.' O Death, where is your sting? O Hades, where is your victory?" (1 Corinthians 15:54-55).

Questions for Discussion:

1. Is Thomas right to stand up to the king?
2. What is God's view of divorce?
3. Isn't Thomas called to obey all authority?
4. Is Thomas rebellious? Why not?
5. How does the screenwriter show Thomas's faith?
6. How are we as Christians to react to those who disobey God?
7. How does Thomas model a Biblical approach to prayer?
8. Why doesn't Henry listen to Thomas More?
9. Does Thomas's vulnerability negate his faith?
10. Does Thomas triumph in the end?
11. What is the premise of *A Man for All Seasons*? Do you agree with it?

Forbidden Planet
Analysis by Bruce Grimes

In *Forbidden Planet*, a classic science fiction film, Dr. Morbius (played by Walter Pidgeon) and his daughter Altaira (played by Anne Francis) are living on a distant planet where they were space-shipwrecked many years before. They are visited by United Planets' Cruiser C-57-D, on a mission from Earth to track down the expedition that landed on Altair 4 twenty years earlier and has not been heard from since.

The commander of the ship, requesting to land, is told sternly by Dr. Morbius, one of the scientists of the original expedition, to turn back. Refusing, he sets the cruiser down on the dusty, desert-like terrain of the planet.

From Morbius the crew learn how the settlers of the first expedition succumbed to a "dark, planetary force here . . . some dark, terrible, incomprehensible force." Only Morbius and his daughter survived.

Altaira has never before seen a man other than her father. She is beautiful and mature, so the ship's officers pay her a great deal of attention. Morbius is furious. His jealous rage over his innocent daughter is matched by the invisible force that enters the space cruiser that night and destroys the radio transmitters.

The commander confronts Morbius, believing he had something to do with the sabotage. Morbius responds by clarifying the situation. "In times long past this planet was the home of a mighty and noble race of beings, the Krel." Morbius goes on to describe the Krel as a million years ahead of the human race. They had conquered all sickness and crime, and "then, seemingly on the threshold of some supreme accomplishment, this all but divine race perished in a single night."

Morbius then displays the Krel equipment. They board a tubular shuttle and descend into the bowels of the planet, where the Krel technology is vividly shown, including mile upon mile of gigantic electrical generating equipment, atomic furnaces, and a generator shaft thousands of levels both up and down. The size of the machinery extends twenty miles in all directions from their vantage point. Morbius, however, is unable to explain the purpose of this vast machinery and why all this energy is being produced.

Altaira falls in love with Commander Adams and wants to leave with him for Earth. That night, an invisible force attacks the spaceship and kills three men in an exciting display of visual effects.

Confronted by Commander Adams, Morbius realizes the truth about the Krel: they had conquered the energy/matter problem and could create anything they imagined with the technology they had devised. Their crowning achievement was their ultimate downfall, as their subconscious thoughts of sinful desires surfaced and manifested themselves in the total annihilation of the Krel race in one night. Commander Adams sums it up by saying, "The secret devil of every soul on the planet was set free all at once to loot and maim, take revenge and kill!"

Morbius refuses to believe that it is the monster of his own sinfulness that haunts them when an invisible force crashes through the outside forest and approaches the house. Commander Adams, Altaira, and Morbius retreat to his private lab hoping to escape, only to have the subconscious "Id monster," powered by the Krel generators, melt through a twenty-six-inch-thick Krel steel door. Morbius confronts his "Id" as it penetrates the door, his conscious battling his subconscious, the good in him fighting his sinfulness. The two forces, good and evil, meet; and Morbius challenges his evil force as it enters the lab. Morbius collapses as his evil side collides with his physical body, and he drops to the floor.

Morbius instructs Commander Adams to activate a switch which will destroy the planet in twenty-four hours. Morbius dies; and the commander, Altaira, and the crew escape Altair 4. The planet explodes as the spaceship leaves for Earth.

There are few films which operate at so many intellectual levels as *Forbidden Planet* does. Even though the film is showing some vestiges of aging (as any science-fiction film will), such as dated slang, costumes, and spaceship equipment, the film still holds interest because of its first-class script and its examination of good and evil. Other attempts to explore the world (or universe) of good and evil, such as *Quatermass and the Pit, Five, Colossus: The Forbin Project;* and *Seconds,* work on a level not quite as thought provoking as *Forbidden Planet.*

Most films, such as *Star Wars,* James Bond films, and westerns work on a straight expository level: the drama is clearly defined good versus evil or protagonist versus antagonist. *Forbidden Planet* presents us with a curious mixture of the basic dramatic elements. Much like Shakespearean drama, the material gives us insight on an exposition level and on an intellectual level for more refined, closer examination of the moral perspectives being presented.

Forbidden Planet shows Morbius, who wants to become godlike, or even a god to the human race, as he doles out bits of the Krel knowledge to earthlings as he sees fit. Morbius and the characters which surround him create an interesting dynamic: good versus evil; the place of religion and law within a technological framework; and the relationship between man and God.

Also, Morbius demonstrates the power of sin to consume oneself with such a vengeance that it destroys everything in sight. By himself, Morbius cannot defeat the sin in him, rather he is defeated by his jealous love for his daughter. Only Jesus could have delivered him, but Morbius knew Him not.

Forbidden Planet is a parable which speaks to the technological immorality of our own age. We believe that we are free to exercise our deepest desires, even if only in the protected environment of our homes in front of our pervasive video players and televisions. However, such hedonism can only lead to death, for sin is self destructive.

Furthermore, God is not mocked. He knows our hearts and judges each of us.

Forbidden Planet also demonstrates that total freedom without restraint leads to anarchy, murder, and suicide. God's law or the liberation from sin found only in Jesus Christ are the sole means of restraining man's destructive sinfulness.

Questions for Discussion:

1. Should the United Planets' Cruiser *C-57-D* have landed when told to turn back? By what right? Cite Scripture.
2. Is anything wrong with Dr. Morbius's protective feelings for his daughter? What? Cite Scripture.
3. What is sin? Does sin have a life of its own? What does the apostle Paul say?
4. Why did the Krel perish?
5. Why can't Dr. Morbius control his sin nature?
6. Does sin always destroy the sinner? Why?
7. Did the destruction of the planet solve the problem?
8. How does Dr. Morbius's desire to be like God fit in with Scripture?
9. Is the film saying that there is a need for religion in a technological society?
10. Is there a need for God in an advanced technological society? Why?
11. Why is Jesus the only answer to the sin problem? Do you think the filmmakers knew this?
12. Is God truly sovereign? What does that mean?
13. What is freedom? Is the license to do anything freedom? Why not?
14. What is the premise of *Forbidden Planet*? Do you agree with it?

The War of the Worlds
Analysis by Ted Baehr

The War of the Worlds, adapted from H. G. Wells's science fiction novel, presents a view of a problem facing humanity, an alien invasion, which can be understood as an allegorical treatment of a demonic attack. In dealing with this attack, *The War of the Worlds* has a very clear, Biblical perspective.

The minister and the Christian faith is portrayed in a very positive light throughout the movie. One of the leading characters says the world was created in six days and wonders if it will be destroyed in the same amount of time. At the end, as the Martians are conducting their final assault on Earth, people are gathered for prayer in various churches.

It is clear that the victory over the alien invaders comes only as a result of God's grace. In fact, the last line tells us, "It is the littlest things that God in his wisdom had put upon the Earth that save mankind."

The movie opens with the explanation that Mars is a dying planet, so the Martians are looking for somewhere to resettle and decide on Earth. When they land in California, the first reaction of the inhabitants is to welcome the aliens, but it's clear that they do not come in peace when they disintegrate the first three greeters. Still, a minister tries to approach the Martians with a message of peace in the Name of God, but they vaporize him.

The war starts and it seems that the Martians are invincible. Dr. Clayton Forrester, from Pacific Laboratories, works with the army to discover a vulnerable chink in the Martian's armor.

In the process, he falls in love with the self-sacrificing minister's niece, Sylvia Van Buren. She leads him back to church and faith in God.

At the end, Los Angeles is being destroyed. Having been separated from Sylvia by the invasion, Clayton searches frantically for her. They are reunited in a church and pray for salvation. God gives it, and all ends well.

The War of the Worlds is just as exciting as any of the science fiction films being released today, and it is Biblical.

Questions for Discussion:

1. Can sin be external, as well as internal? What about a demonic attack? Cite Scripture.
2. Do you find it strange that a six-day view of creation is presented as fact in this film? This film was made thirty years after the Scopes trial invoked the mass media's searing ridicule of creationism. Do you think the writer inserted this perspective on purpose?
3. How were the Martians defeated? Who defeated them?
4. What is the importance of prayer in this film?
5. Could humanity have defeated the Martians?
6. Should the minister have approached the Martians in the Name of God? Why or why not? Cite Scripture.
7. Why does Dr. Forrester come back to church and faith in God?
8. How were Dr. Forrester and Sylvia reunited?
9. What are the Biblical principles put forth in the film?
10. Do you think there could be an alien invasion of Earth? Has there been? Cite Scripture.
11. How does the Biblical perspective of *The War of the Worlds* contrast with *Forbidden Planet?*
12. How does the Biblical perspective of *The War of the Worlds* contrast with *E.T.?*
13. What is the premise of *The War of the Worlds?* Do you agree with it?

Les Miserables
Analysis by Ted Baehr

Les Miserables tells the redeeming story of Jean Valjean who went to jail for stealing a loaf of bread to feed his sister's child. He is captured and sentenced to ten years at hard labor in prison.

When released, he is a hard-bitten, stone-hearted, and utterly unsympathetic creature whose compassion for his fellow man has been hammered out of him by the cruelty of confinement. Rejected and alienated, he comes to the end of his rope. He is starving and prays in desperation. A bishop takes Jean into his home and feeds him.

That night, Jean steals the bishop's only possession, his silver candlesticks. The police arrest him and take him back to the bishop who refuses to prosecute him. When the police leave in frustration, the bishop tells Jean that tonight he has bought Jean's soul for Christ.

Using another name, Jean becomes a new man and dedicates his life to helping others, taking a young waif as his own. He becomes a well-to-do businessman and is elected mayor. Every day of his life is devoted to benefitting his fellow man.

However, the chief of police, Javert, doggedly tracks Jean. To the single-minded Javert the law is to be upheld and enforced at all costs, with no mercy shown to anyone.

One day Jean sees a villager trapped beneath a heavy wagon and, with extraordinary strength, he lifts it so that the man can be saved. Javert watches this feat and is reminded of the unusually strong prisoner he once knew, Valjean.

He investigates the mayor's past and identifies him as Jean Valjean, the wanted criminal, who confesses that he is the real Jean Valjean. Before he can be jailed, he flees to Paris where he assumes another identity.

Javert relentlessly follows him. After a chase through the Paris sewers, Valjean relents to the prodding of his conscience and goes to Javert to surrender.

Although all his life, Javert has denied the power of God to change lives, he has witnessed Valjean's selfless sacrifices on several occasions and finds compassion stirring in is heart, an emotion he cannot understand.

Javert cannot live with Jean's acts of love which prove that Jean was really transformed by Jesus Christ; so, broken, he commits suicide. Valjean is free to live out his life with those who love him.

Les Miserables is a positive, uplifting, Christian story of the struggle between love and hate. It is a witness to the power of God and answered prayer.

Questions for Discussion:

1. Was Jean justified in stealing the bread to feed his sister's baby? Is theft ever justified? Cite Scripture.

2. Should the penal system be blamed for Jean's resentment and anger? Cite Scripture.
3. Is Jean a product of his environment? Or is he merely a sinner? Cite Scripture.
4. How does God get Jean's attention?
5. How did the bishop show forth the love of Christ?
6. Was the bishop acting according to God's word when he refused to prosecute Jean? Cite Scripture.
7. How does Jean repent and come to know God?
8. Was Jean justified in taking a new name and hiding from the law?
9. Did devoting every waking day of his life to benefiting his fellow man compensate for his breaking the law? Cite Scripture.
10. Does coming to know Jesus free us from human authority and law? Cite Scripture.
11. How does Jean demonstrate his conversion?
12. Was Javert right to continue to track Jean?
13. Where was Javert wrong? Cite Scripture.
14. If the opposite of law is lawless, is it true as some contend that the opposite of grace is law? If not, what is the opposite of grace? Cite Scripture.
15. Did Jesus come to do away with the law? Cite Scripture.
16. How does mercy fit in with the law? Should Javert have let Jean go? Cite Scripture.
17. 1 John 3:9 says that no one who is born again of God will continue to sin. How is that Scripture proved in Jean's life?
18. How does Jean show that he is a new man in God?
19. Why can't Javert accept Jean's conversion? Cite Scripture.
20. Why did Javert commit suicide?
21. Is Javert a symbol for law? Or Pharisaism? Or self-righteousness? Or hate? Cite Scripture.
22. Is Jean a model for grace? Or for the Christian pilgrim? Or for transforming love? Cite Scripture.
23. In what way is *Les Miserables* a powerful witness to the power of God and answered prayer? Cite Scripture.
24. In what way is *Les Miserables* a positive, uplifting, Christian story of the struggle between love and hate? Cite Scripture.
25. What is the premise of *Les Miserables*? Do you agree with it?

Jean de Florette and *Manon of the Spring*
Analysis by Ted Baehr

The two-part saga, *Jean de Florette* and *Manon of the Spring*, constitute one of the greatest movie epics, focusing on the moral and ethical values which govern the lives of everyday people living in a small French town. The depth of realism, the essence of the human personalities, and the faithfulness to Biblical justice in these films are extraordinary.

The first film shows the sinfulness of man, while the second shows forth the redeeming grace of God. They are not superficial diatribes but intricate and profound insights into reality from a Biblical perspective. They are not aimed at the choir, but at the average person who may not know God's redeeming grace.

Questions for Discussion Before Viewing:

1. Why would it be important for these films to focus on the moral and ethical values which govern the lives of everyday people?
2. Christians and Jews believe that we live in a real world with real problems and a real God, who is sovereign. Most religions see the world as illusory, transitory, and nominalistic. Why is the real ontology of these films important? Cite Scripture.
3. Why would it be important to portray the essence of the human personalities?
4. What is Biblical justice? Cite Scripture.
5. Why is it important that these films are aimed at the average moviegoer, and not at the committed Christian?

Jean de Florette.

This extraordinary, critically acclaimed movie has no violence, no sex, no nudity, no profanity, and many positive references to God. It shows that good is superior to evil. However, the focus of the film is the sinfulness of man, so Jean's prayers seem to go unanswered and greed seems to triumph over good but this conclusion is reversed in the sequel, *Manon of the Spring*.

Jean de Florette tells the story of Ugolin, who returns home after serving in the army. He is the only relative of his uncle, Cesar, who wants Ugolin to rebuild the family orchards and have children. Ugolin wants to grow carnations, but carnations need lots of water, and the only property with a spring is owned by a neighbor, Pique-Bouffique, who detests Cesar.

Cesar and Ugolin go to Pique to buy his land, but Cesar fights with and accidentally kills him. Pique's heir is Jean de Florette, the hunchback son of Cesar's childhood love, Florette.

Cesar and Ugolin Soubeyran cement the spring before Jean arrives so that Jean's farm will fail and they will get the land they want so badly. Their greed compels them to destroy Jean, although his genius, industry, and faith in God almost get the upper hand.

Jean de Florette cuts deeply into man's sinfulness, making us want to be good, to call out to God, and to encourage others who are motivated by love.

Questions for Discussion:

1. Is it realistic to suggest that Jean's prayers are never answered although he commends and cries out to God? Cite Scripture.
2. Is it troubling to you that greed seems to triumph in this movie?
3. What prompts Pique's death? Cite some similar Biblical stories.
4. What defeats Jean?
5. Do God's people ever struggle? Where is the victory? How should we react?
6. How does *Jean de Florette* make us want to be good, to call out to God, and to encourage others who are motivated by love?
7. In what way is this film an accurate portrait of human relations?
8. Is this film suspenseful without the usual Hollywood devices to portray evil and jeopardy?
9. How does this film portray: Jeopardy? Evil? Good? Love? Greed?
10. What is the premise of *Jean de Florette*? Do you agree with it?
11. How does one murder lead to another? Is that Biblical?

Manon of the Spring

This movie tells the story of Manon, the daughter of Jean de Florette, who died because his greedy neighbors, the Soubeyrans, cemented the spring on Jean's mother's farmland just before Jean moved into his inheritance. Cesar and his nephew, Ugolin, are the perpetrators of this travesty which forced her father to work himself to death trying to be a good steward of his inheritance.

Manon discovers their culpability and longs for revenge. Finding the source of the water for the town, she blocks the spring off.

During a sermon which proclaims Jesus as Lord, the local priest chastises the residents for attending church only when it serves their self-interest and accuses them of perpetrating injustices against their fellow man. This sermon brings out the truth.

Ugolin, who has fallen in love with the beautiful Manon, commits suicide. Cezar learns from an old blind woman that Jean de Florette was more closely related to the town than anyone knew.

Although the miracles in this movie are not spontaneous epiphanies, there are no accidents or coincidences, for it is clear that God is the God of justice who acts through people to bring the unjust to judgment. The fact that the residents interpret Manon's revenge as an act of God seems to be a denial of miracles, but, on reflection, it becomes clear that God acts through Manon's revenge and repentance, as well as the intricate relationships in the town. There is a deeper sovereignty of God here than the superficial magic which so often blinds people to the truth of God's mercy, grace, and justice.

It would be wonderful to recommend this powerful story of repentance and forgiveness without reservation, as *Jean de Florette* and *Manon of the Spring* together offer one of the most Biblical views of sin, judgment, and repentance ever seen in a film.

However, *Manon of the Spring* must be recommended with caution because of a brief, innocent nude scene of the young Manon arising from a bath in a mountain spring. This nonerotic nudity requires that we caution you not to see the film if you will be offended. The problem is not the nudity, which is seen at a great distance, but the witnessing of that scene by Ugolin.

Questions for Discussion:

1. Is it right for Manon to seek revenge? To whom does revenge belong?
2. How does God carry out His justice?
3. Is the priest's sermon accurate? In what way?
4. How does God bring the unjust to judgement?
5. Why does Ugolin commit suicide? Is that God's will?
6. How does God chastise Cezar? What is Cezar's response?
7. Does Manon carry out her own will or God's? How so?
8. Is it clear that God is in control? How so?
9. What do you think about Cezar's deathbed speech?
10. Discuss the theme of forgiveness.
11. What is the premise of *Manon of the Spring*? Do you agree with it?

Repentance
Analysis by Ted Baehr

Repentance was banned for years in its homeland, Russia, because it exposes the evils of communism, statism, and totalitarianism while lifting up the suffering church, the triumphant, eternal church of Christ Jesus. Christians should see and support *Repentance*.

Repentance is an allegory about Russia under Stalin. It tells about Varlam, the communist mayor of a small town who tries to destroy all individuality and Christianity but ends up destroying himself and his family.

It opens with Keti baking cakes in the shape of churches. Then it cuts to Mayor Varlam's funeral. After the burial, Keti exhumes his body because he persecuted unto death both her father, Sandor, an artist who loved Jesus, and her beautiful mother, Nina. Sandor is a Christ figure, who suffers with quiet strength the avaricious machinations of the state.

Varlam is proud of himself. He is full of banal wit and pretends to deal with every situation with aplomb. He is the devil incarnate, as we see when his son confesses to a priest, only to find that the priest is Varlam the devil.

In the end, Varlam's grandson takes his own life because of the atrocious sins of his father and his grandfather. The boy's father repents, exhumes Varlam, and throws him off a cliff. Likewise, *Repen-*

tance calls the people of the world to repent of the sin of communism by renouncing it, turning away from it, exorcising it, and throwing it into the dustbin of history.

God is the center of this film. The Spirit He gives us cannot be defeated by the devil or petty Marxist tyrants. The last dialogue in this heartrending film captures its essence:

Old Woman: "Does this road lead to a church?"
Keti: "This is Varlam Street. It will not take you to a church."
Old Woman: "What good is a road, if it doesn't lead to a church?"

This is a powerful and beautiful movie, with moments of great suspense and moments of laughter. There is a brief scene of shadow nudity, an unfortunate blemish in one of the most Christian films to come along in years.

Also, some parts of *Repentance* may fail for some Americans because it has references that only Russians will understand, but it is well worth seeing, even with these obscure moments.

Questions for Discussion:
1. In what way is the church eternal? In what way is it triumphant? Cite Scripture.
2. What is the premise of *Repentance*? Do you agree with it?
3. Why is Varlam so evil?
4. In what way is Sandor a Christ figure? In what way is Nina a Mary figure?
5. Does Varlam accurately model the devil? Cite Scripture.
6. Why can't the people just bury communism and forget it? Why must they repent?
7. Why does Varlam's son throw him off the cliff? Cite Scripture.
8. How is God shown to be triumphant in this film?

Burke and Wills
Analysis by Ted Baehr

Burke and Wills, a story of courage and perseverance in the face of insincerity, epitomizes every man with a mission. It relates the adventures of the first Europeans to cross the Australian outback in 1860-61 and clearly presents the meaning of covenant.

Mr. Wills, a refined gentleman from England, is a curious naturalist, who travels to Australia to explore the uncharted wilderness.

Mr. Burke, a romantic Irishman who has been chasing the local music hall beauty for years, seizes upon the idea of rushing across the Australian desert to make his fame and fortune.

Mr. Burke and Mr. Wills set out with too many men and supplies to cross Australia from coast to coast. The outback is a terrifying place, and they shed supplies along the way. When they reach the last known landmark, Cutters Creek, they leave their best man, William, with three other men and supplies to hold a little fort until they return.

Racing across the desert in the summer heat, miraculously they make it to the gulf. On the way back, crazed by the sun and the 140-degree heat, they lose one man and all but one of their camels. Months later, they arrive at Cutter's Creek the same day that William left to take his men and supplies back to civilization. The group who was to supply William never arrived because the businessman who agreed to finance the operation reneged on his commitment.

Mr. Burke and Mr. Wills and John King, the young aide-de-camp, find themselves stranded in the desert. They try to make it to civilization, but their last camel dies. John is found by a search party prompted by the outcries of an angry press, shocked that Burke and Wills have been abandoned. The movie ends with the testimony of John King as he addresses the people of Melbourne who let Burke and Wills down by failing to keep their word.

There are positive references to prayer, faith, talking to God, and knowing God intimately. John King, the survivor, is a praying man. His prayers prompt Mr. Burke to ask how to talk to God.

The movie focuses on the fact that trust is a basic building block of civilization. The men who gave their word to support Mr. Burke and Mr. Wills break that trust. In heroic contrast, Mr. Burke and Mr. Wills keep their word.

As Christians, we live in covenant with God and our fellow man. When we fail to keep our word, we break that covenant relationship. *Burke and Wills* summarizes Psalm 15:1, 4b in which God replies to the psalmist that the man who keeps his word, no matter what the cost, will be allowed to live in His sanctuary.

Burke and Wills is a great movie: the photography is beautiful; the story is magnificent; the literary references are wonderful; and the adventure is exciting. There is some earthy obscenity, but no profanity. There is a brief, conjugal bedroom scene with Burke and his bride under the covers, but it is innocuous.

Questions for Discussion:

1. In what way is *Burke and Wills* the story of every man with a mission?
2. What is the premise of *Burke and Wills*? Do you agree with it?
3. What is wrong with insincerity? Cite Scripture.
4. Why did John survive?
5. Where did Mr. Burke and Mr. Wills succeed? Where did they fail?
6. What is John's testimony? Do you agree? Cite Scripture.
7. Why is trust so important?
8. How important is it to keep one's word? Cite Scripture.
9. What is a covenant? Why is it important?
10. How does *Burke and Wills* present the meaning of covenant?

Babette's Feast
Analysis by Bruce Grimes

Set in Sweden during the late 1800s, this remarkable film tells the story of two sisters with a strong faith in God. These women, Filippa (named after the Christian reformer Philip Melanchthon) and Martine (named after Martin Luther), spend their years helping the needy, sick, and poor, while sacrificing their own interests. *Babette's Feast* is a portrait of Christian love.

The sisters need a housekeeper/cook. They meet Babette, a young French woman forced into exile after the Paris uprising of 1871. She has nowhere to go and the sisters give her a home. Babette becomes their humble servant, even though the sisters are unable to provide any remuneration beyond room and board. Babette gains the respect and admiration of the devout, but poor, Christian community on the North Sea Coast.

Babette's arrival comes during a period of dissension within the small community, after the death of the sisters' godly father who served as vicar for the village. Now the sisters try to hold the religious community together with prayers, hymns, and homilies in their humble abode.

Babette, who serves cakes and refreshments after informal worship, always takes her own meals in the kitchen, assuming the role of the faithful servant, never complaining about the staple diet of bread and soup. While the few remaining members of the congregation idly speak of being servants of the Great King, only Babette demonstrates the spirit of servanthood and humility, to everyone's constant dismay.

For years, the three women serve others: the sisters serve those in the village and Babette serves the sisters. However, the rewards of serving are costly. One of the sisters, courted by a noble army officer, declines his offer of marriage because she cannot serve both her calling and him.

The years pass and the sisters, now in their sixties, have slowed in their activities. Babette has remained faithful for many years. Then news arrives that Babette has won the national French lottery, 20,000 francs! Everyone is elated, but the sisters are saddened that Babette will return to her homeland.

Babette proposes to use the money to cook a grand French feast for the sisters and their friends, a feast so special that she must go back to France to purchase the seafood, yeasts, and wine. She asks the sisters' permission to go. They grant it but believe that Babette will stay in France.

However, Babette returns with wheelbarrows full of the finest ingredients, including vintage wines, fine game birds, fresh vegetables, assorted cheeses, fruits, and other delicacies. She serves them the finest meal of their lives. In the midst of the feasting, all jealousies and rivalries evaporate and merriment prevails. The huge banquet, which takes many days for Babette to prepare, is symbolic of our Lord's preparation of His communion table, which cost His life and now serves as a source of joy for the Christian. Also, it prefigures the banquet we will find when we enter into His eternal kingdom in heaven.

As Babette finishes her tasks, everyone realizes that this woman once was one of the finest chefs in the world, who had humbled herself to work for the two sisters, never hinting at her true profession. Furthermore, the sisters discover that Babette has spent all her winnings on the feast and has no desire to return to Paris. She is content to remain a humble servant. She gives up everything, yet gains so much more. It is an act of sacrifice which humbles everyone.

The film is awesome in its Biblical message, but never heavy-handed. Like many European films, it starts slowly. However, the photography is magnificent; the acting, flawless; the story, captivating; and the hymnology and sacramental themes are woven throughout the narrative.

Babette's Feast won an Academy Award for Best Foreign Picture in 1987. Depicting Christian love and humility, it is an example of how the good, the true, and the beautiful can be portrayed in an entertaining, uplifting, and endearing way.

Questions for Discussion:

1. In what do the sisters demonstrate their faith in God? Cite Scripture.
2. How does Babette show forth her commitment to God?
3. What is the cost of service? The reward? Cite Scripture.
4. Why is there dissension in the community?
5. Why does Babette spend her money on a feast instead of something more practical, such as clothes or books?
6. Who in the Bible does Babette typify?
7. Who in the Bible do the sisters typify?
8. Why are the sisters suspicious of the feast? Is that a common problem among Christians? Cite a Biblical parallel.
9. Why in the midst of the feasting, do all jealousies and rivalries evaporate and merriment prevail? Is this Biblical?
10. How is this feast symbolic of communion? How is this feast symbolic of the heavenly banquet which we will enjoy with Christ Jesus? Cite Scripture.
11. What is the premise of *Babette's Feast*? Do you agree with it?
12. How do the guests react to the feast?
13. What opened the community's eyes to godly service and humility?
14. What did Babette gain?
15. What are the sacramental themes woven throughout the narrative? What is the hymnology woven throughout the narrative?
16. What other Christian themes do you find?

The Devil and Daniel Webster
Analysis by Gary DeMar

"I would say to any man who follows his own plough, and to every mechanic, artisan and laborer in every city in the country—I would say to every man, everywhere, who wishes by honest means to gain an honest living, 'Beware of wolves in sheep's clothing!'"

This dialogue is in the opening scene of *The Devil and Daniel Webster* (1941), a sometimes comedic but always authentic portrayal of the devil and his schemes. Its style is reminiscent of C.S. Lewis's *Screwtape Letters*. As in *Screwtape*, the viewer comes away with some idea of Satan's secret councils.

In this flawlessly styled period piece, a simple, down-and-out farmer sells his soul to the devil in exchange for seven years of fame and fortune. Farmer Stone is told that "the soul is nothing." Fame and fortune cannot be compared to "nothing," so why not give up that nothing of a soul? It seems like such a good deal. The covenant is signed in the farmer's own blood, and God responds with thunder and a setting sun.

At the end of the seven years, finally and fully comprehending the "deal" he had made, the farmer changes his mind. He may have gained the world's riches, but he's about to lose it all and then some.

Scratch, the devil's wily assistant played by Walter Huston, is more than accommodating. In exchange for an extension on farmer Stone's contract, the devil will take the soul of the farmer's infant son.

Horror grips him as he comprehends the full impact of his bargain with the devil. What will he do? He turns to the great nineteenth-century orator and lawyer Daniel Webster to find a loophole in the contract. However, the devil always seems to be one step ahead of man, because the devil never plays by the rules. Before Stone and Webster do battle with Scratch, farmer Stone's wife leaves her husband with this Biblical encouragement: "Set me as a seal upon thine heart, as a seal upon thine arm. For love is as strong as death."

Standing on the Constitution, Daniel Webster, in hopes of beating the devil, asks for a jury trial of the farmer's peers. Surely they will understand. However, Webster goes even farther. "If I can't win this case with a jury, you'll have me too," Webster boasts.

This gets the attention of Scratch as the soul of Daniel Webster would be quite a prize. However, Scratch will not be undone: "But you'll have to admit that this is hardly a case for an ordinary jury." Webster quickly responds with, "Be it of the quick or the dead."

Old Scratch accepts the famous lawyer's request. A jury of long-dead scoundrels, traitors, and opportunists, who had likewise sold their souls, is called from the pit of hell to sit in judgment, Benedict Arnold being the most recognizable. The despair of hell is etched in every line of the jurists' faces. Their pact with the devil haunts them, even in death.

We will not reveal the conclusion, but old Scratch is ready at the end to make a deal with any new prospect, a reminder that "Your adversary the devil walks about like a roaring lion, seeking whom he may devour" (1 Peter 5:8).

Questions for Discussion:
1. Why does the movie open cautioning us to "Beware of wolves in sheep's clothing"? What is the Biblical perspective toward trusting others? Cite Scripture.
2. How is *The Devil and Daniel Webster* authentic?
3. Discuss the parallels between this film and C.S. Lewis's *Screwtape Letters.*
4. Can we really sell our soul to the devil? How? Who in Scripture sold his soul to the devil? Cite Scripture.
5. What is the soul? The spirit? How much is the soul worth?
6. Can a pact with the Devil be broken? Cite Scripture.
7. What brought Stone to his senses?
8. Is there a loophole in the contract? If so, what is it?
9. If God is sovereign, what power does the devil have?
10. In what way is love as strong as death?
11. Is Daniel Webster arrogant?
12. What is the premise of *The Devil and Daniel Webster*? Do you agree with it?
13. Are these people naive?
14. Should we fear the devil? How should we treat him? Cite Scripture.

Journey to the Center of the Earth
Analysis by Gary DeMar

Jules Verne's classic thriller, *Journey to the Center of the Earth,* begins on the streets of Edinburgh, Scotland, in 1880. However, the viewer is soon taken to the depths of the earth's core to encounter a glistening cavern of quartz crystals, luminescent algae, a forest of giant mushrooms, dinosaurs thought to be extinct, and the lost city of Atlantis.

Alec (Pat Boone) presents a rare geological find to Sir Oliver Lindenbrook (James Mason), a professor of natural science at the University of Edinburgh: an unusually heavy piece of lava. The professor is intrigued with the lava's peculiar weight and spends an evening in his laboratory attempting to burn away the porous crust. The oven in which the meltdown was to occur explodes.

The accident reveals the rock's core, a plumb bob, a common surveyor's instrument. However, this is no ordinary plumb bob. There is writing on it, and it is signed in what seems to be the blood of a long-lost scientist and explorer, Arnie Saknussemm.

Nearly 300 years earlier, Saknussemm had startled the world with his tales of a domain below the earth's crust, a world accessible to man. He was ridiculed, but the laughter stopped when he failed to return from his trek to the center of the earth.

Professor Lindenbrook and Alec prepare to set off for Iceland to retrace their predecessor's steps to the deepest regions of the earth accompanied by an Icelandic guide and the widow of a scientific competitor. They begin their journey with the prayer, "May the good Lord be with us."

They descend following the carefully notched marks chiseled in stone by Saknussemm three centuries before. Saknussemm's heir, however, is out to sabotage the expedition. He follows behind, initially undetected by the Lindenbrook expedition. At one point, he chisels a new set of three notches to divert the quartet from the marked path. In addition to this menace, there are numerous geological hazards that frustrate the explorers but offer the viewer an array of special effects.

At one point, Alec becomes separated from the expedition, and, through a freakish accident, the remaining trio are cornered in a ravine by a charge of rushing, rising water. There is no place to turn but to flow upward with the rising water. They are soon confronted by a rock ceiling seemingly with no way of escape. However, God answers the professor's earlier prayer by providing a passageway through a dislodged stalactite. When the professor sees the opening, he cries out, "Praise the Lord!"

But what has happened to Alec? The expedition is delayed looking for the young Scot. They are soon reunited when the trio hears a gun shot. Alec has met Count Saknussemm. Alec is soon rescued by the professor, Saknussemm is disarmed, and the expedition continues.

Now the real fun begins. An underground sea, with waves and currents, forces the expedition to leave the security of the earlier Saknussemm notches and to trust Providence once again. Before they can traverse the eerie waters, they must deal with flesh-eating dinosaurs. Of course, they slay the overgrown serpents and continue their journey on a raft constructed from the hardened stems of giant mushrooms. A fierce magnetic storm and an immense whirlpool send the explorers to parts unknown.

God has not deserted them. The wild gyrations of the sea take them to the final resting place of the late Arnie Saknussemm, the lost city of Atlantis with all its attendant idols. They find Saknussemm's skeleton, his hand pointing the way of escape.

Two obstacles remain: one more giant serpent to slay and an obstructed volcanic chimney to ascend. Their only hope is to use the gunpowder that they find in Saknussemm's sack to dislodge a rock barrier in the chimney. A final prayer is offered by Alec as they kneel before a heathen altar stone, "Dear God, ruler of heaven and earth. . ." At this point Professor Lindenbrook interjects, "Don't set any limits to His realm, Laddie." Alec continues, "God of the universe, we are in Thy merciful hands." The explosion not only removes the obstruction, but sets off an enormous volcanic explosion that pushes the quartet up and away from the volcano into the sea.

The Lindenbrook expedition returns to Edinburgh triumphant. These final words are offered to the gathered crowd: "We returned by the grace of God in a heathen altar stone."

The entire family will enjoy this splendidly produced and color-enriched look into the imaginary world below. God is acknowledged as the Creator and Sustainer of the universe. Greed and human autonomy have no place in God's good creation as the arrogant Count Saknussemm is buried by the world over which he claimed to be lord. The mythical pagan city of Atlantis was judged when God opened the sea to bury it forever.

Questions for Discussion:

1. This film has a classic storyline; what is it? What other stories use the same storyline?
2. Is the storyline Biblical? Cite Scripture.
3. Do the explorers start out following God? What is their mission and their goal?
4. How does God intervene to protect and rescue these adventurers?
5. How does *Journey to the Center of the Earth* show that God is sovereign?
6. How is redemption shown in this film?
7. What is the premise of *Journey to the Center of the Earth?* Do you agree with it?
8. What is condemned in this movie? What is the role of evil in *Journey to the Center of the Earth?*
9. How does the film show that God condemns paganism and idolatry?
10. What allegorical elements are present in this film?
11. What is unique about *Journey to the Center of the Earth?*
12. In what ways is this film similar to *Pilgrim's Progress?* The *Odyssey?* Dante's *Inferno?*

A Tale of Two Cities
Analysis by Gary DeMar

The causes and effects of the French Revolution come alive through this cinematic rendering of the Charles Dickens's classic novel *A Tale of Two Cities* published in 1859. As we will see, there's more to *A Tale of Two Cities* than the bloodstained blade of the guillotine.

The movie opens in 1775 with England and France unaware of the forthcoming tumult. A Mr. Lorry, representing a London banking firm, is en route to Dover where he is to meet Lucie Manette, the only surviving daughter of Dr. Manette, eighteen years a prisoner in the Bastille at the hands of the Marquis St. Evremonde (Basil Rathbone). She is told that her father is not dead as she supposes. He had been incarcerated by the French government while she was yet an infant. The London banking firm that Mr. Lorry represents has been safeguarding the small fortune that had been invested by Lucie's father.

Dr. Manette has just been released, and Lucie accompanies Mr. Lorry to Paris to meet her aged and frail father for the first time. His imprisonment has taken its toll, however. The once vibrant and skilled doctor sits at a shoemaker's bench able to do little but stare. The doctor is escorted to London where he is nursed back to health by his loving daughter. On the ship, Lucie Manette meets a young French aristocrat, Charles Darney, a relative of the despised Evremonde family, who caused Dr. Manette's sufferings.

Upon his arrival in England, Charles Darney is charged with spying for the French. The Manettes are called as witnesses against him. However, a clever lawyer, Sydney Carton (Ronald Colman) defends the falsely charged French aristocrat, and he is released.

The movie now focuses on the wasted life of Sydney Carton. He and Darney, whom he physically resembles, are often received at the Manette home and both fall in love with Lucie; but it is Darney's affections that she returns. While outwardly showing little grief over the loss, inwardly Carton begins to examine his life and laments over what could have been. A wasted life is about to be transformed into a self-sacrificing life.

In France, the seeds of revolution have been planted. There are many who want to water the seeds with the blood of aristocrats. One woman in particular, Madame Defarge, has awaited the day of reckoning with controlled agitation. Her knitting records an accounting of the horrors inflicted on the people by the oppressive aristocrats. Highest on her list is the Marquis St. Evremonde. Madame Defarge is present at the storming of the Bastille on July 14, 1789.

For three years the expiating blood of the guillotine drips. The aristocrats are not alone in their brutality. The mob has replaced the court.

Lorry is sent again to Paris on banking business. Darney is called to Paris to act as a witness in defense of an old and faithful servant who served in the Evremonde household. Linked with the Old Regime, he too had to die. Lorry, being an Englishman, is safe. However, Darney is arrested as an aristocrat.

They soon learn that Darney is also an Evremonde, and he must stand trial for the "sins of the fathers." Madame Defarge is pleased. Dr. Manette, Lucie, and their little girl travel to Paris in defense of Charles.

They believe that Dr. Manette, once a prisoner in the Bastille at the hands of the Marquis St. Evremonde, will have some influence over the court. During the trial, Darney and Dr. Manette convince the bloodthirsty mob that he, Darney, is a friend of the people. He had renounced his uncle's bloodletting and had forsaken his French entitlements.

However, Madame Defarge is present at the trial. She will have no part in a verdict of innocence. Her family had been ruined by the Evremondes. She calls into question the testimony of the doctor who had forgiven and accepted Charles, not counting the sins of the fathers to him. He showed his forgiving spirit by giving Charles Darney his own daughter in marriage. Madame Defarge offers in evidence a letter written by Dr. Manette, written while he was suffering under the oppression of the Evremondes, swearing revenge on the Evremonde family. The jury votes for the death penalty.

Sydney Carton, also in Paris, blackmails a man who has access to the prison where Darney is being held for execution. Carton visits Darney, drugs him, changes clothes with him, and has Darney carried out. In the end, it is Carton who gives his life so Darney might live and be reunited with his wife and daughter.

In the tumbrel on the way to the guillotine, a seamstress is startled by the fact that Carton has taken the place of Darney. "You're going to die in his place. Why?" Carton responds, "He's my friend." These words of Jesus come to mind: "Greater love has no one than this, than to lay down one's life for his friends" (John 15:13).

Carton is not without hope. As he contemplates giving up his life for his friend, his arms rests on the mantle of the fireplace over which hangs these embroidered words: "I am the Resurrection and the Life." The movie closes with: "I am the resurrection and the life. He who believes in Me, though he may die, he shall live" (John 11:25).

Questions for Discussion:

1. What is the premise of *A Tale of Two Cities*? Do you agree with it?
2. Do you agree that as a man sows, so shall he reap? Why?
3. In what way is redemption the real message of this film?
4. How has Sydney Carton wasted his life?
5. How does God get Carton's attention?
6. Who is Madame Defarge and why is she so obsessed? Cite Scripture.
7. What is wrong with mob rule?
8. Why are the people as cruel, if not worse, than the aristocrats? Cite Scripture.
9. Why does Darney go to France?
10. Is it right for Darney to stand trial for the "sins of the fathers"?
11. How does Madame Defarge turn the court around?

12. Why can't Madame Defarge forgive?
13. Did Carton do the right thing by giving his life?
14. What is Carton's hope?

Metropolis
Analysis by Ted Baehr

Metropolis opens on a 1927 projection of a city of the year 2000. The sky is almost blotted out by the immense architecture. Quartered below are the workers. Identically uniformed, they toil around the clock, cogs in the machines that power the city.

The elite live in sun-drenched luxury, frolicking in lush pleasure gardens. As Freder Fredersen, son of the master industrialist Jon Fredersen, laughs and sports, Maria, a worker's daughter, leads a few ragged children into the garden. She implores the mercantilists, "These are your brothers." Freder is smitten. He has never thought of the workers or of the huge machines that run the city.

Ignoring his caste, he follows Maria down to the machines. Huge pistons, dynamos, and furnaces stretch as far as the eye can see. High as a mountain, the massive control center has an army of workers swarming over its sides like ants, regulating dials and levers. Amidst clouds of scalding steam, Freder hallucinates that row upon row of workers are sacrificing themselves in the yawning mouth of the monster machinery.

Agitated, Freder rushes to his father's office, high above the city. Jon is not pleased with what his son has done and rebukes him. Jon then goes to see Rotwang, a mad scientist, who has cast a female figure in metal. He proclaims, "I have created a machine in the image of man that never tires or makes a mistake!"

Freder descends to a worker's assembly where Maria is preaching a Biblical hope to the workers, "Today, I will tell you the story of the Tower of Babel." She relates that the toilers knew nothing of the dreams of those who conceived the tower, who in turn cared nothing for the workers. "Between the brain that plans and the hands that build, there must be a Mediator. It is the heart that must bring about an understanding between them," the girl exhorts in an allegorical reference to Jesus Christ, the Mediator between God and man and between men.

Fredersen and Rotwang watch from a spy hole. Jon orders Rotwang to make his robot in the likeness of Maria to teach the workers a lesson. Rotwang kidnaps Maria and transforms his mechanical woman into a duplicate of her.

The robot Maria is sent below to sow discord among the workers and destroy their confidence in her. Inflaming the workers like a revolutionary Barabbas or antichrist, the robot intones, "I have preached patience . . . but your mediator has not come—and will never come! Why should you sweat yourselves to death for the lord of Metropolis?

Who keeps the machines going? Let the machines stop. Destroy the machines!"

The workers revolt, destroying the dikes, thus flooding the underground city and their homes as well. The riot spreads to the surface. The real Maria escapes from Rotwang's laboratory just in time to rescue the workers' children from the flood. Joined by Freder, she leads the children to the safety of the surface. On the surface, a mob of workers spot the robot. Believing their children have drowned, they burn her at the stake.

Freder hears a scream from the roof of a building. Maria is being pursued by Rotwang, who thinks the mob will kill him if they learn there is a second Maria. Dashing to her rescue, Freder attacks Rotwang, who loses his balance and falls to his death.

Freder and Maria descend to the square below. The workers have been told it was Fredersen's son who saved their children. The master industrialist is there himself. Together, hand, heart, and brain, they enter into a partnership to rebuild Metropolis for the benefit of all the people, not just the privileged few.

Metropolis is full of Biblical symbolism and allegory. The city represents heaven and earth, as well as the caste distinctions to be found in a mercantilist/socialist state. Maria preaches reconciliation and new life through the intervention of a mediator between the rulers and the people, between God and man. Rotwang, the priest/scientist wants to be like God by creating creatures who will serve him. He is the adversary who wants to make the world over in his image. Freder becomes the mediator, Christlike and full of love, ready to sacrifice himself to save the children and Maria. Freder reconciles Jon to the workers, and the workers to Jon. The robot is the revolutionary leader who sows discord, not peace. Her lies incite the people to rebel.

As Adam Smith, the father of the free market, did in his *Wealth of Nations*, the filmmakers in *Metropolis* rebuke mercantilism wherein the bonds of privilege wed the rulers of the state and the rulers of the socialized business cartels. This film calls for reconciliation and freedom of opportunity so people work together in partnership. This movie rebukes the mercantilism which was rearing its ugly head as National Socialism in Germany and international socialism in Russia.

The film condemns revolution and the revolutionary leader, the robot Maria, a counterfeit savior in the tradition of Barabbas, Hitler, and Lenin, who leads the people to death and destruction. At the same time, it lifts up the Mediator and Reconciler, who comes not to sow discord, but to bring peace.

There are many levels of symbolism in this masterpiece, which are fun and enlightening to explore. However, in the final analysis all the elements have been woven together into a seamless fabric which is a delight to behold and a pleasure to watch. For this reason, *Metropolis* has stood the test of time, even though it is a silent film.

Questions for Discussion:

1. What is your impression of the city in *Metropolis*? What does it represent?
2. Who are the workers? Is the movie just in its presentation of their plight?
3. What is the root problem in the city? Is technology a problem or a symptom?
4. How can Maria say that the children are Freder's brothers? How would a humanist, a Communist, or a National Socialist look at these two groups of people?
5. How does God get Freder's attention? What other movies suggest the same thing?
6. What is wrong with the conditions wherein the workers live? Cite Scripture.
7. From a Biblical perspective, who does Jon represent?
8. Rotwang is a high priest figure; what is his religion? What are the Biblical and historical parallels?
9. From what is Rotwang suffering?
10. Can man create anything that never makes a mistake? What is the human condition?
11. Is Maria's insight into the story of the Tower of Babel Biblical? Is her story Biblical?
12. Why do Fredersen and Rotwang want to teach the workers a lesson? Cite Scripture.
13. What is the difference between Maria's message for the workers and the robot's message? What is the difference between Jesus' message and Barabbas' message?
14. Why is rebellion wrong? Cite Scripture.
15. Why is mob rule wrong?
16. Does Freder kill Rotwang?
17. How do the two factions in *Metropolis* become reconciled?
18. What is the future of *Metropolis*? What would God want for them?
19. How did Freder sacrifice himself for others?
20. What is wrong with mercantilism, communism, and statism? Cite Scripture.
21. How does Freder bring peace? How does Jesus bring peace?
22. Discuss some of the symbolism you find in *Metropolis*.
23. Is *Metropolis* as interesting as a modern movie? Why, or why not?
24. What is the premise of *Metropolis*? Do you agree with it?

REVIEWS OF SELECTED MOVIES

5

REVIEWS

My people are destroyed from lack of knowledge.
                                        —*Hosea 4:6*

This is a second volume of *The Christian Family's Guide to Movies and Video*, which is published every two years. Most of the reviews appeared in *MovieGuide: A Biblical Guide to Movies and Entertainment*—a daily two minute syndicated radio program, a newspaper/magazine column and a bi-monthly newsletter.

These reviews will help you to select movies to watch on television and to rent from your local video store. This book includes reviews of both good and bad movies to help you have a better idea about their content and thus determine which movies are acceptable for viewing, which movies should be avoided and why.

Parents often call me to ask if a movie is alright for their teenager to see with their friends. The parents often say that their teenager told them the movie wasn't so bad and all their friends have seen it. Or, they note that the advertisement on television made the movie look acceptable. However, when the parents see the movie they are shocked by the offensive elements. Armed with these detailed reviews, the parents have the right information to explain to their teenagers exactly why they should not go to the movie in question. Christian teenagers also appreciate these reviews to help them ward off peer pressure and to help them discern which films are good and which are bad.

Ratings, no matter who determines them, have failed to guide individuals in their choice of motion pictures because they do not give enough information to make an informed decision. The ratings assigned by the Motion Picture Association of America are usually merely a means of advertising the movie in question, not a way to intelligently guide patrons and protect families. Robert Redford asked for an R-rating for *The Milagro Beanfield War* even though it had no nudity, sex, or violence because he was concerned that the movie would not attract an audience if it had a PG-rating. Conversely, other movies, such as the *Police Academy* series, are given a PG-rating even though they are filled with offensive elements because the producers want to capture the teenage moviegoers.

Often, ratings have kept people from movies which have a Biblical worldview, such as *The Prodigal*, or which are worthwhile viewing and yet have been given restrictive ratings for political, economic or ideological motives, as was the case with *Eleni*. On the other hand, ratings have not kept people from movies which they would have avoided if they had known more about the movie than just the rating, the advertisements and the trumped-up word of mouth.

Therefore, *The Christian Family's Guide to Movies and Video* gives you a detailed review of each movie so that you can clearly discern which movies to see and which movies to avoid. Even more important than helping you select movies to see, the detailed review lets you know why you would want to see or avoid the movie in question. Best of all, the detailed review gives you a Biblical perspective toward each movie, so that you, your family and your friends can develop your and their Biblical worldview and discernment.

In addition to the detailed review, we have provided a brief description of each movie using standardized categories. Most of these categories need no explanation. However, the category designated as "Quality" (which rates the general artistic quality of the movie) uses the following star system: ★★★★ = Excellent; ★★★ = Good; ★★ = Fair; ★ = Poor. And in the "Content" category, we attempt to briefly summarize the objectionable as well as the acceptable elements in the movies using some specifically defined words. When we use the word *profanity* in describing the content of a movie, we mean any language which profanes or defiles that which is sacred. Usually, *profanity* refers to taking God's—particularly the Lord Jesus'—name in vain. The word *blasphemy* refers to language or actions which curse, revile, mock, or blaspheme God, His Holy Spirit, the Lord Jesus, or His Church. And finally the word *obscenity* is used to indicate foul, disgusting, offensive, lewd, or filthy language.

In accordance with God's Word written, this book commends "those who do right" (1 Peter 2:14) and exposes "the fruitless deeds of darkness" (Ephesians 5:11) so that standing together Christians can make a difference in the mass media and take every thought captive for Jesus Christ (2 Corinthians 10:3–6). By using discernment in your choice of movies and entertainment, you will be casting your vote for better movies, either by your financial support of good movies, or by withholding financial support from immoral and anti-biblical movies.

We pray that you will be blessed by *The Christian Family's Guide to*

Movies and Video, and that it will help you, your family and your friends.

TITLE:	**THE ACCIDENTAL TOURIST**
QUALITY:	★★★
RECOMMENDATION:	Bad
RATING:	PG
RELEASE:	1988
STARRING:	William Hurt, Geena Davis, and Kathleen Turner
DIRECTOR:	Lawrence Kasdan
GENRE:	Romance/Drama
CONTENT:	Some profanity; marital infidelity; and, brief upper back nudity
INTENDED AUDIENCE:	Adults
REVIEWER:	Nancy Hanger

Macon Leary, who hates to travel, writes travel books for the businessman who hates to travel. Macon's story parallels his books as he tries to remain unruffled by his son's tragic death by a gunman at a burger joint; and, his wife's departure a year later when she is unable to deal with Macon's concealed pain.

Dog trainer Muriel Prichett meets Macon when he boards his dog at her kennel during a trip. Outrageously dressed, she says anything that comes to mind and ends up teaching Macon to live an unexpected, "face the music" life. After a year's separation (during which Macon lives adulterously with Muriel), Sarah and Macon attempt reconciliation at Sarah's suggestion. It doesn't work because Macon refuses to honor his marriage vows. Muriel's unglamorous, yet lighthearted presence captures him. He has been infected by license, and rejected integrity.

God hates divorce and adultery. This accidental tourist is headed straight for hell: "This is the way of an adulteress: She eats and wipes her mouth and says, 'I've done nothing wrong'" (Proverbs 30:20). The house of the adulteress "leads down to death and her paths to the spirits of the dead. None who go to her return or attain the paths of life" (Proverbs 2:18-19). *The Accidental Tourist* does not receive our recommendation.

TITLE:	**THE ACCUSED**
QUALITY:	★★★
RECOMMENDATION:	Bad
RATING:	R
RELEASE:	1988
STARRING:	Kelly McGillis and Jody Foster
DIRECTOR:	Johnathan Kaplan

GENRE:	Drama
CONTENT:	Graphic sexuality, obscenities, and profanity throughout
INTENDED AUDIENCE:	Adults
REVIEWER:	Gene Burke

Last year, *Fatal Attraction* hit the nerve of married men and single women with equal horror. *The Accused* is brought to us by the same folks, at the same time of year, with the same desire, to reap a colossal profit. Instead of adultery, it is the rape of a woman by three men who are being "egged on" by the male on-lookers in a public bar. The assailants were not the only ones on trial: the cheering spectators were as well.

The courtroom proceedings unravel the sordid activities in the bar that led to the most graphic violation of a woman ever filmed. It not only angered me toward any man that would degrade a woman, but also angered me toward those who felt the need to show it so explicitly. The effect, without that scene, was powerful enough. This scene in *The Accused* is one that I pray to forget.

Unquestionably, this formula picture should be avoided in the hope that the talented people who brought this subject so vividly to the screen would venture a production that would encourage us as much as this one depresses us. Why this was nominated for an Academy Award is an extremely perplexing question.

TITLE:	**ACTION JACKSON**
QUALITY:	★ ★ ★
RECOMMENDATION:	Extreme Caution
RATING:	R
RELEASE:	1988
STARRING:	Carl Weathers, Vanity, and Craig T. Nelson
DIRECTOR:	Craig R. Baxley
GENRE:	Action adventure
CONTENT:	Violence, nudity, and profanity
INTENDED AUDIENCE:	Teens
REVIEWER:	Doug Brewer

There are too many supercop adventures around, getting bloodier all the time. *Action Jackson* starts out with people being executed by a gang of killers. Jackson gets a tip that the man behind it is Dellaplane, the father of a sex offender Jackson arrested years earlier. Vanity is a singer who also happens to be Dellaplane's mistress. Jackson woos her, and Dellaplane sends thugs to shut her up.

Though the film is well paced and acted, the language is needlessly graphic and the violence is too explicit. At times, it is funny, but mostly it is disturbing. Do not bother with *Action Jackson*.

☆☆☆ CLASSIC ☆☆☆

TITLE:	**ADVENTURES OF A YOUNG MAN**
QUALITY:	★★★
RECOMMENDATION:	Caution
RATING:	Not rated
RELEASE:	1962
STARRING:	Richard Beymer, Ricardo Montalban, Eli Wallach, Paul Newman, Susan Strasberg, Jessica Tandy, and Diane Baker
DIRECTOR:	Martin Ritt
GENRE:	Adventure/Drama
CONTENT:	Some rough moments
INTENDED AUDIENCE:	Family
REVIEWER:	Protestant Motion Picture Council

Taking its plot from Ernest Hemingway's Nick Adams stories, this suspenseful and immensely appealing drama is an episodic memory ride through the past. A wide-eyed, curious youth, feeling the tightness of his mother's apron strings and the smallness of the Michigan country village, runs away from home and hits the open road to New York and some vague awaiting fame.

He wants to write, but has nothing to say, as he has not yet lived. His escapades on the way involve some rough and tumble encounters, but these pale when he joins an ambulance driving unit on the Italian front during WW I. There, he meets love . . . and death. It is in this process that he attains maturity.

He returns home where he finds himself a stranger, and leaves to make his place in the world. There is no soft-pedaling in the sufferings exacted by life, nor in the juxtaposition and conflicts in family relationships. There is powerful competition between the characters, as should be expected.

The selection of the cast is especially noticeable. The performances deserve highest praise.

TITLE:	**ADVENTURES OF BARON MUNCHAUSEN**
QUALITY:	★★
RECOMMENDATION:	Caution
RATING:	PG
RELEASE:	1989
STARRING:	John Neville, Eric Idle, Sarah Polley, Oliver Reed, Uma Thurman, and Jonathan Price.
DIRECTOR:	Terry Gilliam

GENRE:	Children/Comedy/Action adventure
CONTENT:	Some crude, lewd, and vulgar moments
INTENDED AUDIENCE:	Adults
REVIEWER:	John Evans, Movie Morality Preview

In a city under siege, Henry Salt and his actors are presenting a play: *The Adventures of Baron Munchausen*. Their performance is interrupted by the real Baron. He tells the "true" story. The Sultan is fighting a war because of a bet he lost with the Baron. No one believes this except Sally, Henry Salt's daughter. Her faith inspires the Baron to find four men to save the city. The Baron seeks four amazing men: the fastest runner; the strongest man; a man with awesome hearing; and one with stupendous accuracy as a marksman. Their journey spreads to the moon and then to the volcanic home of Vulcan and Venus. The men are found. However, they believe that they are too old to save the city.

This is a fantasy of imagination's triumph over reason, but it is marred. The fantastic exploits are coupled with lewd scenes: the bare buttocks of the Sultan's harem, the birth of Venus made too revealing, and the pursuits of the moon people. The story is long and overly involved. The crude moments rule out this film for children. Therefore, the film loses its most appropriate audience. You will want to look for better entertainment.

☆☆☆ CLASSIC ☆☆☆

TITLE:	**THE ADVENTURES OF HUCKLEBERRY FINN**
QUALITY:	★★★★
RECOMMENDATION:	Must for children
RATING:	Not rated
RELEASE:	1960
STARRING:	Tony Randall, Eddie Hodges, Archie Moore, and Patty McCormack
DIRECTOR:	Michael Curtiz
GENRE:	Adventure
CONTENT:	Nothing objectionable
INTENDED AUDIENCE:	Family
REVIEWER:	Protestant Motion Picture Council

Who has not read Mark Twain's novel, perhaps even many times, about the irrepressible "Huck"? It can be enjoyed once more in this film version which is concerned almost entirely with his journey on a raft down the Missouri and Mississippi rivers.

Huck and Jim, a black slave, run away together to escape the wrath of Huck's drunken father. Only the boy's inventiveness (a polite word for some useful lying—which is wrong!) saves them from the clutches of some crooks, as well as from the eagerness of a "slave catcher" coveting Jim for the promised reward. They join a circus, board a river boat after the ramming of their raft, and with the continuous race with fate and pursuers never lagging, suspense is supreme.

With all his pretended "tough" ways, Huck wants to be good, though he doesn't know that the answer is Jesus Christ. However, he always manages to get himself out of tight places, in unexpected ways.

Perhaps, no one will ever fulfill the Twain image of Huck, half boy, half man, pushing his nose into any available adventure with delightful curiosity, innocence and courage. Eddie Hodges has the innocence and decency of Huck, but he strikes one as weak and artificial which Huck never was. He was the essence of unwitting bravery and boyish confidence.

The sequence of events is also somewhat changed from that of the novel but this is of little consequence. It catches fully its spirit.

The acting is excellent. The outdoor photography is beautiful. Also, there is an appropriate musical score, with some good songs.

TITLE:	**AFTER THE RAIN**
QUALITY:	★★★
RECOMMENDATION:	Caution
RATING:	PG
RELEASE:	1988
STARRING:	Brian Keith, Ned Beatty, Alexandra Paul, and Dee Law
DIRECTOR:	Harry Thompson
GENRE:	Romance
CONTENT:	Some vulgar language
INTENDED AUDIENCE:	Adults
REVIEWER:	John Evans, Preview's Movie Morality Guide

Annie Bonner is greeted by her parents when she returns from college in 1929. Her father becomes concerned when she is attracted to one of his workmen, Jessie Monroe. Annie and Jessie are married when Annie becomes pregnant. Annie's father disowns his daughter. Annie and Jessie have a good marriage, which engenders three boys and a baby daughter. Annie longs to be accepted by her family. It appears there could be a reconciliation.

Although predictable, *After the Rain* is a heartwarming story of conflict and love. The characters have their weaknesses, but they respect traditional values and try to live decent lives. Scripture and praying are a part of family life, and the family members share a loving relationship. A sexual encounter is implied, but it is not explicit nor condoned. Under stress, a few vulgar words are used, but there is no profanity.

After the Rain is a bit simplistic, but it is enjoyable to view a film which is not filled with crudities and violence. If it were not for a few vulgar words, we could give *After the Rain* our wholehearted recommendation.

☆☆☆ **CLASSIC** ☆☆☆

TITLE:	**THE AGONY AND THE ECSTASY (136 Minutes)**
QUALITY:	★★★★
RECOMMENDATION:	Acceptable for all ages
RATING:	None
RELEASE:	1965
STARRING:	Charlton Heston, Rex Harrison, and Diane Cilento
DIRECTOR:	Carol Reed
GENRE:	Biography
CONTENT:	Nothing objectionable
INTENDED AUDIENCE:	Adult
REVIEWER:	Protestant Motion Picture Council

This movie is for lovers of Michelangelo's art. (In theatrical distribution, before the drama began, viewers were treated to a ten minute film featuring his famous statues.) Remarkable photography and superb color aid in presenting these masterpieces.

We view St. Peter's Cathedral against a pale blue sky with clouds repeating the church's aged white. A narrator sets the scene: from Michelangelo's birthplace in Tuscany, to Florence under Lorenzo the Magnificent where Michelangelo's early work in stone looked like alabaster, then his fame spread to Rome and his sculpture in marble culminated in the *David, Moses,* and the *Pieta.*

The story begins with scenes of the Carrara quarries in the Alps and the delivery of a block of marble by an ox-driven cart to Michelangelo's home in Rome. Rubbing his hands lovingly across the stone he exclaims, "Look. Moses, here in the marble! Moses down from Sinai. God's anger in his eyes. Here alive, sleeping in the stone. God sets them in there: the sculptor cuts them loose."

Pope Julius II commissions him to paint the Sistine Chapel in the Vatican. It is a curved ceiling seventy feet up in the air, but he tells the Pope, "I am a sculptor, not a painter," and that there is no inspiration in painting ceilings. However, he begins the task.

After several pictures, or frescoes, are finished, he enters the Chapel alone one night and destroys them. He runs to the rock quarries to hide from the Pope who is also a military leader. While hiding, he has time to think. He looks at the sky and God inspires him through the cloud formations to paint what the Lord wants painted—the Story of Genesis. This gigantic task occupies four of Michelangelo's eighty-seven years of life.

Humorous moments occur when church services are being held in the Chapel. Since Michelangelo is always working, red paint drips on the white-robed priests below. The Pope, impatient for the work to be completed, yells, "When will you make an end?" Michelangelo simply answers, "When it's finished."

The character of the artist, the fire which consumes him as he creates, the struggle between his divine gift of creation and his human frailties are glimpsed. A woman who loves Michelangelo cares for him when he is sick, motivates him when he is discouraged, and tries to understand when he tells her he is in love with his work.

A war is raging and invaders are being driven out of Italy. Pope Julius II is serving God by force of arms because that is what is required. He is the figure that moves the plot, around whom significant events occur. The Pope's exploits on the fields of battle and his capricious passions occupy time and attention. After deploying masses of men in full battle dress across the Italian hills and valleys, not enough film footage is left to delineate in depth the fascinating growth of the artist.

The final viewing of the Sistine Chapel is during a mass, and the frescoes almost seem secondary to the ritual of worship. The technical details, casting, settings, and particularly Alex North's music are excellent. Michelangelo's work seems even more sacramental knowing *The Agony* he suffered painting for years on a ceiling *and the Ecstasy* of seeing this masterpiece completed.

TITLE:	**ALL'S FAIR**
QUALITY:	★ ★
RECOMMENDATION:	Extreme Caution
RATING:	PG-13
RELEASE:	1989
STARRING:	George Segal, Sally Kellerman, and Robert Carradine
DIRECTOR:	Rocky Lang
GENRE:	Comedy
CONTENT:	Foul language, profanities, sexual jokes, and sexual innuendos
INTENDED AUDIENCE:	Teenagers and adults
REVIEWER:	Nancy Hanger

All's Fair features women fighting to beat men at their own game. A war-crazed old colonel, the CEO of Chunky Chunks Candy Company, takes his men every weekend to the woods for combat. Promotions are given only for feats on the "battlefield." Although Anne is the most conscientious worker, she is demoted. The Colonel tells her, if she wants a promotion, she must raise an army. She recruits and trains women tired of being treated like servants, co-led by the Colonel's wife, Florence, who cares only for shopping and draining her husband's bank accounts. The women hire a Rambo-type expert to train them. The stakes are raised when it turns out Florence has been buying shares of Chunky Chunks for a hostile takeover. Ultimately, love wins out. At the final showdown, a housewife declares her love for her husband, Anne's colleague declares his love for her, and the colonel and Florence are reconciled.

Unfortunately, the producers turned a potentially funny movie with a positive resolution into an infantile, stupid, and ridiculous film. The language is bad, and sexual "jokes" are constant. Avoid *All's Fair*. It's unfair to both sexes.

TITLE:	**AMAZING GRACE AND CHUCK**
QUALITY:	★★
RECOMMENDATION:	Bad
RATING:	PG
RELEASE:	1987
STARRING:	Jamie Lee Curtis, Gregory Peck, William L. Peterson, Alex English, and Joshua Zuehlke
DIRECTOR:	Mike Newall
GENRE:	Drama/War/Science fiction
CONTENT:	Humanism, Zen mysticism, profanity, blasphemy, and anti-Americanism
INTENDED AUDIENCE:	Families
REVIEWER:	Ted Baehr

Amazing Grace and Chuck is a sorry movie with absurd dialogue, an absurd plot, absurd motivations, and an absurd caricature of the President who delivers obsequious platitudes to an uninteresting, unattractive, spoiled brat. What is even sadder is the fact that this Chamberlainesque defeatism will only lead to totalitarian expansion throughout the world.

Amazing Grace and Chuck fails on all counts. It is anti-Biblical, anti-American, anti-freedom, and anti-future. Christians should boycott this insidious movie. Profanity, blasphemy, humanism, and nominalism pervades this evil film. Avoid *Amazing Grace and Chuck*.

TITLE:	**ANGEL HEART**
QUALITY:	★★★
RECOMMENDATION:	Evil
RATING:	R
RELEASE:	1987
STARRING:	Mickey Rourke, Robert DeNiro, and Lisa Bonet
DIRECTOR:	Alan Parker
GENRE:	Horror/Drama/Mystery
CONTENT:	Voodoo, sex, nudity, violence, profanity, and obscenity
INTENDED AUDIENCE:	Adults
REVIEWER:	Ted Baehr

Angel Heart accurately portrays evil from a Biblical perspective. It is so cruel, violent, and sexually explicit that Christians must avoid it.

Angel Heart tells the story of a detective, Harold Angel, who is commissioned by the malevolent Louis Cyphre, to find a singer named Johnny Favorite, who disappeared thirteen years earlier. Johnny skipped out on a contract with Cyphre, and Cyphre wants to be paid. While searching for Johnny, Harry gets caught in a nightmare of confusion, voodoo, and death.

Johnny had amnesia and a destroyed face from a bomb blast during a battle in World War II. When Harry goes to track Johnny down at the nursing home, Harry finds that Johnny had been whisked away soon after he arrived, but Dr. Foster continued to send Mr. Cyphre records claiming that Johnny was in the home.

When Harry returns to talk with Dr. Foster, he finds him dead. Harry tracks down Toots, a black jazz musician with whom Johnny used to sing, and Margaret, Johnny's fortune teller girlfriend. Both moved to New Orleans many years before.

In New Orleans, everybody Harry interviews dies soon thereafter in gruesome ways. Mr. Cyphre arranges to meet Harry in a church and tells Harry to mind his language in respect for God. Harry replies that he is an atheist.

In the end, it becomes clear that Harry is Johnny Favorite, whose soul was sold to the devil many years before and who tried to escape that contract by taking the identity of a Harold Angel in a gruesome voodoo rite. Louis Cyphre is Lucifer, and Harry (alias Johnny) goes to Hell.

Explicit sex and violence makes *Angel Heart* off-bounds for Christians. However, it shows that the wages of sin is death and the devil is devouring the souls of those who do not choose Jesus as their Lord and Saviour. Lucifer recognizes God's authority and chides Johnny/Harry for his atheism. We can only pray that pagans will be so frightened by this vision of evil that they will call out to Jesus Christ.

TITLE:	**ANNA**
QUALITY:	★★★
RECOMMENDATION:	Bad
RATING:	PG-13
RELEASE:	1987
STARRING:	Sally Kirkland and Pauline Porizkova
DIRECTOR:	Yurek Bogayevicz
GENRE:	Drama
CONTENT:	Some obscenity and brief frontal nudity
INTENDED AUDIENCE:	Adults
REVIEWER:	Ted Baehr

Anna is a powerfully acted movie about a Czech movie star who participated in the 1968 revolution against Russian imperialism. She was sent to a concentration camp where she lost her baby. After her release, Anna escaped to New York.

The film opens as she is tracked down by Krystin who, as a child, idolized Anna. Krystin incorporates Anna's past into her own to enhance her success; whereas, Anna refused to promote herself by feeding the media her tragic past. Anna drifts into despair and has a nervous breakdown. Finally, she tries to kill Krystin, her alter ego.

Written, produced, and directed by Czech refugees, *Anna* shows that the state is not the solution to one's problems. Unfortunately, nobody has a relationship with God, and so they are aimlessly adrift in the sea of life. Also, *Anna* contains some off-color language and brief frontal nudity which predetermine that *Anna* cannot be recommended for Christians in spite of its powerful message that communism and humanism destroy everything, including hope.

TITLE:	**ANOTHER WOMAN**
QUALITY:	★★★
RECOMMENDATION:	Caution
RATING:	PG
RELEASE:	1988
STARRING:	Gena Rowlands, Mia Farrow, Gene Hackman, and John Houseman
DIRECTOR:	Woody Allen
GENRE:	Drama
CONTENT:	No physical sex, but sexual conversation; language, not bad
INTENDED AUDIENCE:	Adults
REVIEWER:	Troy Schmidt

Although thoughtful, intelligent and well-acted, *Another Woman* pounds us unrelentingly with its sadness. Unfortunately, the characters in *Another Woman* are profoundly sad, and no one would particularly care to identify with them.

Marion is a successful writer and professor of German philosophy. She has entered a crossroads in her life, reevaluating her past, present and future relationships after eavesdropping on the miserable troubles of a next-door psychologist's patient. The painful memories and present revelations bring despair and loneliness into Marion's life, to say the least.

I remember reading the reviews for *September* earlier this year where someone said that with an artist as creative as Woody Allen, one bomb always means a success the next time up. Well, maybe next time. Woody clearly needs Jesus Christ. He seems to have abandoned all hope.

TITLE:	**APPOINTMENT WITH DEATH**
QUALITY:	★★
RECOMMENDATION:	Caution
RATING:	PG

RELEASE:	1988
STARRING:	Peter Ustinov, Lauren Bacall, and John Gielgud
DIRECTOR:	Michael Winner
GENRE:	Mystery/Detective/Comedy
CONTENT:	Profanity
INTENDED AUDIENCE:	Adults
REVIEWER:	Ted Baehr

This Agatha Christie mystery tells about a mean stepmother, whose wealthy husband died, leaving two wills. She destroys the will that benefits her stepchildren, and claims despotic rule over the family through the earlier will. Hercule Poirot hears the children plot to kill their stepmother. When she dies, he sets out to find who did it.

Appointment with Death might have worked, if corners had not been cut in production. The soundtrack was weak, almost annoying. The costuming was cheap. The photography did not capture the exotic locations. There should have been some effort made to polish each scene. There was one annoying profanity. Also, the ending of the movie condoned deceit which God abhors. We suggest you save your money and avoid *Appointment with Death*.

TITLE:	**ARTHUR 2: ON THE ROCKS**
QUALITY:	★★
RECOMMENDATION:	Caution
RATING:	PG
RELEASE:	1988
STARRING:	Dudley Moore, Liza Minnelli, and John Gielgud
DIRECTOR:	Bud Yorkin
GENRE:	Comedy
CONTENT:	Profanity, obscenity, and mild violence
INTENDED AUDIENCE:	Adults
REVIEWER:	Rebecca Wayt

Arthur and his wife are unable to get pregnant, so they decide to adopt. He loses his inheritance to his ex-fiance's father (this is a frame-up to force Arthur to marry her). Arthur takes a job at a hardware store on the lower East Side. His would-be father-in-law purchases the store just to fire Arthur. Arthur continues his heavy drinking and joins the homeless. His deceased valet, Hobson, comes back as an angel to convince Arthur to stop drinking. Arthur convinces his father-in-law to return the $750 million. Arthur wins back Linda, they adopt a baby, and Linda becomes pregnant.

This is mindless entertainment. Don't bother, unless you just want to sit and eat popcorn. It is sad that Arthur is no longer funny when he is sober. *Arthur 2* is *On the Rocks*—stranded and unsalvageable. Save your money.

TITLE:	**THE ASSAULT (Subtitles)**
QUALITY:	★★★
RECOMMENDATION:	Caution
RATING:	None
RELEASE:	1987
STARRING:	Derek De Lint, Mark Van Uchelon, and Monique Van De Ven
DIRECTOR:	
GENRE:	War/Drama
CONTENT:	A few profanities, some obscenity
INTENDED AUDIENCE:	Adults
REVIEWER:	Bruce Grimes

Winner of 1987 Academy Award for Best Foreign Picture, *The Assault* is a complicated, yet understandable story that spans several decades of Anton Steenwijk's life. Anton is a man haunted by the memory of the murder of his family by the National Socialists (Nazis) in World War II.

The story begins in the small Dutch city of Haarlem, Holland in January 1945. One night, a Nazi collaborator is shot by the Dutch Resistance in front of a neighbor's house. The neighbors drag the body in front of the Steenwijk's house. The Nazis arrive and execute all the Steenwijk family, except Anton.

The story follows Anton as he ages over the next forty years, possessed by the tragedy which slew his family. Anton cannot live in the present until he understands the past which he slowly pieces together by interviewing everyone who had anything to do with the night his family died.

Like the famous *Rashomon*, *The Assault* uses flashback not only from the perspective of the central character, but also of the secondary characters, so that the story is told and retold with subtle variations from several points of view. All of this is brilliantly woven into one of the finest screenplays written during the last few years.

The Assault is an exciting, riveting film and would have been highly recommended, except for the fact that there is a small amount of off-color language and profanity. Therefore, caution is advised. Also, Anton's coming to grips with his past seems to incline him to a pacifist political stance which is a denial of the truth that he has learned. However, in the final analysis, Anton's journey through life is a captivating story which helps us to understand his life in depth.

TITLE:	**AU REVOIR LES ENFANTS**
QUALITY:	★★★
RECOMMENDATION:	Caution
RATING:	PG
RELEASE:	1987

STARRING:	French children
DIRECTOR:	Louis Malle
GENRE:	Drama/War
CONTENT:	Sexual innuendoes
INTENDED AUDIENCE:	Adults
REVIEWER:	Ted Baehr

Au Revoir les Enfants treats once more the evil of National Socialism. This time the courage of Christians who sheltered Jews during World War II is also portrayed. Jean is a young Jewish boy who is placed in a Catholic school to hide him from the Nazis. After many conflicts and adventures, he becomes best friends with Julian, the smartest boy in the school. Eventually, the Nazis take Jean away, along with four other boys and the priest who runs the school. They die in concentration camps.

Au Revoir les Enfants should make us aware of the evils of statism. Unfortunately, the movie is slow and tedious. However, the importance of the subject matter and the keen insights into the characters of the boys will win an audience for this film. We recommend *Au Revoir les Enfants* with the caution that there is a flippant attitude toward sexual promiscuity in the movie.

☆☆☆ MASTERPIECE ☆☆☆

TITLE:	**BABETTE'S FEAST**
QUALITY:	★★★★
RECOMMENDATION:	Acceptable
RATING:	Not rated
RELEASE:	1987
STARRING:	Bibi Anderson and Stephanie Audran
DIRECTOR:	Gabriel Axel
GENRE:	Drama/Religious/Christian
CONTENT:	Nothing objectionable
INTENDED AUDIENCE:	Adults
REVIEWER:	Bruce Grimes

Set in Sweden during the late 1800's, this film tells the story of two sisters with a strong faith in God. These women, Filippa (named after the Christian reformer Philip Melanchthon) and Martine (named after Martin Luther), spend their years helping the needy, sick and poor, while sacrificing their own interests. *Babette's Feast* is a portrait of Christian love.

The sisters need a housekeeper/cook. They meet Babette, a young French woman, who was forced into exile after the Paris revolt of 1871. She has nowhere to go, and the sisters give her a home. Babette becomes their humble servant, even though the sisters are unable to provide any remuneration beyond a simple room and board. Babette gains the respect and admiration of the devout, but poor, Christian community on the North Sea Coast.

Babette's arrival comes during a period of dissension within the small community, and after the death of the sister's godly father, who served as vicar for the village. Now the sisters attempt to hold the religious community together with prayers, hymns, and homilies in their humble abode.

Babette serves simple cakes and refreshments after informal worship. Babette always takes her own meals in the kitchen after serving the remnant congregation, always assuming the role of the faithful servant, never complaining about the staple diet of bread and soup. While the few remaining members of the congregation idly speak of being servants of the Great King, only Babette demonstrates the spirit of servanthood and humility, to everyone's constant dismay.

For years, the three women serve others: the sisters serve those in the village, and Babette serves the sisters. The rewards of serving has its costs. One of the sisters, courted by a noble army officer, declines on his offer of marriage because she cannot serve both her calling and him.

The years pass and the sisters, now in their sixties, have slowed in their activities. Babette has remained faithful for many years. The dissension in the community becomes too vocal for Martine and Filippa to suppress.

Unexpectedly, in the midst of the bickering, news arrives that Babette has won the National French Lottery: 20,000 Francs! Everyone is elated, but the sisters are saddened that Babette will return to her homeland.

Babette proposes to use the money to cook a grand French feast for the sisters and their friends. This feast is so special that she must cautiously venture back to France in order to purchase the seafood, yeasts and wine herself. She asks the sisters' permission first, and after it is granted, the sisters believe that Babette will use the remainder of the money to make a permanent move back to France.

Babette returns with wheelbarrows full of the finest ingredients from France, including: vintage wines, fine game birds, fresh vegetables, assorted cheeses, fruits, and other delicacies. The sisters become suspicious of such extravagance and scrutinize the contents of the feast. All of the guests are prepared for the worst. Having seen a pig's head and other unusual items arrive, they anticipate a horrific evening, but will agree to pretend to enjoy the meal, so as not to hurt Babette's feelings.

However, Babette serves them the finest meal of their lives. In the midst of the feasting, all jealousies and rivalries evaporate, and merriment prevails. The huge banquet, which takes many days for Babette to prepare, is symbolic of our Lord's preparation of His communion table which cost His very life to offer and which now serves as a source of joy for the Christian. It also prefigures the banquet we will find when we enter into His eternal Kingdom in Heaven.

The guests are amazed at the courses, and the wines astonish their palates. As Babette finishes her tasks, they salute her and everyone realizes that this woman was one of the finest chefs in the world, who had humbled herself to work with the two sisters, never once hinting at her true profession. Furthermore, the sisters discover that Babette has spent all her winnings on the feast and has no desire to return to Paris where she served as the premier chef de cuisine at the Cafe Anglais. She is content to remain a humble servant.

Babette had given up everything, yet gained so much more. It was a act of sacrifice which humbled everyone.

The film is awesome in its Biblical message, but never heavy-handed. Like many European films, it starts slowly, but stay with it. When I screened Babette's Feast, I noted that many of the critics and distributors in the audience were openly crying by the end of this film.

The photography is magnificent. The acting is flawless. The story is captivating. Hymnology and sacramental themes are woven throughout the narrative.

Babette's Feast won an Academy Award for Best Foreign Picture in 1987. It exudes with Christian love and humility and is an example of how the good, the true, and the beautiful can be portrayed in an entertaining, uplifting, and endearing way.

TITLE:	**BABY BOOM**
QUALITY:	★★★
RECOMMENDATION:	Extreme Caution
RATING:	PG
RELEASE:	1987
STARRING:	Diane Keaton and Sam Shepard
DIRECTOR:	Charles Sheyer
GENRE:	Comedy
CONTENT:	Cohabitation and casual sexual relationships
INTENDED AUDIENCE:	Adults
REVIEWER:	Glennis O'Neal

Diane Keaton's metamorphosis from a career woman to a loving mother is superb. Diane Keaton stars as J.C. Wyatt, who wants to succeed. The company president lets her know he is preparing to make her the first female partner.

However, a phone call tells her that a relative died and left her baby Elizabeth. Elizabeth steals J.C.'s heart, and J.C.'s position is given to an underling.

J.C. leaves for a Vermont farm. The heating fails, the roof caves in and the well runs dry. With everything depleted except apples, she makes a special apple sauce for Elizabeth and, as a last gasp, promotes her product as gourmet baby food. Skyrocketing sales cause her former company to make a lucrative buy-out offer. Motherhood brings true success.

Unfortunately, *Baby Boom* has a cavalier attitude about co-habitation and sex out of wedlock. Furthermore, the language leaves much to be desired.

TITLE:	**BACK TO THE BEACH**
QUALITY:	★ ★
RECOMMENDATION:	Caution
RATING:	PG
RELEASE:	1987
STARRING:	Frankie Avalon, Annette Funicello, Connie Stevens, Ed Byrnes, Dick Shawn, Bob Denver, Don Adams, Pee Wee Herman, David Rasche, Eddy, Wally and Mom from "Leave It to Beaver," and Alan Hale, Jr.
DIRECTOR:	Lyndall Hobbs
GENRE:	Comedy
CONTENT:	A few expletives; one plea to the Almighty; one brief, innocuous bed scene; and drinking and dancing in questionable taste
INTENDED AUDIENCE:	Teenagers and adults
REVIEWER:	Kay M. Black

When last we saw the "corniest couple" in America, over twenty years ago, the Great Kahuna had met his match with the "humanga cowabunga . . . from down unda." Annette is the same tiny, high-haired ingenue. Frankie moved his family to Ohio and is obsessed with sales. College-aged Sandy lives in a pier apartment on Mom's and Dad's old beach. Bobby is a punk copy of his father.

Annette has become very domesticated. Frankie is so tightly wound on sales that he hardly knows the family. Everyone decides Frankie must get away. They decide to vacation in Hawaii. They have a few hours lay-over in L. A. and decide to visit Sandy, who has been afraid to tell her parents she is engaged to Michael. The visit goes from one delay to another. Frankie and Annette take Sandy to her work at the old Daddy O's. Dick Dale is still playing. Kids over twelve will identify with Sandy and Bobby. Almost everyone over thirty-nine will identify with our "older" favorites. This is "corny," and hysterically funny if you were the "typical teenager" of the early 60's. This is the same pure fluff of the original series of "beach" pix. However, caution is urged for Christians because of the loose moral perspective.

☆☆☆ MASTERPIECE ☆☆☆

TITLE:	**BAMBI**
QUALITY:	★ ★ ★ ★
RECOMMENDATION:	Acceptable
RATING:	G
RELEASE:	1942
STARRING:	Animation

DIRECTOR:	David Hand and Perce Pearce
PRODUCER:	Walt Disney
GENRE:	Animated/Nature/Drama
CONTENT:	Nothing objectionable
INTENDED AUDIENCE:	Children of all ages
REVIEWER:	Hannah Jackson

Walt Disney's animated classic opens with an animated forest scene which redefines excellence. Thumper exclaims "It's happened. The new prince is born!" Bambi, the new prince, is the offspring of the Prince, the buck who has eluded "Man" longer than any other deer.

Bambi takes us through a year in the life of the forest denizens. He makes friends with Thumper, the baby rabbit who imparts such pearls as, "If you can't say something nice, don't say nothing at all." Thumper teaches Bambi about birds, butterflies and flowers. Winter comes and Bambi learns about snow and about going hungry. Bambi's mother sacrifices what bark she can get for her growing fawn. Then spring comes! There are fresh new blades of grass and "Man" comes into the forest, bringing destruction. With summer, we find the animals reaching maturity, and Thumper and Bambi become enamored with the female variety of their respective species.

Bambi is a movie the entire family can enjoy. Lovingly, it teaches us about life. At 101, we will not be too old for *Bambi*.

TITLE:	**BANDITS**
QUALITY:	★★★★
RECOMMENDATION:	Extreme Caution
RATING:	None
RELEASE:	1988
STARRING:	Jean Yanne, Marie-Sophie, L. Patrick Bruel, Charles Gerard, and Corinne Marchand
DIRECTOR:	Claude Lelouch (*A Man and a Woman*)
GENRE:	Action adventure
CONTENT:	Semi-nude scene
INTENDED AUDIENCE:	Adults
REVIEWER:	Joseph L. Kalcso

Bandits utilizes the established language of film to achieve its aims in a brilliant and effective manner. Simon contracts with Mozart to fence some jewels which Mozart's gang stole from Cartier's. Simon's wife is kidnapped by a masked man and killed. Simon suspects one of the gang members. He goes to jail, but not before taking his twelve-year-old daughter to boarding school. Father and daughter exchange letters through a ten year span. These letters reveal the truth of the mother's death and the father's incarceration.

Simon is released and reunited with his daughter. Those responsible for his wife's murder are unmasked. The movie comes to a warm, though farfetched, conclusion.

The acting is superb, the camera choreographed masterfully and the musical soundtrack just so. There are scenes which are offensive, or open to interpretation. All in all, this is a film which may be seen by adults for its beauty, but with a discerning eye for its moral and philosophical pitfalls. Extreme caution is advised.

TITLE:	**BAT 21**
QUALITY:	★ ★ ★
RECOMMENDATION:	Extreme Caution
RATING:	R
RELEASE:	1988
STARRING:	Gene Hackman, Danny Glover, David Marshall Grand, and Jerry Reed
DIRECTOR:	Peter Markle
GENRE:	War
CONTENT:	Continuous profanity, obscene language, and violence
INTENDED AUDIENCE:	Adults
REVIEWER:	Russ Houck

Lt. Col. Hambleton is shot down in hostile Viet Nam territory. His rescue is coordinated by Captain "Bird Dog" Clark. After several days, Col. Hambleton, for the first time in his long military career, comes to grips with the reality of war.

This moving story of a rescue under fire is excellent. This film is well directed with just enough humor to allow breathing space before jumping back into the struggle. Christopher Young kept the emotional pulse in total control with his musical score. Hackman, Glover and Grand develop such irresistible characters that the viewer is drawn to the very core of the story. The movie deals brilliantly with the horrors of war. The references to family life are positive. There is also a love story here . . . about "love for your fellow man."

Unfortunately, the only religious points focused on a young sergeant who was into Eastern religion. Worse, the opening scene takes God's name in vain. This is repeated throughout, with four letter words added for variation. In a day when we desperately need heros for our children, why can't Hollywood make great movies that I can take my wife and children to see?

TITLE:	**BATTERIES NOT INCLUDED**
QUALITY:	★ ★
RECOMMENDATION:	Caution
RATING:	PG

RELEASE:	1987
STARRING:	Hume Cronyn, Jessica Tandy, and Elizabeth Pena
DIRECTOR:	Terry Robbins
GENRE:	Comedy/Science fiction
CONTENT:	Occasional profanity
INTENDED AUDIENCE:	Young teens
REVIEWER:	Doug Brewer

The Rileys run a cafe in the bottom floor of their apartment building. The buildings around them have all been cleared away in order to make way for Lacey Plaza. Adorably daft, Faye Riley suffers from premature senility caused by the death of their only son. When two little space ships appear on the scene to help fight progress, the grade school crowd should go wild.

This movie is so predictable I caught myself imagining story lines. The action is slow and painful. *Batteries Not Included* is no *E.T.* Unfortunately, there is some profanity in this movie which makes it unacceptable for Christian families.

☆☆☆ CLASSIC ☆☆☆

TITLE:	THE BATTLE OF THE SEXES (88 Minutes, Black and White)
QUALITY:	★★★★
RECOMMENDATION:	Acceptable
RATING:	Not rated
RELEASE:	1960 (British)
STARRING:	Peter Sellers, Robert Morley, and Constance Cummings
DIRECTOR:	Charles Crichton
GENRE:	Comedy
CONTENT:	Nothing objectionable
INTENDED AUDIENCE:	Adults and mature teenagers
REVIEWER:	Protestant Motion Picture Council

James Thurber's "The Catbird Seat" comes to the screen with a Scottish accent and locale. A meek and timid-looking character with an iron will, a canny wit and a whimsical disposition is opposed to a shrewd American woman efficiency expert and all her wiles. This makes an unbeatable combination in entertaining farcical comedy.

The moot question being, "Shall the House of MacPhereson, purveyors of woolen goods in Edinburgh, be modernized?" Mr. Martin, the trusted employee, is against modern ideas and the disturbances they would bring. He plans to eradicate the proponent of such measures, but the near revolution subsides with a more peaceful solution. In his own words: "No need to use violence; many a battle has been won without striking a blow."

The large cast gives excellent characterizations. The shining star being the versatile Peter Sellers as Mr. Martin. He is well seconded by Robert Morley as the blustering MacPhereson and Constance Cummings as the efficiency expert.

TITLE:	**BEACHES**
QUALITY:	★★★
RECOMMENDATION:	Caution
RATING:	PG-13
RELEASE:	January 1989
STARRING:	Bette Midler and Barbara Hershey
DIRECTOR:	Garry Marshall
GENRE:	Drama
CONTENT:	Bawdy jokes and obscenity
INTENDED AUDIENCE:	Adults
REVIEWER:	Ted Baehr

At age twelve, the precocious singer C.C. Bloom meets the well-bred Hillary Whitney. They write each other for years. C.C. is singing in a dive when Hillary comes to visit. She has renounced her fortune so she can work with the poor.

Hillary is called back to San Francisco to care for her dying father. C.C. becomes a star. When they meet again, their friendship cracks under the strain of Hillary's envy that C.C. has achieved her goals and C.C.'s disgust for Hillary's Junior League life.

However, after Hillary divorces her philandering husband, C.C. re-adopts her as a friend. Hillary is dying of a rare heart disease. C.C. becomes the surrogate mother of Hillary's little girl, Victoria. In the end, C.C. moves beyond her ambition to pick up where Hillary left off as a mother.

This movie doesn't make it, not just because it has obscenities, but also because the audience can't understand why these women like each other. Nevertheless, Bette makes a valiant attempt to carry the entire movie, and she can't do it. We suggest that you avoid it.

TITLE:	**THE BEAST**
QUALITY:	★★★★
RECOMMENDATION:	Extreme Caution
RATING:	R
RELEASE:	1988
STARRING:	George Dzundza, Jason Patric, and Steven Bauer

DIRECTOR:	Devin Reynolds
GENRE:	War
CONTENT:	Violence and obscenity
INTENDED AUDIENCE:	Adults
REVIEWER:	Bill Myers

Far too seldom there comes a movie made with such intelligence and intensity that it is both a joy and a horror to watch. However, such is the case with *The Beast*, the story of a Russian tank driver, Koverchenko, who struggles with the brutality of his comrades in Afghanistan. This is a film of cultures colliding: their people, their lifestyles, their values, and their epoches.

All of this is encapsulated in the story of a handful of Afghans pursuing a lone Russian tank, the "armored beast," with stones and discarded Soviet hardware. Koverchenko is eventually captured and joins up with the small tribe to destroy his own tank.

A severed hand here, bullet-ridden bodies there, and the agonizingly slow, intentional death of a captured Afghan under the track of the tank does not make for easy viewing. Yet, the violence is never gratuitous. It is simply a fact of war. Also, these men talk like soldiers. *The Beast is not easy viewing. It dos not contain easy answers, except, perhaps, that the only way to truly hate your enemy is to make sure you never see his heart.*

TITLE:	**BEETLEJUICE**
QUALITY:	★★★
RECOMMENDATION:	Evil
RATING:	R
RELEASE:	1988
STARRING:	Alec Baldwin, Geena Davis, and Michael Keaton
DIRECTOR:	Tim Burton
GENRE:	Comedy/Horror
CONTENT:	Demonic themes
INTENDED AUDIENCE:	Teenagers
REVIEWER:	Doug Brewer

Beetlejuice is haphazardly constructed around an excessive number of special effects. The Maitlands are a nice New England couple who die in an automobile accident. They don't go to heaven, nor to hell; they go back to their house. They are content until a trendy New York family buys their house and hires a chic interior decorator. At that point, Adam and Barbara decide to try and scare the new family out of the house.

The idea of redoing *The Exorcist* from the point of view of the ghosts is an intriguing intellectual pose, but the approach is uneven. Furthermore, God condemns spiritism and any consultation with demons (see Deuteronomy 18:10), and anyone or anything which panders to spiritism must be condemned by Christians in no uncertain terms.

The message that people and spirits can live peaceably side by side since ghosts are just nice folks who don't want to be dead, must be rebuked. Christians should boycott *Beetlejuice* by telling everyone they know not to see it.

TITLE:	**THE BELIEVERS**
QUALITY:	★ ★
RECOMMENDATION:	Evil
RATING:	R
RELEASE:	1987
STARRING:	Martin Sheen, Helen Shaver, Robert Loggia, Richard Masur, Harley Cross, and Jimmy Smits
DIRECTOR:	John Schlesinger
GENRE:	Horror/Detective
CONTENT:	Violence, satanism, child sacrifice, profanity, and nudity
INTENDED AUDIENCE:	Young adults
REVIEWER:	Bret Senft and Kathy Wallace

This is a movie which Christians must boycott. *The Believers* lifts up ancient Baal worship and undermines the church. Underlining how evil this movie is, the teenagers in the theater laughed at the human sacrifices to Satan. *The Believers* is straight from Hell. In order to take a stand against evil, Christians must boycott *The Believers*.

☆☆☆ CLASSIC ☆☆☆

TITLE:	**THE BELLS ARE RINGING (126 Minutes)**
QUALITY:	★ ★ ★ ★
RECOMMENDATION:	Acceptable
RATING:	Not rated
RELEASE:	1960
STARRING:	Judy Holiday, Dean Martin, Fred Clark, Eddie Foy, Jr., Jean Stapleton, Ruth Storey, Dort Clark, and Frank Gorshin
DIRECTOR:	Vincente Minnelli
GENRE:	Musical comedy
CONTENT:	Nothing objectionable
INTENDED AUDIENCE:	Adults
REVIEWER:	Protestant Motion Picture Council

This is an amusing musical comedy, enlarged from the stage play and equally entertaining. It tells about an answering service operator who gets passionately involved in the lives of her customers.

Her main concern is a young playwright who has trouble concentrating on his writing. She succeeds in urging him to work. Also, she manages to find jobs for other customers.

A few of her customers are gamblers, who conduct their illegal activities by means of the telephone. As a cover, they pretend to sell musical records over the phone.

The frustrated playwright drowns his disappointment in a drinking episode which adds to the mix-up before all ends well. The young operator with love to spare finds her own true love while she is helping everyone else.

Judy Holiday keeps the film bubbling with her effervescent personality.

TITLE:	**BENJI: THE HUNTED**
QUALITY:	★★★
RECOMMENDATION:	Acceptable
RATING:	G
RELEASE:	1987
STARRING:	Joe Camp, Steve Zanolini, Karen Thorndike, Nancy Francis, Ben Vaughn, Mike Francis, Red Steagall, TV cameraman (as himself), and Benji (as himself)
DIRECTOR:	Joe Camp
GENRE:	Nature
CONTENT:	Nothing objectionable
INTENDED AUDIENCE:	All ages
REVIEWER:	Peirce (age 6) & James (age 4) Baehr

The movie opens with a newscast: Benji, the famous canine star, is lost at sea. The film crew was on a boat which capsized in a storm. Everyone was rescued, but Benji. Benji is washed ashore. From now on, there is practically no dialogue. The adventure is with Benji and other small animals which he encounters.

Benji witnesses a cougar shot down by a hunter. Benji takes care of the cubs while attempting to locate another mother for them. They have adventures with bears, raccoons, fawn, owls, eagles, and a big, bad wolf! In the meantime, Benji's trainer, Frank, is searching for him via helicopter. Benji avoids the helicopter as he wants to find a mother for the cubs first. In the end, Benji succeeds.

If you love animals, you will love this film. The director was able to get the most amazing expressions from the animal-actors. Benji, as usual, is wonderful and lovable. *Benji: the Hunted* has a very good moral, that there is no higher calling than sacrificing yourself for others and accepting your responsibilities. *Benji: the Hunted* is recommended for everyone who loves nature, beautiful photography and animals.

TITLE:	**BERNADETTE**
QUALITY:	★ ★ ★
RECOMMENDATION:	Acceptable
RATING:	None
RELEASE:	1988
STARRING:	Sydney Penny, Roland Leseffre, and Michele Simonnet
DIRECTOR:	Jean Delannoy
GENRE:	Religious
CONTENT:	Nothing objectionable except three minor expletives
INTENDED AUDIENCE:	All ages
REVIEWER:	Bruce Grimes

Based on the life of a French girl, this true story begins in the 1850's in a small rural village called Lourdes. Her loving father looses his business, and the family must move to a tenement. Bernadette contracts a lung infection and moves to her uncle's farm to recuperate. On a walk, Bernadette and her friends gather firewood near a spring. Bernadette has a vision of the Virgin Mary. The impact on others becomes hysterical and chaotic. The army steps in to protect the site as people flock from everywhere to drink the waters of the spring. Bernadette is questioned before a group of Bishops and Cardinals. Her story is accepted by the church. To this day, Lourdes is visited by millions each year seeking a cure.

Bernadette is a beautifully photographed biography with the excellent music of Francis Lai ("A Man and a Woman") and good supporting characters. In spite of the mariology with which many would disagree, *Bernadette* is a warm and gentle film suitable for the entire family.

TITLE:	**BERT RIGBY: YOU'RE A FOOL**
QUALITY:	★ ★
RECOMMENDATION:	Extreme Caution
RATING:	R
RELEASE:	1989
STARRING:	Robert Lindsey, Robbie Coltrane, Jackie Gayle, Bruno Kirby, and Corbin Bernsen
DIRECTOR:	Carl Reiner
GENRE:	Musical Comedy
CONTENT:	Profanity, blasphemy, and sexual innuendos
INTENDED AUDIENCE:	Adults
REVIEWER:	Ted Baehr

Bert Rigby tells the story of an English miner, Bert Rigby, who loves to sing and dance. He is infatuated with the movies of Gene Kelly and Fred Astaire and wants to revive the Ritz theater in his home town. His girlfriend wants to settle down. Bert wins an amateur night contest, and thus starts a roller coaster ride to fame and fortune in Hollywood. After adventures in Hollywood, he returns home to fulfill his dream.

The dancing and humor are entertaining. However, blasphemy, profanity, sexual innuendo, and other sleazy touches ruin the ride. Robert Lindsey is a talented dancer. He should have taken a stand against the writer who threw in these demeaning elements, since this movie was made to showcase his talents and did not need the gratuitous gutter language of Hollywood. As it is, we cannot recommend *Bert Rigby: You're a Fool.* "The fool says in his heart, 'There is no God.' They are corrupt, and their ways are vile; there is no one who does good" (Psalm. 53:1).

☆☆☆ CLASSIC ☆☆☆

TITLE:	**THE BEST OF ENEMIES**
QUALITY:	★★★★
RECOMMENDATION:	Acceptable
RATING:	Not rated
RELEASE:	1962
STARRING:	David Niven, Michael Wilding, Harry Andrews, Noel Harrison, Ronald Fraser, and Bernard Cribbins
DIRECTOR:	Guy Hamilton
GENRE:	War Comedy
CONTENT:	Nothing objectionable
INTENDED AUDIENCE:	Adults
REVIEWER:	Protestant Motion Picture Council

To use the concept of war in the desert and make it real enough to be taken seriously, yet personalized enough to remove the horror, then to satirize the characteristics common to men of different origins, is pure genius. We find this genius amply demonstrated in this comedy which describes the events resulting from the crash landing of a British oberservation plane in the Ethiopian desert in 1941.

Two men are taken in by an Italian patrol. The Italian commander lets them go free when his patrol is promised refuge in an old fort. Later, one of the British men is ordered to attack that fort and does so with great annoyance as it means breaking his word.

The British and Italian officers are individualists who differ from the usual patterns. Their behavior leads to some unusual situations, at times furious with one another, and then most congenial in a humorous way.

The inevitable snafu of war and the satire evolved from the changing positions of victor and vanquished are wonderfully done. This film has drama and tension, chuckles, guffaws, witticisms, pathos, and sentimentality. It is intellectually and emotionally rewarding.

TITLE:	**BETRAYED**
QUALITY:	★ ★
RECOMMENDATION:	Bad
RATING:	R
RELEASE:	1988
STARRING:	Debra Winger, Tom Berenger, John Heard, Betsy Blair, John Mahoney, Ted Levine, Maria Valdez, and Joey Simmons
DIRECTOR:	Costa-Gavras
GENRE:	Drama/Detective
CONTENT:	Raw violence, language, and sex
INTENDED AUDIENCE:	Adults
REVIEWER:	Glennis O'Neal

"Frightening," "Sickening," "Shameful," "Dangerous," aptly describe the emotions saturating the viewers of this production. This is another sick attempt to make money by fanning the flames of bigotry.

A trucker is listening to a Jewish radio host. He parks to sub-machine gun the talk-jock. The FBI suspects Gary, a farmer, and plants Katie, aka Cathy Weaver, to trap him. His first wife was accidentally killed. Katie, attached to his children, accompanies them to church and other activities where she photographs the gatherers for FBI scrutiny. Wes warns Gary not to trust Katie. Gary invites her to go hunting. A black man is hunted. She, Gary and the children attend a meeting of the KKK, where they wave American, Rebel and Nazi flags while singing "Amazing Grace." Target practice is given with heads and bodies of Negroes and Jews as targets. Katie tries to escape. Gary pursues her. The duty of each to kill the other for their separate causes is the culmination of the film.

Hauntingly ugly is the only way to remember this movie. The one redeeming feature is Katie's attempt to save the children. But, who is going to rescue people from this movie? This film tries to make money by aggravating racial and religious bigotry. Christians should avoid this yellow filmmaking by a myopic political ideologue.

TITLE:	**BEYOND THE NEXT MOUNTAIN**
QUALITY:	★ ★ ★
RECOMMENDATION:	Acceptable
RATING:	PG
RELEASE:	1980
STARRING:	Alberto Isaac, Barry Foster, Saeed Jeffrey, and Richard Lineback
DIRECTOR:	Rolf Forsberg and James Collier
GENRE:	Drama/Biography

CONTENT:	Nothing objectionable
INTENDED AUDIENCE:	All ages
REVIEWER:	Ted Baehr

Beyond the Next Mountain tells the story of a young Welshman, Mr. Roberts, who goes into India and brings the gospel to the Hmar tribe. The missionary societies are upset with Mr. Roberts because he does not use the traditional missionary techniques. He succeeds, however, where missionary organizations have failed. After he leaves, his converts set up churches throughout the tribe.

The son of one of the tribesmen who was converted, Rochunga Pudaite, at the age of ten, is sent off by his father to become educated so he can translate the Bible into Hmar. He faces the prejudice of those who do not know Jesus as Lord and Saviour. He has many heartbreaks, but God leads him from victory to victory. After an extensive education, he ends up translating the Bible and returning to his people.

Beyond the Next Mountain is beautifully filmed, entertaining and recommended for your whole family. If you would like to order a copy, call *Bibles for the World* at (800) 323-2609.

TITLE:	**BIG**
QUALITY:	★★★★
RECOMMENDATION:	Caution
RATING:	PG
RELEASE:	1988
STARRING:	Tom Hanks, Elizabeth Perkins, Robert Loggia, and John Heard
DIRECTOR:	Penny Marhsall
GENRE:	Comedy
CONTENT:	Sexual innuendo, obscenity, and expletives
INTENDED AUDIENCE:	Adults (Not Children)
REVIEWER:	Bret Senft

Big is a wonderful comedy, a well-drawn presentation of sexual politics in the 1980's which succeeds where other films have failed. Thirteen-year-old Josh approaches Zoltar the robotic fortune teller to express his wish: for bigness (note: magic is an anathema to God). Next morning, Josh has been transformed into an adult, who travels to New York, gets work at a toy manufacturer and falls in love with Susan, who is trying to balance career and personal life. She falls for Josh because he is sweet, honest, caring, and lovable—in short, he is thirteen years old! The "adult" men in her life act like children, while Josh is the perfect grown up. The statement here is to present another career woman looking for Mr. Right, only to discover that he is a mere fantasy.

Unfortunately, there is sexual innuendo, obscenity and a few expletives. This movie should not be seen by little children. Also, the plot device is occultic. Therefore, we caution you to exercise discretion with regard to *Big*.

TITLE:	**BIG BUSINESS**
QUALITY:	★★★
RECOMMENDATION:	Caution
RATING:	PG
RELEASE:	1988
STARRING:	Bette Midler and Lily Tomlin
DIRECTOR:	Jim Abrahams
GENRE:	Comedy
CONTENT:	Obscenity and sexual innuendo
INTENDED AUDIENCE:	All ages
REVIEWER:	Ted Baehr

In the 1940s, a businessman and his wife are driving to West Virginia when she goes into labor. He buys a local company so she can be admitted to the company hospital. A local is having her baby at the same time. They both have twin girls and the nurse mixes up one of each. Both couples name their daughters Rose and Sadie. Cut to New York in the 1980's. Sadie and Rose are running Moramax. Sadie is a tough business woman. Rose keeps thinking she should be in the country. Sadie has decided to sell Jupiter Hollow to an Italian conglomerate. Cut to Jupiter Hollow, where the other Rose is trying to protect the simple life of the town from the evil developers from the city, while the other Sadie feels out of place. The sisters travel to New York to confront Moramax. Confusion reigns as these mixed up pair of identical twins throw Moramax and the Plaza Hotel into conniptions. This mix-up is often funny, but often tedious.

Although there are obscenities, *Big Business* never descends into the profanity and blasphemy of previous Touchstone/Disney movies. There are even positive references to God. However, caution is recommended because of the language and the casual references to sex.

TITLE:	**THE BIG MAN ON CAMPUS**
QUALITY:	★★★
RECOMMENDATION:	Caution
RATING:	PG
RELEASE:	1989
STARRING:	Cindy Williams
DIRECTOR:	Jeremy Kagan
GENRE:	Romantic comedy
CONTENT:	Obscenity and frank conversations about the sexual questions that would be asked by most twelve year olds

INTENDED AUDIENCE:	Teenagers and adults
REVIEWER:	Ken Kistner

This romantic comedy is a delightful blend of *My Science Project* and *The Hunchback of Notre Dame*. When a college co-ed finds herself in distress, Bob, the resident of the campus bell tower, comes to her aid. However, Bob is viewed as a monster by some.

Dr. Webster and Dr. Girard, two professors in the Psychology Department, set out to prove that Bob can be a productive citizen if given the chance. Alex, a student that just hasn't been able to decide what he wants out of school, is enticed into living in the bell tower with Bob as part of Bob's re-introduction into society. The movie has many wonderful moments as we see Bob's childhood innocence transformed by the joys and pains of adolescence.

We must caution you about a few obscenities in this movie. There is no nudity, but there are frank conversations about sex. The sexual questions are ones that would be asked by most inquisitive twelve year olds. Children are exposed to far worse on network TV. The film makes very clear how wrong it is to make value judgments based on physical appearance and socio-economic background. We recommend caution.

TITLE:	**BIG TIME**
QUALITY:	★
RECOMMENDATION:	Caution
RATING:	PG
RELEASE:	1988
STARRING:	Tom Waits
DIRECTOR:	Chris Blum
GENRE:	Documentary/Comedy
CONTENT:	Musical "performance art"
INTENDED AUDIENCE:	Followers of Tom Waits
REVIEWER:	F. L. Lindberg

To a fan of Tom Waits, *Big Time* would rate three stars. If you are not a fan, it is simply boring. *Big Time* is a memorandum from the outer limits of creativity. This is not a concert movie. I describe it as "performance art." Some of the movie was shot on tour; some of it was staged like a rock video. The mood is the message. There is a smoky, bluesy, not quite boozy mood to the whole production. Tom Waits' coarse voice bellows and whispers, unmelodiously chewing and savoring words that express counterculture impressions of a hardened world. The music is to be experienced, not really examined closely.

Some of Tom Waits' lyrics and spoken words are very abstract. Often, I simply could not catch the mumbled words. The language is mostly unobjectionable, but caution is recommended due to odd lyrics and remarks. *Big Time* is creative, but inaccessible to the great majority of us. We simply become baffled, then bored.

TITLE:	**BIG TOP PEE WEE**
QUALITY:	★★
RECOMMENDATION:	Caution
RATING:	PG
RELEASE:	1988
STARRING:	Pee Wee Herman, Kris Kristofferson, Susan Terrill, and Valeria Golino
DIRECTOR:	Randal Kleiser
GENRE:	Comedy/Children
CONTENT:	Sexual innuendo
INTENDED AUDIENCE:	Children
REVIEWER:	Debi Mulligan

Pee Wee lives on a farm populated by a talking pig, a cow that gives chocolate milk, and animals that sleep in beds. The circus lands in his backyard during a tornado. A trapeze artist knocks Pee Wee off his feet. Sounds great, except he is engaged to Winnie, the school teacher. Pee Wee's next problem is his small town neighbors, who threaten to send poor Pee Wee to jail if the circus doesn't pack up and move on. Pee Wee single-handedly changes their minds with a bizarre, yet ingenious tactic.

Considering how the circus centers on freaks, oddities and impossibilities, Pee Wee Herman seems very much at home in the "big top." The supporting cast is good; definitely better than the script. *Big Top Pee Wee* is light entertainment with no redeeming social value, except laughter, juvenile humor and nothing to be taken seriously. Unless you are a fan, he is annoying. It's tacitly portrayed that he and Gina sleep together, but the allusion might not be picked up by children. Not being a Pee Wee Herman follower, I found *Big Top Pee Wee* to be moronic fun.

TITLE:	**BILL AND TED'S EXCELLENT ADVENTURE**
QUALITY:	★
RECOMMENDATION:	Bad
RATING:	PG
RELEASE:	1989
STARRING:	Alex Winter and George Carlin
DIRECTOR:	Steve Herk
GENRE:	Comedy
CONTENT:	Instances of mystical powers and an anti-word, anti-authoritarian message
INTENDED AUDIENCE:	Teenagers
REVIEWER:	Gene Burke

Bill and Ted, two high school students, take nothing seriously, except for "picking" guitars they can't play. They joke about the meaning of discipline and education, then look for ways to pass a final history exam even though neither has the vaguest understanding of history. Miraculously, Rufus is sent from the future to help them pass. He gives them a means to transport notable historical figures to their classroom for their final exam. They capture people like Lincoln, Socrates, Freud, and Genghis Khan. With their help, they pass with flying colors.

This philosophy angers me. It teaches that there is a way to beat the system without hard work. It exhibits total disrespect for parental and educational authority, and even portrays Bill and Ted to be the "fathers" of a future society just like themselves. This is not a funny movie. This film resonates the need for a Saviour in the entertainment business. Save your money and don't waste your time on this imbecilic mess. It's opposed to all family values, even though it is dressed in a "PG outfit." As God says: "If a man will not work, he shall not eat" (2 Thessalonians 3:10).

TITLE:	**BILOXI BLUES**
QUALITY:	★★★
RECOMMENDATION:	Extreme Caution
RATING:	R
RELEASE:	1988
STARRING:	Matthew Broderick and Christopher Walken
DIRECTOR:	Mike Nichols
GENRE:	Comedy/Drama/Biography/War
CONTENT:	Profanity and prostitution
INTENDED AUDIENCE:	Adults
REVIEWER:	Doug Brewer

Eugene Morris Jerome is a Brooklynite on his way to World War II by way of Biloxi, Mississippi. He is there for Basic Training, under the watchful and easily disturbed eye of Sgt. Merwyn J. Toomey. The interactions of these two, as well as a romance that develops between Eugene and Daisy are the basis of this coming-of-age movie. It is funny and sweet, and Matthew Broderick is excellent as Eugene, the diarist and future writer in the barracks.

Unfortunately, because this is a movie about people in the Army, there is an enormous amount of off-color language. There is also a scene in which Eugene visits a prostitute. As was the case with the play, we must recommend that you avoid *Biloxi Blues*. Prostitution and profanity are evil, and we should never condone either. In this day and age of AIDS, we don't need this coming-of-age treatment of prostitution.

TITLE:	**BIRD (160 Minutes)**
QUALITY:	★★★
RECOMMENDATION:	Extreme Caution

RATING:	R
RELEASE:	1988
STARRING:	Forest Whitaker and Diane Venora
DIRECTOR:	Clint Eastwood
GENRE:	Biography/Drama
CONTENT:	No nudity, but infidelity, substance abuse, and obscene language
INTENDED AUDIENCE:	Adults
REVIEWER:	Don Vice

Charlie Parker was one of the most famous jazz saxophone players from WW II to his untimely death at age thirty-four on March 12, 1955. This film is a powerfully told story of a talented personality trying to make it and failing. It depicts the power of alcohol and drugs to destroy people's lives.

New York City's fast life hooks Parker with opportunities to play jazz. Nicknamed "Bird," he becomes famous. Romance with a white woman, Chan, intensifies Parker's life. Although she bore him three children, their marriage was tempestuous. The pressure to be "on top" and "on" caused Bird to increasingly use drugs and booze. Bird dies at the age of thirty-four while watching TV in another woman's apartment.

Bird gave his fans what they wanted—jazz. In return, he received an early death. There are no sex or nude scenes. Four letter obscenities are repeated throughout the film. You will have to judge, after reading this review, whether or not to see this movie. We recommend it with extreme caution only for adults.

☆☆☆ CLASSIC ☆☆☆

TITLE:	**BIRDMAN OF ALCATRAZ**
QUALITY:	★ ★ ★ ★
RECOMMENDATION:	Caution
RATING:	Not rated
RELEASE:	1962
STARRING:	Burt Lancaster, Karl Malden, Thelma Ritter, and Betty Field
DIRECTOR:	John Frankenheimer
GENRE:	Biography
CONTENT:	Prison life, some objectionable scenes
INTENDED AUDIENCE:	Adults
REVIEWER:	Protestant Motion Picture Council

Robert Stroud had spent fifty-three years of his life behind prison bars at the time this movie was released, mostly in solitary confinement, on two first degree murder charges. Burt Lancaster's bravura performance as Stroud, the "birdman," holds this lengthy chronicle together, long after the mystique of the character would have faded at the hands of another.

Stroud is seen as a savage and violent man going through every stage of revolt, animosity and resistance. The uncompromising inmate's life is changed when a small bird, lost in a storm, flies into his cell. He manages to cure the sick bird by putting together some homemade medicine. This leads to Stroud's obsession with birds which made him into one of the world's most learned ornithologists, developing cures for ill birds, even the most exotic.

His concern spreads to other inmates, and the atmosphere of the prison is changed. A kindly, compassionate guard provides Stroud with implements and chemicals, but he receives not a whit of thanks from the truculent prisoner.

Adverse circumstances, strict regulations and severe prison officials create parallel problems. Several characters move in and out of the story. The passing of time is felt mainly through the commentary.

Oddly, Stroud was nothing like the tough, taciturn character Lancaster embodies. He was a sneaky, whining, cringing type whose raging homosexuality, more than anything else, caused him to be permanently confined in isolation.

In fact, as good as this movie is, it has an unbiblical worldview. This movie extols the rights of criminals while demeaning those in authority, in accordance with a Marxist perspective, which has the stated goal of abolishing all authority.

In contrast, God calls us to:

> Submit yourselves for the Lord's sake to every authority instituted among men: whether to the king, as the supreme authority, or to governors, who are sent by him to punish those who do wrong and to commend those who do right. (1 Peter 2:13–14)

TITLE:	**BITTER HARVEST**
QUALITY:	★ ★ ★
RECOMMENDATION:	Acceptable
RATING:	None
RELEASE:	1981
STARRING:	Ron Howard, Art Carney, and Richard Dysant
DIRECTOR:	Roger Young
GENRE:	Drama
CONTENT:	Nothing objectionable
INTENDED AUDIENCE:	Teenagers and adults
REVIEWER:	Betty Hill

This true story tells about a young Christian couple who own a dairy farm. A calf is born who won't nurse. When the calf dies, a government autopsy reveals death due to malnutrition. The report implies the farmer was at fault. This infuriates the farmer. He suspects something much worse. His neighbor's cows are also dying.

Dead rats are discovered in the barn. Doing his own autopsy, he sees a tablet of food additive in the rat's stomach. A researcher discovers that poison was manufactured by the same chemical company that produced the food additive. Poison was accidentally placed in the food additive sacks.

Their own baby develops a rash. Since the mother has eaten meat and drank milk from sick cows, her own milk is poisoned. She becomes hysterical and depressed because she wanted to breast feed their baby.

They visit another farmer. His son is wearing a baseball cap to hide bald patches in his hair and there is a rash on his mouth. His cattle are infected, but when milk production went down he sold them to make baby food. "Do you think I would have sold them if I knew? I'm a Christian," he states.

Desperate for the public to know the truth, he calls TV stations and tells them the story. With full media coverage, he destroys his entire herd with rifles. The bulldozers cover them up.

The farmer exposed a serious scandal, even though it meant financial ruin. Five hundred farms were infected and 30,000 cows had to be destroyed.

TITLE:	**BLOODSPORT**
QUALITY:	★ ★
RECOMMENDATION:	Extreme Caution
RATING:	R
RELEASE:	1988
STARRING:	Jean Claude Van Damme
DIRECTOR:	Newt Arnold
GENRE:	Action adventure/Kung fu
CONTENT:	Violence
INTENDED AUDIENCE:	Teenagers
REVIEWER:	Christopher Farrell

Kumite is an underground, full-contact, martial arts championship. This is your classic *Rocky* plot; the good guy, Frank W. Dux fights his way to the championship for the honor of his master, while the bad guy brutalizes his opponents, dishonors the noble tradition, and inflates his ego. This formula movie includes the required bungling FBI men and the gorgeous blonde reporter who is desperate enough for the story to work undercover. Also, the good guy's sidekick gets beaten up by the bad guy and has to be avenged.

This film is not bloody, although a good amount of red syrup is spit out of mouths upon impact to body or head, and there's a weak attempt to shock the audience with an overdone broken leg. There are no actors in *Bloodsport*, but there are some amazing athletes. The variety of fighting styles is fascinating, but there's not enough here to spend your time or money.

TITLE:	**BLUE VELVET**
QUALITY:	★★★
RECOMMENDATION:	Evil
RATING:	R
RELEASE:	1986
STARRING:	Kyle MacLachlan, Isabella Rossellini, Dennis Hopper, Laura Dern, and Hope Lange
DIRECTOR:	David Lynch
GENRE:	Mystery/Detective
CONTENT:	Nudity, profanity, sexual violence, and pornography
INTENDED AUDIENCE:	Adults
REVIEWER:	Donna Jackson

Blue Velvet is the type of film which is being given a big advertising push to capture a large audience, and which Christians must not only avoid, but also boycott. This movie is pure evil. The language is filthy, and the sexual violence is disgusting.

Blue Velvet involves a continuing stream of sexual abuse with people being beaten, raped, cursed, hit, and sodomized in a disgusting portrait of evil. *Blue Velvet* is the type of movie which causes susceptible people to go out and commit sexually related crimes. It portrays women as masochists who want to be abused. It convinces men that they will get pleasure from abusing women. It promotes violence as something enjoyable. These images will be burned into the viewer's mind and scar him or her for life. It is evil. Boycott it, no matter what other people say.

TITLE:	**BOYFRIENDS AND GIRLFRIENDS**
QUALITY:	★★★
RECOMMENDATION:	Caution
RATING:	PG
RELEASE:	1988
STARRING:	Emmanuelle Chaulet, Sophie Renoir, Anne-Laure Meury, Eric Viellard, and Francois-Eric Gendron
DIRECTOR:	
GENRE:	Romance
CONTENT:	No moral standard
INTENDED AUDIENCE:	Young adults
REVIEWER:	Ted Baehr

Blanche, employed by the Ministry of Arts and Culture, is new in town. Introverted and waiting for the ideal relationship, she is afraid of one-night stands. After meeting in a cafeteria, she and Lea become friends. Lea, it turns out, is living with Fabien, but has her eye on Alexandre. Always the conniver, Lea convinces Blanche that Blanche is in love with Alexandre. When Lea and Fabien break up, it becomes clear that Blanche and Fabien are perfect for each other, but duped by Lea, Blanche makes a fool of herself pursuing Alexandre. Our heart goes out to Blanche, who wants so much to be loved and yet fumbles every opportunity because she is insecure.

These are very attractive people who want to do the right thing, but don't know what it is. This is a horrible comment on a valueless society that has forgotten what mutual responsibility is all about. We cannot recommend *Boyfriends and Girlfriends* because of the references to cohabitation. However, it provides an insight into the barriers people erect for themselves in trying to establish relationships. It's a pity that this movie was not built on a Biblical foundation!

☆☆☆ CLASSIC ☆☆☆

TITLE:	**THE BOY WHO STOLE A MILLION**
QUALITY:	★ ★ ★ ★
RECOMMENDATION:	Acceptable
RATING:	Not rated
RELEASE:	1960 (British)
STARRING:	Virgilio Texera, Maurice Reyna, Marianne Benet, and Harold Kasket
DIRECTOR:	Charles Crichton
GENRE:	Comedy
CONTENT:	Good lesson on honesty
INTENDED AUDIENCE:	Family
REVIEWER:	Protestant Motion Picture Council

Paco, a twelve-year-old messenger boy in Valencia, overhears his father discussing the repairs of his bread-earning taxi with the garage owner who will not give him credit. Working in a bank and surrounded by large amounts of money, Paco wishes to help his father and "borrows" a million pesetas.

He and his lively dog Pepe are soon the objects of pursuit by the police, several ruffians who hear of the burglary, his father who nearly disowns him, and the garage owner. The chase through Valencia (Keystone Cops style), showing faithfully many of the details, with the bells toiling, the organ grinder grinding, the city throbbing with life, is the story.

A happy ending with the cooperation of the bank manager gives a satisfactory solution and a lesson on honesty. Light, whimsical comedy about a boy and his dog but entertaining for more than children.

TITLE:	**BRADDOCK: MISSING IN ACTION III**
QUALITY:	★ ★ ★
RECOMMENDATION:	Caution

RATING:	R
RELEASE:	1987
STARRING:	Chuck Norris
DIRECTOR:	Aaron Norris
GENRE:	War
CONTENT:	Violence and some rough language
INTENDED AUDIENCE:	Adult
REVIEWER:	Richard White

Braddock: Missing in Action III is full of love, praises of God and dreams of freedom. The violence is redeemed by hope and loyalty. If Braddock's victory over impossible odds seems a bit far-fetched, it is. Movies are sometimes made as dreams, showing us who we want to be and what we could do, not who we are and what we do. *Braddock: Missing in Action III* reminds us that we were once in Vietnam and our children are still there: fifteen thousand tormented outcasts—marked and condemned.

Col. Braddock believed that his Vietnamese wife had been killed before the American army retreated. More than ten years later, a priest named Polanski tells Braddock his wife and son are alive. Braddock takes on the CIA and the entire Vietnamese army to rescue them. In the process, he manages to break out Fr. Polanski (whose line throughout the movie is, "Thank God") and all the children in his orphanage.

This film offers one of the best love scenes around when Braddock finds his family in a candle-lit shack. He emerges out of the rain and shadows to see his wife and son cringing on the floor, expecting to see a policeman. She recognizes him, stands, walks to him. "I didn't know," Braddock says. "It doesn't matter," she whispers and embraces him. "I prayed you would come for us and you are here."

The violence and rough language in this one is redeemed by scenes that should be remembered: the retreat from Saigon; the lives of the Amerasian children; and, the torture, murder, and overwhelming police presence that is part of everyday life in communist countries. When will Americans admit that our only shame in Vietnam was to prefer defeat rather than victory—to condemn those who looked to us for help and those who served America?

☆☆☆ CLASSIC ☆☆☆

TITLE:	**BRAINWASHED**
QUALITY:	★★★★
RECOMMENDATION:	Caution
RATING:	Not rated
RELEASE:	1961
STARRING:	Curt Jurgens, Claire Bloom, Jorg Felmy, and Mario Adolrf
DIRECTOR:	Gerd Oswald
GENRE:	War

CONTENT:	Nothing objectionable, but some caution for children
INTENDED AUDIENCE:	Adult
REVIEWER:	Protestant Motion Picture Council

This is a highly suspenseful, gripping and fascinating psychological melodrama, though somewhat deliberate. It tells about an Austrian aristocrat who is thrown into solitary confinement by the Nazis upon their takeover in 1938.

While they mentally torture him to obtain vital secrets, he attempts to retain his sanity by stashing a book on chess in his cell and concentrating on the complexities of the chessboard to keep his mind stimulated and clear. His mind finally functions only in terms of a chess game.

This is a sinister, well-developed, believable story, told in flashbacks, expertly directed and convincingly acted. It is remarkable in what it leaves to deduction rather than to dialogue.

The photography is important, filmed on locations in Austria and Yugoslavia. Music is an excellent accompaniment to the dark mood of the picture.

TITLE:	**BRAVESTAR, THE MOVIE**
QUALITY:	★★★
RECOMMENDATION:	Caution
RATING:	PG
RELEASE:	1988
DIRECTOR:	Tom Tataranowicz
GENRE:	Animated/Children/Science fiction
CONTENT:	Violence
INTENDED AUDIENCE:	Children
REVIEWER:	John Evans, Movie Morality Preview

Adapted from a TV cartoon series, *Bravestar, the Movie* features animated, futuristic characters on an alien planet in a faraway galaxy. Two forces are locked in a fierce battle throughout the film. The evil force is led by the large bull-like Stampede. He's opposed by an American Indian type leader who has preserved his son, Bravestar, with his magical powers to fight Stampede in the future. Stampede recruits many evil followers on another planet to join him in the battle, but Marshall Bravestar is brought in to fight his evil domination. Aided by townspeople and critters, Bravestar fortifies a Western-like town and the battle rages.

The overall quality of this animated film is quite good. The plot and dialogue are strong and fascinating. Almost continuous violence dominates the action. While the film is filled with fighting and evil powers, other conventional offensive elements, such as vulgar and profane language and sexual content, have been eliminated. Though *Bravestar, the Movie* is an innovative, well-done cartoon film, its over emphasis on violence keeps us from recommending it.

☆☆☆ CLASSIC ☆☆☆

TITLE:	**THE BRIDAL PATH**
QUALITY:	★ ★ ★
RECOMMENDATION:	Acceptable
RATING:	Not rated
RELEASE:	1959 (British)
STARRING:	Bill Tavers, Alex MacKenzie, Eric Woodburn, and Jack Lambert
DIRECTOR:	Frank Launder
GENRE:	Romantic Comedy
CONTENT:	Nothing objectionable
INTENDED AUDIENCE:	Adult
REVIEWER:	Protestant Motion Picture Council

A resident on a remote island is ordered to go from his homeland to the Scottish mainland in search of a wife. Her specifications have been determined by the elders of the village, so that no more first cousins marry in the cloistered community.

With the best of intentions, this romantic comedy's hero acts as a lumbering innocent whose every move seems to be misinterpreted. When he is mistaken for a salmon poacher, he must flee from the police. His escape leads through many places and awkward situations, including the great event of the Scottish games.

The running man proves to himself there is "no place like home," and no winsome lassie like the one waiting for him on his island.

There is beautiful photography of the scenery. Local customs and good settings abound. A fine musical background is provided by the Campbeltown Gaelic Choir. The acting is excellent.

TITLE:	**BROADCAST NEWS**
QUALITY:	★ ★ ★
RECOMMENDATION:	Extreme Caution
RATING:	R
RELEASE:	1987
STARRING:	William Hurt, Holly Hunter, and Albert Brooks
DIRECTOR:	James Brooks
GENRE:	Drama/Comedy
CONTENT:	Profanity, brief nudity, and adult situations

INTENDED AUDIENCE:	Adults
REVIEWER:	Bret Senft

Broadcast News moves *Terms of Endearment* into the newsroom. The focus remains the same: personal relationships in the Eighties, amid changing mores.

Holly Hunter plays a news producer obsessed with her work and repelled by the commercialism and sensationalism pervading the industry. Hurt is a handsome anchorman with no experience and no particular interest in news. Brooks is a Pulitzer Prize winning reporter with no audience appeal. Brooks loves Hunter, who loves Hurt, who loves himself and his future as a national anchorman of the Peter Jennings variety.

Unfortunately, this is a film with no moral center. *Broadcast News* is a failed attempt to treat perhaps the most important subject of our time. Therefore, we recommend you avoid this superficial humanist portrait of the media elite who shape our society.

TITLE:	**BULL DURHAM**
QUALITY:	★ ★
RECOMMENDATION:	Evil
RATING:	R
RELEASE:	1988
STARRING:	Kevin Kostner, Susan Sarandon, and Tim Robbins
DIRECTOR:	Ron Shelton
GENRE:	Comedy/Romance
CONTENT:	Profanity, blasphemy, nudity, obscenity, sex, occultism, and as much garbage as the writer/director could include
INTENDED AUDIENCE:	Adults
REVIEWER:	Ted Baehr

Putting down Jesus and Christianity, *Bull Durham* worships baseball as a religious metaphor. Annie Savoy's internal dialogue dictates a New Age melange tied together by her masochistic nymphomania. Annie worshipped Buddha and then Jesus (who made her feel guilty) until she decided to devote the rest of her life sleeping with a different baseball player every season.

Her intentions change when she meets Crash Davis, who exhibits a tender cynicism which appeals to her. Although she falls for Crash, she chooses to have her yearly affair with a young pitcher, Nuke LaLoosh, who manifests unrestrained prowess in all that he does. In the end, thanks to Crash's tutoring, Nuke goes to the majors and Annie ends up with Crash.

Bull Durham is tedious. The writer/director throws as much sex, nudity, profanity, and blasphemy as he can at the audience to hold their attention. Occultism, reincarnation and everything God abhors is stuffed into this movie. It is unbearably awful. Boycott *Bull Durham*.

TITLE:	**BURBS**
QUALITY:	★★★
RECOMMENDATION:	Bad
RATING:	PG
RELEASE:	1989
STARRING:	Tom Hanks and Bruce Dern
DIRECTOR:	Joe Dante
GENRE:	Comedy
CONTENT:	Obscenity and occultism
INTENDED AUDIENCE:	Teenagers
REVIEWER:	Marty Zinger

Burbs is a typical suburban community, located at the end of a cul-de-sac. The fireworks start when a new family moves into a house on the cul-de-sac. No one knows anything about them, except they rarely leave their house and appear suspicious. Suspicions turn into paranoia when one of the neighbors disappears. This leads the community into fabricating stories. The sleuths get so worked up they break into the house and go on a wild digging party. They do not find any bodies, but Tom Hanks continues to dig until he bursts a gas line. The house blows up just as the owners return to see their house ablaze.

Hanks ends up in an ambulance. A doctor accompanies him, intent on adding Hanks to his "collection of dead bodies." He nearly wrestles Hanks to death. The neighbors rescue Hanks, after finding evidence against the doctor. This time the nosey neighbors turn out to be heroes.

This is a lightweight, nothing. Bruce Dern's young wife is slightly dingy and promiscuous. There is also an impression of something demonic going on, which turns out not to be the case, but it is abhorrent and unnecessary. What's worse, it is boring. Avoid this rotten movie at all costs.

☆☆☆ MASTERPIECE ☆☆☆

TITLE:	**BURKE AND WILLS**
QUALITY:	★★★★
RECOMMENDATION:	Caution
RATING:	PG-13
RELEASE:	1987
STARRING:	Jack Thompson, Nigel Havers, and Greta Scacchi
DIRECTOR:	Graeme Clifford
GENRE:	Action adventure/Historical/Biography/Western

CONTENT: Some earthy language, rough situations, and a very brief
                            conjugal scene

INTENDED AUDIENCE: Adults

REVIEWER: Ted Baehr

Burke and Wills is a story of courage and perseverance in the face of insincerity. It is the story of every man with a mission. It is the story of the first Europeans to cross the Australian outback in 1860–61.

Mr. Wills is a refined gentleman from England. A curious naturalist, Mr. Wills travels to Australia to explore the uncharted wilderness.

Mr. Burke is a romantic Irishman who has been chasing the local music hall beauty for years. He seizes upon the idea of rushing across the desert of Australia to make his fame and fortune.

Mr. Burke and Mr. Wills set out with too many men and supplies to cross Australia from coast to coast. The outback is a terrifying place. They shed supplies along the way. They reach the last known landmark, Cutters Creek, and leave their best man, William, with three other men and supplies to hold a little fort until they return.

They race across the desert in the summer heat. Miraculously, they make it to the gulf. On the way back, crazed by the sun and the 140 degree heat, they lose one man and all but one of their camels. Months late, they arrive at Cutter's Creek on the very day that William left to take his men and supplies back to civilization. The group who was to supply William never arrived because the businessman who agreed to finance the operation reneged on his commitment.

Mr. Burke, Mr. Wills and John King, the young aid de camp, find themselves stranded in the desert. They try to make it to civilization, but their last camel dies. John is found by a search party prompted by the outcries of a angry press, shocked that Burke and Wills have been abandoned. The movie ends with the testimony of John King as he addresses the people of Melbourne who let Burke and Wills down by failing to keep their word.

There are positive references to prayer, faith, talking to God, and knowing God intimately. John King, the survivor is a praying man. His prayers prompt Mr. Burke to ask how to talk to God.

The movie focuses on the fact that trust is a basic building block of civilization. Each of the men who gave their word to support Mr. Burke and Mr. Wills breaks that trust. In heroic contrast, Mr. Burke and Mr. Wills keep their word. When people play fast and loose with their promises, civilization dies.

As Christians, we live in covenant with God and our fellow man. When we fail to keep our word, we break that covenant relationship. *Burke and Wills* summarizes Psalm 15 verses 1 and 4b where God replies to the psalmist that the man who keeps his word no matter what the cost will be allowed to live in His sanctuary.

Burke and Wills is a great movie: the photography is beautiful; the story is magnificent; the literary references are wonderful; and, the adventure is exciting. There is some earthy obscenity, but no profanity. There is a brief, conjugal situation between Burke and his bride under the covers, but it is innocuous.

Burke and Wills is a must for every adult Christian. It clearly presents the meaning of covenant. If you can, see it.

TITLE:	**BURNING SECRETS**
QUALITY:	★ ★ ★
RECOMMENDATION:	Caution
RATING:	Not available
RELEASE:	1988
STARRING:	Faye Dunaway, Claus Maria Brandauer, Ian Richardson, and David Eberts
DIRECTOR:	Andrew Birkin
GENRE:	Romance
CONTENT:	No nudity, no profanity, and shows respect for elders, but focuses on an incipient illicit affair
INTENDED AUDIENCE:	Adults
REVIEWER:	Lauren Neal

A young boy and his mother visit an exclusive lodge in the Austrian countryside, leaving his father at work in the city. A baron eyes the beautiful mother and establishes a relationship with the boy. The boy is smitten with the baron's entertaining war stories.

However, as the baron focuses on his mother, the young boy becomes jealous. The boy's mother almost falls prey to the baron, but is stopped by the boy. The baron admits he does not love her, but had a passion for the conquest. Hurt and confused, the boy runs to catch a train home to his father. The mother arrives home shortly after, to find that the boy has not told his father, but rather covered up his mother's actions. A child within the boy is dead forever.

The movie deals with the very real and serious issues of friendship, love, faithfulness, lust, and growing up. Although, the subject matter is true to life, it is not the way God chooses for His children. God is not included in the movie, rather it centers around desire. We recommend caution.

TITLE:	**BUY AND CELL**
QUALITY:	★ ★
RECOMMENDATION:	Extreme Caution
RATING:	R
RELEASE:	1989
STARRING:	Robert Carradine, Michael Windslow, Ben Vereen, and Malcom McDowell
DIRECTOR:	Robert Boris
GENRE:	Comedy
CONTENT:	Rough prison language and nudity

INTENDED AUDIENCE: Adults

REVIEWER: Ken Kistner

Herbie Altman, a stock analyst, is framed and takes the fall for his company's improper activities in some Wall Street deals. The warden seeks his opinion on the market. Herbie refuses, because the money the warden wants to invest is money he has diverted from prison programs. However, when cellmate Sly is threatened with death for bad gambling debts, Herbie comes to the rescue. He convinces the inmates to pool their money and invest it according to his advice. They amass a fortune. Through a "moving wall," the prisoners keep the warden in the dark about their business deals, a disco stage, and hot tubs used for relaxation after a day of at their computer terminals. James Bond would be proud!

Adults can separate fact from fantasy, but many times children do not. Since most children get their first impressions of our penal system through the media, we need to make sure they realize that the majority of the people filling our prisons are not there for bootlegging firecrackers and that teaching someone to use a computer does not change their moral ethics. Avoid *Buy and Cell*; it's not worth the price of admission or rental.

TITLE:	**CADDYSHACK II**
QUALITY:	★★
RECOMMENDATION:	Caution
RATING:	PG
RELEASE:	1988
STARRING:	Jackie Mason, Robert Stack, Dyan Cannon, Dina Merrill, Randy Quaid, Chevy Chase, and Dan Aykroyd
DIRECTOR:	Allan Arkush
GENRE:	Comedy
CONTENT:	Obscenity, sexual innuendo, and adolescent humor
INTENDED AUDIENCE:	Teens and adults
REVIEWER:	Anne Machell

Kate and her father, Jack Hartoonian, are denied country club membership after Jack's embarrassing behavior. Jack purchases the 53 percent of club's stock and transforms the club into a Wacky Golf Course. The father of Kate's friend Miffy hires Captain Everett, a deranged Viet Nam veteran, to do away with Jack. Kate is so embarrassed by her father that she moves in with Miffy until Miffy suggests Kate change her last name to Hart. Kate "comes to her senses" and apologizes to her father. Captain Everett's efforts at destroying Jack are unsuccessful when our gopher friend sabotages the exploding golf balls meant for Jack, and Elizabeth falls in love with Jack. The good guys win, and everyone lives happily ever after.

If you think the plot was boring, you should hear the jokes. At the screening, there was a conspicuous absence of laughter. Positives for this film are the lack of nudity, and Christians were not mocked, nor is the Lord's Name taken in vain. This is not an evil film, but just a waste of time and money.

TITLE:	**CAMPUS MAN**
QUALITY:	★★
RECOMMENDATION:	Caution
RATING:	PG-13
RELEASE:	1987
STARRING:	John Dye, Kim Delaney, Kathleen Wilhoite, and Morgan Fairchild
DIRECTOR:	Ron Casden
GENRE:	Comedy
CONTENT:	Very little off-color language
INTENDED AUDIENCE:	Adults
REVIEWER:	Ken Kistner

Campus Man is a light comedy with no nudity and very little off-color language. In it, a college student named Todd doesn't win his scholarship, so he badgers Brett, a champion diver, into posing for his "Men of Arizona State University" pin-up calendar, which he hopes will earn him $10,000 for tuition. It costs him $12,000 to print the calendar which he borrows from Cactus Jack. Todd makes money from the calendar sales, but can't pay both Cactus Jack and his tuition. He pays his tuition.

Catherine from *Image* magazine comes along to find the "Man of the '80's." Todd talks Brett into signing up. Brett, who is headed for the Olympics, loses his eligibility because of this contract. Todd gets Catherine to tear up the contract, but now, Catherine is in trouble because she is committed to introducing the "Man of the 80's" at the charity diving match. Todd cleans up Cactus Jack so he becomes the "Man of the 80's." Brett gets his amateur standing back, and everyone lives happily ever after.

Ingenuity triumphs over adversity. However, there are some loose moral ends in *Campus Man*, such as the fact that Todd manipulates people to achieve his goals. In the final analysis, *Campus Man* is a cute movie. You could do much worse. *Campus Man* is recommended with caution.

TITLE:	**CAUGHT**
QUALITY:	★★
RECOMMENDATION:	Caution
RATING:	PG-13
RELEASE:	1987
STARRING:	John Shephard and Jill Ireland
DIRECTOR:	James Collier
GENRE:	Drama

CONTENT: Homosexuality and drugs

INTENDED AUDIENCE: All ages

REVIEWER: Ted Baehr

Caught is another Billy Graham Organization/World Wide Pictures evangelistic film. As an evangelistic tool, it may work; however, as a feature film, it is unfulfilled potential.

Caught tells the story of a young man, Timothy, who discovers that he was born out of wedlock and goes off to Europe to search for his father. He gets caught up in the drug scene and the male prostitution trade in Amsterdam. Tim is befriended by an Indian boy, Raji, who is coming to the Billy Graham evangelistic training session. Raji witnesses the Gospel to Timothy, and helps Timothy find his father. Timothy comes to Christ and goes home to his mother and his girlfriend.

This is an interesting storyline. However, the realization of the film leaves much to be desired. There is an excessive focus on homosexuality. The first part of the film is dull. *Caught* is okay, but not great. It won't hurt anybody.

TITLE: **CHANCES ARE**

QUALITY: ★ ★ ★ ★

RECOMMENDATION: Extreme Caution

RATING: PG

RELEASE: 1989

STARRING: Cybill Shepherd, Robert Downey, Jr., and Ryan O'Neal

DIRECTOR: Emile Ardolino

GENRE: Romance

CONTENT: Reincarnation, a few profanities, and premarital sex

INTENDED AUDIENCE: Adults

REVIEWER: Dak Ming

The deceased Federal prosecutor Louie Jeffries realizes his soul has been "recycled" to Alex Finch, a graduate of Yale University, who is seeking a job at the *Washington Post*. Louie was improperly processed in the clouds so the Louie in Alex remembers inside information that gives Alex a D.C.-sized exposé for an article. Alex re-encounters Phillip, Louie's best man at his wedding to Corine. His faithful bride has never in twenty-three years since Louie's fatal accident let anyone distract her from her total devotion to Louie. Phillip patiently consoles her, waiting until she forgets her husband. Miranda, Louie's daughter, born after his death, is smitten by Alex, who is anxious to get back to life as Louie, Miranda's father and Corine's husband. They work out a solution with divine intervention. To help dispel any confusion, in one scene where Corine tries to tell Phillip that Louie is back, Phillip tells her no one has ever come back, "except Jesus Christ."

This growingly popular New Age concept of reincarnation is an anathema to God. Also, this film condones pre-marital sex which is totally irresponsible in our age of AIDS and abuse. Avoid this deranged movie.

A man is destined to die once, and after that to face Judgment. (Hebrews 9:27)

☆☆☆ **MASTERPIECE** ☆☆☆

TITLE:	**THE CHARGE OF THE LIGHT BRIGADE (115 Minutes, Black and White)**
QUALITY:	★ ★ ★ ★
RECOMMENDATION:	Acceptable
RATING:	Not rated
RELEASE:	1936
STARRING:	Errol Flynn, Olivia de Havilland, Patric Knowles, Donald Crisp, Henry Stephenson, Nigel Bruce, and David Niven
DIRECTOR:	Michael Curtiz
GENRE:	War
CONTENT:	Nothing objectionable
INTENDED AUDIENCE:	Adult
REVIEWER:	Ted Baehr

In northwest India in 1850, a British officer, Major Geoffery Vickers is sent to the remote fortress of Chukoti after saving the life of a scheming Indian Raj, Surat Khan. Unexpectedly, Khan's tribesmen attack. It is a massacre. Vickers and the remnants of the 27th Lancers vow revenge.

The light calvary unit, part of the Light Brigade, is removed to the Crimea where British troops face the Russian forces, entrenched on Balaclava Heights. Vickers receives an order for the general's signature which directs the withdrawal of the Light Brigade. Knowing that Khan is with the Russians and consumed by vengeance, he rewrites the order to direct the Light Brigade to attack and signs the general's name.

He then leads the magnificent charge of the doomed 600 calvarymen into the "Valley of Death." They are decimated by Russian artillery as they race forward, but nothing can stop this heroic charge. Not a trooper turns back. The British fall in whole ranks as the Russian general and Khan stand on Balaclava Heights in shock and awe.

Even the counter-attacking Russian calvary cannot stop the lancers who break through the final barricades, Vickers leading the way. He spots Khan and raises his lance. Khan shoots him fatally, but Vickers manages to hurl his lance through the Khan's evil heart. Vickers falls from his horse and watches rider after rider drive lances into Khan's body. Vickers dies knowing that the Chukoti massacre has been avenged.

At headquarters, the general takes full responsibility for ordering the suicidal charge. Alone, he reads Vicker's letter of confession. However, rather than hold up this dead hero to shame, the general tosses the letter into a fire, whispering, "For conspicuous gallantry."

TITLE:	**CHILD'S PLAY**
QUALITY:	★★
RECOMMENDATION:	Evil
RATING:	R
RELEASE:	1988
STARRING:	Catherine Hicks and Chris Saranson
DIRECTOR:	Tom Holland
GENRE:	Horror
CONTENT:	Profanity, obscenity, bloody violence, and gory dismemberment
INTENDED AUDIENCE:	Teenagers and adults
REVIEWER:	Don Vice

This madness begins with a detective engaged in a gun battle with a weirdo. The bad guy is hit, but before departing for his reward, he calls upon God to place his soul into a nearby doll so he can take revenge against the detective and his partner, who drove off and left him for the cops. Andy's mother, who bought a "good guy" doll, "Chucky," appears on the scene. No one knows at this point that the "good guy" doll has turned into a "bad guy." The doll talks to Andy and commits a murder, but when Andy tries to tell Mom or anyone else, no one will believe him. After Chucky takes care of a baby-sitter, his partner and former mentor, he then determines he must transfer his talent into Andy. The end of Chucky takes an endless amount of time designed to keep the audience on the edge of their seats. It does not work.

Save your time and money. *Child's Play* is evil trash full of profanity, obscenity, bloody violence, and gory dismemberment. This is the bottom of the barrel. Unfortunately, *Child's Play* is one of the top-grossing films of the season. If people would avoid films like this, Hollywood would stop making them.

TITLE:	**THE CHIPMUNK ADVENTURE**
QUALITY:	★★
RECOMMENDATION:	Acceptable
RATING:	G
RELEASE:	1987
STARRING:	The Chipmunks and the Chipettes
DIRECTOR:	Janice Karmen
CONTENT:	Nothing objectionable
GENRE:	Children
INTENDED AUDIENCE:	Children

REVIEWER: Peirce and James Baehr

The Chipmunk Adventure is a film which little children will love and adults will endure. It is a pure action adventure, cartoon.

Dave, who is the human surrogate parent for the three Chipmunks (Simon, Theodore and Alvin), departs for Europe and leaves the Chipmunks with Mrs. Miller. The Chipmunks are playing the video arcade game of *80 Days Around the World* with the Chipettes.

Claudia and Klaus are trying to figure out how to smuggle some diamonds around the world without being caught by the nefarious Jemal. They use the Chipmunks to deliver the diamonds by daring them to undertake a real life version of the video game. They challenge the Chipettes and the Chipmunks to race each other around the world following different routes, dropping dolls concealing diamonds at twelve different points and picking up complimentary dolls concealing dollars at each point.

The Chipmunks and Chipettes go off in balloons, followed by Jemal's henchmen. After several stops around the world, the Chipettes find that the dolls contain diamonds. They find and rescue the Chipmunks from cannibals and come back to Los Angeles, arriving at the same time Dave is returning from Europe. They are captured by Claudia and Klaus. Dave sees them, and gets into the police car with Jemal. Claudia and Klaus are captured and thrown into jail. The Chipmunks go back home.

The Chipmunk Adventure has no occultism, no evil plot devices, no gnosticism, and no heresies. There is also no divinity, no grace and nothing great in the movie. However, your children will like it.

TITLE:	**CLARA'S HEART**
QUALITY:	★★★★
RECOMMENDATION:	Caution
RATING:	PG-13
RELEASE:	1988
STARRING:	Whoopi Goldberg, Michael Ontkean, and Kathleen Quinlan
DIRECTOR:	Robert Mulligan
GENRE:	Drama
CONTENT:	Two expletives and one profanity
INTENDED AUDIENCE:	Adolescents and adults
REVIEWER:	Bruce Grimes

Leona and Bill Hart have a serious problem. Their infant daughter just died. Leona has difficulty adjusting. Their son David, age twelve, is given to Clara Mayfield, a Jamaican housekeeper who moves in with the family. The Hart family has it all: a mansion on the bay, limousines, and money. The Hart family also has pain, because they have no love, only things. David finds the love he needs from Clara. Bill is caught cheating on Leona, and Leona becomes involved with a psychiatrist who writes books on *Losing Guilt*. The family destroys itself. Only Clara remains a bedrock, with her foundation: Jesus Christ.

This excellent film conveys to the audience the necessity of humility and faith in God. Whoopi Goldberg shines as Clara, a determined woman with a love for Jesus Christ, as evidenced by her convictions and service to others. This film is highly recommended. It is an example of how Hollywood can create magnificent films without having to rely on sex, violence, or foul language.

TITLE:	**CHOOSE ME**
QUALITY:	★ ★ ★
RECOMMENDATION:	Extreme Caution
RATING:	PG-13
RELEASE:	1986
STARRING:	Genevieve Bujold, Keith Carradine, and Leslie Ann Warren
DIRECTOR:	Allen Rudolph
PRODUCERS:	Carolyn Pfeiffer and David Blocker
GENRE:	Romance
CONTENT:	No nudity, but profanity, obscenity, and implied sex
INTENDED AUDIENCE:	Adults
REVIEWER:	Ted Baehr

Choose Me has the simple premise that love triumphs over everything. This premise is realized in a modern realistic fairy tale set in the shadows of the seediest part of town.

It is the story of three outcasts. Eve owns a bar, loves men, and fears permanent relationships. Mickey has just been released from a mental institution. Once upon a time he was a professor at Yale, a poet, a CIA agent, and a test pilot, but he cracked up along the way.

Dr. Nancy Love motivates the relationship between Mickey and Eve. Nancy is a famous radio talk show host who has been bottled up for years and learns from Mickey and Eve how to accept herself and others. Eve and Mickey find each other in spite of the destructive temptations of the world, and, in the end, get married and head off into the sunset together on a bus.

Casual sex, profanity, and the seedy setting undermines the positive premise. The story emerges from the bottom of the sinful human condition and ends affirming goodness, grace, and love. *Choose Me* is fast-paced and beautifully photographed. It is a powerful love story which ends with Nancy, the psychologist, admitting, "I am not God," and with Eve affirming, "Marriage is a sacred thing."

It would be encouraging if pagans would hear the premise and the messages at the end of *Choose Me*. Unfortunately, many might be led astray by the surplus of casual sexual matter which is shown to be wrong, but is still present. However, it must be noted that there is no pornography, graphic sex, or nudity in this film. In the final analysis, *Choose Me* is a movie Christians should avoid.

TITLE:	**CINDERELLA**
QUALITY:	★★★
RECOMMENDATION:	Caution
RATING:	G
RELEASE:	1950, re-release 1987
STARRING:	Cinderella, a handsome prince, and assorted others
DIRECTOR:	Wilfred Jackson, Hamilton Luske, and Clyde Geronomie
PRODUCER:	Walt Disney
GENRE:	Animated/Children/Romance
CONTENT:	Nothing objectionable
INTENDED AUDIENCE:	Everyone
REVIEWER:	Lauren Neal, and Peirce and James Baehr

Cinderella slaves to take care of her two stepsisters and stepmother. Her gentle nature permeates all that she does. The stepmother and stepsisters resent her for this. The King sends out an invitation inviting all single women to a ball in honor of his son. The three women leave a sad Cinderella at home. Cinderella's fairy godmother prepares a way for the young girl to go. After dancing with the prince, Cinderella flees to return home by midnight. In her hurry, she leaves a glass slipper behind. The prince searches the kingdom to find the foot that fits the slipper.

Unfortunately, *Cinderella* suggests that magic and wishful thinking can overcome evil. In truth, only Jesus can and has defeated the Evil One. *Cinderella* is recommended with the caveat that children need to be informed that Jesus is the Answer to evil, not Prince Charming nor a fairy godmother.

TITLE:	**COBRA VERDE**
QUALITY:	★★★★
RECOMMENDATION:	Caution
RATING:	Not Rated
RELEASE:	1988
STARRING:	Klaus Kinsky and Peter Berling
DIRECTOR:	Werner Herzog
GENRE:	Historical
CONTENT:	Mild expletives and inoffensive tribal "National Geographic" nudity
INTENDED AUDIENCE:	Adults
REVIEWER:	Bruce Grimes

With passion, flair and energy, *Cobra Verde* captures the last years of the slave trade. The U.S. ended slavery in the mid 1800's, but Brazil continued since slaves worked the sugar plantations. Francisco M. da Silva's story personifies the shame of slavery. da Silva conquers the Africans by pitting tribe against tribe. His trade flourishes, and da Silva becomes a man who is feared. However, his power wanes when Brazil abandons slavery, and he becomes nothing in the eyes of men.

This powerful film provides viewers with much of what makes a film good: tension between characters; fine performances; a well-written script with moral undertones; exotic locations; and a cornucopia of moral issues to examine. *Cobra Verde* makes the Biblical point that we are answerable ultimately to God. Unfortunately, it contains natural, inoffensive tribal nudity and a few expletives. However, it is a highly entertaining, beautifully made film which makes an extremely important Biblical point. We highly recommend *Cobra Verde*.

TITLE:	**COCKTAIL**
QUALITY:	★ ★ ★
RECOMMENDATION:	Extreme Caution
RATING:	R
RELEASE:	1988
STARRING:	Tom Cruise, Bryan Brown, and Elisabeth Shue
DIRECTOR:	Roger Donaldson
GENRE:	Romance/Comedy
CONTENT:	Profanity, obscenity, and explicit sex
INTENDED AUDIENCE:	Adult
REVIEWER:	Ted Baehr

Cocktail is a morality play for immoral people. Brian Flanagan seeks his fortune in New York City. After being rejected by Wall Street, he gets a job working with a bartender named Doug Coughlin. Doug teaches Brian everything he knows.

Brian heads for Jamaica where he falls for artist Jordan Mooney until Doug shows up with his wealthy bride. Doug challenges Brian to land someone with money. Brian follows this advice, losing Jordan while indenturing himself to a businesswoman.

After months, Brian goes back to Jordan, who tells him she's pregnant and kicks him out. When Doug commits suicide, Brian kidnaps Jordan. They get married in a renovated bar to live happily ever after in the ethnic outskirts of New York City.

The authors show that the profanity and sexual immorality in their movie is wrong, but they seem to be saying that marriage will save you from the wicked world. Christians know this is not the case. We cannot recommend *Cocktail* because of the explicit sex and foul language.

TITLE:	**COCOON: THE RETURN**
QUALITY:	★ ★ ★
RECOMMENDATION:	Extreme Caution
RATING:	PG
RELEASE:	1988
STARRING:	Don Ameche, Steve Guttenberg, Jack Gilford, Wilford Brinley, Maureen Stapleton, and Courteney Cox
DIRECTOR:	Daniel Petrie
GENRE:	Science fiction/Comedy
CONTENT:	Vulgarities, three profanities, and an allusion to sexual relationships
INTENDED AUDIENCE:	All ages
REVIEWER:	Nancy Hanger

The elderly people, who left for space and perpetual youth, return to visit their friends and family in Florida while the Antareans recover the cocoons not rescued five years earlier. During the week-long visit, the Antareans encourage their friends to enjoy everything that is not available on their new planet: young children, pretty girls, hot dogs, basketball, roses, and nightclub dancing. They begin experiencing homesickness, the natural effects of aging, and even death for one of them. Several decide to stay on earth because of the value they place on their earthly relationships. Ben acknowledges that parents shouldn't outlive their children and that their grandson's growing up is too valuable for them to miss.

Cocoon: The Return is a funny film with an uplifting emphasis on caring relationships. Unfortunately, it is full of vulgar language, as well as "extra-terrestrial hope" which doesn't acknowledge that our true hope of salvation and everlasting life is Jesus Christ. Therefore, we recommend that you skip *Cocoon: The Return*.

TITLE:	**THE COLOR OF MONEY**
QUALITY:	★ ★ ★
RECOMMENDATION:	Extreme Caution
RATING:	R
RELEASE:	1986
STARRING:	Paul Newman and Tom Cruise
DIRECTOR:	Martin Scorsese
GENRE:	Drama/Action adventure
CONTENT:	Profanity, sexual situations, and nudity
INTENDED AUDIENCE:	Adults

REVIEWER: Ted Baehr

The Color of Money is a twenty-five-year later sequel to *The Hustler* which does not compare with the original masterpiece. *The Hustler* has some of the greatest dialogue ever written; *The Color of Money* is adrift in a sea of self-consciousness.

Once more, Paul Newman plays "Fast Eddie" Felson, who has given up pool to sell cheap alcohol to bars. Eddie discovers a young pool player, Vincent, who can make it to the top. Eddie undertakes the education of Vince and his girlfriend so that they can hustle their way to fame and fortune. On the way, Eddie decides he isn't over the hill and drops Vince so he can start playing pool to win all over again. Eddie and Vince make it to the top of the ladder in the Atlantic City pool championship matches. Vince throws the game so he can hustle more money at the practice tables just as Eddie taught him. Eddie is furious, defaults on his last game and challenges Vince to a game. The movie ends before this game between the giants is played.

The Color of Money is too long. As is the case with most of Scorsese's movies, there is a selfish, macho attitude which demonstrates the hero's immaturity and inability to love. To make such selfish men the heroes is quite sad. These men have no way of giving of themselves to anyone else, especially the women who love them. They need Jesus Christ.

Also, there is no reason for the nudity and sexual promiscuity in this movie, which makes the film off limits to Christians. Avoid *The Color of Money.*

TITLE:	**COLORS**
QUALITY:	★ ★ ★
RECOMMENDATION:	Bad
RATING:	R
RELEASE:	1988
STARRING:	Sean Penn, Robert Duvall, and Maria Conchita Alonzo
DIRECTOR:	Dennis Hopper
GENRE:	Detective
CONTENT:	Sexual situations, profanity, obscenity, and violence
INTENDED AUDIENCE:	Adults
REVIEWER:	Rick Hight

Two policemen hit the streets of L.A. as members of the "LAPD Crash Unit." These honest cops want to rid the streets of gangs. Penn is a "let's take a bite out of crime" cop. Duvall builds relationships by showing gang members he doesn't want to send them to jail, he just wants them to get out of the gangs. The Crypts prey on the Blood in drive-by shootings. Innocent bystanders are killed. All the gang members end up dead or arrested.

Colors is frightening because of its reality. It's educational, not exploitative. The question is, how much education can you handle?

The cinematography is gritty and bleak, like the walls of east L.A. The script is weak and there are two gratuitous sex scenes. The main problem is that Christ is not presented as the answer to the problem. We cannot recommend *Colors*.

TITLE:	**COMING TO AMERICA**
QUALITY:	★★★
RECOMMENDATION:	Extreme Caution
RATING:	R
RELEASE:	1988
STARRING:	Eddie Murphy, Arsenio Hall, James Earl Jones, John Amos, Madge Sinclair, and Shari Headley
DIRECTOR:	John Landis
GENRE:	Comedy
CONTENT:	Profanity, obscenity, and brief nudity
INTENDED AUDIENCE:	Teenagers and adults
REVIEWER:	Abby Flanders

Where would a foreign prince find a good catch? Queens, N.Y., where else? So, forfeiting his money, this prince takes his servant and jumps into the lifestyle of the poor and proud. His search introduces him to hilarious characters, most of whom are played by Hall and Murphy. He finds a job at a fast-food establishment, and the owner's daughter becomes the object of his affection. Prince falls for the girl and finds greater wealth within: life, love, and people.

Is this the Eddie Murphy of *Raw* fame? No. This is a more mature entertainer who has created a fantasy that may be his dream of how things could be when the prince of comedy forfeits his kingdom for something greater—values!

However, *Coming to America* is not recommended because it does contains profanity, obscenity, lewdness, and brief nudity. Eddie Murphy has moved away from his previous foul-mouthed, rebellious persona, but not far enough.

TITLE:	**COMING UP ROSES (Subtitles)**
QUALITY:	★★★
RECOMMENDATION:	Caution
RATING:	PG
RELEASE:	1987
STARRING:	Dafydd Hywel, Iola Gregory, Marri Emlyn, and Olive Michael
DIRECTOR:	Stephen Bayly
GENRE:	Drama/Romance
CONTENT:	Nothing offensive and much to be commended

INTENDED AUDIENCE:	Adults
REVIEWER:	Ted Baehr

Coming Up Roses is an upbeat, positive, uplifting film. It is rare to find a film which is so positive.

Set in a small town in Wales where the mines have been shut down by the state, *Coming Up Roses* tells the story of three employees of the Rex Cinema: Trevor, the projectionist; Mona, the concession girl; and, Mr. Davies, the manager. In its inexplicable wisdom, the city council decides to close the Rex. The bureaucracy has made it impossible to do anything but live on the dole.

Mr. Davies talks Trevor into becoming the caretaker for the theater. Trevor believes that the city council will re-open the theater until Mona tells him that the theater is dead. At this point, spurred by financial needs, Trevor becomes an entrepreneur and turns the theater into a mushroom farm, rock-and-roll band practice studio, and an old-age recreational hall.

This free enterprise captures everybody's imagination, and they start to succeed in their mushroom business. The last crop, which is dedicated to repaying a loan to Mr. Davies to pay for his eminent funeral, fails. Mr. Davies dies, and Trevor keeps his promise to give him a spectacular funeral by selling the spoiled mushroom crop as enhanced compost. While free enterprise is giving new life to this small South Wales town, Trevor and Mona are falling in love with each other. Everyone ends up happy ever after.

Coming Up Roses is highly recommended as a positive, realistic look at the world. Everything about this movie is worthwhile, including Trevor's prayers for Mr. Davies. *Coming Up Roses* shows what a little freedom can do for a town which has been suffocated by socialism.

Coming Up Roses is a gem which you will not want to miss.

TITLE:	**COMMISSAR (Subtitles)**
QUALITY:	★★★★
RECOMMENDATION:	Acceptable
RATING:	No rating
RELEASE:	1988
STARRING:	Nonna Morduka, Rolan Bykov, and Raisa Nedaskovkaya
DIRECTOR:	Alexandere Askoldov
GENRE:	War/Drama
CONTENT:	Children bathing, mother breast feeding, nothing really objectionable
INTENDED AUDIENCE:	Adults
REVIEWER:	Wendell B. Rhodes

Banned twenty-one years ago, *Commissar* is the story of a ruthless, female Red Commissar. She is a self-appointed judge and jury, sentencing a deserter to death.

Her life takes a turn when she discovers she's pregnant. Yefim and Mariya, a poor Jewish couple, give up their bed for "the cause," and sleep with their six children and elderly mother. Yefim's family life is one of poverty, yes, but also of great love. In one marvelous scene, Mariya explains the importance of motherhood to Klavidia: "Raising children," she says, "is much harder than making wars." The love and tenderness that suddenly wells up within Vavilova is beautiful to behold. In fact, this love for her child and adopted family sends the Commissar back to the battleground. She fights the war once more. This time for different reasons.

We highly recommend *Commissar*. The humanity and respect of God and family will surely touch each viewer. If this is what glasnost makes available, whatever the reasons, then it is a breath of fresh air. It would be well for the "land of the free" to produce such wholesome and moving stories.

Editor's Note: This film has yet to be released in the USSR, and the director has never been allowed to make another movie.

TITLE:	**THE COMPUTER ANIMATION SHOW**
QUALITY:	★★★
RECOMMENDATION:	Caution
RATING:	None
RELEASE:	1987
STARRING:	Various computers and their programmers
DIRECTOR:	Several people
GENRE:	Animated
CONTENT:	Nothing objectionable
INTENDED AUDIENCE:	Teens and adults
REVIEWER:	Doug Brewer

For those technophiles and artists around who enjoy what is being created on computers lately, *The Computer Animation Show* is worth seeing. There are some amazing effects here. Along with a series of "presentations" for those firms who sell this stuff and some graphic research efforts, there is a short film called "Dance of the Stumblers," produced by Steve Segal on an inexpensive PC in his bedroom. Pixar gets my vote for best work with the last short film in the show, "Luxo, Jr."

If you enjoyed *Tron* and *The Black Hole* and can remember the effects those films demonstrated, you will appreciate the advances these shorts showcase. However, if you're looking for a plot, or anything like that, forget this showcase.

TITLE:	**COOKIE**
QUALITY:	★★★
RECOMMENDATION:	Extreme Caution
RATING:	PG-13

RELEASE:	1989
STARRING:	Peter Falk, Emily Lloyd, and Diane Weist
DIRECTOR:	Susan Seidelman
GENRE:	Comedy
CONTENT:	Vulgar language and ridicule of the marriage covenant
INTENDED AUDIENCE:	Adult
REVIEWER:	Patricia Sharp

Cookie unfolds from the elaborate funeral of Dino Capisco, a labor racketeer recently paroled from prison. From the cemetery, the film reviews the events leading up to Dino's funeral. We meet Cookie, his illegitimate daughter whom Dino arranges to get off the streets by putting her to work in the Garment District. Cookie resents Dino's intrusion into her life after his thirteen-year absence and is jealous of her mother Lenore's rekindled romance with him.

As a stipulation of Dino's parole, he must reside with his estranged legal wife, Bunny, another tough cookie. *Cookie* is very predictable, with the exception of an unexpected twist at the end. The characters could have been a cliché of every mafia mobster imaginable were it not for the capable acting of the talented cast.

Even though the story is farcical, *Cookie* is a mildly amusing, entertaining film. Unfortunately, the first few minutes are filled with obscenities. Also, the final scene makes a total mockery of Christian marriage. There is no nudity or explicit sex in *Cookie,* and it could be recommended for adult audiences were it not for the vulgar language and ridicule of the marriage covenant. As it is, avoid *Cookie.*

☆☆☆ CLASSIC ☆☆☆

TITLE:	**THE COUNTERFEIT TRAITOR**
QUALITY:	★★★★
RECOMMENDATION:	Caution
RATING:	Not rated
RELEASE:	1962
STARRING:	William Holden, Lilli Palmer, and Hugh Griffith
DIRECTOR:	George Seaton
GENRE:	War/Spy drama
CONTENT:	Execution of a spy
INTENDED AUDIENCE:	Adult
REVIEWER:	Protestant Motion Picture Council

A fascinating and absorbing true spy melodrama, with much suspense and excitement, about an American-born Swede who is an oil trader doing business with the Nazis during WW II. His oil dealings with both sides get him on the Allied enemies list.

A British Intelligence officer shows him how he can redeem himself by obtaining information on locations and capacities of oil depots in Germany. He consents to the scheme, using his business contacts to obtain his goal, and thus becomes a "counterfeit traitor."

His coworker is a German woman who is eventually discovered and executed by the Nazis before his very eyes. A deep attachment had grown between them, but, when her death separates them, he must find a way to escape.

This becomes the most exciting part of the story as it is fraught with danger and can be accomplished only with the assistance of underground workers (which incidentally gives a good idea of such activities during the war).

Since this is based on a real life story and directed with great skill, with excellent acting, and set in the actual places in West Germany, Denmark and Sweden, it is all the more impressive.

☆☆☆ CLASSIC ☆☆☆

TITLE:	**THE COURT-MARTIAL OF BILLY MITCHELL**
QUALITY:	★ ★ ★
RECOMMENDATION:	Acceptable
RATING:	None
RELEASE:	1955
STARRING:	Gary Cooper, Rod Steiger, Ralph Bellamy, and Elizabeth Montgomery
DIRECTOR:	Otto Preminger
GENRE:	War/Biography
CONTENT:	Nothing objectionable
INTENDED AUDIENCE:	Adults (Slow-moving with many adult conversations)
REVIEWER:	Betty J. Hill

In this true story, we realize Billy Mitchell was a man ahead of his time. Billy Mitchell questions orders, but only to improve America's air power.

He believes airplanes can carry bombs and sink battleships, so he flies at a lower altitude with bombs heavier than regulations allow. When a battleship is sunk, the press loves it, but Mitchell is sent to General John Pershing's office. Since Mitchell won't work with the team, he's relieved of command and transferred to Fort Sam Houston.

The Navy orders Zack to take the balloon Shenandoah to a state fair. It's a death trap due to the stormy weather. In fear of a court martial, Zack ignores the weather warning and Mitchell's advice: "It is wrong to follow orders that take you and your men to your deaths." Newspapers tell of the crash.

Mitchell's desire to expose an archaic air force led him to make a statement to the newspapers. The military resented the bad publicity, ordering a court-martial. Mitchell was glad to have his day in court to let America know how inadequate our air power was.

Ideas brought out during the trial were: Mitchell's desire that the Air Force be a separate branch from the Army and Navy; an aviation academy; planes that would fly over 1,000 miles per hour; planes crossing the Atlantic and Pacific Oceans; and planes to protect Hawaii which would be an easy enemy attack from the air. In 1925, he tells how easily the Japanese could attack Pearl Harbor.

He was suspended from the military for five years, but decided to resign instead. As the movie ends, we see tiny two-winged planes flying in the air and then jets zoom across the sky in formation.

TITLE:	**COUSINS**
QUALITY:	★ ★
RECOMMENDATION:	Bad
RATING:	R
RELEASE:	1989
STARRING:	Ted Danson, Isabella Rosselini, and Sean Young
DIRECTOR:	Joel Schumacher
GENRE:	Comedy/Romance
CONTENT:	Bad language, profanity, and extra-marital affairs
INTENDED AUDIENCE:	Adult
REVIEWER:	Nancy Hanger

> If a man commits adultery with another man's wife . . . both the adulterer and the adulteress must be put to death. (Leviticus 20:10)

Maria is married to Tom, who runs around with women. Larry is a dance teacher with a beautiful wife, Tish. Maria and Larry meet at the wedding of his uncle, Phil, and her mother, Edie. When Tom and Tish disappear, the spouses wait for them after the festivities.

The next day, Maria tracks down Larry and asks him, "Do you think our spouses slept together?" They spend time together because they have an affinity for each other, and they want to make their spouses nervous. They fall in love, but refuse to give in to their desires. Their spouses are consumed with jealousy. Maria and Larry consummate their desire at another wedding, the union of Maria's mother (uncle Phil died suddenly) and Larry's father.

This movie is boring and poorly made. Tom's repentance is unexplained. Larry and Tish did not seem like a feasible couple. Larry and Maria's spouses' immorality becomes an excuse for their own. The message is: If you've been hurt, you have the right to indulge yourself. This film that justifies self-indulgence at the expense of marriage. God has made it very plain: "You shall not commit adultery" (Exodus 20:14). We cannot, therefore, recommend *Cousins*.

TITLE:	**CRIME ZONE**
QUALITY:	★★
RECOMMENDATION:	Bad
RATING:	R
RELEASE:	1989
STARRING:	David Carradine, Peter Nelson, Sherilyn Fenn, and Michael Shaner
DIRECTOR:	Luis Llosa
GENRE:	Science fiction/Detective
CONTENT:	Vulgarities, obscenities, nudity, and excessive violence
INTENDED AUDIENCE:	Adults
REVIEWER:	Bruce Grimes

Set in the future, in the city-state of Soliel, a young man named Bones decides to buck the system. The authorities control every aspect of life. Bones decides to take his girl and escape to Frolan, a city-state with which Soliel is at war. Jason, a wealthy manipulator with access to money and guns, will allow them to rob a bank and get away. It turns out Jason is a cop who creates criminals, since the police have decided that total power is worthless if they can't be seen going after headline criminals. Bones and Helen escape with millions.

The set decoration of *Crime Zone* mimics *Bladerunner*. However, it has no subtleties. The actors shout obscenities. The film lacks imagination and polish. This film says that three things can make life better: money, sex, and a new place to live. Unfortunately, seeking those three things are always man's downfall. *Crime Zone* is not recommended.

> Then, after desire has conceived, it gives birth to sin; and sin, when it is full-grown, gives birth to death. (James 1:15)

TITLE:	**CRIMINAL LAW**
QUALITY:	★★
RECOMMENDATION:	Bad
RATING:	R
RELEASE:	1989
STARRING:	Gary Oldham, Kevin Bacon, Tess Harper, and Joe Don Baker
DIRECTOR:	
GENRE:	Drama
CONTENT:	Profanity and brief rough nude scene

INTENDED AUDIENCE:	Adults
REVIEWER:	Tim Berends

Get ready for open season on pro-lifers. For years, some in Hollywood have portrayed Christians as kooks and psychopaths. Now, Hemdale, who brought you *The Last Emperor* and *Platoon,* is targeting a new enemy, those who don't think babies should be murdered in their mothers' wombs.

Gary Oldham is a successful, young criminal lawyer who defends Kevin Baker. Kevin's mom is an OB/GYN. Kevin is killing girls who have been given abortions by his mom. As Kevin also kills his mom, the last line she hears is, "Have you killed any babies today, Mom?" Eventually, Kevin is himself killed.

There is a some swearing and a brief unnecessary nude scene. However, what is worse is the support this movie gives to the notion that those who want to save the life of little babies are kooks and killers, when, in fact, the killers are those who are murdering the babies. Send the money you would have spent on this deceit to a worthy ministry involved in the fight against abortion. Don't patronize a movie that is going to be loved by the folks at Planned Parenthood.

TITLE:	**CROCODILE DUNDEE II**
QUALITY:	★★★
RECOMMENDATION:	Caution
RATING:	PG
RELEASE:	1988
STARRING:	Paul Hogan and Linda Kowslowski
DIRECTOR:	John Cornell
GENRE:	Comedy/Action adventure
CONTENT:	Obscenity and sexual innuendo
INTENDED AUDIENCE:	Teenagers and adults
REVIEWER:	Ted Baehr

Crocodile Dundee II is a "good triumphs over evil," 1940s movie with a twist: a good-natured country hero has unlimited *savoir-faire* while the city folk have lost all common sense. Unfortunately, Mick and his lady love, Sue, are living in the same apartment, although she makes it clear to a curious friend that they haven't slept together as he still sleeps on the floor.

Sue is sent some photographs showing the evil drug dealer, Ricco, killing a man. Mick intercepts the photos. Sue is taken hostage by Ricco. Mick rescues Sue from Ricco's fortified estate. Ricco chases Sue and Mick to Australia. There Mick humorously captures the drug dealer's henchmen one by one by using every Tarzan trick in the book. Ricco eventually gets his come-up-ence.

This is great fun, humorous and enjoyable. We object to the repeated obscenities, but there is no profanity. *Crocodile Dundee II* is recommended with caution. *Crocodile Dundee I* is a better movie.

TITLE:	**CROSSING DELANCEY**
QUALITY:	★ ★ ★
RECOMMENDATION:	Extreme Caution
RATING:	PG
RELEASE:	1988
STARRING:	Amy Irving, Peter Riegert, and Reizl Bozyk
DIRECTOR:	Joan Micklin Silver
GENRE:	Romance
CONTENT:	Casual sex, minimal profanity, and lingerie but no nudity
INTENDED AUDIENCE:	Adults over 25
REVIEWER:	F. L. Lindberg

Crossing Delancey is a warm, modern Jewish morality play. Isabel sells books in Manhattan. She is intellectual and liberal. I cringed at her casual sex with a friend whose wife was out of town. She is not hardened. She loves her grandmother "Bubbie." Bubbie sets her up with a marriage broker! Isabel is matched with Sam Posner, a pickle maker. Meanwhile, she is developing an interest in a Dutch novelist with a new book out and an eye for women. Isabel comes to her senses in the end. "How could I have been so stupid?" she cries.

Crossing Delancey starts too slowly. This movie captures the texture and flavor of Manhattan better than any other movie ever has. *Crossing Delancey* is a carefully crafted, "small" work. There are laughs and smiles of recognition, lots of warmth, and a message to settle down to marriage (and maybe children?). However, because of the casual sex and the profanity, we cannot recommend *Crossing Delancey*.

TITLE:	**CRY FREEDOM**
QUALITY:	★ ★
RECOMMENDATION:	Evil
RATING:	PG
RELEASE:	1987
STARRING:	Kevin Kline and Denzel Washington
DIRECTOR:	Sir Richard Attenborough
GENRE:	Drama
CONTENT:	Profanity and violence
INTENDED AUDIENCE:	All ages
REVIEWER:	Ted Baehr

As Adolph Hitler and Vladimir Lenin pointed out so frankly in their writings, neither

National Socialism (Nazism), nor International Socialism (communism) can capture the imagination of the people without being bathed in the Big Lie. Only lies can make people elevate the state to the level of godhood.

In the Marxist-socialist mold, *Cry Freedom* attempts to turn a legitimate problem, apartheid, into a device for deceitfully advocating Marxist revolution. The word *apartheid* could be substituted for the word *sin*, because one of the Biblical meanings of sin is separation from God, and, consequently, our fellow man. The solution to the sin problem is Jesus the Christ, not a change in political structure as claimed by socialism. Trying to solve the sin problem by changing political structures would be similar to trying to change one's character by moving from a Georgian Colonial house to a Victorian house.

What is amazing about *Cry Freedom* is not the inordinate amount of press which has been given to this dishonest, mediocre movie; but rather, the fact that the press admits the deceitfulness of this movie. These cinematic lies will capture the consciousness of the people who watch this film, and cause many of them to advocate the revolutionary Barabbas, rather than the one true Saviour, Jesus Christ.

The goal of this multi-million dollar propaganda and disinformation is to encourage increased sanctions against South Africa, which will only cause more blacks to starve (1.4 million blacks in South Africa are suffering some of the worst starvation on the continent of Africa) and aid the cause of the Marxist revolutionaries, such as the African National Congress.

Two wrongs do not make a right. Opposing apartheid does not call for advocating starvation, lies and totalitarian communism. Cry Freedom is merely a deceitful cry for death. There is very little truth in this movie, and what truth there was was edited out between the press screenings and the theatrical run. No one should support this type of evil. Those who do may very well have the blood of black and white Africans on their hands.

We pray that Christians will find out the truth before being caught up in this deception. If you would like the true story from a Christian perspective, Good News Communications has several video documentaries available on South Africa which we will send you upon request.

We also pray that *Cry Freedom* does not succeed at the box office. It is so well-made that its failure would be a miracle. Furthermore, Christians should preach the gospel of Jesus Christ with greater urgency to all so that the Good News may be made manifest in the lives of fallen men. We should point out to people that neither the state, nor a revolution can save them: only Jesus can.

If you would like to write Universal Pictures to protest this propaganda, the address is:

Mr. Lew Wasserman
MCA-Universal
Universal City, CA 91608

TITLE:	**CRY FROM THE MOUNTAIN**
QUALITY:	★ ★
RECOMMENDATION:	Acceptable
RATING:	PG

RELEASE:	1985
STARRING:	James Cavan, Wes Parker, Rita Walters, and Chris Kidd
DIRECTOR:	James F. Collier
GENRE:	Religous
CONTENT:	Adventure/Drama with moral and religious messages
INTENDED AUDIENCE:	All ages
REVIEWER:	F.L. Lindberg

Cry from the Mountain tackles the problems of a troubled family. The father and son are leaving for a kayak trip in Alaska. The pregnant wife stays home. There is another woman.

Twenty minutes into the film, the father and son are separated in an accident. Son saves injured dad and goes for help. A crusty hermit cares for them.

Cut to the upset wife. Her mother recommends prayer, but the wife grapples with problems from a secular viewpoint. She ponders abortion.

The father collapses. The hermit sets off for help. Soon the main characters meet at the hospital. The stage is set to resolve crises. Dad survives, but will the family?

A Billy Graham Crusade is underway, which the hermit wants to see. The son rushes down front to thank God that his father will recover. Then the mother follows, and, finally, the hermit. Unfortunately, during the Crusade, we have a serious break in continuity. The outcome is good, however. Hearts are opened by forgiveness. The last scene shows the hermit beginning a hopeful letter to his estranged son.

☆☆☆ MASTERPIECE ☆☆☆

TITLE:	**CRY IN THE DARK**
QUALITY:	★★★★
RECOMMENDATION:	Caution
RATING:	PG
RELEASE:	1988
STARRING:	Meryl Streep and Sam Neill
DIRECTOR:	Fred Schepisi
GENRE:	Drama/Biography/Christian
CONTENT:	Obscene and profane language, but in context with story structure
INTENDED AUDIENCE:	Adults
REVIEWER:	Glennis O'Neal

Michael Chamberlin, a minister, takes his wife Lindy, two children and ten week old baby girl on a camping trip at Australia's Big Rock. After Lindy puts her baby to bed, a cry causes Lindy to rush back to the baby's empty, bloody bed. Her small son mumbles, "dingo (an Australian 'coyote') take baby." Lindy screams. Police sweep the area, yet no clue is uncovered.

They comfort each other with prayer and Scripture. The media manipulates the facts and testimony of the Bible-quoting couple. They are accused of murder and brought to trial. The jury sentences Lindy, now seven months pregnant, to prison as the murderer of her baby. Four and one-half years later the police accidentally find evidence of the baby's clothing which substantiates Lindy's testimony, proving her innocence.

Cry in the Dark has strong Christian content and should encourage all those who take a stand for the truth. The Chamberlins lift up Jesus and Scripture throughout the film. Unfortunately, the pagans in the film utter some profanity. We commend Warner Brothers for releasing a film which affirms a Biblical worldview, but we hope the time will come when filmmakers avoid all profanity in an excellent movie such as this.

TITLE:	**DA**
QUALITY:	★ ★ ★
RECOMMENDATION:	Caution
RATING:	PG
RELEASE:	1988
STARRING:	Martin Sheen, Barnard Hughes, and William Hickey
DIRECTOR:	Matt Clark
GENRE:	Drama
CONTENT:	Profanity
INTENDED AUDIENCE:	Adults
REVIEWER:	Ted Baehr

Da inspires you. Charlie goes back to Ireland to attend the funeral of his Da (Dad). Throughout the movie, Charlie sees Da as a tangible memory with whom he can discuss the past. Charlie recalls being brought up by a loving couple who took him in as a baby when he was abandoned by his real mother. He was frustrated with Ma and Da. They loved the land and their family, but had no desire to achieve anything great. Whereas Charlie wanted to be a writer, Da was contented to be a humble gardener for the town's wealthy Protestant family. Yet, as he remembers them, Charlie realizes how much he loves them.

Da helps the generations to understand each other and family members to love each other. However, there is frequent use, as Ma says, of the "Sacred Name." It is not a curse, but an exclamation, a prayer and a hope rolled into one. We recommend *Da* with caution for those of you who can see beyond the misuse of the "Sacred Name" to the love that helped Charlie become not only the great playwright God intended him to be, but also the loving son he should have been all along.

TITLE:	**DAKOTA**
QUALITY:	★★★
RECOMMENDATION:	Acceptable
RATING:	PG
RELEASE:	1988
STARRING:	Lou Diamond Phillips, Herta Ware, Deedee Norton, E. Cummins, and Jordan Burton
DIRECTOR:	Fred Holmes
GENRE:	Action adventure
CONTENT:	Nothing objectionable except a dream replay of an accidental death
INTENDED AUDIENCE:	Adults and teenagers
REVIEWER:	John Evans, Movie Morality Guide

Dakota is the first feature film produced by the Kuntz Brothers, who previously specialized in Christian comedy films for young people.

John Dakota leaves home after his younger brother is killed in an accident. He ends up as a ranch hand in Dillon, Texas. He's attracted to the ranch manager's spirited daughter, Molly, but she has a steady boyfriend. Dakota is a conscientious young man who's been deeply hurt by the implication he was responsible for his brother's death. Seemingly to make amends, he helps the ranch manager's twelve-year-old handicapped son achieve a hill climbing "quest."

Dakota's plot seems a bit contrived at times, but it has plenty of realism, action, and young love to make it good viewing. Dakota's character is beyond question and, although he pursues Molly, he doesn't become sexually involved with her. The film's dialogue has a few rough words, but no profanity. Dakota eventually must choose between running from his troubles again, or facing them squarely and responsibly. This is a fine film which the whole family can enjoy.

> He will eat curds and honey when he knows enough to reject the wrong and choose the right. (Isaiah 7:15)

☆☆☆ CLASSIC ☆☆☆

TITLE:	**DAMN THE DEFIANT!**
QUALITY:	★★★
RECOMMENDATION:	Acceptable
RATING:	Not rated
RELEASE:	1962 (British)
STARRING:	Alec Guinness, Dirk Bogarde, Maurice Denham, Nigel Stock, Richard Carpenter, Peter Gill, and David Robinson

DIRECTOR:	Lewis Gilbert
GENRE:	War
CONTENT:	British sea adventure
INTENDED AUDIENCE:	Adults
REVIEWER:	Protestant Motion Picture Council

Set in the late 1700s during the Napoleonic wars, serious trouble aboard ship threatens the HMS Defiant. Because of unspeakable living conditions prevailing on vessels at sea, the crew has planned to participate in a fleet-wide mutiny against the British Navy. The Defiant is under the command of Captain Crawford (Alec Guinness), who would like to improve the lot of his men, as well as to stop certain abuses by the "press gangs" who "shanghai" prospective sailors to furnish crews.

His First Lieutenant is a brilliant, but brutal man, who impertinently questions the authority of the Captain and takes sadistic satisfaction in the punishments he inflicts for the slightest infractions. The Captain is unaware of the lieutenant's cruel treatment of the sailors, but when the lieutenant inflicts a vicious flogging upon the Captain's son, who serves as a midshipman on the vessel, he begins to see the light.

Just when mutiny is about to boil over, the Defiant is engaged by a French frigate. The Defiant wins the contest, but it costs the Captain his arm. Patriotism overcomes craving for revenge in the men, and there is victory at sea.

This absorbing story, which does not spare any unpleasant details, points up a serious condition that created a desire for change which eventually took place. The film has excellent photography, especially of the nautical scenes, and good acting.

TITLE:	**DANCERS**
QUALITY:	★★★
RECOMMENDATION:	Acceptable
RATING:	PG
RELEASE:	1987
STARRING:	Mikhail Baryshnikov, Alessandra Ferri, Leslie Browne, Thomas Rall, and Julie Kent
DIRECTOR:	Herbert Ross
GENRE:	Dance/Musical
CONTENT:	Nothing objectionable
INTENDED AUDIENCE:	Adults
REVIEWER:	Joe Kalcso

Dancers does not have great dancing, although a great dancer stars in it; nor does it have great music, even though the London Symphony provides a pleasant score. However, *Dancers* offers a respite from the violence, sex, and foul language in almost every other contemporary movie. Therefore, we recommend it.

An American dancer arrives in Italy to take part in the movie version of *Giselle*. She spots Tony, the greatest living dancer. The infatuation is immediate and innocent. The ballet mirrors their relationship. In one satisfying sequence, the action alternates between the ballet and reality. This screen play was written from a secular perspective, but the emotion, beauty, and creativity manifested in the characters, dancing, and musical score are the realm of human beings under God, whether they acknowledge Him or not.

TITLE:	**DANGEROUS LIAISONS**
QUALITY:	★ ★ ★
RECOMMENDATION:	Evil
RATING:	R
RELEASE:	1989
STARRING:	Glenn Close, John Malkovich, Uma Thurman, and Michelle Pfeiffer
DIRECTOR:	Stephen Frears
GENRE:	Drama/Historical
CONTENT:	Decadence, nudity, and evil
INTENDED AUDIENCE:	Adults
REVIEWER:	Ted Baehr

Dangerous Liaisons is an immoral period piece set during the *fin de siecle* France of the 1780s. It is based on the French epistolary novel about a pair of fiendish seducers, the Marquise de Merteuil and the Vicomte de Valmont, but does not have the moral perspective of the novel.

The Marquise's pleasure is revenge and deception. She enlists a rakish paramour, the Vicomte, to corrupt the innocent Cocille, betrothed to her former lover. The Vicomte has his eyes on a devout wife, Madame de Tourvel. Slowly, the movie develops these destructive conquests. Then, it reveals that the true object of the Marquise's hate is the Vicomte. However, he forces a duel with her young lover and allows himself to be pierced by his opponent. As he dies, the Vicomte takes revenge on the Marquise by giving her letters of revenge to her lover to publish. Parisian society turns on the Marquise.

Not even the most dedicated effete will be entertained by this lifeless piece. This movie tries to be evil and ends up being boring. The fact that it was nominated for an Academy Award indicates how confused the Hollywood elite are.

From a Biblical perspective, it tries to mock God and portrays Christianity as a "works" religion rather than the loving grace of God. Christians should shun *Dangerous Liaisons* and pray for all those involved who are trapped in their own stylized arrogance.

TITLE:	**DARK EYES**
QUALITY:	★ ★ ★ ★
RECOMMENDATION:	Extreme Caution

RATING:	R
RELEASE:	1987
STARRING:	Marcello Mastroianni
DIRECTOR:	Nikita Mikhalkov
GENRE:	Drama
CONTENT:	Semi-nudity and adultery which is shown to be wrong
INTENDED AUDIENCE:	Adults
REVIEWER:	Ted Baehr

Dark Eyes is the story of a man who fritters away his life only to face the awesome question he dreams the Lord asks upon his death, "Romano, what have you done with your life?" Romano is a chronic liar and an adulterer. He has no compassion for anyone, including himself. He is a paradigm of the selfish egoists of our age.

Dark Eyes is recommended with extreme caution, especially for pagans who need to come face to face with the wages of sin. There is no profanity, or obscenity, but there is brief semi-nudity from a distance and promiscuity. Christians may note that there are a growing number of foreign films, like *Dark Eyes*, with Biblical perspectives. God willing, this trend will influence Hollywood.

☆☆☆ CLASSIC ☆☆☆

TITLE:	**THE DAY THE EARTH CAUGHT FIRE**
QUALITY:	★★★★
RECOMMENDATION:	Acceptable
RATING:	Not rated
RELEASE:	1961
STARRING:	Janet Munro, Leo McKern, Edward Judd, and Michael Goodliffe
DIRECTOR:	Val Guest
GENRE:	Science Fiction
CONTENT:	Nothing objectionable
INTENDED AUDIENCE:	Adult
REVIEWER:	Protestant Motion Picture Council

"Within the next few hours, the world will know whether this is the End, or another Beginning: the rebirth of man, or his final obituary" is the arresting commentary greeting the audience of the opening of this British presentation.

A reporter discovers that the Earth has been knocked off its axis by simultaneous nuclear bomb tests conducted on the same day by the Americans and Russians on opposite sides of the planet. Because of the different orbit, the Earth is now moving toward the sun and will eventually burn up.

The results are terrifying as they affect natural resources and the forces of life and death, especially the behavior of those threatened, some of whom set aside moral restraints.

Most of the action takes place in the newspaper offices of the *The London Daily Express* which lends a documentary-like quality to the proceedings as the world gets warmer. Extreme suspense is created by the reporting of a skillful journalist, while the conclusion is left to the judgment of the viewer.

The emotional impact is overwhelming. Acting is superb, settings are realistic, and a few light touches relieve the tension of this thought-provoking melodrama.

Christians should rejoice in the fact that the good news is that the bad news is wrong. We need to rebut the theology of fear in this film which is still prevalent today. Jesus triumphed on the Cross, and He has made us more than conquerors. Fear is of the Adversary, and those who are born of the Spirit of God are freed from a bondage to fear.

TITLE:	**THE DEAD**
QUALITY:	★★★★
RECOMMENDATION:	Acceptable
RATING:	PG
RELEASE:	1987
STARRING:	Angelica Huston and Donal McCann
DIRECTOR:	John Huston
GENRE:	Drama
CONTENT:	Nothing objectionable
INTENDED AUDIENCE:	Adults
REVIEWER:	Doug Brewer

Almost all the action takes place at a party given by the Misses Morkan and their niece Mary Jane, who was following in their spinsterly footsteps. It is an annual affair, their Feast of the Epiphany, and always a big hit with their friends, relatives and pupils. The conversation is trivial and friendly. Soon most of the guests have departed, and Gabriel is waiting for his wife, Gretta. As she starts down the stairs, Bartell D'Arcy, a singer attending the party, begins singing "The Lass of Aughrim." Gretta stops and listens. When they reach their hotel, Gretta tells Gabriel a story about her life, and he realizes he has no idea of the depth of her passions.

As the film (based on a story by James Joyce) ends, the viewer is so filled with a sense of Joyce's poetic vision, that words cannot contain a correct description. There are few movies to which deserve four stars: *The Dead* is highly recommended.

TITLE:	**DEADLINE**
QUALITY:	★★★
RECOMMENDATION:	Caution

RATING:	Not rated
RELEASE:	1987
STARRING:	Christopher Walken and Marita Marschall
DIRECTOR:	Nathaniel Gutman
GENRE:	Action adventure
CONTENT:	Violence
INTENDED AUDIENCE:	Adults
REVIEWER:	Doug Brewer

The background plays a larger role than the story in *Deadline*. Don Stevens is a television reporter who covers fashion shows in Paris. He is sent to Beirut to replace a man with an ulcer. Hanging out by the pool, Stevens is approached by an Arab girl who offers him a chance to interview a ranking member of the Palestine Liberation Organization. He causes a worldwide stir with the interviewee's plea for moderation. Thus begins an account of the duplicity, confusion, and violence that rules the streets of Beirut.

Deadline brings the fighting to the screen without glorifying or condemning. Stevens' adventures are exciting, but it is the soldiers, the explosions and the armed children who are the stars of this film. The PLO, Israelis, the Druse, and the Christians all think they are in charge of Beirut. In reality, everybody is a villain. In one memorable line, a fellow reporter says, "It's not, 'kill who you want,' it's, 'kill who you can.'"

Deadline should be seen by those who wish to understand what is going on in Beirut. However, be warned that there are killings galore. While Stevens searches for answers, Beirut itself never asks why and never says die. Caution is recommended.

TITLE:	**DEAR AMERICA: LETTERS HOME FROM VIETNAM**
QUALITY:	★ ★ ★
RECOMMENDATION:	Caution
RATING:	PG-13
RELEASE:	1988
STARRING:	The American Men and Women who served in Vietnam
DIRECTOR:	Bill Couturie
GENRE:	Documentary
CONTENT:	Objectionable language
INTENDED AUDIENCE:	Adults
REVIEWER:	Christopher Ferrell

Dear America provides an eye witness account of Vietnam. It is a documentary composed of unreleased news footage and home movies. The narration is letters from soldiers enlivened by background music from the sixties. This film is not exciting, glamorous, or shocking. It grips you with the honesty of its testimony and the stirring familiarity of recent history. For those who served in the war, or survived the loss of a loved one, *Dear America* will appear as a powerful scrapbook. For the rest of us, it will answer many questions.

There is a moderate amount of profanity in this film. The imagery is not so graphic as the theatrical productions, but it is real, making it harsh because of its nature. Vietnam memorials have become our wailing walls in modern America. The realities of preserving freedom has a cost which many want to overlook. *Dear America* reminds us of those men and women who paid the ultimate price. *Dear America* is recommended with caution.

TITLE:	**DEEP STAR SIX**
QUALITY:	★ ★ ★
RECOMMENDATION:	Bad
RATING:	R
RELEASE:	1989
STARRING:	Taurean Blacque, Nancy Everhard, Greg Evigan, Miguel Ferrer, Nia Peeples, Matt McCoy, Cindy Pickett, and Marius Weyers
DIRECTOR:	Sean S. Cunningham
GENRE:	Science fiction
CONTENT:	Blasphemy, vulgar language, and graphic sex scenes
INTENDED AUDIENCE:	Adult
REVIEWER:	Glennis O'Neal

Subs launch out from their underwater mother ship in search of sites for missile installation. We explore the seascape with two encapsulated explorers when the sea floor collapses. The crew realizes they've lost an irreplaceable piece of equipment. Pursuing it, the pilots are so fascinated that they go farther and farther, unaware that they are being drawn into a place of no return. Not only does the territory slide in around them, but an unseen presence is "felt" lurking in the strange waters. Dr. Van Gelden and Scarpelli, a female scientist, pilot their capsule to the same depths. They also wreck. The Mission Captain takes over a third search. Again, it is a costly rescue, requiring the sacrifice of life. "The thing," a prehistoric frog with claws and fangs, enters the mothership, putting each crew member on an alert to kill anything that moves.

This film, from the beginning, has to be labeled a "wash out." Sex scenes are obviously planted for "turn-on" purposes, along with polluted, repulsive language. Too bad, because it could have been an enjoyable adventure. As it is, send Hollywood a message and avoid *Deep Star Six*.

TITLE:	**DEFENSE OF THE REALM**
QUALITY:	★ ★
RECOMMENDATION:	Extreme Caution

RATING:	PG
RELEASE:	1987
STARRING:	Gabriel Byrne, Greta Scacchi, Denholm Elliott, Ian Bannen, Bill Patterson, and Fulton MacKay
DIRECTOR:	David Drury
GENRE:	Spy
CONTENT:	Some profanity
INTENDED AUDIENCE:	Adults
REVIEWER:	Ted Baehr

Defense of the Realm starts with a chase and quickly moves to a frame-up, a double-cross and an unexpected ending. Suspense builds throughout. The camera work is good. The direction is good. The acting is good. However, the script fails within the last few minutes because it becomes a political diatribe.

Nick and Vernon are two reporters following up a story about Dennis Markhem, a Member of Parliament (MP), who has been visiting the same call girl as a Major in the East German Diplomatic Corps. Through Nick's keen reporting, Dennis is hounded out of Parliament. However, all along, Vernon has told Nick to slow down because Dennis has been framed. After Vernon's suspicious death, Nick starts to search for the truth and finds a fantastic cover-up. The suspense throughout his search for the truth is excellent. The trouble is that the reason for a cover-up is a contrived way to include an anti-nuclear statement. This is unfortunate because up to the weak ending, *Defense of the Realm* was very realistic and exciting.

There are a few exclamatory profanities in the movie and some background "pin-up girls" in one of the offices. Given the profanity and the weak ending, it is recommended that you avoid *Defense of the Realm*. It is not worth your time or effort to get caught up in this mystery—only to have it turn out to be a dud!

TITLE:	**DIE HARD**
QUALITY:	★★★★
RECOMMENDATION:	Bad
RATING:	R
RELEASE:	1988
STARRING:	Bruce Willis, Alan Rickman, and Alexander Gudonov
DIRECTOR:	John Mctiernan
GENRE:	Action adventure
CONTENT:	Extreme violence, nudity, and foul language
INTENDED AUDIENCE:	Adults
REVIEWER:	Debi Mulligan

John McClaine is a New York City policeman who visits his estranged wife in L.A. for Christmas. Arriving on Christmas Eve, McClaine crashes the party thrown by the corporation which employs his wife. Soon, the party is crashed by twelve terrorists. With ruthless efficiency, the terrorists take each guest hostage. McClaine begins a one man crusade against the "bad guys." Although a familiar set-up, it is done with enough tongue-in-cheek to come across as a fresh idea.

Die Hard sustains an almost unbearable suspense from open to close. *Die Hard* moved the audience to applause at the finish. However, the bloodshed is overwhelming, and there is brief nudity, frequent foul language, and drug abuse. Therefore, we do not recommend *Die Hard*.

Recalling the Motion Picture Code, films can be even more entertaining without sex, violence, and profanity. One reviewer saw an edited version of *Die Hard* with no profanity nor nudity on a cross-county flight and was impressed. The edited film was just as exciting as the original without being offensive.

☆☆☆ MASTERPIECE ☆☆☆

TITLE:	**THE DEVIL AND DANIEL WEBSTER (107 Minutes, Black and White)**
QUALITY:	★★★★
RECOMMENDATION:	Acceptable
RATING:	None
RELEASE:	1941
STARRING:	Edward Arnold, Walter Huston, Jane Darwell, Simone Simon, Gene Lockhart, John Qualen, and Frank Conlan
DIRECTOR:	William Dieterle
GENRE:	Drama/Religious
CONTENT:	Nothing objectionable
INTENDED AUDIENCE:	Adults
REVIEWER:	Gary DeMar

I would say to any man who follows his own plough, and to every mechanic, artisan and laborer in every city in the country—I would say to every man, everywhere, who wishes by honest means to gain an honest living, "Beware of wolves in sheep's clothing!" (From the opening scene)

Until Hollywood undergoes its revival, Christians will have to be content with movies that were produced when, at least, both God and the devil were real. *The Devil and Daniel Webster* is a sometimes comedic, but always authentic, portrayal of the devil and his schemes. Its style is reminiscent of C.S. Lewis' immortal Screwtape Letters. As in Screwtape, the viewer comes away with some idea of Satan's secret councils.

In this flawlessly styled period piece, a simple, down-and-out farmer sells his soul to the devil in exchange for seven years of fame and fortune. Farmer Stone is told that "the soul is nothing." Fame and fortune cannot be compared to "nothing," so why not give up that nothing of a soul? It seems like such a good deal. The covenant is signed in the farmer's own blood, and God responds with thunder and a setting sun.

At the end of the seven years, finally and fully comprehending the "deal" he had made, the farmer changes his mind. He may have gained the world's riches, but he's about to lose it all and then some.

"Scratch," the devil's wily assistant played by Walter Huston, is more than accommodating. In exchange for an extension on farmer Stone's contract, the devil will take the soul of the farmer's infant son.

Horror grips him as he comprehends the full impact of his bargain with the devil. What will he do? He turns to the great nineteenth-century orator and lawyer Daniel Webster to find a loophole in the contract. However, as we soon learn, the devil always seems to be one step ahead of man. You see, the devil never plays by the rules. Before Stone and Webster do battle with Scratch, farmer Stone's wife leaves her husband with this Biblical encouragement:

"Set me as a seal upon thine heart, as a seal upon thine arm. For love is as strong as death."

Standing on the Constitution, Daniel Webster, in hopes of beating the devil, asks for a jury trial of the farmer's peers. Surely, they will understand. However, Webster goes even farther. "If I can't win this case with a jury, you'll have me, too," Webster boasts.

Well, this gets the attention of Scratch. The soul of Daniel Webster would be quite a prize. However, Scratch will not be undone: "But you'll have to admit that this is hardly a case for an ordinary jury." Webster quickly responds with, "Be it of the quick or the dead."

Old Scratch accepts the famous lawyer's request. A jury of long-dead scoundrels, traitors and opportunists, who had likewise sold their souls, is called up from the pit of hell to sit in judgment, Benedict Arnold being the most recognizable. This scene is one of the most chilling in the entire film. The despair of hell is etched in every line of the jurists' faces. Their pact with the devil haunts them, even in death. After hearing the pleading by Webster, the jury of the damned . . .

Well, I don't want to give away the ending. *The Devil and Daniel Webster* is filled with striking rural scenes and spirited character acting. As a viewer, you are taken back to the halcyon era of sunrise-to-sunset work days. The people are trusting, but wise. They seem naive, but their spiritual instincts tell them that man is not designed to get something for nothing. The farmer, as well as some other devil-enriched gentlemen in the county, learn this the hard way.

Old "Scratch" comes in at the end of the movie ready to make a deal with any new prospect. It's a reminder that:

> Your Adversary, the Devil, prowls about like a roaring lion, seeking someone to devour. (1 Peter 5:8)

☆☆☆ CLASSIC ☆☆☆

TITLE:	**THE DEVIL AT FOUR O'CLOCK**
QUALITY:	★★★★
RECOMMENDATION:	Acceptable

RATING:	Not rated
RELEASE:	1961
STARRING:	Spencer Tracy, Frank Sinatra, Kerwin Matthews, Jean Pierre Aumont, Gregoire Aslan, and Alexander Scourby
DIRECTOR:	Mervyn LeRoy
GENRE:	Adventure/Disaster
CONTENT:	Nothing objectionable
INTENDED AUDIENCE:	Adult
REVIEWER:	Protestant Motion Picture Council

Three manacled convicts are on their way to jail in Tahiti when their small plane stops for the night on a French South Seas island in the Pacific. Also aboard the plane is a young Roman Catholic priest who is going to take the place of Friar Doonan, a cleric on the island who has lost his faith in God and found new hope in a bottle.

There is a children's leper hospital up in the mountains, however, and some work has to be completed on the chapel before the young priest can depart. He asks the governor of the island for permission to put the three convicts to work, and it is granted.

The island's volcano (the devil) is making gurgling sounds, and slight earthquakes signal the onset of the volcano's activity. When the island is rocked by a huge quake, Doonan enlists the convicts to get the children down from the mountain, through the jungle and down to the sea where a large schooner will wait until the outgoing tide at four o'clock— but not a second longer.

The plot holds together through the details inherent to the care of leprosy, the work of rescue and the imperative of service, so that the eventual sacrifice of a few seems natural in the saving of many. Although the convicts make a show of mocking religion, it is merely a cover-up for emotion.

Of high value dramatically and artistically, this film is well cast and beautifully acted. The title comes from a non-Biblical proverb: "It is hard for a man to be brave when he knows he is going to meet the devil at four o'clock."

TITLE:	**DIRTY DANCING**
QUALITY:	★★★
RECOMMENDATION:	Extreme Caution
RATING:	PG-13
RELEASE:	1987
STARRING:	Patrick Swayze, Jennifer Grey, and Cynthia Rhodes
DIRECTOR:	Emile Ardolino
GENRE:	Romance/Dance
CONTENT:	Mild language and suggestive dancing, but no nudity
INTENDED AUDIENCE:	Teenagers and adults

REVIEWER: Ken Kistner

Dirty Dancing is a portrait of the romantic awakening of a seventeen-year-old girl. Frances "Baby" Houseman is vacationing with her family at a Catskills Resort in the early 1960's. Baby is attracted to a young dance instructor, Johnny, who comes from a poor background. The elite's perception of Johnny makes him a prime suspect in a resort theft. He is also assumed to be the irresponsible individual who has gotten a young female employee "in trouble." Baby comes to Johnny's defense.

The dance routines would make Elvis Presley's mother blush. The movie deals with moral questions of fidelity, pre-marital sex, abortion, and social prejudice. There are instances of implied infidelity in the movie, but such immorality is shown as wrong. Because of the implied sex, off-color language and 'dirty dancing,' we cannot recommend *Dirty Dancing*, and we urge Christians to avoid this movie and keep their teenagers and their friends away from it. Christians should never support movies that pander to prurient interests.

TITLE:	**DIRTY ROTTEN SCOUNDRELS**
QUALITY:	★ ★ ★
RECOMMENDATION:	Caution
RATING:	PG
RELEASE:	1988
STARRING:	Michael Caine and Steve Martin
DIRECTOR:	Frank Oz (of Sesame Street fame)
GENRE:	Comedy
CONTENT:	One innuendo of sexual activity
INTENDED AUDIENCE:	Teenagaers and adults
REVIEWER:	Gene Burke

Michael Caine plays a well-mannered con artist who does not con anyone who cannot quite "afford" his schemes. Clearly, "a fool and his money are soon parted." He meets Steve Martin, a sloppy, drifting con artist, with no moral code or conscience about his "profession." When Caine discovers Martin's intentions to "work" his coastal European community, he devises a scheme to run Martin out. It does not succeed, but Martin is so impressed by the tactics of the well-versed Caine that he blackmails him into teaching him all that he knows. They realize that the town is too small for both. They decide on a contest between them, with the winner staying and the loser leaving. They find an heiress, then appoint her to be "the contest." It just so happens that she is the best con artist of all and "stings" them both. All ends happily with the three working cooperatively.

We must caution you about one scene where reference is made toward premarital sex that is ultimately discovered as having never taken place. Of course, all their "Robin Hood" talk is a cover for dishonesty, which God abhors. Robin Hood was a thief. However, this plot device works as a way of revealing some interesting, albeit charming, characters whom we should recognize if we meet them on the street. Overall, this is a entertaining movie which will not hurt anyone if they look at it from a Biblical perspective. However, you can do much better.

TITLE:	**D.O.A.**
QUALITY:	★★★★
RECOMMENDATION:	Extreme Caution
RATING:	R
RELEASE:	1988
STARRING:	Dennis Quaid and Meg Ryan
DIRECTOR:	Rocky Morton and Annabel Jankin
GENRE:	Detective
CONTENT:	Violence, implied sexual looseness, and scattered profanities
INTENDED AUDIENCE:	Young adults
REVIEWER:	Doug Brewer

D.O.A. is a stylish, innovative thriller about Dexter Cornell, an English Professor with five published novels, tenure, and a soon-to-be finalized divorce. His prize student has written a novel. Dex writes an "A" on the cover. Minutes later, he watches the student bounce off his window on the way to the sidewalk, an apparent suicide. Upset over this, Dex drinks too many martinis. Since he can't shake his hangover, Dex goes to see his doctor, where he is informed he has been poisoned and might live twenty-four hours. He gets to his house in time to see his wife murdered. He sets out to discover who murdered her. Everyone appears to be involved as Dex and his student friend Sydney uncover clues in a complex series of events covering several years and some of his closest friends.

There are some caveats about *D.O.A.* that should be mentioned. A couple of violent scenes may disturb some folks, and a sex scene is implied. Furthermore, there is some profanity which is never excusable. Therefore, we cannot recommend *D.O.A.* It is sad that a mystery of this calibre is undermined by immorality.

☆☆☆ CLASSIC ☆☆☆

TITLE:	**A DOG OF FLANDERS**
QUALITY:	★★★★
RECOMMENDATION:	Acceptable
RATING:	Not rated
RELEASE:	1959
STARRING:	David Ladd, Donald Crisp, Theodore Bikel, and Max Croiset
DIRECTOR:	James B. Clark
GENRE:	Children
CONTENT:	Nothing objectionable

INTENDED AUDIENCE:	Family
REVIEWER:	Protestant Motion Picture Council

This film is based on one of Ouida's best known dramas, written in 1872. It mainly concerns a Flemish boy's affection for his grandfather, his care for his dog and his yearning to become an artist.

It is an inspiring drama. It is more than the traditional story of "a boy and his dog." It is told in calmness and beauty, revealing what goes into the making of a character, the realization of a vocation and the influences which bear upon a child's life.

A Dutch boy, who aspires to become a painter but seems to have no chance of ever attaining his dream, lives with his grandfather in Flanders, where they eke out a living by delivering milk from neighboring farms into Antwerp. When they find a sickly dog and nurse it back to health, it becomes their cart dog.

Those involved are portrayed with sympathetic appeal to form an entertaining whole: the humble old man who has so much to bequeath to his grandson, not in riches, but in integrity and honor; the artist who sees the possibility in a boy's desire to describe what he sees; the dog who becomes a friend after being rescued from a cruel master; and the simple life of the industrious laborer. This is brought to the screen with the beauty of the great cathedral and the wonder of a Ruben's painting. Settings of the Low Countries have an air of authenticity and the music is outstanding. The acting is natural.

It is a film to be enjoyed by family audience.

TITLE:	**DOMINICK AND EUGENE**
QUALITY:	★★★
RECOMMENDATION:	Extreme Caution
RATING:	PG-13
RELEASE:	March 18, 1988 (Limited Release)
STARRING:	Tom Hulce, Ray Liotta, and Jamie Lee Curtis
DIRECTOR:	Robert M. Young
GENRE:	Drama
CONTENT:	Cursing, sexual suggestions, and child abuse
INTENDED AUDIENCE:	Adults
REVIEWER:	Lauren Neal

Dominick and Eugene Luciano are extremely close brothers due to their mother's death at childbirth and their father's childhood abandonment of them. They live alone in an old building. Dominick, known as the "slow" one because of a childhood accident, works as a trash collector. He is not only their sole means of financial support but is also putting Eugene through medical school. Dominick is trusting and innocent, yet often confused and frightened by things he cannot understand. He begins to doubt Eugene's loyalty when Eugene begins dating a a fellow student. Eugene, hard working and ambitious, is strained by his brother's demands. Nevertheless, he is bound by love and commitment, as well as a secret that Dominick has not yet discovered.

This movie is one of love, courage, and responsibility in rare form. Jesus is referred to as Saviour, and Dominick goes to church several times to appeal to his Lord. Extreme caution should be exercised due to language, sexual suggestions, and child abuse. It is unfortunate that an outstanding movie like this, which lifts up Jesus, should be marred by unnecessary language and sexual innuendo.

☆☆☆ CLASSIC ☆☆☆

TITLE:	**DON QUIXOTE**
QUALITY:	★ ★ ★ ★
RECOMMENDATION:	Acceptable
RATING:	Not rated
RELEASE:	1961 (USSR)
STARRING:	Nikolai Cherkassov, Yuri Tolubeyev, and T. Agamirova
VOICES:	Arnold Diamond, Howard Marion Crawford, and Bettina Dickson
DIRECTOR:	Grigoriy Kozintsev
GENRE:	Drama
CONTENT:	Nothing objectionable
INTENDED AUDIENCE:	Adults, and mature young people
REVIEWER:	Protestant Motion Picture Council

This Russian production based on the novel by Miguel de Cervantes is a warmly human presentation of the ludicrous adventures of a good, but foolish man who, in his foolishness is wiser than his contemporaries. The tale is told with gusto, but Don Quixote's simple goodness is always apparent.

It is impossible to give more than a sampling of Cervantes's masterpiece which is a philosophical satire on a 17th-century Spanish gentleman. He is so full of reading that he becomes a visionary, setting out to right the wrongs of the world with his faithful, but ignorant companion Sancho Panza. Clad as a knight and riding his tired white horse Rossinante, he protects the oppressed, releases the accused, rescues fair ladies in distress, only to meet ridicule and abuse.

The settings and artistry catch the flavor of the story. The English dubbing is wonderfully handled. The English-language actors' voices are well-cast to suit the roles.

TITLE:	**DRAGNET**
QUALITY:	★ ★
RECOMMENDATION:	Bad
RATING:	PG-13
RELEASE:	1987

STARRING: Harry Morgan, Dan Aykroyd, Tom Hanks, Christopher Plummer, and Dabney Coleman

DIRECTOR: Tom Mankiewics

GENRE: Comedy

CONTENT: Foul language, blasphemy, sexual innuendos, drugs, and violence

INTENDED AUDIENCE: Young adults

REVIEWER: Brandy-Brooke Egan

Dan Aykroyd plays the namesake nephew of Detective Sergeant Joe Friday. Tom Hanks plays his hip partner, Pep Streebek. Harry Morgan reprises his role as Bill Gannon, Friday's partner in the 1960's television program, whose years of service have now earned him the rank of Captain.

Besides Gannon's promotion to Captain, the only difference between this movie and the old television series is the great abundance of profanity and sexual innuendos in the film. Like the television series, Friday and Streebek answer several radio calls to get "just the facts, Ma'am."

The profanity is *too much!* *Dragnet* would have been a lot funnier without the profanity and the blasphemy. Christians will not be able to tolerate this film because of the blasphemy and the way the priest is portrayed. Christians should boycott *Dragnet!*

TITLE: **DREAM A LITTLE DREAM**

QUALITY: ★

RECOMMENDATION: Caution

RATING: PG 13

RELEASE: 1989

STARRING: Jason Robards, Meredith Salenger, Corey Feldman, Piper Laurie, Corey Haim, and Harry Dean Stanton

DIRECTOR: Marc Rocco

GENRE: Comedy

CONTENT: Obscenities and crude humor

INTENDED AUDIENCE: Teenagers

REVIEWER: Phil Boatwright

Dream a Little Dream is not only unbelievable, it is inconceivable. Corey Feldman and Corey Haim have no acting ability, and it is preposterous to believe that girls find Corey Feldman "cute."

An old man, Robards, wants to find a way of remaining with his wife forever. He thinks the answer lies in a "dream state" (the writer has overlooked Heaven; perhaps, because he doesn't know Jesus—the only Way to eternal life). Robards and his wife are "dream stating" when along comes Feldman and Salenger. They collide, and suddenly everybody is in everybody else's body. Soon each wants to get back to their old selves. They spend the next eighty minutes trying to reverse the process.

The movie is a grab bag of crude humor, bad language, and a silly story. It has a few nice moments and a happy ending, but as it is, avoid *Dream a Little Dream*.

> And as it is appointed unto men once to die, but after this the judgment.
> (Hebrews 9:27)

TITLE:	**THE DREAM TEAM**
QUALITY:	★ ★
RECOMMENDATION:	Bad
RATING:	PG-13
RELEASE:	1989
STARRING:	Michael Keaton, Christopher Lloyd, Peter Boyle, and Stephen Furst
DIRECTOR:	Howard Zieff
GENRE:	Comedy
CONTENT:	Many profanities, blasphemies, obscenities, and rear nudity
INTENDED AUDIENCE:	Adults
REVIEWER:	Diane Rich

The Dream Team has an inventive, but implausible story line. Though it has a good cast, their foul language and blasphemous nature do not allow us to recommend this comedy for Christian families.

Four patients of a mental institution in New Jersey, bound together as a team in therapy, are taken by their doctor on an outing to a baseball game at Yankee Stadium. The doctor, while taking one of the patients to an alleyway to relieve himself, witnesses the murder of a policeman by two other police officers in New York City. The doctor is attacked by the policemen and ends up being taken unconscious to a hospital somewhere in the city. The rest of the story revolves around the experiences and escapades of the four patients as a team.

This would have been a fairly funny movie except for one patient's personality identification with Jesus Christ. He utters blasphemies about communion, healing, and other Christian doctrines. His propensity toward nudity makes this movie extremely offensive to Christians.

The Dream Team uses Christianity as a vehicle for humor, in a vile and contemptuous affront to Jesus Christ.

> Do not be deceived: God cannot be mocked. A man reaps what he sows.
> (Galatians 6:7)

TITLE:	**EAT THE PEACH**
QUALITY:	★★★
RECOMMENDATION:	Caution
RATING:	None
RELEASE:	1987
STARRING:	Stephen Brennan, Catherine Byrne, and Eamon Morrissey
DIRECTOR:	Peter Ormron
GENRE:	Drama
CONTENT:	Very mild, off-color language
INTENDED AUDIENCE:	Young adults and adults
REVIEWER:	Doug Brewer

With so many Rambos and Bonds rifling across America's screens today, this small tale of Irish folk is especially refreshing and poignant.

The story opens sadly with the demise of a micro-computer plant. Two friends, Vinnie and Arthur, who are rabid Elvis Presley fans, decide to build a motorcycle stunt ride, "wall of death," like the one in Presley's movie, *Roustabout*. They set to work, undaunted by the lack of funds or support of their relatives and friends. Scraping together what money they can, the wall gradually takes shape.

As we watch, Vinnie and Arthur's enthusiasm becomes contagious until we are caught up with every board and nail with which they build their hopeful futures. Nora, Vinnie's wife, leaves him only to return when she realizes the validity of his venture.

With a jaunty score by Donal Lunny and lush photography for a background, the acting of these characters stand out against all odds. The big day arrives fraught with nerves and a chilly wind. The television station has been called. A local priest is on hand. The local member of Parliament is there to cut the ribbon. The "wall of death" opens to the public only to . . .

The ending is the most heart-warming and hopeful I have witnessed in many a film. This is filmmaking on a local, personal level about people the audience will come to love.

Eat the Peach is highly recommended. Be ready to stand up and cheer!

TITLE:	**EIGHT MEN OUT**
QUALITY:	★★★★
RECOMMENDATION:	Caution
RATING:	PG
RELEASE:	1988
STARRING:	John Cusack, Clifton James, Michael Lerner, Christopher Lloyd, Charlie Sheen, David Strathairn, and D. B. Sweeney

DIRECTOR:	John Sayles
GENRE:	Drama/Historical
CONTENT:	A few obscenities
INTENDED AUDIENCE:	Young adults and up
REVIEWER:	Wendell B. Rhodes

There are tyrants who prey upon the greed of unwary victims. For all who succumb, there are tragic consequences. In 1919, eight Chicago White Sox baseball players conspired to throw the World Series. We clearly see legitimate needs become reasons for greed. After all, when you work for a miser who promises you a $10,000 bonus if you pitch thirty wins, but then ditches you when you win twenty-nine, what do you do? Who can keep a dry eye when one young street urchin pleads with his hero "Tell me it ain't so, Joe. Tell me it ain't." But it is so, and everyone knows it.

The acting is superb. There isn't a better looking movie anywhere. This movie is one of the best of the year! Any parent with a teenager needs to drag their son or daughter to see it.

It might be well to study Psalm 73 before going. If the eight players had lived the lesson discovered by the Psalmist, perhaps they never would have "betrayed [a] generation of children" (Psalm 73:15b).

TITLE:	**18 AGAIN**
QUALITY:	★ ★ ★
RECOMMENDATION:	Caution
RATING:	PG
RELEASE:	1988
STARRING:	George Burns and Charlie Schlatter
DIRECTOR:	Paul Flaherty
GENRE:	Comedy
CONTENT:	Scattered sexual remarks and brief back nudity
INTENDED AUDIENCE:	Teenagers, young adults, and George Burns fans
REVIEWER:	Doug Brewer

Jack Winston is a rich, opinionated grandfather who wishes to be eighteen again. His grandson takes a drive with him and an accident causes them to switch places. Taking David's place at college, Jack finds out that David is scorned by all. His frat brothers force him to do their homework, girls ignore him, and worst of all, he wants to be an artist. With Jack's help, David makes a social about-face and wins the respect he deserves.

18 Again is a funny movie. Seeing Charles Schlatter performing a perfect George Burns impersonation is worth the price, and the film has a quality that has been lacking in *Like Father, Like Son* and *Vice Versa*. *18 Again* gives not only the high points of doing it over again; it also shows that it wouldn't all be easy. If it is remembered that *18 Again* is a fantasy, with no connection to real life, it will be enjoyable.

Caution is recommended because there are a few scattered sexual remarks and some obscenity. Also, there is a scene in a college art class with a model in the background. We caution George Burns against switching places in reality. To be trapped on earth for more than one's appointed time, even in a younger body, when one could be with God in Heaven, is a nightmare of eternal proportions.

TITLE:	**84 CHARING CROSS ROAD**
QUALITY:	★★★★
RECOMMENDATION:	Caution
RATING:	PG
RELEASE:	1987
STARRING:	Anne Bancroft and Anthony Hopkins
DIRECTOR:	David Jones
GENRE:	Drama
CONTENT:	Mild expletives
INTENDED AUDIENCE:	Adults
REVIEWER:	Diane Rich

84 Charing Cross Road is a film about relationships. It opens with Helene Hanph, portrayed by Anne Bancroft, taking a first time flight to London from her home in New York City. Her taxi ride from the airport to 84 Charing Cross Road brings Helene to the empty shop which once housed Marks and Cohen and Co., a bookshop specializing in out-of-print books. As she stands in the empty rooms, we are transported back in her memories about thirty years to the early 1950's.

Helene, a struggling script reader and aspiring writer, is frustrated in her fruitless search in New York City for out-of-print English literature. She finds the advertisement in a trade magazine for Marks and Cohen and Co. at 84 Charing Cross Road in London, and writes a candid, funny letter describing her frustrations and including a list of the books she is seeking. She adds that none of them must cost over $5.

Weeks later, several of these books are mailed to her from the London shop with a short note from F.P.D. of Marks and Cohen and Co. This begins a twenty-year exchange of many books and many letters, developing a relationship between Helene and: Frank (F.P.D.), the other employees, and after a time, even their families. All of this weaves in and out of Helene's life, work, and circle of friends in New York City.

The writer and the director beautifully involve the audience in the characters' daily lives. Helene is a sharp-witted, funny, totally lovable single Jewish woman making her way through life, forming lasting friendships. Those relationships in London were bonded by Helene's generous and timely gift packages sent each holiday to everyone at 84 Charing Cross Road. The most poignant and touching relationship was the closeness developed over the years between Helene and Frank, and eventually Frank's family.

Years before Helene regretfully canceled a trip to London to visit Marks and Cohen and Co. When Helene learns of Frank's sudden, tragic death, she mourns the loss of her friend and suddenly decides to take the long delayed trip to London. This brings us to the present where Helene stands in Frank's empty office, and simply says, "Here I am Frank. I finally made it."

This film is a gently paced, delightful story of relationships; probably more appealing to the adults in your family. There is nothing offensive to the Christian viewer beside a very few expletives which flow from the situations. We recommend *84 Charing Cross Road*.

☆☆☆ MASTERPIECE ☆☆☆

TITLE:	**EL CID (180 Minutes)**
QUALITY:	★★★★
RECOMMENDATION:	Acceptable
RATING:	Not rated
RELEASE:	1961
STARRING:	Charlton Heston, Sophia Loren, John Fraser, and Raf Vallone
DIRECTOR:	Anthony Mann
PRODUCER:	Samuel Bronston and Anthony Mann
GENRE:	Historical drama
CONTENT:	Nothing objectionable
INTENDED AUDIENCE:	Family
REVIEWER:	Protestant Motion Picture Council

A spectacle that is really Colossal! Three dramas unfold together:

- 11th century Spain is cleared of Moors by the battling Rodrigo Diaz de Bivar, better known as El Cid;
- the kingdoms within Spain fight one another over the spoils at the death of King Ferdinand;
- and, the personal life of Spain's greatest hero, the legendary soldier El Cid and his romance with the Lady Chimene who loved him.

Here is a panoply of knighthood in a pageant of color, rich reds and russets and olive greens, pearls and gold braid. There is a medieval church, carved masonry, embossed doors, riding horsemen, armor, broadswords and scimitars, while the whiz of arrows, sword against sword, the roar of thunder and the ringing of bells fill the air.

The legend which has gone down through the centuries through various dramatizations is glorified and grows into an exaggerated symbol of a man with noble ideas and intent; not of the soldier of fortune known to history, the man who fought Moors or Christians for his own gain, his services sold to the highest bidder. The photography is spectacular.

☆☆☆ CLASSIC ☆☆☆

TITLE:	**ELENI**
QUALITY:	★ ★ ★ ★
RECOMMENDATION:	Acceptable
RATING:	PG
RELEASE:	1986
STARRING:	John Malkovich and Kate Nelligan
DIRECTOR:	Peter Yates
GENRE:	Historical
CONTENT:	Nothing objectionable
INTENDED AUDIENCE:	Adults
REVIEWER:	Ted Baehr

Eleni is a must for anyone who cares about their children, freedom, and the future. *Eleni* is the true story of a mother who was murdered by the communists during the Greek Civil War; and how her son, Nicholas Gage, a *New York Times* reporter, goes looking for her murderer thirty years later. In his search, he finds that his mother was murdered because she saved her children from the communists who took 28,000 children from their families to reeducate them in Soviet satellite countries.

Eleni clearly shows the deceit and cruelty of communism. In the beginning of the film, Eleni hides one of the communists, a local teacher, from the government, thinking that he is being wrongly persecuted. The teacher returns her kindness when he becomes commandant of the peoples revolutionary army by stealing her house, taking all she has, torturing her, and killing her.

Eleni portrays the true horrors of communism and should be seen by anyone who wants to know what the people's revolution is all about. It is incredible to me that one secular reviewer questioned the fact that Nicholas Gage intended to kill his mother's killer and relented when confronted by the opportunity—the choice between love and hate. Gage's story not only rings true, but it is his story, and he was both the producer and the author. However, the worldly perspective of the reviewer did not allow for someone to be motivated by sin and have to choose life over death.

Eleni has a redemptive message and some clear Christian overtones, although evangelicals will be put off by the one reference to Mariology. Other than that, Eleni proclaims, "Christ is risen" on Easter, prays to God and concludes before her execution with the touching statement that "It is such a joy to be a mother that I thank God for letting me know it."

There is no sex or profanity in *Eleni*. It is a powerful, good movie which will leave you in tears. *Eleni* is the type of movie Christians should support if they want better movies.

TITLE:	**EMMA'S SHADOW (Subtitles)**
QUALITY:	★★★
RECOMMENDATION:	Acceptable
RATING:	Not rated
RELEASE:	1989
STARRING:	Line Kruse and Morje Ahlstedt
DIRECTOR:	Soeren Kragh-Jacobsen
GENRE:	Drama
CONTENT:	Nothing objectionable
INTENDED AUDIENCE:	Teenagers and adults
REVIEWER:	Ted Baehr

Scandinavian films are now focusing on love and salvation, looking for a deeper meaning in life. *Emma's Shadow,* representing Denmark, is a film that Christians can support.

Emma is a twelve-year-old girl from an upper class family living in Copenhagen during the 1930's. She is an only child neglected by a mother, who cares more for her own amusements. Her father, a prominent businessman, is too busy to notice that his daughter is lonely and unhappy.

Emma runs away, making it look like a kidnapping. She finds herself in a poor section of the city, hungry and lost. She loses her footing on the slick cobblestones and falls down. Malthe, a kindhearted, simple man, who works in the sewers, takes her to his house to clean her bleeding knee and lets her stay the night.

The next morning Emma decides to return home and overhears the chauffeur say that her parents hardly miss their daughter. Emma returns to Malthe. She realizes that Malthe is the butt of jokes and tries to protect him from the unkindness of others. In turn, Malthe cares tenderly for his new charge. Together they discover that love is caring and giving, not taking.

When the police catch up with Emma after a chase through the sewers, they are ready to execute Malthe, but he has committed no wrong. In the end, love triumphs, in her home and in the streets.

Christianity is lifted up in this film. Selfishness is rebuked. We recommend *Emma's Shadow.*

TITLE:	**EMPIRE OF THE SUN**
QUALITY:	★★★
RECOMMENDATION:	Caution
RATING:	PG
RELEASE:	1987

STARRING:	Christian Bale and John Malkovich
DIRECTOR:	Steven Spielberg
GENRE:	War
CONTENT:	Infrequent profanities
INTENDED AUDIENCE:	Adults
REVIEWER:	Doug Brewer

Mr. Spielberg has created an exciting epic. In the opening days of World War II, Jim and his parents live in Shanghai. As the Japanese army advances, the Grahams try to get out but are too late. First, his father is swept away, and then his mother's hand slips out of Jim's. He is placed in an internment camp. He develops a respectful relationship with the Japanese, but he has a precarious hold over his own mind.

This is a storybook style movie with characters more like people described by a child. When Jim is faced with a power he cannot comprehend, he attributes it to God.

While there are a scattered profanities in this film, the overall quality of *Empire of the Sun* deserves our recommendation with a sad caution about the language. Please write Mr. Spielberg at Warner Brothers to express your disappointment about the profanity and your encouragement about the positive reference to God.

> Mr. Steven Spielberg
> Warner Brothers
> 4000 Warner Drive
> Burbank, CA 91522

TITLE:	**END OF THE LINE**
QUALITY:	★★★
RECOMMENDATION:	Caution
RATING:	PG
RELEASE:	1988
STARRING:	Wilford Brimley and Levon Helm
DIRECTOR:	Jay Russell
GENRE:	Drama
CONTENT:	Obscenity
INTENDED AUDIENCE:	Adults
REVIEWER:	Doug Brewer

Set in the fictional little burg of Clifford, *End of the Line* tells the story of Haney and Leo. Their railyard, where they have worked some thirty years, is closed in the name of progress. Southland, the owner, is switching to air freight. Haney and Leo hatch a plan to steal a locomotive, and drive it to Chicago to try to get their jobs back. Failing to get any support from their fellow ex-employees, they take off, just the two of them.

End of the Line is a sweet, well-meaning little film about two men who want to do their jobs. Unfortunately, the dialogue is occasionally obscene in order to receive the PG-rating, but the discussion between Haney and Leo about the Pledge of Allegiance should not be missed. *End of the Line* is recommended with caution.

TITLE:	**ERNEST GOES TO CAMP**
QUALITY:	★ ★ ★
RECOMMENDATION:	Caution
RATING:	PG
RELEASE:	1987
STARRING:	Jim Varney, Iron Eyes Cody, and John Vernon
DIRECTOR:	John R. Cherry, III
GENRE:	Comedy
CONTENT:	Some scatological humor and occult references
INTENDED AUDIENCE:	All ages
REVIEWER:	Susan Klaudt and Brandy Egan

Ernest Goes to Camp is a funny film with no profanity nor sexual permissiveness. However, there is crude humor and occult references which are annoyingly unnecessary in this movie which could easily have been good clean fun.

An Indian boy is tied to a tree in an initiation ritual. A warrior throws a knife, a stone, and then shoots an arrow at the young brave. If the brave's courage is great enough, he comes out a warrior.

Cut to modern Camp Kekakee where all-American boys are learning about nature. Enter a group of tough boys from Mid-State Boys Detention Center. The result is an outlandishly funny clash. The Mid-State Boys are assigned to Ernest. Ernest is chased by badgers, rolled in gauze and bitten on the nose by his turtle as he tries to teach the boys about nature.

Krader Inc. wants the Camp Kekakee land because it contains petrocide, which is essential for the space program. Nurse St. Cloud's aging Indian grandfather refuses to give up the land. Due to Ernest's misunderstanding the land is lost. Ernest, feeling guilty, rights the wrong and saves Camp Kekakee!

This movie does have some pretty funny lines, and Jim Varney's expressions are hilarious! However, some viewers may find this movie slightly crude. Though in the final analysis, *Ernest Goes to Camp* is harmless and funny. Jim Varney, as Ernest, is simply lovable as the Camp Counselor.

TITLE:	**ERNEST SAVES CHRISTMAS**
QUALITY:	★ ★ ★ ★
RECOMMENDATION:	Caution

RATING:	PG
RELEASE:	Fall 1988
STARRING:	Jim Varney, Douglas Seale, Oliver Clark, Noelle Parker, Gailard Sartain, and Billie Bird
DIRECTOR:	John R. Cherry, III
GENRE:	Comedy
CONTENT:	Nothing objectionable except a secular view of Christmas
INTENDED AUDIENCE:	Family
REVIEWER:	Hannah Jackson

On December 23rd, two business men walk through the airport. "What line of business are you in?" asks the younger. "Toys," replies the older man. "But I am here for a replacement. . . . I can't remember names, or what toys they wanted." This bearded old man is Santa Claus.

Ernest, a taxi driver with a sign saying, "Put Christ Back into Christmas" in his glove compartment, finds "Santa" looking for a hack. Ernest delivers Santa to the Children's Museum to find Joe, his replacement. While Santa is trying to convince Joe to come with him, Joe's fast-talking agent whisks him away to have his beard shaved for an audition for an upcoming movie. Santa is arrested for vagrancy, loses his red bag and Ernest gets fired. Santa must get out of jail, find his bag and Joe by 7:00 P.M. Christmas Eve or Christmas is over forever. And then: *Ernest Saves Christmas*.

I was surprised at the humor and wit in the film. Never is the slightest foul language uttered. Love is a constant theme. However, this is a secular view of Christmas. Had it not been for the birth of Jesus Christ, we would continue to live as unforgiven sinners in a meaningless world. If you see *Ernest Saves Christmas*, first discuss with your children the true meaning of Christmas.

TITLE:	**EVERYBODY'S ALL-AMERICAN**
QUALITY:	★ ★
RECOMMENDATION:	Extreme Caution
RATING:	R
RELEASE:	1988
STARRING:	Dennis Quaid, Jessica Lange, and Timothy Hutton
DIRECTOR:	Taylor Hackford
GENRE:	Romance
CONTENT:	Profanity, obscenity, nudity, and adultery
INTENDED AUDIENCE:	Adults
REVIEWER:	Ted Baehr

The first twenty minutes of the movie had me hoping for another *Tucker*. The remainder of the movie had me hoping for a quick ending which never came. Gavin Grey, the Grey

Ghost, was LSU All-American in 1957. He's not only a great football player, but he really wants to help others, though he tries to adopt the attitude of a "good ol' boy." His girlfriend, Babs, is more problematic. She loves him, but part of her love involves his image, so they get married. His younger cousin, Cake, looks up to Gavin, and idolizes Babs. Cake loves her, and she likes him, so she commits adultery with him. From then on it's hard to look at her without feeling disgusted.

Babs becomes the provider. Cake becomes a professor. Gavin asks Cake to write his story, and this movie may be that story which rambles along until the closing five minutes. Between the first third and last five minutes there is boredom, adultery, profanity, and nudity. The first third avoided all of that and was the most interesting part of the movie. You will be thankful if you avoid this dud.

TITLE:	**THE FAMILY (Subtitles)**
QUALITY:	★ ★ ★ ★
RECOMMENDATION:	Acceptable
RATING:	PG
RELEASE:	1988
STARRING:	Vittorio Gassman, Fanny Ardent, and Stefania Sandrelli
DIRECTOR:	Ettore Scola
GENRE:	Drama
CONTENT:	One expletive
INTENDED AUDIENCE:	Adults
REVIEWER:	Doug Brewer

The Family is a fabulous tale, a chronological record of one man and his family. Beginning with Carlo's christening and fading out with his eightieth birthday party, *The Family* takes place entirely within the walls of a single apartment in Rome, showing us the love and sniping, the regrets and celebrations, of life. Though centered around Carlo, it does not tell the tale from his point of view. He is shown to be vain and selfish at times, calling into question several of his decisions about the way he chooses to live.

This is a busy movie, with around forty people appearing in it. They fall in and out of love, have children, work, and argue among themselves. They are a family, with all of the troubles and warts, and all of the happiness. This is a life-affirming film, a heart-warming film and a must-see. There is one expletive, but that is the extent of any objectionable elements. *The Family* is highly recommended.

TITLE:	**FAREWELL TO THE KING**
QUALITY:	★ ★
RECOMMENDATION:	Extreme Caution
RATING:	PG 13
RELEASE:	1989

STARRING:	Nick Nolte, Nigel Havers, Marius Weyers, and Frank McRae
DIRECTOR:	John Milius
GENRE:	Drama
CONTENT:	Profanity, obscenity, and sexual immorality
INTENDED AUDIENCE:	Adults
REVIEWER:	Harold Buchholz

Borneo, 1942: an American soldier, Sgt. Learoyd, deserts his shipwrecked comrades and heads into the jungle. He is discovered by the head-hunting Dayaks, and becomes their leader. A plane drops two parachutes into the jungle. Captain Fairbourne, a British officer, and Sergeant Tenga, a radio technician, have come to incite the tribes of the interior to rebel against Japanese rule. They are astonished to encounter Learoyd, who has shaped his own paradise. Learoyd strikes a bargain: his men will fight if he is guaranteed autonomy from outside forces once WW II is over.

Milius tries sandwiching a number of philosophical inclinations into his hero with little success. The result is a shallow characterization by Nolte.

The film has a smattering of profanity. Battle scenes are not too violent, although there is cannibalism and head-hunting. Free sex abounds for the Europeans who have left their wives at home. The bottom line, however, is that inept storytelling makes the *Farewell to the King* worthless as dramatic entertainment. This is paganism presented as paradise, a lie which we should abhor.

TITLE:	**FATAL ATTRACTION**
QUALITY:	★ ★
RECOMMENDATION:	Bad
RATING:	R
RELEASE:	1987
STARRING:	Michael Douglas and Glenn Close
DIRECTOR:	Adrian Lyne
GENRE:	Drama
CONTENT:	Foul language, nudity, violence, and adultery
INTENDED AUDIENCE:	Adults
REVIEWER:	Ken Kistner and Doug Brewer

Glenn Close's portrayal of Jessica Walter's role in *Play Misty for Me* leaves much to be desired. This is another story of a one night stand which turns into a nightmare for the adulterous husband, as his date throws herself at him jeopardizing his marriage and his life. When Alex appears in Dan's house and attacks Dan's wife Beth with the cliched piece of cutlery in the bathroom, the theft of *Play Misty for Me* is complete.

Fatal Attraction gets the message across that extra-marital affairs are dangerous. We should all know that. So why do we need to see two people having amplified sex in a freight elevator?

On our way out of the screening, a young man was heard to say, "If I have anything to do with it, a lot of people will not see this movie." We will end this review in the spirit of that unknown young man. Pass on this film, and pass the word.

TITLE:	**FEDS**
QUALITY:	★★★
RECOMMENDATION:	Caution
RATING:	PG-13
RELEASE:	1988
STARRING:	Rebecca De Mornay, Mary Gross, Ken Marshall, and Fred Dalton Thompson
DIRECTOR:	Dan Goldberg
GENRE:	Comedy
CONTENT:	Vulgarity and implied immorality
INTENDED AUDIENCE:	Adults
REVIEWER:	F.L. Linberg

DeWitt is just mustering out of the Marines and seeking admission to the FBI Academy. She gets in and rooms with Zuckerman, her opposite. DeWitt is bright but unschooled, physically fit but socially inept. Zuckerman is an old-moneyed preppie and inclined to say "please" if asked to put the cuffs on someone. After a slow start, they learn from each other's strengths. They become distinguished graduates in their class. Along the way, they get into some hilarious spots. The high water marks include: a single-handed shootout with heavily armed bank robbers; Zuckerman turning the tables on a macho classmate; and the climax, when the two girls out-smart "stars" of the Academy.

There are several good laughs in this movie and many grins. This is not the bathroom humor of *Police Academy.* The humor is more intellectual, mixed with slapstick, like *The Odd Couple.* Caution is recommended, because some language and situations are vulgar. Nevertheless, you have to give the movie credit for omitting nudity, gratuitous sex, and floods of four-letter words. If you like to laugh and are not easily offended, this may be worth a look. Otherwise, avoid *Feds.*

TITLE:	**FIGHTING THOROUGHBREDS**
QUALITY:	★★★
RECOMMENDATION:	Acceptable
RATING:	Not rated
RELEASE:	1939
STARRING:	Bob Allen, Mary Carlisle, Ralph Byrd, and George Hayes

DIRECTOR:	Sidney Salkow
GENRE:	Drama
CONTENT:	Nothing objectionable
INTENDED AUDIENCE:	Family
REVIEWER:	Ted Baehr

Self-made millionaire, Mr. Beaureguard, moves to Kentucky to become a country-gentleman. He acquires the premiere race horse, Battleguard, and puts several of his neighbors out of business.

His son, Brad, comes home from college to take over the thoroughbred farm. He wants to reestablish a relationship with Marian Montrose. Unfortunately, Brad finds that Marian and her father hate the Beaureguard name since his father took everything they had except one prize mare.

Ironically, Battleguard escapes one night to mate with Mary's prize horse, siring a foal, Sweet Revenge. Sweet Revenge is soon taking the honors that Brad's father believes should belong to the Beaureguard-Battleguard Line.

In the end, good will and justice triumph. This film is an endearing and entertaining lesson in loving your neighbor; the type of movie we all wish they would make today. *Fighting Thoroughbreds* is a classic movie from the 1930's. It is as entertaining today as it was then. If you can find it at your video store, you'll love it.

TITLE:	**FIRE AND ICE**
QUALITY:	★ ★
RECOMMENDATION:	Caution
RATING:	PG
RELEASE:	1987
STARRING:	John Eaves and Susie Chaffee
DIRECTOR:	Willy Bogner
GENRE:	Docu-drama
CONTENT:	Mild swearing, vulgarity, and sexual innuendos
INTENDED AUDIENCE:	Adults
REVIEWER:	Bruce Grimes

Fire and Ice is a beautiful "quasi-documentary" about two world-class skiers. The film captures some of the most exciting skiing and hang gliding imaginable, in the most spectacular locations.

The plot line is a flimsy vehicle for the skiing sequences. It's a "boy sees girl, boy chases girl, boy gets girl" scenario that detracts from the the film.

Overlooking the minor sexual innuendos and other objectionable material, the film will appeal to ski enthusiasts who are willing to sit through boring interludes between action sequences. Others may wish to avoid *Fire and Ice*.

TITLE:	**A FISH CALLED WANDA**
QUALITY:	★ ★ ★
RECOMMENDATION:	Bad
RATING:	R
RELEASE:	1988
STARRING:	John Cleese, Jamie Lee Curtis, Kevin Kline, and Michael Palin
DIRECTOR:	Charles Crichton
GENRE:	Comedy
CONTENT:	Sexual immorality, profanity, and obscenity
INTENDED AUDIENCE:	Adults
REVIEWER:	Nancy Hanger

There is nothing sloppy about the action or the comedy in *A Fish Called Wanda*. Unfortunately, the humor revolves around sex and deceit. Otto, Wanda, George, and Ken pull off the heist of the decade, and then each plots to keep the jewels for himself. Wanda and Otto, lovers posing as brother and sister, turn in George to the police. George has hidden the jewels and left a key with Ken. Wanda attempts to seduce George's lawyer Archie Leach to find the diamonds. Otto is jealous and foils her attempts to get information. The ending is not surprising, but comedy, not suspense, is the intent.

There are some funny scenes, and there is a fish called Wanda, in Ken's aquarium. Wanda is really the fish with all her slippery tactics of persuasion.

Unfortunately, the subject matter and language are just plain offensive to Christians. Wanda excuses her lack of character and conscience by saying that "all Americans are like that." Let's prove her wrong. Avoid *A Fish Called Wanda*.

TITLE:	**FIVE CORNERS**
QUALITY:	★ ★ ★ ★
RECOMMENDATION:	Extreme Caution
RATING:	R
RELEASE:	1988
STARRING:	John Patrick Shanley, Jodie Foster, and Tim Robbins
DIRECTOR:	Tony Bill
GENRE:	Drama
CONTENT:	Some rough street language and sexual laxity
INTENDED AUDIENCE:	Adults
REVIEWER:	Ted Baehr

Five Corners is a gritty movie set in the Bronx in the 1960's. Harry is a street kid who becomes a civil rights activist after hearing Martin Luther King, Jr. speak about the power of love. Harry comes home to pack and head South to fight for the rights of blacks. Heinz has just been let out of prison, and the girl Heinz tried to rape is afraid Heinz will try again. Harry saved her the first time, and she wants Harry's protection again. Heinz kidnaps the object of his twisted desires and proceeds to kill several people, including his mother. Heinz forces Harry to fight. Harry asks Heinz for his forgiveness. Heinz refuses and is killed by neighborhood vigilantes.

This is a film about trying to live as a loving person in a sinful world. Harry doesn't realize that true love cannot be divorced from justice. Although Jesus' love can be read into the film, Jesus, Lord and Saviour, has been left out. *Five Corners* contains rough language and tough subject matter, but it seriously considers the power of love. Extreme caution is recommended.

☆☆☆ CLASSIC ☆☆☆

TITLE:	**FLAME OVER INDIA (130 Minutes)**
QUALITY:	★ ★ ★
RECOMMENDATION:	Acceptable
RATING:	Not rated
RELEASE:	1960 (British)
STARRING:	Kenneth More, Lauren Bacall, Herbert Lom, and Wilfred Hyde
DIRECTOR:	J. Lee Thompson
GENRE:	Historical Adventure
CONTENT:	Nothing objectionable
INTENDED AUDIENCE:	Adults and mature young people
REVIEWER:	Protestant Motion Picture Council

A Moslem siege of a British fortress town in rural India in 1905 threatens the life of a young Hindu Prince. The mission is to get him away from the trouble spot and save him at all costs as his succession to his father's position as the Maharajah insures stability and continuity.

The British governor, his wife, the boy's American governess, and a British officer are entrusted with the boy's safety. This begins a series of exciting adventures as the party is joined by a dubious character with dark intentions, and they depend on an old locomotive to reach their goal in a rickety train. Before the mission is accomplished, dangerous situations call for the best in everyone.

This is a very enjoyable film, loaded with action, excellent color photography, interesting backgrounds, maintained suspense, good acting, and an imaginative plot.

TITLE:	**FLETCH LIVES (II)**
QUALITY:	★★
RECOMMENDATION:	Extreme Caution
RATING:	PG-13
RELEASE:	1989
STARRING:	Chevy Chase, Julie Anne Phillips, and Hal Halbrook
DIRECTOR:	Michael Ritchie
GENRE:	Comedy
CONTENT:	Many sexual references and several vulgarities
INTENDED AUDIENCE:	Young adults
REVIEWER:	Gene Burke

Fletch, the outlandish investigative reporter with his unlimited disguises for fact finding, returns. *Fletch Lives* contains the same irreverent sarcasm and silly gags as the original.

Fletch inherits a Louisiana plantation and envisions himself in the splendor of a southern mansion. He resigns and flies to Louisiana only to find that his inheritance is a dilapidated mansion. His disillusionment is compounded when the attorney handling the inheritance is murdered. An anonymous offer to buy the property is made. Disguised as such "southern" characters as a tennis player, a contract worker, and a part time preacher, Fletch investigates the underhanded going-ons. The major suspect is a noted TV evangelist. Fletch discovers that the evangelist is clean, and that the town lawyer is the real crook. All returns to normal.

This film makes fun of televangelism. Furthermore, *Fletch Lives* is not recommended because of crude sexual references and because the last half is completely boring— without a single laugh!

TITLE:	**FLY II**
QUALITY:	★★
RECOMMENDATION:	Bad
RATING:	R
RELEASE:	1989
STARRING:	Eric Stolz
DIRECTOR:	Chris Wales
GENRE:	Science fiction
CONTENT:	Rough language, vivid gore, instances of sexual activity, and nothing uplifting
INTENDED AUDIENCE:	Young adults
REVIEWER:	Gene Burke

Fly II is just as forgettable as the original. This film opens with the birth of Martin Brundle, the offspring of Seth, who perfected a transporter to convert matter into energy, move it through space and convert it back again at the other end. While doing so, a fly was mistakenly transported with Seth causing his genes to mix with that of the fly. Martin is secretively raised in a totally experimental environment by his adopted father, Mr. Bartoc, owner of Bartoc Industries. Martin meets Beth Logan, a night shift employee, and they become inseparable. When Mr. Bartoc discovers Martin is developing certain "buggie" characteristics, Beth is transferred. Martin runs away with her. When he all but becomes a fly, she can't handle it and returns him to Bartoc. He retaliates by killing some of his captors and placing himself in Mr. Bartoc's hands for one final attempt at returning to normality through the transporter. It is successful for Martin, but Mr. Bartoc is now the hideous creature that is left to be researched. Martin and Beth live happily ever after, hopefully without plans for another sequel.

This film has no redeeming social values and I suggest you spare yourself this nauseating stomach-churner. We recommend that you avoid *Fly II*.

> If a woman approaches a beast to have sexual relations with it, kill both the woman and the beast. They must be put to death; their blood will be on their own heads. (Leviticus 20:16)

☆☆☆ MASTERPIECE ☆☆☆

TITLE:	**FORBIDDEN PLANET**
QUALITY:	★★★★
RECOMMENDATION:	Acceptable
RATING:	Not rated
RELEASE:	1956
STARRING:	Walter Pidgeon, Anne Francis, Leslie Nielsen, Warren Stevens, Richard Anderson, Earl Holliman, and Jack Kelly
DIRECTOR:	Fred Wilcox
GENRE:	Science fiction
CONTENT:	Nothing objectionable
INTENDED AUDIENCE:	All ages
REVIEWER:	Bruce Grimes

MGM released this big budget, class "A" science fiction film in the mid-50's. Today, *Forbidden Planet* is considered a classic, perhaps the finest science fiction film to come out of the 1950's.

Forbidden Planet is based in large part on William Shakespeare's *The Tempest*. Dr. Morbius (Shakespeare's Prospero), played expertly by Walter Pidgeon, and his daughter Altaira (Shakespeare's Miranda), played by Anne Francis, are living on a distant planet where their spaceship wrecked many years before. They are visited by United Planets Cruiser C-57-D which is on a mission from Earth to track down the expedition that landed on Altair 4 twenty years earlier and has not been heard from since.

There are few films which operate at so many intellectual levels as *Forbidden Planet* does. Even though the film is showing some vestiges of aging (as any science-fiction film will), such as dated slang, costumes, and spaceship equipment, the film still holds interest because of its first-class script and its examination of good and evil. Other attempts to explore the world (or universe, as the case may be) of good and evil, such as *Quatermass and the Pit, Five, Colossus, The Forbin Project,* and *Seconds,* work on a level not quite as thought-provoking as *Forbidden Planet.*

Most films, such as *Star Wars,* the James Bond films, and westerns, work on a straight expository level: the drama is presented with clearly-defined good versus evil, or protagonist versus the antagonist. *Forbidden Planet* presents us with a curious mixture of the basic dramatic elements. Much like Shakespearean drama, the material gives us insight on an exposition level and on an intellectual level for more refined, closer examination of the moral perspectives being presented.

Forbidden Planet presents us with Morbius, who wants to become godlike or even a god to the human race. He doles out bits of the Krel knowledge to earthlings as he sees fit. Morbius and the characters which surround him create an interesting dynamic: good versus evil; the place of religion and law within a technological framework; and the relationship between man and God.

This thought-provoking film is a must of the science fiction genre.

TITLE:	**THE FOURTH PROTOCOL**
QUALITY:	★★★
RECOMMENDATION:	Extreme Caution
RATING:	R
RELEASE:	1987
STARRING:	Michael Caine and Pierce Brosnan
DIRECTOR:	John McKenzie
GENRE:	Spy
CONTENT:	Moderate violence and profanity
INTENDED AUDIENCE:	Adults
REVIEWER:	Doug Brewer

In 1968, the United States and Russia entered into a strategic arms agreement which included four secret protocols. The fourth is an agreement not to construct nuclear weapons inside the other's boundaries or the boundaries of their allies.

Discovering an integral component to an atomic bomb concealed in the personal effects of Petrofsky, a Russian sailor, Preston sets out to find the man putting them together. As the hunt draws to a close, both men start to crack, Petrofsky more so. The final minutes of the film are a heart-pounding, shallow-breathing exercise in suspense.

Unfortunately, *The Fourth Protocol* can not be recommended. Although there is only moderate violence, there is a nude female corpse. Also, there are a few profanities which are never excusable.

TITLE:	**THE FOURTH WISE MAN**
QUALITY:	★ ★ ★
RECOMMENDATION:	Acceptable
RATING:	Not rated
RELEASE:	1985
STARRING:	Martin Sheen, Lance Kerwin, Alan Arkin, Harold Gould, Eileen Brennan, Ralph Bellamy, Adam Arkin, and Richard Libertini
DIRECTOR:	Michael Ray Rhodes
GENRE:	Religious/Christian
CONTENT:	Nothing objectionable
INTENDED AUDIENCE:	Family
REVIEWER:	Betty Hill

A young physician, Arteban, sells his possessions to follow the three wise men who are following the Star of Bethlehem. Arteban lost all hope when his wife and children were killed in a fire, so he is searching. A slave is sent with him with the promise that the father will give him his freedom when his son's mission is completed. The slave's letters to his master tell the story.

Arteban's presents for the newborn king are an emerald, a ruby, and a pearl. However, he has to sell the emerald to buy supplies to cross the desert. On the journey, Arteban stops to help many people. A beggar along the road begs for help and receives it.

The three wise men go on to Bethlehem without him. A woman in Bethlehem takes Arteban to the place of Jesus' birth. Soldiers start slaughtering babies. Arteban runs to the door to keep a soldier from entering. The ruby is given to the soldier. The child's life is spared. The woman says Jesus has been taken to Egypt.

In Egypt, he meets a phony Mary, Joseph and son Benjamin. The slave arranged the charade in hopes he could return home. A Rabbi is consulted. He says to look in Jerusalem among the poor.

As Arteban and the slave walk past a leper colony, they are attacked by robbers. The woman leader learns Arteban is a physician and asks him to cure her son. He intends to stay one day; however, it turns into many years. Arteban teaches them to raise crops. He's an old man, and his ambition hasn't been realized.

A friend tells him his father is dead. The slave is released from his vow. The slave goes to Jerusalem and witnesses Palm Sunday. He returns with news of the Messiah, "A man named Jesus was surrounded by poor people and a blind man was healed." Arteban and the freed slave, whom he calls brother, head toward the crucifixion, Arteban sees a friend's daughter about to be sold to pay for her father's debts. Arteban uses his last gift, the pearl, to purchase her freedom. Soon after, he has a heart attack. As Arteban is dying, Jesus "appears" to him: "Whenever you did these things for the least of these, my brother, you have done it unto me."

Beautifully produced and acted, this story, based on the novel *The Other Wise Man* by

Henry Van Dyke, speaks for itself. It is a special witness to Him who gave His life for us.

TITLE:	**FRANTIC**
QUALITY:	★★★★
RECOMMENDATION:	Extreme Caution
RATING:	R
RELEASE:	1988
STARRING:	Harrison Ford and Emmanuelle Seigner
DIRECTOR:	Roman Polanski
GENRE:	Mystery/Romance
CONTENT:	Some obscenity, sexual lewdness, and brief silhouette nudity
INTENDED AUDIENCE:	Adults
REVIEWER:	Ted Baehr

Frantic argues for a loyal marital relationship at all costs. Dr. Richard Walker goes to Paris for a medical conference and takes his wife for a romantic vacation. By mistake, they end up with the wrong suitcase. Mrs. Walker is kidnapped, and Richard sets out to find her. He is confronted by the seamy underworld of drugs, sex, and crime, but he never wavers in his loyalty to his wife. He discovers that the bag he possesses contains a detonator for a nuclear weapon and belongs to the smuggler Michelle. Finding Michelle is his only hope of reuniting with his wife . . . Christians should appreciate this storyline. Unfortunately, some off-color language, seamy locations, lewdness, and silhouette nudity are is used to tell this suspenseful story. Because of these defects, we can only advise extreme caution.

TITLE:	**FUNNY FARM**
QUALITY:	★★★
RECOMMENDATION:	Caution
RATING:	PG
RELEASE:	1988
STARRING:	Chevy Chase, Madolyn Smith, Joseph Maher, Jack Gilpan, and Brad Sullivan
DIRECTOR:	George Roy Hill
GENRE:	Comedy
CONTENT:	Some rough language
INTENDED AUDIENCE:	Adults
REVIEWER:	Nancy Hanger

Except for expletives and obscenities, Funny Farm would be enjoyable. Unfortunately, it's not very funny. The story reveals insights into human nature in the protagonist's slide into deceit and alcoholism, in the face of failure, and the townspeople's outward friendliness and inward guarded-selfishness.

When Chevy and his wife move to the country so he can write the "great American novel," they find that they are fish out of water. On their very first day, their furniture gets lost and they spend the night on the living room floor. When they find a body in their garden and are charged $4,000 for the burial, they suspect that country folks are not all charm and warmth. Chevy gets writer's block. His wife begins to write a story based on their experiences. His novel turns out flawed while she gets published. Their marriage starts to crumble, but all ends well.

Caution is recommended because of the rough language. It is not the funniest movie of the year, but it won't hurt anyone over 18.

TITLE:	**GABY, A TRUE STORY**
QUALITY:	★ ★
RECOMMENDATION:	Extreme Caution
RATING:	Not rated
RELEASE:	1987
STARRING:	Liv Ullman, Rachel Levin, and Norma Aleandro
DIRECTOR:	Luis Mandoki
GENRE:	Biography
CONTENT:	One profanity and brief nudity
INTENDED AUDIENCE:	Adults
REVIEWER:	Nancy Hanger

Gabriela Brimmer was born with cerebral palsy, the second child of a well-to-do family in Mexico. Florencia, her Nanny, is Catholic and comforts Gaby with "God has a reason for everything." Gaby has a fine mind, but can only move her left foot. She goes to a school for handicapped students which progresses only to the sixth grade.

She enrolls in normal high school and then goes to college, where Florencia must attend classes with her and be her voice, as Gaby types out her communications with her toe. She is very successful academically. She encounters much loneliness and frustration in trying to live a normal life and expresses anger with God, her situation and life in general. There is no resolution of her frustration except for her commitment to an adopted baby. Since it is a true story, it is still in progress. It is unfortunate that Gaby does not know the peace which is Jesus Christ.

We recommend this moving story of devotion with the extreme caution that there is some brief, non-erotic nudity, as well as one profanity. It is unfortunate that the filmmaker did not avoid these elements in telling this poignant story.

☆☆☆ CLASSIC ☆☆☆

TITLE:	**THE GALLANT HOURS (Black and White)**
QUALITY:	★★★★
RECOMMENDATION:	Acceptable
RATING:	Not rated
RELEASE:	1960
STARRING:	James Cagney, Dennis Weaver, Ward Costello, Richard Jaekel, Les Tremayne, Robert Burton, and Raymond Bailey
DIRECTOR:	Robert Montgomery
GENRE:	Biography/War
CONTENT:	Nothing objectionable
INTENDED AUDIENCE:	Family
REVIEWER:	Protestant Motion Picture Council

In this war drama of the fateful days at Guadalcanal, the audience has the feeling of participation in the planning and strategy which insured future victory in the Pacific. This particular five week period in 1942 (October 18 through December 1), at the height of the war effort, is depicted from the vantage point of Admiral Halsey. It is told in flashback manner with the force and feeling of a very truthful documentary.

The characters are identified with factual backgrounds. An intelligent commentary (though at times a bit too much) illumines every scene.

Although the story of a great victory, there is almost no battle action on screen, as the director focuses in on the human side of war. There are occasional glimpses of humor but, on the whole, it is a serious and engrossing film, an uplifting one, as one gets a clear idea of the price at which peace was ultimately secured.

James Cagney plays most successfully a new type of role for him and is, in fact, the perfect choice to play Admiral Halsey. Cagney is subtle in his portrayal, perhaps one of his best, as he uses his superior military strategy to outwit the Japanese Admiral Yamamoto in the battle of Guadalcanal.

All performances are outstanding under the direction of Robert Montgomery. This is a production of real distinction and a fine memorial to a great man.

☆☆☆ CLASSIC ☆☆☆

TITLE:	**THE GENE KRUPA STORY (Black and White)**
QUALITY:	★★★★
RECOMMENDATION:	Caution
RATING:	Not rated

RELEASE:	1959
STARRING:	Sal Mineo, Susan Kohner, James Darren, and Susan Oliver
DIRECTOR:	Don Weis
GENRE:	Biography
CONTENT:	Adult situations
INTENDED AUDIENCE:	Adults and mature young people
REVIEWER:	Protestant Motion Picture Council

An excellent biographical drama about a famous drummer who achieved success the hard way. Gene Krupa was one of ten children in a miner's family. As a youth, he wanted to play drums in a jazz band against his father's will, who wanted him to go into the priesthood.

Antagonism flares up between them. When his father destroys his drums, he leaves home.

Upon his father's sudden death, in a repentant mood, he enters a seminary to fulfill his father's wishes, but, after a year, he returns to his own life: drum playing. This is the beginning of a long road of ups and downs, periods of want and depression, and times of wild living and popularity.

At one time, he was tempted into becoming a marijuana addict and served a prison term for possession of narcotics, which had been planted on him, however. He showed much determination to vanquish the habit and succeeded. In the background, faithful, ready to help and stand by him through time of achievement and of trouble is his high school sweetheart, Ethel, the girl he eventually marries.

Throughout is the music of Gene Krupa and the following numbers: "I Love My Baby," "Memories of You," "Royal Garden Blues," "Cherokee," "Indiana," "Way Down Yonder in New Orleans," "Let There Be Love," "Song of India," and "Drum Crazy." Sal Mineo impersonates Gene Krupa in a brilliant manner and is well-seconded by an excellent cast.

This is the story of a period as well as that of a man. It may point a lesson about the temptations to resist, the things to avoid to the youth whose idea of life is noise and excitement.

TITLE:	**THE GLASS MENAGERIE**
QUALITY:	★ ★ ★
RECOMMENDATION:	Acceptable
RATING:	PG
RELEASE:	1987
STARRING:	John Malkovich, Joanne Woodward, Karen Allen, and James Naughton
DIRECTOR:	Paul Newman

GENRE:	Drama
CONTENT:	Nothing Objectionable
INTENDED AUDIENCE:	Adults
REVIEWER:	Doug Brewer

Paul Newman has given us a faithful, lyrical and magical performance to savor over and over again. The story concerns the Winfield family: Amanda, a deluded Southern Belle; Tom, literary and frustrated at having to work in a shoe factory to support his mother and sister; and Laura, fragile and caught up in the imaginary world of her tiny glass animals. It is Tom's play, a seeking for justification in the rubble of St. Louis, an apology to us, and an appeal to the ghosts of his past for forgiveness.

This movie is slow at times and runs a little long, but as a character study, Mr. Newman has constructed a hauntingly beautiful record of *The Glass Menagerie*.

TITLE:	**GLEAMING THE CUBE**
QUALITY:	★★
RECOMMENDATION:	Bad
RATING:	PG-13
RELEASE:	1988
STARRING:	Christian Slater and Steven Bauer
DIRECTOR:	Graeme Clifford
GENRE:	Action adventure
CONTENT:	Violence, rebellion, and profanity
INTENDED AUDIENCE:	Teenagers
REVIEWER:	Ted Baehr

Bryan Kelly, a rebellious teenager, can't do anything right except skateboard. Vinh, his adopted Vietnamese brother, does everything right. Since Vinh is a star pupil and obedient son, the parents prefer him over Bryan.

While working for a Vietnamese anti-communist Relief Organization, Vinh discovers that the weight of the medical supplies being shipped to Vietnam is way out of whack. We know at this moment that there must be guns in those medical supplies and that the anti-communists are the bad guys. Vinh gets bumped off. Bryan sets out to avenge the murder of his adopted brother. In the process of solving this murder, Bryan cleans up his act and falls in love with Tina, Vinh's former girlfriend.

Skateboarding is an improbable device to solve a mundane mystery, which the audience has solved five minutes into the film. Profanity is frequent, rebellion is extolled, motivations are caricatured, and some moments reveal an embarrassing poverty of script. Furthermore, it seems pretty mean-spirited to portray the freedom-loving people of Vietnam who lost their homes and families to the communists as the bad guys. We recommend that you avoid *Gleaming the Cube*.

TITLE:	**GOOD MORNING, BABYLON**
QUALITY:	★ ★ ★
RECOMMENDATION:	Extreme Caution
RATING:	None
RELEASE:	1987
STARRING:	Vincent Spano and Joaquim De Almeida
DIRECTOR:	Paolo and Vittorio Taviani
GENRE:	Historical
CONTENT:	Some frontal nudity and profanity
INTENDED AUDIENCE:	Adults
REVIEWER:	Marlys M. Moxley

Two Tuscan artisans leave Italy for America, pledging to return to restore their father's studio once they have made their fortune. They hear of work at D.W. Griffith's studios and become the set designers on *Intolerance*. They fall in love with two extras. At the wedding, Griffith defends them as artisans in filmmaking. One wife dies in childbirth. The brothers enlist to fight the Kaiser, one in the Italian forces and one in the American.

Unfortunately, there are brief scenes of nudity and a few unacceptable profanities. This is not a film for children, or teenagers, who will be bored, as will adults who prefer highly emotive films. You may want to avoid *Good Morning, Babylon.*

TITLE:	**GOOD MORNING, VIETNAM**
QUALITY:	★ ★ ★
RECOMMENDATION:	Extreme Caution
RATING:	R
RELEASE:	1987
STARRING:	Robin Williams, Forest Whitaker, and Bruno Kirby
DIRECTOR:	Barry Levinson
GENRE:	Comedy
CONTENT:	Some rough language
INTENDED AUDIENCE:	Adults
REVIEWER:	Doug Brewer

Good Morning, Vietnam is a funny movie. Adrian Cronauer is a disc jockey sent to Saigon during 1965 to boost morale among the troops. What there is of a plot concerns reactions by the Brass to his show and his attempts to catch the eye of a beautiful Vietnamese girl. However, the real reason for this film is to showcase Williams' manic mental leaps and bounds.

Unfortunately, there are some major problems with *Good Morning, Vietnam*. Some aspects are quite anti-Biblical in nature. There was a blatant disregard for authority, and officers are portrayed as imbeciles with an imbalanced love for rules and regulations. Also, the evil of communism is downplayed. For these reasons, along with the salty language employed by Mr. Williams, we do not recommend *Good Morning, Vietnam*.

TITLE:	**THE GOOD MOTHER**
QUALITY:	★★★
RECOMMENDATION:	Bad
RATING:	R
RELEASE:	1988
STARRING:	Diane Keaton, Liam Neeson, and Jason Robards
DIRECTOR:	Leonard Nimoy
GENRE:	Drama
CONTENT:	Nudity, sex, and sexual terms
INTENDED AUDIENCE:	Adults
REVIEWER:	Don Vice

At 1950's family reunion, Annie meets Babe, who is worshipped by younger nieces and nephews because she teaches them how to sin. Following in Babe's footsteps, Annie reappears in the 1960's as a divorcee with her child, Molly. She begins a steamy relationship with Leo, a sculptor. Her first date with Leo leads to a steamy seduction.

When Molly expresses curiosity about Leo's private parts, Leo gives a full explanation, which is repeated to her real father. Enraged, the father sues for full custody of his daughter on grounds of "child molestation." During the trial, Annie takes the stand losing her lover and her child. She somehow holds herself together for another family reunion. This leads into the most unbearable part of the entire movie, the ending, when the grandmother sympathetically responds: "Everybody knows you're a good mother."

Avoid *The Good Mother*, it mocks Biblical values and degrades human relationships. It shows the problems of sinfulness in our age, but never offers the slightest hope of any solution. Jesus is The Answer, but no one in this movie knows that wonderful fact.

TITLE:	**GORILLAS IN THE MIST**
QUALITY:	★★★
RECOMMENDATION:	Caution
RATING:	PG-13
RELEASE:	1988
STARRING:	Sigourney Weaver and Bryan Brown
DIRECTOR:	Michael Apted

GENRE:	Biography
CONTENT:	Unnecessary bad language and suggestive love scene
INTENDED AUDIENCE:	Adults
REVIEWER:	Gene Burke

Gorillas in the Mist is a true story about Diane Fossy, a therapist turned *National Geographic* writer, who studied gorillas. She was able to communicate with them and was allowed to live among them. She became their protector against outsiders coming to capture the babies for sale to zoos. Their welfare and safety become her obsession.

A *National Geographic* photographer also works on the project with Diane. They fall in love. Though he asks his wife for a divorce, this does not materialize. When Fossy's favorite gorilla, "Digit," is mauled, a breakdown begins as she realizes the odds she faces with the poachers and authorities. Just as she began changing laws to protect the gorillas against poachers, she was murdered.

The scenery and soundtrack are wonderful. The scenes of the human annihilation of the gorillas are vivid and violent. However, the language and adulterous affair will also give you good cause to avoid this movie.

TITLE:	**THE GREAT OUTDOORS**
QUALITY:	★ ★ ★
RECOMMENDATION:	Caution
RATING:	PG
RELEASE:	1988
STARRING:	John Candy and Dan Aykroyd
DIRECTOR:	Howard Deutch
GENRE:	Comedy
CONTENT:	Obscenity and sexual innuendo
INTENDED AUDIENCE:	Teenagers and adults
REVIEWER:	Ted Baehr

The Great Outdoors is a mindless comedy set in the north woods about two families who encounter nature and each other in a vacation lodge. Chet drives up to Lake Potowotomimac so he can get closer to his children. Unfortunately, Chet's arrogant brother-in-law, Roman, surprises Chet by driving his family up to join Chet's vacation. Eventually, Chet tells Roman what he thinks of him. Roman, the expert salesman, turns Chet around so that Chet buys some bogus stock from Roman. Convicted by his wife that he took advantage of Chet, Roman gives back Chet's money while admitting he is bankrupt. Chet takes Roman under his wing to help Roman in his hour of need.

There is enough obscenity and sexual humor to caution any family which might be contemplating *The Great Outdoors*. This is not a great film, but it has some funny moments.

☆☆☆ CLASSIC ☆☆☆

TITLE:	**GREYFRIAR'S BOBBY**
QUALITY:	★★★★
RECOMMENDATION:	Acceptable
RATING:	Not rated
RELEASE:	1961
STARRING:	Donald Crisp, Laurence Naismith, and Alexander Mackenzie
DIRECTOR:	Don Chaffey
GENRE:	Children's drama
CONTENT:	Nothing objectionable
INTENDED AUDIENCE:	Family
REVIEWER:	Protestant Motion Picture Council

A most enjoyable, supposedly true story of 1867 set in Edinburgh about Old Jock, a Highlands shepherd, and Bobby, his Skye terrier. The dog has been immortalized in Scotland for his undying faithfulness and love for his master.

When Jock became too old to work and went to live in town, Bobby could not be kept at Cauldbrae farm, but found all kinds of ways to escape to join his master. When his elderly master died, the loyal dog insisted on keeping vigil over Jock's grave and refused to leave. Through adversities and adventures, Bobby became a legendary figure, the "guest of the city."

Beautifully produced, with an appropriate musical score and excellent acting by a cast of well-known British character actors, this is good family entertainment. Bobby is the star throughout.

TITLE:	**GRIEVOUS BODILY HARM**
QUALITY:	★★★
RECOMMENDATION:	Extreme Caution
RATING:	R
RELEASE:	1989
STARRING:	John Friels and John Waters
DIRECTOR:	Mark Joffe
GENRE:	Mystery
CONTENT:	Sexual immorality, nudity, and violence
INTENDED AUDIENCE:	Adult
REVIEWER:	Dak Ming

Tom Stewart is a renowned writer/newspaper reporter. As we watch Tom pursue a series of murders, we see that people tell Tom the truth because he accepts no less. As Tom is on the trail of the murderer and is trying to get to the next intended victim while she is still alive, the police captain is in hot pursuit of Tom. Tom is the last person to speak to a thief dying in his wrecked car after speeding from a robbery where $270,000 was stolen. The money was not recovered from the wreck, and the captain thinks Tom's got the money. The outcome has a Hitchcockian twist.

Because of the slow storyline development and the complex characters, it will not enjoy a long theater engagement. Because of the unnecessary nudity and sexual situations, we cannot recommend *Grievous Bodily Harm*. This pandering to prurient interests places this film on the "to avoid" list for Christians. Sooner or later, Hollywood will get the message, if Christians take a stand.

TITLE:	**HALF OF HEAVEN (Subtitles)**
QUALITY:	★ ★ ★
RECOMMENDATION:	Caution
RATING:	Not rated
RELEASE:	1988
STARRING:	Angela Molina and Margarita Lozano
DIRECTOR:	Manuel Aragon
GENRE:	Drama
CONTENT:	Breast-feeding scene
INTENDED AUDIENCE:	Adults
REVIEWER:	Nancy Hanger

Half of Heaven conveys much about triumph and love. Rosa is an intelligent young widow girl from the country, who goes to Madrid to be a nurse. Later, Rosa decides to open a stall at the market. When Rosa comes up against trials, she grows rather than being dissuaded. She goes on to own a fancy luncheon restaurant where officials dine. She attracts love without being showy, false, or proud. Although she doesn't achieve the traditional love relationship, her virtue and independent success are gratifying to see.

Half of Heaven provides a rich palette of characters. Rosa is close to her grandmother, a country woman who foresees the future. Christians should be aware of this supernaturalism, but it is not strong enough to dissuade viewers from enjoying this entertaining film. Also, the movie provides wonderful comical scenes. You are certain to enjoy this movie for its entertainment value.

TITLE:	**A HANDFUL OF DUST**
QUALITY:	★ ★ ★ ★
RECOMMENDATION:	Caution
RATING:	PG

RELEASE:	1988
STARRING:	James Wilby, Kristin Scott Thomas, Jackson Kyle, Rupert Graves, Judi Dench, and cameos by Anjelica Huston and Alec Guinness
DIRECTOR:	Charles Sturridge
GENRE:	Drama
CONTENT:	Adultery
INTENDED AUDIENCE:	Adults
REVIEWER:	Wendell B. Rhodes

A Handful of Dust is the screen adaptation of Evelyn Waugh's novel. Tony Last, Lord of Hetton Manor, and his wife, Brenda, have what seems to be a stable marriage. Then, Brenda without guilt or apprehension begins to seek the affections of Mr. Beaver, a lazy opportunist, in cahoots with his mother to seek fortunes in adulterous affairs. Tony is ignorant of the whole affair until tragedy strikes their little arrangement. Soon, both are filing for divorce. Tony becomes an explorer in the uncharted wilderness of Brazil. After leaving the Victorian prison of Hetton, he finds himself a prisoner of the great Victorian Charles Dickens.

This movie is elegant. You can't find better cinematography and editing. The acting is superb! It is haunting. However, looking only at the wages of sin leaves us struggling in hopelessness and fear. If you enjoy a deep discussion, this may be for you. However, choose your discussion partner carefully; mine was "bored to tears!"

TITLE:	**HANNA'S WAR (149 Minutes)**
QUALITY:	★ ★
RECOMMENDATION:	Caution
RATING:	PG-13
RELEASE:	1988
STARRING:	Ellen Burstyn, Maruschka Detmers, Anthony Andres, and Donald Pleasence
DIRECTOR:	Menahem Golan
GENRE:	War
CONTENT:	Wartime atrocities and one scene of torture
INTENDED AUDIENCE:	Adult
REVIEWER:	Philip Boatwright

The true story of an Israeli natural heroine, Hanna, a twenty-three year old poet who moved to Israel to escape anti-Semitism in her native Hungary only to return to fight in the World War II Resistance Movement. Hanna is captured by Nazi sympathizers and tortured by Donald Pleasence. With help from David Warner, Pleasence tries to gain information from Hanna about her mission and the names of other Resistance Fighters.

Hanna's War is a mixture of noble intent and mediocre storytelling. For every positive, this film counters with a negative: the cinematography is beautiful—the musical score overbearing; Detmers is lovely and passionate—Pleasence is cartoon-like, playing his part like Simon Legree; the story is powerful—the directional choices are amateurish. We do, however, recommend *Hanna's War*, if for no other reason that it is a reminder of the people who gave their lives so that others might live. We hope that during this age of remote control, we will never forget those who gave their all so that we could enjoy that one ideal we take so for granted—FREEDOM!

TITLE:	**HANOI HILTON**
QUALITY:	★★★
RECOMMENDATION:	Extreme Caution
RATING:	R
RELEASE:	1987
STARRING:	Michael Moriarity, Jeffrey Jones, Paul Le Mat, and David Soul
DIRECTOR:	Lionel Chetwynd
GENRE:	War
CONTENT:	Rough language used as exclamatory remarks, not gratuitously
INTENDED AUDIENCE:	Adults
REVIEWER:	Bruce Grimes

Hanoi Hilton is the story of the American Prisoners of War (POWs) captured and tortured by the Vietcong from the 1960s through the mid-1970s. The film recreates the hell that these men suffered at the hands of their captors.

Brilliantly acted, with a highly polished script, *Hanoi Hilton* is a moving, insightful film that will be too strong for some viewers because of its realism. Although the film does not resort to excessive, gory, distasteful violence, it does realistically portray the war and its prisoners; therefore, there is some male nudity (from behind), as well as profanity, obscenity, and scenes of torture.

Hanoi Hilton is recommended because a film of this nature cannot be so antiseptic as to be a "war is heck" film. However, extreme caution is recommended since *Hanoi Hilton* is a very realistic portrait of the Vietnamese War, much better than the overrated movie, *Platoon*.

TITLE:	**HAPPY NEW YEAR (80 Minutes)**
QUALITY:	★★★
RECOMMENDATION:	Extreme Caution
RATING:	None
RELEASE:	1987

STARRING:	Peter Falk, Charles Durning, Wendy Hughes, and Tom Courtney
DIRECTOR:	John G. Avildsen
GENRE:	Action adventure
CONTENT:	Crime pays; some off-color language; and one mild, brief sexual situation
INTENDED AUDIENCE:	Teenagers
REVIEWER:	Kay M. Black

Happy New Year is set in the Caymen Islands. This nice cast does a fine job in this sophisticated, light-hearted jewelry heist. The story is delightful and fast-paced. The few off-color words are unnecessary, so why have them?

After a lot of planning, Nick and Charlie are ready to rob Winston's jewelry store. Unfortunately, Nick falls in love with Carol Hughes who owns the antique store next door to Winston's. The police capture Nick. Carol moves to New York where Nick goes to prison. Charlie is never apprehended, but safely hides Nick's share. Nick is released, and the police tail him to see if he will lead them to the jewels. The end of the movie is satisfying, but promotes the immoral notion that crime pays.

Happy New Year is fluffy entertainment. Unfortunately, the off-color language, the sexual situation, and the premise that crime pays make *Happy New Year* unacceptable for Christian audiences.

HARRY AND THE HENDERSONS

TITLE:	**HARRY AND THE HENDERSONS**
QUALITY:	★★★
RECOMMENDATION:	Caution
RATING:	PG
RELEASE:	1987
STARRING:	John Lithgow, Melinda Dillon, Don Ameche, David Suchet, Margaret Langrick, Joshua Ruddy, Lainie Kazan, M. Emmet Walsh, and Kevin Peter Hall
DIRECTOR:	William Dear
GENRE:	Comedy/Fantasy
CONTENT:	Some exclamatory profanity
INTENDED AUDIENCE:	All ages
REVIEWER:	Christopher Farrell

While on a camping trip, the Hendersons literally run into "Big Foot." They adopt the Sasquatch and call him Harry. Harry's presence in their lives throws them into bizarre situations which change their lives forever.

Harry and the Hendersons is first rate in its workmanship. The "Big Foot" monster is very convincing, and the cinematography is excellent. Children will love Harry; *Harry and the Hendersons* is warm and emotional.

For the most part, this film has a high moral tone. There are five exclamatory profanities, which are inexcusable, but the characters are chastised for their language on two of these occasions. The family is loving and normal. The turning of the father's heart from selfish ambition to a desire to do the right thing is clearly portrayed. The monster is charming, and the audience is spared any evolutionary editorials about his humanness, although this devaluation of humanity is something you should consider, as noted in the chapter on asking the right questions.

Harry and the Hendersons could be a G-rated film without the aforementioned profanities. One may choose to skip this film because of the profanity. Why Hollywood has to marr a fun film with bad language is a mystery. Please write Universal Pictures and ask them not to use profanities in their movies.

TITLE:	**HEARTBREAK HOTEL**
QUALITY:	★ ★ ★
RECOMMENDATION:	Extreme Caution
RATING:	PG-13
RELEASE:	1988
STARRING:	David Keith, Charlie Schlatter, and Tuesday Weld
DIRECTOR:	Chris Columbus
GENRE:	Comedy
CONTENT:	Several obscenities and one profanity
INTENDED AUDIENCE:	Mature teens and adults
REVIEWER:	Nancy Hanger

The time is 1972. Johnny Wolfe is a teenager who leads a rock 'n' roll band, cares for his sister and tries to make his mother happy. His mother has taken up drinking and running with the wrong crowd since her husband left. Johnny decides to bring Elvis Presley to Taylor, Ohio to cheer her up. He kidnaps Elvis, and then it's time to enjoy a soul-searching Elvis getting in touch with his roots while bringing joy to this family. The events of the next few days help each character to grow and feel renewed.

This compassionate, vulnerable, past-his-prime rock 'n' roll king is very interesting. The music is great and a couple of performances are worthy of goosebumps. Family values are portrayed favorably. Although God is not shown as The Answer, references to Him are favorable. There is none of the drugged, drinking Elvis in this film. Unfortunately, every four letter word comes up in this movie at least once. Otherwise, the film is great fun and ends up being not about Elvis but about a family, helping each other to make dreams come true. In the final analysis, caution is advised because, as usual, there is objectionable language.

TITLE:	**HEART OF MIDNIGHT**
QUALITY:	★ ★ ★
RECOMMENDATION:	Evil
RATING:	R
RELEASE:	1989
STARRING:	Jennifer Leigh, Denice Dummont, and Brenda Vaccaro
DIRECTOR:	Matthew Chapman
GENRE:	Mystery
CONTENT:	Profanity, obscenity, rape/violence, murder, sexual perversion, and child porn suggested
INTENDED AUDIENCE:	Adult
REVIEWER:	Glennis O'Neal

A beautiful woman limps down a street until she stands at the Midnight Theatre, an inheritance from Uncle Fletcher. The red hallway houses many rooms with individual door colors. Carol opens each door exposing different color schemes, costumes and props. Carol pauses at the window long enough for three boozers to get an eye full. The theatre door opens, giving the boozers the idea Carol is signaling them to "come on up." They almost gang-rape her until the black man helps her escape. The police mortally wound the fleeing black man. The police laugh at the idea of her being raped since she's taken up residence in the theatre her uncle used as a front for "sex service." Detectives pursue an investigation into Uncle Fletcher's theatre, and how it almost cost the sanity of the little girl who grew up as the troubled Carol.

Despite interesting color and scene variations, the morbid and pornographic content of this film qualifies it for a one word summary: EVIL! *The Heart of Midnight* is full of profanity, obscenity, rape, violence, murder, and sexual perversion. This is a movie you will be glad you avoided.

TITLE:	**HEAVEN**
QUALITY:	★ ★
RECOMMENDATION:	Extreme Caution
RATING:	PG-13
RELEASE:	1987
STARRING:	Ordinary people and loonies from Hollywood
DIRECTOR:	Diane Keaton
GENRE:	Comedy/Documentary
CONTENT:	Either blasphemy or tough evangelism, depending upon your mood and point of view

INTENDED AUDIENCE:	Adults
REVIEWER:	Ted Baehr

Heaven is Diane Keaton's first film. It is an attempt to find out how normal people think about the hereafter. However, what emerges is not a portrait of how normal people think about Heaven, but a kooky insight into how Hollywood distorts Heaven. Diane doesn't look for the sensitive, the interesting, and the exciting; but rather the tired, weird, and kooky.

The first two-thirds of the film seems to be a tendentious attack on the concept of Heaven. However, as the movie progresses, it moves from being funny to shattering your inhibitions about the thought of Heaven. At the end, it seems to lift up a Biblical vision of Heaven, especially with the narration of the last goodbyes. The ending seems to beckon everyone to accept Christ and come to Heaven.

The question is whether *Heaven* is a piece of tough evangelism, or a piece of punk moviemaking. If it is the latter, then it is blasphemy. If it is the former, then it is extremely clever because the first two-thirds of the film so shatter the pre-conceived prejudices of our age that by the end, you are rooting for God, Christ and Heaven to exist.

It is too bad that Miss Keaton couldn't have done a better job of constructing the film. As far as the believers are concerned, you will be bored and annoyed by *Heaven*. *Heaven* is not a film that should concern Christians, and it is not a film that anyone would want to emulate.

TITLE:	**HER ALIBI**
QUALITY:	★★★
RECOMMENDATION:	Extreme Caution
RATING:	PG
RELEASE:	1989
STARRING:	Tom Selleck and Paulina Porizkova
DIRECTOR:	Bruce Beresford
GENRE:	Action adventure
CONTENT:	Some profanity, strong sexual overtones, and magazine nudity
INTENDED AUDIENCE:	Adults
REVIEWER:	Lauren Neal

A novelist, played by Tom Selleck, seeks to help Nina, a beautiful Romanian, out of a situation which could establish her as a murderess. After Nina's arrest, Tom offers her an alibi that will save her from prosecution. Nina is being pursued by Romanian KGB Agents who want her and her companions to return home to Romania. Tom situates Nina in his country home, while creating a novel based on their encounter. Tom develops the story from the records he keeps on each day's new experiences. Just as he discovers he's falling in love with Nina, he realizes that she could be guilty, in which case his "life" would be the only thing standing in the way of her freedom. After harassment by the

KGB, the involvement of the police force, the help of Tom's publisher, and several encounters between Tom and Nina, the couple concede to their emotions and culminate their relationship.

The movie has funny moments with a minimal amount of offensive language, but has strong sexual suggestions and a brief moment of nudity in a magazine. Good intentions and emotions do not justify loose morals. Avoid *Her Alibi*.

> For her house leads down to death and her paths to the spirits of the dead. None who go to her return or attain the paths of life. (Proverbs 2:18–19)

TITLE:	**HEY BABU RIBA**
QUALITY:	★ ★ ★
RECOMMENDATION:	Extreme Caution
RATING:	R
RELEASE:	1987
STARRING:	Srdjan Todorovic, Dragan Bjelogrlic, Nebosa Bakocevic, Goran Radakivoc, and Gala Videnovic
DIRECTOR:	Jovan Acin
GENRE:	Comedy
CONTENT:	Implied sexual situations
INTENDED AUDIENCE:	Adults
REVIEWER:	Laura Lindley

This gem stresses friendship and would be worth recommending except for a major flaw. The story tells about five schoolmates, four boys and a girl. Set in post-war Yugoslavia, the five valiantly try to be carefree while their world is crumbling around them. While their houses are ransacked by the communists, the five listen to Glenn Miller records, ride around on their bikes and practice boating on the river. All four young men are secretly in love with Mirana, whom they nickname Esther, after Esther Williams. One by one they confess their love to her, but her answer is always the same—she wants the friendship to continue innocently.

The film's flaw is that the boys sacrifice their virginity to a local girl who deals with the black market. She seduces them after they obtain objects from her—blue jeans, valuable medicine, etc. The sex is only implied, but this flaws this otherwise innocent, sweet film.

TITLE:	**THE HIDDEN**
QUALITY:	★ ★ ★
RECOMMENDATION:	Extreme Caution
RATING:	R
RELEASE:	1987

STARRING:	Kyle Maclachlan and Michael Nouri
DIRECTOR:	Jack Sholder
GENRE:	Science fiction/Horror
CONTENT:	Excessive violence, lewdness, and obscenity
INTENDED AUDIENCE:	Adventure fans
REVIEWER:	Doug Brewer

The killer, Nouri, is an alien who inhabits bodies to move around on Earth. He wears the bodies out and gets new ones. The FBI agent, Maclachlan, turns out to be an alien also, an intergalactic bounty hunter who has tracked his slug-thing to Earth. The relationship between Nouri and Maclachlan form the basis for the film's humor, as Nouri's incredulity and Maclachlan's unfamiliarity with Earth set them on opposite poles.

Unfortunately, the almost unending violence and a scene in a strip joint make this film too vulgar for Christian audiences, which is too bad, because take away the blood and there would be a decent unrealistic story about spacemen.

TITLE:	**HIDING OUT**
QUALITY:	★★★
RECOMMENDATION:	Caution
RATING:	PG
RELEASE:	1987
STARRING:	Jon Cryer
DIRECTOR:	Bob Giraldi
GENRE:	Comedy
CONTENT:	Simplistic nothingness
INTENDED AUDIENCE:	Teenagers and young adults
REVIEWER:	Laura Lindley

Hiding Out is the story of a young Boston stockbroker, who pulls a bad deal with the mob and escapes by hiding out as a teenager in a high school with his "nerdy" seventeen-year-old cousin.

This movie is basically a lightweight comedy as he trades his twenty-nine-year-old ways for those of a high-schooler. Along the way he falls for a girl about ten years his junior and gets himself elected senior class president.

The writers are very simplistic in their characterization, choosing to show Cryer as an adult by having him drink Scotch.

Hiding Out does not seek first the kingdom of God, but it doesn't portray teens as pot-smoking rebels, either. Hiding Out probably won't hurt anyone, but we recommend you don't waste your money.

TITLE:	**HIGH TIDE**
QUALITY:	★ ★ ★
RECOMMENDATION:	Caution
RATING:	R
RELEASE:	1988
STARRING:	Judy Davis, Jan Adele, and Claudia Karvan
DIRECTOR:	Gillian Armstrong
GENRE:	Drama
CONTENT:	Vulgarities and some profanity; no nudity, but close
INTENDED AUDIENCE:	Adults
REVIEWER:	Nancy Hanger

Set in Australia, *High Tide* deals with relationships, growth, and commitment. A mother and daughter are reunited after having been separated since the girl was a baby. The daughter, now fourteen, lives with her grandmother and believes her mother is dead. The mother tours as a back-up singer.

When Lilli loses her job, she settles into the Caravan park for a few days and strikes up a friendship with Ally. Lilli discovers Ally is her daughter. At first, Lilli plans to move on, but she finds herself drawn to discover more about the girl. The grandmother urges Lilli to stay away. Lilli realizes she must come to grips with her past and the crossroads where she finds herself.

High Tide has verbal and visual vulgarities peppered throughout the film. While these portray Lilli's nature, they hamper the viewer's ability to be uplifted by the story. Also, basic Christian values are absent from this film. Therefore, we suggest that you avoid *High Tide*.

TITLE:	**HOPE AND GLORY**
QUALITY:	★ ★ ★
RECOMMENDATION:	Extreme Caution
RATING:	PG
RELEASE:	1987
STARRING:	Sarah Miles
DIRECTOR:	John Boorman
GENRE:	Drama
CONTENT:	Some obscene language and sexual immorality
INTENDED AUDIENCE:	Adults
REVIEWER:	Doug Brewer

212 Reviews of Selected Movies

Set in wartime London, *Hope and Glory* tells the story of Bill, who collects shrapnel and marvels at the piles of bricks and piping that were once homes. Around Bill, swirls the adventures of his family: from his father, who joins up to fight the Hun, but ends up fighting a typewriter; to his mother, who tries to understand the influence war has on her children; to his teenage sister, Dawn, who flaunts her will to live with such panache that she nearly steals the show.

At one point, Bill is forced by a gang of local boys to repeat a series of swear words. Later in the story, he rejects such peer pressure when his family is threatened.

Unfortunately, there is some sexual immorality which is not consummated on screen. Also, the film shows the curiosity of young boys as they look through a keyhole. This blemishes an otherwise happy, nostalgic look at family love.

TITLE:	HOT SHOT
QUALITY:	★ ★ ★
RECOMMENDATION:	Caution
RATING:	PG
RELEASE:	1987
STARRING:	Jim Youngs and Pele
DIRECTOR:	Rick King
GENRE:	Drama
CONTENT:	Some profanity, vulgarity, and crude language
INTENDED AUDIENCE:	Young adults
REVIEWER:	John Evans of Movie Morality Ministries

Jimmy Kristidis wants to be a professional soccer player. Jimmy qualifies for the New York Rockers against his parents' will. When the coach puts Jimmy on suspension for his undisciplined behavior, Jimmy takes off for Brazil where he persuades a former soccer player named Santos to train him. Santos sharpens Jimmy's soccer skills and influences his attitude toward team play. Jimmy returns to the New York Rockers and has a successful season.

The theme is Jimmy's change from an undisciplined, cocky young player to a mature team player. The movie also portrays his transformation from an angry, rebellious son to a responsible family member. His concern for his teammates is commendable, and Santos generously devotes time and care to Jimmy's training. However, crude, vulgar, and profane language prevents us from recommending this film.

TITLE:	HOT TO TROT
QUALITY:	★ ★
RECOMMENDATION:	Extreme Caution
RATING:	PG

RELEASE:	1988
STARRING:	Bob Goldthwait, Dabney Coleman, and Virginia Madsen, with John Candy as the voice of Don, the talking horse
DIRECTOR:	Michael Dinner
GENRE:	Comedy
CONTENT:	Profanity, obscenity, and lewdness.
INTENDED AUDIENCE:	Teenagers and adults
REVIEWER:	Ted Baehr

Hot to Trot is the adventures of a foul-mouthed talking horse named Don. Unfortunately, the humor has been spoiled by profanity, obscenity, and other off-color devices.

Don teams up with Fred, who has inherited 50 percent of a stock brokerage firm. The heir of the other 50 percent, Walter, hates Fred. Don gives Fred enough tips to make Fred a multi-millionaire. Walter takes revenge, and the last tip goes sour. To redeem himself, Don runs in a horse race with Fred as his jockey. Walter bets Fred his entire stable of horses that Don can't win. Don wins by telling the other horses off-color jokes and using other methods of psychological warfare.

Hot to Trot alternates between being funny and being boring. It thumbs its nose at the audience. Avoid this affront to your intelligence.

TITLE:	**HOTEL TERMINUS: THE LIFE AND TIMES OF KLAUS BARBIE (4½ Hours, Subtitles)**
QUALITY:	★★★
RECOMMENDATION:	Caution
RATING:	Not Rated
RELEASE:	Fall 1988
STARRING:	A documentary
DIRECTOR:	Marcel Ophuls
GENRE:	Historical/Documentary
CONTENT:	Nazi war crimes, nude women photos in Barbie's cell, one curse word, and profanity
INTENDED AUDIENCE:	Adults
REVIEWER:	Russ Houck

Klaus Barbie was an SS officer stationed in Paris during World War II. Beginning with interviews of some of Barbie's victims and stories about some who did not survive, an opinion of this man forms early. The viewer is shocked by the extent to which the French Police cooperated with the Gestapo.

When the war ends, the film's real surprise happens: Barbie is hired by the American government as a CIA agent. He is protected by the CIA for several years. As time approaches to leave the continent, the CIA involves a Catholic Political Action Group. This particular SS officer, murderer and torturer of thousands of men, women and children, developed some unusual accomplices. Barbie fled to South America, where he lived out his final years.

This film shows how sinful man is apart from God. God is not mocked, and the church must stand against evil, not hide it. Unfortunately, *Hotel Terminus: The Life and Times of Klaus Barbie* is a bit long and tecious, but history and war buffs will enjoy it. Since it is a documentary, there are some profanity and other objectionable elements. Caution is advised.

TITLE:	**THE HOUSE ON CARROLL STREET**
QUALITY:	★
RECOMMENDATION:	Extreme Caution
RATING:	PG
RELEASE:	1988
STARRING:	Kelly McGillis and Jeff Daniels
DIRECTOR:	Peter Yates
GENRE:	Mystery
CONTENT:	One brief instance of nudity
INTENDED AUDIENCE:	Adults
REVIEWER:	Doug Brewer

Kelly McGillis is improbably blacklisted during the McCarthy hearings. During lunch one day, she happens upon the counsel for the Senate committee and discovers he is embroiled in a plot to sneak Nazis into the US. He sends the FBI to lean on her, and one of them becomes involved with her. Jeff Daniels, as the corn-fed cop who ends up on her side, is always showing up to rescue her just in the nick of time.

There seems to be a too much to the story, which makes the film ambiguous. *The House on Carroll Street* is certainly a nice enough place, but it appears that no one is at home. Therefore, there is very little to recommend this regurgitated anti-American movie. The history is flimsy, and the overstuffed story doesn't compensate for the swipe at patriotism. Therefore, avoid *The House on Carroll Street*.

TITLE:	**HOUSEKEEPING**
QUALITY:	★★★
RECOMMENDATION:	Caution
RATING:	PG
RELEASE:	1987
STARRING:	Christine Lahti, Sara Walker, and Andrea Burchill
DIRECTOR:	Bill Forsyth

GENRE:	Drama
CONTENT:	Extreme individualism
INTENDED AUDIENCE:	Adults
REVIEWER:	Ted Baehr

Housekeeping tells the story of two young sisters, Lucille and Ruth, who face one tragedy after another. Their mother commits suicide. Their grandmother dies after a few years and their great aunts contact the mother's sister, Sylvia, who comes to care for them. Sylvia is a wanderer, at home riding the rails with the hobos. She has no concern for anything; therefore, the house runs down, newspapers pile up, food cans stack up, and the steps fall apart. Everything drifts toward disaster. Lucille goes to live with a lady teacher. The police chief decides he is going to take Ruth away from Sylvia. Sylvia cleans the house, but realizes that the people of Fingerbone are still after Ruth. Sylvia and Ruth burn the house down and escape to parts unknown.

There is no profanity, nudity, sex, or violence in *Housekeeping,* but there is aimlessness and insanity. This movie is beautifully made—funny in some parts; sad and maudlin in others. Whoever sees *Housekeeping* will see the futility of being absorbed with one's self. We recommend *Housekeeping.*

TITLE:	**IMAGINE: JOHN LENNON**
QUALITY:	★★
RECOMMENDATION:	Extreme Caution
RATING:	R
RELEASE:	1988
STARRING:	John Lennon
DIRECTOR:	Andrew Solt
GENRE:	Documentary
CONTENT:	Profanity, obscenities, and full nudity
INTENDED AUDIENCE:	Beatles and Lennon fans
REVIEWER:	Nancy Hanger

This portrait of John Lennon and the Beatles is alternately insightful and boring. John was complex and childlike, an example of undisciplined exploration—through drugs, divorce, and the band's breakup. Had Lennon known Christ, he would have been a powerful witness for Him. His death saw his journey unfulfilled.

The movie is a compilation of clips from concerts, the recording studio, interviews, and private moments. It is fun to recall the early days of the Beatles. They were ingenuous in their success. In reflection, they admit they didn't know what to make of it. Anyone inclined to idolize Lennon should pay attention to his lyrics: "How can I go forward when I don't know which way I'm facing," "I don't believe in anything but me," "Mommy don't go; Daddy come home" (he was raised by his aunt after the age of four).

The movie is interesting for its candid portrait. We have seen this type of film in the past, and there is not much to distinguish it. Furthermore, *Imagine: John Lennon* has profanity, obscenity, and nudity. Don't waste your time.

TITLE:	**IN A SHALLOW GRAVE**
QUALITY:	★ ★ ★
RECOMMENDATION:	Extreme Caution
RATING:	R
RELEASE:	1988
STARRING:	Michael Biehn, Maureen Mueller, Michael Beach, and Patrick Dempsey
DIRECTOR:	Kenneth Bowser
GENRE:	Drama
CONTENT:	Emotionally intense with mild profanity, brief violence, and brief partial nudity
INTENDED AUDIENCE:	Adults
REVIEWER:	F.L. Lindberg

The opening scene is on a Guadalcanal beach in 1943. One man opens a pocket watch, showing us a beautiful blonde woman. He shows the picture to his buddy as an attack begins. Next, on a farm a year later, a seedsman tries not to face the owner, disfigured by his war injury. The owner is the buddy we just saw. The beautiful woman, now a widow, lives on a neighboring farm. Daventry, the mysterious drifter, agrees to stay on as a valet for the disabled veteran. Daventry is a comforter to both Garnet and Georgina. Daventry is far removed from conventional views of a Comforter though.

Scenes of extreme intensity occur among scenes that flow quietly, and, often, too slowly. The richness and complexity of emotions is confusing. The film asks you to reexamine your beliefs. It may make you angry. *In a Shallow Grave* affirms that God is at work in the world. The strangeness is that of an allegory. Extreme caution is recommended because *In a Shallow Grave* has profanity and partial nudity which are never acceptable.

TITLE:	**INHERIT THE WIND**
QUALITY:	★ ★ ★ ★
RECOMMENDATION:	Evil
RATING:	Not rated
RELEASE:	1960
STARRING:	Spencer Tracy and Fredric March
DIRECTOR:	Stanley Cramer
GENRE:	Drama
CONTENT:	Blaspheme

INTENDED AUDIENCE: Adults

REVIEWER: Ted Baehr

Inherit the Wind's attack on God and Christianity makes one cringe. The film is adapted from the play by Jerome Lawrence and Robert E. Lee which fictionalizes the famous 1925 Scopes "Monkey" Trial in Tennessee, wherein Clarence Darrow and William Jennings Bryan pitted their legal skills. Thanks to Bryan, creationism won the trial, but, because of the reporting of H.L. Mencken and others, Christians lost the war.

The movie portrays Christians as narrow-minded, fanatical bigots who try to stand against academic freedom. The evolutionists, both the ACLU lawyer, Clarence Darrow, whose name in the film is Henry Drummond, and the teacher, whose name in the movie is Tates, seem to be reasonable, well-intentioned individuals. The journalist, H.L. Mencken, whom the film renames E.K. Hornbeck, aims a steady stream of sarcastic venom at the Christians.

Avoid *Inherit the Wind* unless you want to see how the Adversary digs his own grave. Also, please pray that God will turn our nation from its wicked rebellion.

TITLE:	**IRON EAGLE II**
QUALITY:	★ ★
RECOMMENDATION:	Extreme Caution
RATING:	PG
RELEASE:	1988
STARRING:	Lou Gosset, Jr. and Mark Humphrey
DIRECTOR:	Sydney Furrie
GENRE:	Action adventure
CONTENT:	Verbal expletives and one love scene with mild kissing
INTENDED AUDIENCE:	Youth
REVIEWER:	Gene Burke

Colonel Chappy Sinclair is called to active duty by his Commanding General to lead a secret joint air-strike with the Soviets. The target is a terrorist nation, which is completing construction of a nuclear warhead, threatening the USSR and USA. Two pilots and ground crew from each country are selected for training. Doug Masters' best friend, Cooper, who witnessed Doug's being shot down, is included in the American team. Also included is the Soviet pilot who shot him down.

What a hodgepodge of enemies and poorly written script. The American General has ulterior motives: to prove that Soviet and American personnel cannot work together, even against a common enemy. Colonel Sinclair exposes the dastardly General's plans and pulls everyone together to successfully complete this "impossible" mission.

To enjoy this film, one must not remember the first *Iron Eagle*. This film is disappointing, slow, and boring. Warning should be given for a number of military expletives. Otherwise, this film aligns itself more with an amateurish, melodramatic Saturday morning matinee than an exciting original feature. Don't encourage the filmmakers to produce *Iron Eagle III.* This is enough!

TITLE:	**IRONWEED**
QUALITY:	★ ★ ★
RECOMMENDATION:	Caution
RATING:	R
RELEASE:	1987
STARRING:	Jack Nicholson and Meryl Streep
DIRECTOR:	Hector Babenco
GENRE:	Drama
CONTENT:	One suggestive sexual scene
INTENDED AUDIENCE:	Adults
REVIEWER:	Katie Meyer

Ironweed is the story of two street-people. While helping his wife change their baby's diaper, Francis, a former baseball player, drops the baby, causing a fatal head injury. Unable to face his guilt, he leaves to take up life on the streets. Helen, once a very successful concert pianist, becomes an alcoholic and also lives on the streets.

Ironweed shows us how people can turn their backs on forgiveness and love from friends and family because of their own guilt. There is no vulgarity, obscenity, or foul language, but the movie contains one explicit "petting" scene. *Ironweed* can open our eyes to the compassion we need to give to our destitute, homeless, and poverty stricken neighbors; therefore, it is recommended with caution.

TITLE:	**ISHTAR**
QUALITY:	★
RECOMMENDATION:	Caution
RATING:	PG
RELEASE:	1987
STARRING:	Dustin Hoffman, Warren Beatty, Isabelle Adjani, Charles Grodin, and Jack Weston
DIRECTOR:	Elaine May
GENRE:	Comedy
CONTENT:	Nudity and off-color language
INTENDED AUDIENCE:	Adults
REVIEWER:	Ken Kistner

Dustin Hoffman and Warren Beatty star as a song writing/singing duo who have absolutely no talent. With all of their savings spent and their girlfriends gone, they finally get their first booking in Ishtar, a small Middle Eastern country. Their blindness to their lack of talent is surpassed only by the blind trust they extend to others. Dustin finds himself gathering information for the CIA. Beatty finds himself trying to help a woman who is part of the revolution. Fighting off the vultures, they finally realize that both sides have lied and sent them off into the desert to die.

The first ten minutes of the movie should have ended up on the cutting room floor. *Ishtar* is too long, and the movie lacks the entertainment value. Furthermore, nudity and obscenity make *Ishtar* off limits for Christians. Don't waste your time or money on this bomb.

☆☆☆ MASTERPIECE ☆☆☆

TITLE:	**IT HAPPENED ONE NIGHT (Black and White)**
QUALITY:	★★★★
RECOMMENDATION:	Acceptable
RATING:	Not rated
RELEASE:	1934
STARRING:	Clark Gable, Claudette Colbert, Roscoe Karns, Henry Wadsworth, Clair McDowell, and Walter Connolly
DIRECTOR:	Frank Capra
GENRE:	Comedy/Romance
CONTENT:	Nothing objectionable
INTENDED AUDIENCE:	Adult
REVIEWER:	Ted Baehr

A millionaire is upset with his spoiled daughter who is engaged to a fortune hunter. The cigar chomping tycoon has private detectives kidnap his daughter to save her from the error of her ways. They bring her to his yacht where he chastises her. She won't hear a word of criticism about the man she claims she loves. Strong-willed, she sasses her father to the point where he loses control and slaps her, instantly regretting it.

When the yacht anchors off Miami, she dives overboard. She buys a ticket for New York, trying to evade her father's detectives. In the bus station is a two-fisted newspaper reporter (Clark Gable). He is on the phone denouncing his editor for firing him for drinking on an assignment; "When you fired me you fired the best news-hound your filthy scandal sheet ever had . . . You gas-house palooka!"

They meet. He learns that her father has offered a $10,000 reward for her recovery. He's interested in staying close to her to get the scoop and win back his newspaper job.

Social barriers come down, as this down-to-earth love story unfolds. It is a reverse Cinderella tale where the rich girl accepts middle-class values and gets the poor boy.

☆☆☆ MASTERPIECE ☆☆☆

TITLE:	**IT'S A WONDERFUL LIFE**
QUALITY:	★★★★
RECOMMENDATION:	Acceptable for all ages
RATING:	Not rated
RELEASE:	1946
STARRING:	Jimmy Stewart, Donna Reed, Thomas Mitchell, Lionel Barrymore, and Ward Bond
DIRECTOR:	Frank Capra
GENRE:	Drama
CONTENT:	Nothing objectionable
INTENDED AUDIENCE:	All ages
REVIEWER:	Bruce Grimes

It's snowing on Christmas Eve, and the camera pans across the town's houses, circa 1946. The voices of the individual people are heard as they pray to God, petitioning the Lord for help in their lives. The camera tilts up, and distant galaxies are seen. A voice from one of the galaxies says, "looks like we'll have to send someone down. Got a lot of people asking for help for a man named George Bailey."

We flashback to 1919, as young boy George Bailey, while playing on the frozen lake, saves his younger brother from drowning. As a result, he partially loses his hearing.

The story follows George through the years, and he develops into a respectable, earnest, concerned businessman and citizen. However, George feels that life is passing him by. He is bitter and depressed because of his perceived failures in life.

George, not knowing where to turn for help, ends up in the local tavern. As he sits at the bar, he whispers into his hands, "Dear Father in Heaven, I'm not a praying man, but, . . . show me the way. I'm at the end of my rope. Show me the way, God." Then, a stranger slugs George, knocking him off the chair.

George leaves, drunk and bitter, thinking that the only thing left to do is to commit suicide. Wandering through the snow, he halfway crosses the town's bridge, thinks seriously about jumping, when a man standing next to him jumps. George jumps into the freezing water and saves the man.

The man explains that he is George's guardian angel. George tells the angel to go "haunt somebody else" and says he wishes he never was born. Hearing this, the angel has an idea. Consulting with "Above," the angel tells George his wish is granted: he was never born.

Retracing his steps back into town, George realizes that Bedford Falls is now "Pottersville" and never had his influence. The people, the history of the town and the world are different because of George's wish to never be born. He sees what the world is like without him, and this "funny dream" descends quickly into a nightmare.

The town, which was a respectable community partially due to George, is now a honkytonk, raunchy town. His friends, his own mother don't know him. Realizing his mistake, he asks the angel Clarence and, finally, God to return him to his "wonderful life."

George returns home to a joyous Christmas Eve in Bedford Falls with family and friends who know him and with an entirely new outlook on his life. The townspeople, gathered in the Bailey living room, sing together as George picks up a book that his guardian angel had been carrying and reads the inscription inside, which says "remember, no man is a failure who has friends."

Time magazine said of the film, "*It's a Wonderful Life* is a pretty wonderful movie. It has only one formidable rival (Goldwyn's *Best Years of Our Lives*) as Hollywood's best picture of the year." An interesting note is that Capra began filming *It's a Wonderful Life* the same day, April 8, 1946, William Wyler began his picture, *Best Years of Our Lives*. However, I far as I am concerned *It's a Wonderful Life* is one of the greatest, if not the greatest, movie of all times—and, it is a testimony to the Good News!

TITLE:	**I'VE HEARD THE MERMAIDS SINGING**
QUALITY:	★ ★ ★
RECOMMENDATION:	Extreme Caution
RATING:	Not rated
RELEASE:	1987
STARRING:	Shelia McCarthy, Paula Baillarge, and Ana-Marie MacDonald
DIRECTOR:	Patricia Rozema
GENRE:	Drama
CONTENT:	Implied homosexual relationship which is shown as wrong
INTENDED AUDIENCE:	Art film buffs
REVIEWER:	Kay M. Black

Most of us have our secret lives; therefore, we are like mermaids: half seen and half hidden. Polly is an unsuccessful woman who applies for a job at a new gallery. Polly lives a dull existence in a colored world, but she dreams a fantastic life of beauty and success in black and white. Polly sends her photographs to the gallery. The curator tells Polly that these hold no talent. Polly tells the curator off. The curator is ashamed. Polly asks if they would like to see more of her art. She opens the door to the darkroom and they step out into a beautiful woods.

If you like thinking "art" pictures, you'll find *I've Heard the Mermaids Singing* interesting. This is not a family film, though there is nothing objectionable except an implied homosexual relationship which is shown as wrong. Understanding is shown, but God's real solution is never given.

TITLE:	**JACKNIFE**
QUALITY:	★★
RECOMMENDATION:	Extreme Caution
RATING:	R
RELEASE:	April 1989
STARRING:	Robert De Niro, Ed Harris, and Kathy Baker
DIRECTOR:	David Jones
GENRE:	Drama/Romance
CONTENT:	Much profanity and obscenity
INTENDED AUDIENCE:	Adult
REVIEWER:	Russ Houck

Jacknife is the story of three young men who go to Vietnam. One doesn't come home. Bobby is killed in a Viet Cong ambush trying to pull his buddy, Jacknife, to safety. Fifteen years pass. Jacknife works as a mechanic. In the same town lives Dave, the other survivor of that tragic incident. The two have not seen each other since the Army. Still guilt-stricken and traumatized by nightmares, Jacknife pays Dave a visit.

This is an intense drama. The movie is full of profanity and obscenity, and is not recommended. It's also full of truth and good therapy. There's a chance that this film will help either veterans themselves, or possibly friends or families of the veterans. The movie deals with touchy issues and doesn't do it delicately. Guilt and cowardice are hit right between the eyes. At one point Jacknife admits that he finally broke down and prayed, and it helped.

Veterans who are withdrawn will benefit most from the film. There is some superb acting, writing, and directing, but I wouldn't recommend it for anyone who doesn't need to see it.

TITLE:	**JAWS: THE REVENGE**
QUALITY:	★★
RECOMMENDATION:	Caution
RATING:	PG-13
RELEASE:	1987
STARRING:	Lorraine Gary, Lance Guest, Mario Van Peebles, and Michael Caine
DIRECTOR:	Joseph Sargent
GENRE:	Action adventure
CONTENT:	Some gore, mild language, and implied marital sex
INTENDED AUDIENCE:	Late teens and adults
REVIEWER:	Loralee Lindley

Just when you thought it was safe to go back to the theater, summer brings an inevitable *Jaws* sequel. Old razor tooth is at it again, this time seeking revenge on the family of Ellen Brody. Not content with killing Ellen's husband in the first Jaws adventure, the beast returns to devour Ellen's son, Sean Brody! Ellen flees to the sunny Bahamas with her eldest son, marine biologist Michael Brody, where she hopes to be safe from the shark's craving for Brody blood. Guess again, folks, no safety for this little family.

Despite promises to the contrary: the acting is spotty and lacks depth and development; the plot is simple; and, the shark is eminently forgettable. This time the film falls as flat as a rubber jellyfish on a novelty store shelf.

TITLE:	**JEAN DE FLORETTE (Subtitles)**
QUALITY:	★ ★ ★ ★
RECOMMENDATION:	Acceptable
RATING:	PG
RELEASE:	1987
STARRING:	Yves Montand, Gerard Depardieu, and Daniel Auteuil
DIRECTOR:	Claude Berri
GENRE:	Drama/Historical
CONTENT:	Nothing objectionable
INTENDED AUDIENCE:	All ages
REVIEWER:	Ted Baehr

Jean de Florette (based on the novel my Marcel Pagnol) is extraordinary, a critically acclaimed movie which has no violence, no sex, no nudity, no profanity, and many positive references to God. *Jean de Florette* shows that good is far superior than evil. Unfortunately, unlike *Les Miserables*, God never answers Jean's prayers, and greed seems to triumph over good, though this conclusion is reversed in the sequel, *Manon of the Spring*.

Jean de Florette tells the story of Ugolin, who returns home after serving in the army. He is the only relative of his uncle, Cesar, who wants Ugolin to rebuild the family orchards and have children. Ugolin wants to grow carnations, but carnations need lots of water, and the only property with a spring is owned by a neighbor, Pique-Bouffique, who detests Cesar.

Cesar and Ugolin go to Pique to buy his land, but Cesar fights with and accidentally kills him. Pique's heir is Jean de Florette, the hunchback son of Cesar's childhood love, Florette.

Cesar and Ugolin cement up the spring so that Jean's farm will fail and they will get the land they want so badly. Their greed compels them to destroy Jean, although his genius, industry, and faith in God almost get the upper hand.

Jean de Florette cuts deeply into man's sinfulness. *Jean de Florette* makes us want to be good, to call out to God and to encourage others who are motivated by love.

Jean de Florette is an accurate portrait of human relations. *Jean de Florette* shows that the filmmaker does not need to resort to profanity, obscenity, and other trash to communicate the wretchedness of mankind and the power of good. We highly recommends *Jean de Florette*.

TITLE:	**JOHNNY BE GOOD**
QUALITY:	★ ★ ★
RECOMMENDATION:	Extreme Caution
RATING:	PG-13
STARRING:	Anthony Michael Hall and Robert Downey, Jr.
DIRECTOR:	Bud Smith
GENRE:	Action adventure
CONTENT:	Profanity, crudity, and implied sex
INTENDED AUDIENCE:	Teenagers
REVIEWER:	Rebecca M. Robbins

High school football star Johnny Walker has a dilemma: where to attend college. He tries to decide by considering his girlfriend, his need for an education and the recruiters who promise money, women, and more if he will attend their schools. After the winning game, Johnny is whisked away to schools all over the country. He is almost seduced by a recruiter's wife and watches nude dancing at a nightclub. Johnny is almost sucked into a world of college football glamor, but, just in time, he realizes the importance of his education and his family's happiness.

The film is irreverent and crude. The two redeeming factors are the star's realization of the evil of selfishness, and his decision to "get an education," instead of attending a "football factory." *Johnny Be Good* plays fast and loose with sexual morality and profanity. In His Word written, God clearly states that sexual immorality and profanity are as sinful as greed (see His Ten Commandments), and so should we.

☆☆☆ MASTERPIECE ☆☆☆

TITLE:	**JOURNEY TO THE CENTER OF THE EARTH**
QUALITY:	★ ★ ★ ★
RECOMMENDATION:	Acceptable
RATING:	Not rated
RELEASE:	1959
STARRING:	Pat Boone, James Mason, Arlene Dahl, and Diane Baker
DIRECTOR:	Henry Levin
GENRE:	Science Fiction/Fantasy
CONTENT:	Nothing objectionable

INTENDED AUDIENCE:	Family (especially children)
REVIEWER:	Gary DeMar

This Jules Verne thriller begins on the streets of Edinburgh, Scotland, in 1880. You are soon taken to the depths of the earth's core where you encounter a glistening cavern of quartz crystals, luminescent algae, a forest of giant mushrooms, dinosaurs thought to be extinct, and the lost city of Atlantis.

This exciting, suspenseful melodrama was produced in a straight forward manner which proves entertaining and captivating. Half camp, half serious, and all silly fun, this is an excellent combination of witty scripting and fine acting.

Alec presents a rare geological find to Sir Oliver Lindenbrook, a professor of natural science at the University of Edinburgh: an unusually heavy piece of lava. The professor is intrigued with the lava's peculiar weight and spends an evening in his laboratory in an attempt to burn away the porous crust. The oven in which the meltdown was to occur explodes.

The accident reveals the rock's core, a plumb bob, a common surveyor's instrument. However, this is no ordinary plumb bob. There is writing on it, and it is signed in what seems to be the blood of a long-lost scientist and explorer, Arnie Saknussemm.

Nearly 300 years before, Saknussemm startled the world with his tales of a domain below the earth's crust, a world that was accessible to man. He was ridiculed, but the laughter stopped when he failed to return from his trek to the center of the earth, that is, until the providential find of the plumb bob with Saknussemm's blood-stained scrawl indelibly etched in the iron top.

Professor Lindenbrook and Alec prepare to set off for Iceland to retrace their predecessor's steps to the deepest regions of the earth. They are delayed by the cunning of a jealous scientific competitor and the murderous intentions of a descendant of Arnie Saknussemm, who has claimed the nether world for himself. With these challenges out of the way, the professor, Alec, an Icelandic guide and the widow of the now-deceased scientific competitor, they begin their journey with these words: "May the good Lord be with us."

The entire family will enjoy this splendidly produced and color-enriched look into the imaginary world below. God is acknowledged as the Creator and Sustainer of the universe. Greed and human autonomy have no place in God's good creation. The arrogant and egotistical Count Saknussemm is buried by the world over which he claimed to be lord. The mythical pagan city of Atlantis was judged when God opened the sea to bury it forever. A Sodom and Gomorrah-like fire of lava entombs it as the God-fearers ascend by the only means of escape. Not even the serpent (dinosaur) can keep them from being lifted up by the merciful and mighty hand of God.

☆☆☆ MASTERPIECE ☆☆☆

TITLE:	**JUDGMENT AT NUREMBERG (190 Minutes)**
QUALITY:	★★★★
RECOMMENDATION:	Caution
RATING:	Not rated

RELEASE:	1961
STARRING:	Spencer Tracy, Burt Lancaster, Richard Widmark, Marlene Dietrich, Maximillian Schell, Judy Garland, Montgomery Cliff, William Shatner, Edward Binns, and Werner Klemperer
DIRECTOR:	Stanley Kramer
GENRE:	Drama
CONTENT:	Some actual footage of concentration camp atrocities
INTENDED AUDIENCE:	Adult
REVIEWER:	Protestant Motion Picture Council

This is the emotive story of one of the most famous trials in history. Held in Nuremberg, Germany in 1948, the trial attempted to determine the legal and moral guilt of those committing crimes while obeying their government's orders to enforce questionable laws in time of war. This trial is dramatized in a powerful, yet sensitive, manner.

At the bar of justice are four German judges who have rendered verdicts in harmony with National Socialist decrees which sent millions of innocent victims to death, promoted personal persecution and encouraged sadism. The presiding judge is an American. The prosecuting attorney, an Army Colonel, is also an American. He opens the film with a seething indictment of the German judges on trial who abandoned law in order to enforce Hitler's mad mandates.

Three of the accused voice their own defense. Maximillian Schell, in a powerful performance, roars back that his clients were merely upholding Hitler's laws and to place them on trial is to judge all of Germany. The fourth, refusing to speak, has an attorney who makes impassioned pleas on his behalf.

In his desire for fairness, the judge seeks to inquire into the circumstances in which the accused functioned, their background and the attitudes of the German peoples, most of whom denied participation in or knowledge of the dreadful events. The prosecuting attorney produces vital witnesses and brings forth evidence by showing some of the films made at the opening of the concentration camps by the Allies. None of the horror is avoided.

The characters of the accused, the witnesses, the participants, and the details of court procedure create mounting interest. Some tragic moments, added to the poignancy of the human factors, produce a highly emotional and convincing experience.

However, the film is overlong and at times quite static, but through it all a calm determination that right must prevail. The judge's comment that "the first crime was that of finding an innocent man guilty" is a fitting climax to the whole account.

Magnificently acted under exceptionally faultless direction, this is an epochal production which stands apart. It is a restrained statement of facts. It is not mongering hate and does not aim at being sensational. It is history, well told and to be remembered.

> You, therefore, have no excuse, you who pass judgment on someone else, for at whatever point you judge the other, you are condemning yourself, because you who pass judgment do the same things. Now we know that God's judgment against those who do such things is based on truth. So when you, a

mere man, pass judgment on them and yet do the same things, do you think you will escape God's judgment? (Romans 2:1-3)

☆☆☆ CLASSIC ☆☆☆

TITLE:	**JUMBO (123 Minutes)**
QUALITY:	★ ★ ★
RECOMMENDATION:	Acceptable
RATING:	Not rated
RELEASE:	1962
STARRING:	Doris Day, Stephen Boyd, and Jimmy Durante
DIRECTOR:	Charles Walters
GENRE:	Musical
CONTENT:	Nothing objectionable
INTENDED AUDIENCE:	Family
REVIEWER:	Protestant Motion Picture Council

Gay, fast-moving and beautifully colored scenes of circus life with daring acrobats and performances by well-known circus artists bring back all the delights of the old-time circus as presented in the original Billy Rose's Jumbo. Because Jumbo the elephant and his wink is so dear to the heart of many, he will satisfy their nostalgia and bring to the young real entertainment.

Pop and Kitty Wonder are father-and-daughter circus owners who do not remain solvent because of Pop's gambling disposition. Things look better when a jack-of-all trades is hired to help out, but unbeknownst to them he is the son of a rival circus owner. The ending is in a riot of color of the "Sawdust, Spangles, and Dreams" of which the circus is made.

TITLE:	**KAMILLA AND THE THIEF**
QUALITY:	★ ★ ★ ★
RECOMMENDATION:	Acceptable
RATING:	Not rated
RELEASE:	1988
STARRING:	Veronika Flaat, Dennis Storhoei, and Agnete Haaland
DIRECTOR:	Grete Salomonsen
GENRE:	Action-adventure (English dubbing)
CONTENT:	Evangelistic

INTENDED AUDIENCE: Families

REVIEWER: Ted Baehr

Praise God! Foreign films are becoming overtly Biblical. *Kamilla and the Thief* (based on the novel by Kari Vinje) is overtly evangelistic, even though it is a major feature film.

It tells the story of little Kamilla, who lives in a sleepy town in southern Norway around 1913. Her parents died, and she now lives under the strict regime of her formidable Aunt Louise. Her kindhearted uncle sends Kamilla to live with her older sister, Sophie, who lives in a remote rural mountain community working at a wealthy landowner's home.

The carriage driver has no time for Kamilla either, so he drops her off in the village, scared and alone, hours before the train. Some ruffians try to steal Kamilla's tiny bag. Young Sebastian comes to her aid, but Kamilla misses her train. Committed to helping those in need, Sebastian decides to deliver Kamilla safely to her sister.

Sebastian's compassion, however, is not balanced by integrity. Since his mother died in jail for stealing a loaf of bread to keep him alive as a child, he sees no reason not to steal from the rich to give to the poor. Kamilla remembering the Bible, which her mother taught her, pricks Sebastian's guilt by asking him if he is a thief.

On their cross-country journey they encounter an escaped convict. The terrifying experience serves only to unite Kamilla and Sebastian, who become the best of friends. Sebastian comes to Christ after reading Kamilla's Bible. The end of the movie is worth its weight in gold—spiritual gold, because it clearly presents the truth of the gospel.

That a Norwegian film company would produce such a Biblical movie is quite extraordinary. This entertaining fable is beautifully filmed and suitable for everyone. There is nothing offensive and everything to commend. The filmmakers should be congratulated.

☆☆☆ CLASSIC ☆☆☆

TITLE:	**KING OF KINGS**
QUALITY:	★★★★
RECOMMENDATION:	Acceptable
RATING:	Not rated
RELEASE:	1961
STARRING:	Jeffrey Hunter, Sioban McKenna, Hurd Hatfield, Ron Randell, Carmen Sevilla, Rip Torn, and Robert Ryan
DIRECTOR:	Nicholas Ray
GENRE:	Religious/Biblical Epic
CONTENT:	Nothing objectionable
INTENDED AUDIENCE:	Family
REVIEWER:	Protestant Motion Picture Council

This episodic presentation of Jesus' life is preceded by a short commentary with brief, accompanying scenes setting the historical background for the events to come. This commentary underscores the fact that His coming was in troubled times, with conflicting forces aiming at the supremacy finally achieved by the Romans.

The well-known Bible record is followed in simple fashion at first and gathers dramatic importance as it progresses. The events of the Nativity are short (only the visit of the Kings from the East is noted). The flight to Egypt, the childhood and youth periods of Jesus are passed over rather quickly. The years of public ministry, beginning with Jesus' baptism by John the Baptist to the post-resurrection episodes are then depicted.

Liberty is taken with the Bible narrative. On several occasions the Scriptural account has to make room for the exigencies of the "script." While the baptism takes place in the river, there is evidence that a gourd is used to pour the water. It is expected that immersionists will not find this acceptable.

Certain characters are developed out of proportion, as in the case of Barabbas, who is made to be the leader of a violent insurrection, with much bloodshed and a tremendous revolutionary following. The Bible merely speaks of "sedition made in the city . . . and murder" as the cause of his imprisonment (Luke 23:19).

Certain comparisons are intimated between Jesus' times and present events, so that His life, ministry and mission acquire subtle ideological overtones. Jesus offers freedom of the spirit and advocates the peaceful methods, while Barabbas insists on fighting for it, achieving his results through violence. Judas is a co-conspirator with Barabbas, who uses this relationship to betray Jesus. Nothing is said about the price of betrayal. The bargain of the thirty pieces of silver remain unnoticed.

Some events are reported, but not witnessed, such as Jesus appearing before the Sanhedrin, their questioning and their leading Him to Pilate. Pilate's judgment is a private affair, in an empty court with one defender assigned to "the accused."

The climax of the Crucifixion is rather hastily treated, with only a few witnesses, and not enough attention is given to the facts attendant upon the Resurrection. Two of Jesus' apparitions are related. The final one ends abruptly when He speaks to His disciples as they are returning from fishing. It is then that Jesus gives them the Great Commission.

Thus the story ends, rather incomplete, before the Ascension. One feels that at the start some efforts were made to give a simple, dignified account of Jesus' ministry, but that the dramatic possibilities of such a portrayal got out of hand so that the final effect does not bring about the inspirational or esthetic feelings desired.

TITLE:	**KINJITE: FORBIDDEN SUBJECTS**
QUALITY:	★ ★
RECOMMENDATION:	Extreme Caution
RATING:	R
RELEASE:	1989
STARRING:	Charles Bronson, Peggy (Mob Squad) Lipton, James Pax, Kumiko Hayakawa, and Juan Fernandez
DIRECTOR:	J. Lee Thompson
GENRE:	Action Adventure/Kung fu

CONTENT:	Violence, obscene language, and child prostitution
INTENDED AUDIENCE:	Adults
REVIEWER:	Gene Burke

Hiroshi Hada is about to be transferred from the Orient to the States. While in Japan, he notices an executive on the subway fondling a female passenger. Surprised that the woman offers no resistance, the act plants a fantasy in his mind that brings him close to confrontation with Lt. Crowe. In the States, Hiroshi exercises his fantasy by fondling Lt. Crowe's thirteen-year-old daughter on a crowded city bus. The girl screams, causing him to flee. He confesses the incident to his wife which allows him to forget it. Hiroshi's eleven-year-old daughter is forced into prostitution. Lt. Crowe is assigned the case, forcing him to help locate the young girl. After much ado, he eliminates the prostitution ring and rescues the little girl. Our oriental family is so overjoyed by the return of their daughter, they bring a gift to Lt. Crowe's family. Crowe's daughter realizes that Hiroshi Hada is the same man who violated her on the bus. The film ends with her shrugging it off.

Due to violence and an abundance of indecent, obscene, sick subjects, *Kinjite: Forbidden Subjects* should be avoided. "Then when lust hath conceived, it bringeth forth sin: and sin, when it is finished, bringeth forth death" (James 1:15).

TITLE:	**KNIGHTS AND EMERALDS**
QUALITY:	★★★
RECOMMENDATION:	Caution
RATING:	PG
RELEASE:	1987
STARRING:	Warren Mitchell, Rachel Davies, Christopher Wild, Beverley Hills, and Bill Leadbitter
DIRECTOR:	Ian Emes
GENRE:	Drama
CONTENT:	Some off-color innuendo and some exclamatory language
INTENDED AUDIENCE:	Adults
REVIEWER:	Ted Baehr

Knights and Emeralds is set in an industrial town in England. It tells the story of an old-fashioned, all-white marching band led by Mr. Kirkpatrick. This band used to win all the national band contests, but has seen better days. They are opposed by a black marching band which is walking away with all the honors.

Kevin, the drummer for the white band, is intrigued by the blond majorette who becomes interested in black music and goes over to play with the black band. Then, he falls in loves with the black drummer girl, Melissa.

The white band doesn't make it into the championships, but the black band does. However, the first routine that the black band does is a traditional routine, and they don't win enough points. They decide that they have nothing to gain by playing traditional music, so they go out and finish with an incredible number which wins the championship.

There is no sex and no violence. There is a little off-color innuendo and exclamatory language. Overall, *Knights and Emeralds* is an enjoyable film. It should be recommended with caution because of the exclamatory language.

TITLE:	**LA BAMBA**
QUALITY:	★★★★
RECOMMENDATION:	Extreme Caution
RATING:	PG-13
RELEASE:	1987
STARRING:	Lou Diamonds Phillips, Esai Morales, and Rosana Desoto
DIRECTOR:	Luis Valdez
GENRE:	Drama/Biography
CONTENT:	Some obscenity, magic, and risque scenes
INTENDED AUDIENCE:	Adults
REVIEWER:	Lili Baehr

La Bamba is the true story of Ritchie Valens. Born Ricardo Valenzuela to a poor Mexican family, Ritchie became a rock-and-roll star in eight short months and then was tragically killed in an airplane crash at the age of seventeen.

A slow-motion, grainy scene of children playing in a playground shows a plane flying overhead and then blowing up in mid air. It is Ritchie's nightmare—a premonition. Cut to 1957 in Northern California. Bob, Ritchie's brother, is coming back from prison. Ritchie, his mother and two younger siblings are living in the fruit pickers' camps. "I am gonna get you out of this dump," says Bob to his mother as he hands her some money. "I don't want dirty money," she says, but she takes it.

The next scene shows the family in Southern California in a poor neighborhood. Ritchie is motivated by his music. His brother is a troublemaker, in contrast to Ritchie who is clean-cut. This contrast is the theme of the movie. Bob feels that mother prefers Ritchie to him. Both have talent. Bob is a good artist, however he is self-destructive. Ritchie is focused on what he wants to do. He's going to make it!

Ritchie falls in love with Donna, but her family is not happy about the relationship. One of Ritchie's most famous songs was written in Donna's honor. It is refreshing to see a teenage romance in a movie without sex.

The entire family gets together to promote Ritchie's singing debut. However, a drunken Bob starts a fist-fight. A record promoter signs Ritchie up. This is the beginning of a short, fast rise to the top of the charts. Eight months later, his plane crashes and Ritchie dies with Buddy Holly and the Big Bopper.

The movie has strong performances, excellent direction, and excellent depiction of that era. Unfortunately, there are dirty words and bad scenes. In one scene, Bob takes his brother to a whore house, but Ritchie is more interested in music and discovers the song, "La Bamba."

La Bamba depicts very low life, however it does not depict it in pathetic terms. Although poor, the family members love each other and are sympathetic characters for whom the audience cares. *La Bamba* is a tough, poignant movie, but it cannot be recommended because of its language and immoral situations. Extreme caution is advised.

TITLE:	**LAND BEFORE TIME**
QUALITY:	★★★
RECOMMENDATION:	Caution
RATING:	G
RELEASE:	1988
STARRING:	Animation
DIRECTOR:	Don Bluth, Gary Goldman, and John Pomeroy
GENRE:	Animated/Children
CONTENT:	Some minor, frightening scenes which may scare young children
INTENDED AUDIENCE:	Children
REVIEWER:	Gene Burke

Journeying to the Great Valley where everyone lives happily together, five childlike dinosaurs are separated from their parents during an earthquake. The mother of a long neck called "Little Foot," dies during the earthquake, leaving him with only one clue to discover the way to the Great Valley and a reunion with his grandparents. That clue is to use his heart as well as his mind.

He is joined by four other orphaned dinosaurs. One was raised with the philosophy that Long Necks are different and must stay with "their own kind." Ultimately, their need to help each other supercedes the barriers of prejudice. Little Foot victoriously leads his friends into the Great Valley for a joyful reunion with their respective families.

Don Bluth's Mormonism may be showing in this film. Salvation here comes through works, not faith in Jesus Christ, who is the only way into the Kingdom of God. We've seen the story of *Land Before Time* many times before. Nothing will be missed by overlooking this film and choosing another.

TITLE:	**THE LAST EMPEROR**
QUALITY:	★★★
RECOMMENDATION:	Extreme Caution
RATING:	PG-13
RELEASE:	1987
STARRING:	John Lone, Joan Chen, and Peter O'Toole
DIRECTOR:	Bernardo Bertolucci
GENRE:	Historical
CONTENT:	Some sex and pro-communism

INTENDED AUDIENCE: Adults

REVIEWER: Bret Senft

The Last Emperor is a small docudrama told in epic form. It is the story of Pu Li (1906—1967), the last emperor of China. With the death of the Empress Dowager, the Forbidden City becomes an island of dynastic rule in a sea of social and political change. While Sun Yat Sen struggles to construct a republic, Pu Li and his two wives cavort beneath the royal sheets.

The Japanese invade China. Pu Li and his friends simply play tennis while Beijing burns. Eventually, the Japanese escort Pu Li back to his ancestral homeland of Manchuria where he serves as their public ruler. He is captured by the Russians and ends up in a communist prison camp. He is released after ten years to spend his last days as a gardener in Beijing.

Shot on location, *The Last Emperor* presents the communists as benevolent saviors of a country lost to imperialism, opium, and decadence. The ruthless murder of over thirty million people by the communists is never addressed. However, the film does make communism look pathetic and depressing.

Beautifully photographed, the film is a picturesque documentary without a dramatic center. Save your money for a better movie.

TITLE:	**THE LAST TEMPTATION OF CHRIST**
QUALITY:	★
RECOMMENDATION:	Evil
RATING:	R
RELEASE:	1988
STARRING:	Willem Dafoe, Harvey Keitel, and Barbara Hershey
DIRECTOR:	Martin Scorsese
GENRE:	Religious
CONTENT:	Blasphemy, nudity, blood, and evil
INTENDED AUDIENCE:	Adults
REVIEWER:	Ted Baehr and Evelyn Dokovic

The Last Temptation of Christ is the most blasphemous movie ever made. As if that wasn't bad enough, it is boring.

To show how bad it is, here are some quotes from the July 12 screening by Evelyn Dokovic from Morality in Media. This is not pleasant, but it is clear that God is using *The Last Temptation of Christ* to separate the sheep from the goats. If we love Him, we will stand against this blasphemy in any way we can.

> Film opens with the Jesus character, a carpenter putting the finishing touches on the horizontal portion of a cross. Judas enters and berates Jesus for making crosses that are used by the Romans to kill Jews. As they talk, Jesus indicates that he is struggling. . . .

(Viewer observation: This is typical of the exchanges between the two throughout the film. Judas is strong, knows exactly who he is and what he wants. Jesus is weak, confused, fearful, doesn't know who he is, from time to time falls on the ground in a faint after hearing voices. He doesn't know if the voices come from God or the devil.)

Jesus seems to be helping them crucify the man.

He revives and says he wants God to hate him. He makes crosses because he wants God to hate him.

The viewer sees a bare-breasted woman sitting at a well. There is no dialogue between Jesus and the woman, as Jesus proceeds on his way to Mary Magdalene's house. He has to wait in line to get in. When he does the room is filled with men sitting down, watching Mary have sex with a customer. Jesus sits down and watches, too. . . .

Jesus says: "I'm a liar, a hypocrite, I'm afraid of everything. . . . Do you want to know who my God is? They're fear . . . Lucifer is inside me. He tells me I am not a man, but the Son of Man, more the Son of God, more than that, God."

The Last Supper. After the apostles partake of the Bread and the Cup, blood and flesh are seen dripping from the mouths of some.

Mary Magdalene dresses his wounds. They make love and Mary breathes: "We can make a baby."

Jesus is walking with his wives and children, and stops to listen to a preacher—St. Paul. He is telling the people that Jesus of Nazareth was the Son of God, that he was tortured and crucified for our sins, and that three days later He rose from the dead.

Jesus asks Paul if he ever saw Jesus of Nazareth. Paul replies: "No, but I saw a light." Jesus screams: "Liar." Jesus tells Paul that he is Jesus, asks why he is telling these lies. Jesus says: "I was saved. I have children." Paul tells him to look around him and see how unhappy the people are. Their only hope is the resurrected Jesus. Paul says: "They need God. If I have to crucify you, I'll crucify you. If I have to resurrect you, I'll resurrect you. My Jesus is more important than you are. I'm glad I met you. Now I can forget about you."

This is a unique opportunity for Christians to continue to take a stand for Jesus. Hollywood is watching the Church to see if they can continue to exploit blasphemy as a money-making attraction. We need to stop this evil.

TITLE:	**LAWRENCE OF ARABIA (222 Minutes with 16-Minute Intermission)**
QUALITY:	★★★★
RECOMMENDATION:	Acceptable
RATING:	PG
RELEASE:	1962
STARRING:	Peter O'Toole, Omar Sharif, Alec Guinness, Anthony Quinn, Jack Hawkins, Jose Ferrer, Anthony Quayle, Claude Rains, Arthur Kennedy, Donald Wolfit, Michel Ray, and John Dimech

DIRECTOR:	David Lean
GENRE:	Historical/Drama/War
CONTENT:	Nothing objectional
INTENDED AUDIENCE:	Adults
REVIEWER:	Wendell B. Rhodes and Troy Schmidt

How does a person of insignificance, a military mapmaker of low rank, a common man from the very "basement" of influence, become both a maker of history and a puppet of political advantage?

We are introduced to Mr. T.E. Lawrence at a memorial in his honor. Some consider him a pompous, egotistical power-grabber. Others believe him to have been a humble servant and liberator of the Arab nation. So who was T.E. Lawrence?

Cut to Lawrence at British headquarters in Cairo during WW I. He is granted a transfer to Arabia. Once there, he unites the Arabs in their rebellion against the Turks. Upon arriving at the Arab outpost, Lawrence finds the army in disarray. They are being bombarded by Turkish artillery. Lawrence forms his own impossible plan. With fifty Arabs, he treks across the sands to capture the strategic port of Aqaba from a superior Turkish garrison. This solidifies Lawrence's authority in the eyes of the Arabs, and even deifies him.

This film is a study in self-identity. The English have an identity. The Turks have an identity. Even the feuding Arabs have an identity. But who is T.E. Lawrence? His life is ambiguous. He is an ordinary man meeting impossible odds and beating them! He writes his own history, yet he disintegrates at the fulcrum of his power.

This is a masterpiece. Peter O'Toole portrays Lawrence with such believability that we cheer for his cause, hurt with his hurts, pity his foolishness, flinch at his arrogance, and admire his humility. This is a film of epic measurements about a character larger than life, in a story larger than life. Sweeping desert vistas and a stark story combine to totally immerse the viewer. See it on a large screen if you can.

TITLE:	**LEAN ON ME**
QUALITY:	★ ★ ★ ★
RECOMMENDATION:	Extreme Caution
RATING:	PG-13
RELEASE:	1989
STARRING:	Richard Guillaume
DIRECTOR:	John Avildsen
GENRE:	Drama/Biography
CONTENT:	Dramatization of a true story with realistic vulgar language and some violence
INTENDED AUDIENCE:	Adult
REVIEWER:	F.L. Lindberg

Lean on Me is an inspiring true story which deals with tough situations. Eastside High School of Paterson, New Jersey has become a nightmarish jungle of drugs, violence, and illiteracy. Joe Clark is called back from a quiet elementary school to save the school board and mayor from further public embarrassment. Later, he notes that God called him to this school. Joe Clark is the principal who chained the doors shut to keep drug dealers out of his school. This man carried a baseball bat and a bullhorn.

Crime and immorality are consistently rebuked in this film. Compassion is shown for repentance, followed by help. Things do not miraculously get better; hard work is the only way out. No budget increases are asked, just hard work from students and faculty alike. The focus is on Joe Clark, a rough personality—ruthless in opposing evil, hopelessness, and ignorance.

Despite the rugged atmosphere of Eastside and urban decay, *Lean on Me* passed the test. Maybe all is not lost, if good people can take a stand and lean on each other.

TITLE:	**LEONARD, PART 6**
QUALITY:	★
RECOMMENDATION:	Bad
RATING:	PG
RELEASE:	1987
STARRING:	Bill Cosby, Tom Courtney, and Joe Don Baker
DIRECTOR:	Paul Wieland
GENRE:	Comedy
CONTENT:	Occult practices
INTENDED AUDIENCE:	Teenagers and adults
REVIEWER:	Doug Brewer

Bill Cosby has bought himself a movie to break into the world of the big screen. He has made a ninety-minute sit-com, complete with Coke commercials. Bill plays Leonard Parker, a multi-millionaire, former CIA agent. There have been a rash of attacks by small creatures on CIA agents, and Leonard is needed to find out who trained these creatures to kill. What follows is a dumb, mostly unfunny stab at satirizing the James Bond series. All of this is ultimately harmless, but Cosby resorts to some nonsense about a fortune teller and several talismans she gives him to help him save the world. Up until then the movie had been nice and stupid; and, afterward, it was still stupid, but not so nice.

There is certainly something Christians can do about *Leonard, Part 6*. We can ignore it. Maybe it will go away.

☆☆☆ MASTERPIECE ☆☆☆

TITLE:	**LES MISERABLES (Black and White)**
QUALITY:	★★★★
RECOMMENDATION:	Acceptable

RATING:	Not rated
RELEASE:	1935
STARRING:	Fredic March, Charles Laughton, Cedric Hardwicke, Rochelle Hudson, and Marilyn Knowlden
DIRECTOR:	Richard Boleslawski
GENRE:	Historical Drama
CONTENT:	Nothing objectionable
INTENDED AUDIENCE:	Adult
REVIEWER:	Ted Baehr

Les Miserables tells the redeeming story of Jean Valjean who went to jail for stealing a loaf of bread to feed his sister's child. Jean is captured and given ten years at hard labor in prison.

When he finally escapes prison, he is a hard-bitten, stone-hearted, and utterly unsympathetic creature whose compassion for his fellow man has been hammered out of him by the cruelty of confinement. Rejected and alienated, he comes to the end of his rope. He is starving and prays in desperation. A bishop takes Jean into his home and feeds him.

That night, Jean steals the bishop's only possession, his silver candlesticks. The police arrest him and take him back to the bishop. The bishop comes to Jean's aid and refuses to prosecute him. When the police leave in frustration, the bishop tells Jean that tonight he has bought Jean's soul for Christ. Jean repents and totally reforms.

Jean becomes a new man and dedicates his life to helping others. He works night and day to build a new life for himself using another name, taking a young waif as his own. He becomes a well-to-do businessman and, moving to another town, becomes so widely liked that he is elected mayor. Every waking day of his life is devoted to benefiting his fellow man.

However, the chief of police, Javert, who was his guard in prison, doggedly tracks Jean so he can drag Jean back to prison. To the single-minded Javert the law is to be upheld and enforced at all costs, with no mercy shown to anyone.

One day Jean sees a villager trapped beneath a heavy wagon and, with extraordinary strength, he puts his back to the wagon and lifts it so that the man can be saved. Javert watches this feat and is reminded of the prisoner he once guarded.

He begins to investigate Jean's past and identifies him as Jean Valjean, the wanted criminal. He is then confused when another prisoner is found, a mindless inmate who resembles Valjean and admits that he is him, but the honest Valjean admits that he is the real Jean Valjean. Before he can be jailed, he flees to Paris where he assumes another identity.

Javert is right behind him. After a chase through treacherous chest-high waters in the Paris sewers, Jean relents to the prodding of his conscience and goes to Javert to surrender.

All his life, Javert denied the power of God to change lives and served the humanist fallacy that people can not change and can only be incarcerated. Javert has witnessed Valjean's selfless sacrifices on several occasions and finds compassion stirring in his heart, an emotion he cannot understand, nor abide.

Javert cannot live with Jean's acts of love which proves that Jean was really transformed by Jesus Christ; so, broken, he commits suicide. Jean is free to live out his life among those who love him.

Les Miserables is a positive, uplifting, Christian story of the struggle between love and hate. It is a powerful witness to the power of God and answered prayer. Les Miserables is great. If you have the blessed opportunity to see it, do so.

TITLE:	**LEVIATHAN**
QUALITY:	★★★★
RECOMMENDATION:	Extreme Caution
RATING:	R
RELEASE:	1989
STARRING:	Peter Weller, Richard Krenna, Ernie Hudson, and Hector Elizondo
DIRECTOR:	George Cosmatos
GENRE:	Science fiction
CONTENT:	Some gory violence, though not explicit; partial nudity; obscenities; vulgarities; and blasphemies
INTENDED AUDIENCE:	Adults
REVIEWER:	Bruce Grimes

A conglomerate begins to mine the ocean bottom. Located in "Shack 7" are men and women miners, plus geologist Weller. A slip sends one crewman over the edge of a ridge. His backup follows and her camera transmits the image of a rusted Russian freighter on the ocean floor. Two items are found in the ship's vault. One is a videotape, the other a bottle of vodka. The crewman who found the ship slips a flask into his pocket. He drinks the few ounces and shares it with a female crew member. Within 24 hours, he is dead. As the female crew member begins to die, we realize the other crewman is not dead: his body is transforming into something grotesque. A Russian geneticist had put a virus in the vodka, and the crew had mutated. The ship was sunk to prevent the infection from reaching land. From this point, the movie is a copy of Alien and Aliens. It becomes a battle to the last man and woman as they fight the creature throughout the complex.

It is sad that such a potentially entertaining film must "contaminate" itself with so much foul language. We cannot recommend Leviathan in its original release. Perhaps, it will be edited for television.

TITLE:	**LICENSE TO DRIVE**
QUALITY:	★★
RECOMMENDATION:	Bad
RATING:	PG
RELEASE:	1988

STARRING:	Corey Haim, Corey Feldman, and Heather Graham
DIRECTOR:	Greg Beeman
GENRE:	Comedy
CONTENT:	Theft, dishonesty, rebellion against authority, materialism, profanity, and obscenity
INTENDED AUDIENCE:	Teenagers
REVIEWER:	Rebecca Wayt

The promotional material contends: "It is the most important thing a young person will ever possess." All Biblical virtues are ignored in this materialistic destruction derby which is rife with envy, lust, and jealousy.

Set in a Los Angeles suburb, this comedy is about a fifteen-year-old boy, Les, flunking a driver's test. Les pretends he passed. Motivated by a date with Mercedes, he steals his grandfather's Cadillac and ends up in a series of mishaps. He brings the car home, "totaled."

What happened to the car should have happened to the film. Unfortunately, teenagers pay big money for this type of entertainment. There is no excuse for a movie such as this which promotes theft, dishonesty, rebellion against authority, and materialism. Avoid this film-accident.

TITLE:	**THE LIGHTHORSEMEN**
QUALITY:	★★★
RECOMMENDATION:	Caution
RATING:	R
RELEASE:	1988
STARRING:	Jon Blake, Peter Phelps, Anthony Andrews, and Sigrid Thornton
DIRECTOR:	Simon Wincer
GENRE:	War
CONTENT:	Profanity and some violence
INTENDED AUDIENCE:	Adults
REVIEWER:	Ted Baehr

The Lighthorsemen tells the story of the Australian Lighthorse mounted infantry which turned the tide at the battle of Beersheba in 1917. The movie focuses on four men who are trying to deal with the war. Frank dies and is replaced by Dave. Since Dave wasn't with them at Gallipoli, Scotty, Taz and Chill doubt his ability to guard their flank in a battle. Their suspicions prove correct when he is unable to kill a retreating Turk during a major battle. Dave is reassigned to the medical support unit, but during the attack on Beersheba, he breaks from the medical unit and rides to save his compatriots.

The Lighthorsemen is a true story of valor, love, and reconciliation which could have been recommended except for the constant use of the Lord's Name in vain. This profanity is inexcusable.

☆☆☆ CLASSIC ☆☆☆

TITLE:	**THE LION**
QUALITY:	★★★
RECOMMENDATION:	Acceptable
RATING:	Not rated
RELEASE:	1962 (British)
STARRING:	William Holden, Trevor Howard, Capucine, and Pamela Franklin
DIRECTOR:	Jack Cardiff
GENRE:	Drama/Nature
CONTENT:	Nothing objectionable
INTENDED AUDIENCE:	Family
REVIEWER:	Protestant Motion Picture Council

An American lawyer, Robert Haywood, is summoned to the Dark Continent by his ex-wife who fears that their daughter has become overly fond of the jungle and too attached to Zamba, a lion she has raised from birth. The current husband is a game warden who oversees the preserve and is skeptical about the appearance of the girl's father. He doesn't mask his jealously well.

When an old tribal chieftain is left to die at the mercy of the elements (the custom of that tribe), Haywood can't bear it and saves the man's life. This precipitates a battle between Zamba and the chieftain's son, who must kill a lion to take over the tribe.

The family difficulties are solved plausibly in honorable fashion. All those involved seem especially honest and understanding.

Photographed in East Africa, on the game reserves of Uganda, Kenya, and Tanganyika, before socialism destroyed those countries, this film is dramatically and artistically superb, with a good story woven in and around beautiful scenery.

TITLE:	**THE LITTLE DEVIL (Subtitles)**
QUALITY:	★★★
RECOMMENDATION:	Extreme Caution
RATING:	None
RELEASE:	1989
STARRING:	Robert Benigni and Walter Matthau
DIRECTOR:	Robert Benigni

GENRE:	Comedy
CONTENT:	Brief naturalistic nudity and lewdness
INTENDED AUDIENCE:	Adults
REVIEWER:	Ted Baehr

The Little Devil is a morality play full of humor and profound insights into temptation and sin.

A priest named Maurice falls in love with one of his parishioners, Patricia. At that moment, this funny-looking, Woody Allen type man appears from out of nowhere, and Maurice asks what is that foul smell. That foul smell is the little demon who Maurice has let into his life through his lust.

Humorously, the demon makes life impossible for Maurice, who doesn't believe in demons, being a very modern priest. Eventually, Maurice sees the connection and understands that demons do exist. When he turns from temptation, the little devil flees from him.

This is a very Biblical allegory. There are some earthy moments which we must caution you about. These are not repulsive as one would find in an American film, but conform to the earthiness of the Italian cinema. Although we object to those elements, the moral of this story is worthwhile.

TITLE:	**LITTLE DORRIT: A Story Told in 2 Films—Part One: Nobody's Fault—Part Two: Little Dorrit's Story (150 minutes and 180 minutes)**
QUALITY:	★★★★
RECOMMENDATION:	Acceptable
RATING:	G
RELEASE:	1988
STARRING:	Derek Jacobi, Alec Guinness, Joan Crenwood, Rashan Seth, Cyril Cusack, and Sara Pickering
DIRECTOR:	Christine Edzard
GENRE:	Drama/Historical
CONTENT:	Absolutely wonderful truth and hope in the face of great despair
INTENDED AUDIENCE:	Adults
REVIEWER:	Wendell B. Rhodes

Little Dorrit is Dickens' monumental story of the human spirit and love. Part One focuses on Arthur, a forty-year-old bachelor coming home from China. His father has died, and he returns to make things right with his past. Standing in the way of reconciliation is his embittered mother. She manipulates everyone. Arthur blames no one; she blames everybody. A quiet servant named "Little Dorrit" is hardly noticed until Arthur asks her a question. He discovers a wonderful person living an extraordinary life.

Part Two is the story through Little Dorrit's eyes. You will laugh with delight at her slightly different viewpoint. She seems to know who is at fault, without fixing blame. She takes responsibility for her life.

I highly recommend *Little Dorrit!* However, let me caution you of one thing: *This is an event!* You must view it as such, or you may not enjoy it. Television junkies should avoid it. Readers of great novels should not miss it! You will feel like we did: "Let's go back and see it again!" Even after six hours . . . it is that good!

TITLE:	**LITTLE NIKITA**
QUALITY:	★ ★
RECOMMENDATION:	Caution
RATING:	PG
RELEASE:	1988
STARRING:	Sidney Poitier and River Phoenix
DIRECTOR:	Richard Benjamin
GENRE:	Detective/Spy
CONTENT:	Obscenity
INTENDED AUDIENCE:	Teenagers and young adults
REVIEWER:	Doug Brewer

FBI agent Roy Parmenter, who harbors bad feelings for one of the local Russian spies in San Diego, figures out that his spy is killing the other spies. When Jeff Grant applies to attend the Air Force Academy, Parmenter is asked to screen him. Feeding Jeff's parents' names into the computer, he discovers they do not compute. Roy interviews Jeff, trying to find out if Jeff knows his parents are "sleepers." Roy asks Jeff to spy on his parents. Jeff is taken aback, with good reason, and the film really gets rolling. *Little Nikita* plays for the cloak-and-dagger suspense while examining the consequences of revealed secrets on the family unit. Jeff confronts his parents, who have recently been contacted after twenty years of inactivity. They are scared and vulnerable, as is he.

The climax is exciting and heart-warming, with just enough ambiguity to show that the family will deal with their problems together. *Little Nikita* is surprisingly absorbing. In the end, good does triumph over evil.

TITLE:	**THE LIVING DAYLIGHTS**
QUALITY:	★ ★
RECOMMENDATION:	Extreme Caution
RATING:	PG
RELEASE:	1987
STARRING:	Timothy Dalton and Joe Don Baker
DIRECTOR:	John Glen

GENRE:	Action adventure/Spy
CONTENT:	Sexual innuendoes and violence
INTENDED AUDIENCE:	Adults
REVIEWER:	Doug Brewer

James Bond movies are formula films with enough casual sex, blood, death, and destruction to keep several critics busy for weeks. By way of a plot, we had one Russian Intelligence Officer's defection, an alleged plan to kill British and American spies, arms-selling, CIA surveillance, Afghan rebels, heroin trafficking, an assassination, and one vaguely Slovak looking, pretty, female cello player. Your usual Bond labyrinth.

Dalton, who looks like a thin, dead George Segal, fights a desperate battle with an inane script and looses. He does not have the staying power of Sean Connery, or the aloofness of Roger Moore. Joe Don Baker, as the unbalanced arms dealer, turns in a passable performance, although he is too loud.

On the whole, the movie is tedious and disjointed. Bond appeared monogamous, even though his love interest seemed hardly worth the effort. While *The Living Daylights* is a superficial romp through Ian Fleming's repetitive imagination, the worldliness and fleshliness leave much to be desired.

☆☆☆ CLASSIC ☆☆☆

TITLE:	**THE LEGEND OF LOBO**
QUALITY:	★★★
RECOMMENDATION:	Acceptable
RATING:	Not rated
RELEASE:	1962
STARRING:	Rex Allen (Narrator and singer)
DIRECTOR:	James Algar
PRODUCER:	Walt Disney
GENRE:	Nature/Action adventure
CONTENT:	Nothing objectionable
INTENDED AUDIENCE:	Family
REVIEWER:	Protestant Motion Picture Council

Based on a story by Ernest Thompson-Seton, this nature drama is about a wolf whose name has become a legend. During the settling of the West, wolves running in packs were a menace to the herds and flocks which they destroyed in great numbers. For a period, bounties were put on their pelts. When they were nearly eliminated, they became their own defenders against men's killing devices.

Lobo was a mighty pack leader in the Southwest. This film tells of his adventures. When his mate is captured by a hunter, Lobo outsmarts the man and gets his mate back.

The production is artistically superb. It is more than just an "animal picture." The photography and animal lore are unusual. Rex Allen is splendid as narrator and singer. An excellent musical score is provided.

☆☆☆ MASTERPIECE ☆☆☆

TITLE:	**LONELY ARE THE BRAVE**
QUALITY:	★★★★
RECOMMENDATION:	Caution
RATING:	Not rated
RELEASE:	1962
STARRING:	Kirk Douglas, Gena Rowlands, Walter Matthau, Michael Kane, Carroll O'Connor, and George Kennedy
DIRECTOR:	David Miller
GENRE:	Western
CONTENT:	One violent bar room fight
INTENDED AUDIENCE:	Adult
REVIEWER:	Protestant Motion Picture Council

This Western is quite different from the usual "cowboy and his horse" stories. This is a genuine cowboy, one of the last real cowboys. He is being engulfed by the modern world—the world which is slowly crushing the Old West. He resents all restrictions, fences, regulations, and boundaries, as he fights a losing battle.

As the film opens, Jack Burns (Kirk Douglas) is resting beneath clear and spacious skies, when the broad peace is split by the sound of a jet plane passing overhead. This brings a wry smile to his face.

Because a friend of his has been jailed for helping some "wetbacks" come over the border, he determines to help him escape. He gets himself imprisoned, but his pal wants no help in breaking out. He will serve his brief time. He tells Burns he intends to play out his hand with the law and refuses to become a fugitive.

Burns breaks out himself and heads for the hills, with Sheriff Johnson (Walter Matthau) organizing a pursuit. He is an understanding sheriff, who tries his best to capture a man he does not want to see in irons.

During the pursuit, Burns second-guesses Sheriff Johnson and his men at every turn, which earns the sheriff's respect. He secretly admires Burns and his individualistic ways, but he knows the cowboy represents a wild way of life that is no more and that "either you go by the rules or you lose." The sheriff pursues Burns with his posse, using a Jeep, short-wave communications, and a helicopter borrowed from the Army, but Burns dodges and shifts his trail through thick forests and up high mountain trails into New Mexico.

This is a tough story, including a violent barroom fight. His loyalty spins a cocoon around him from which he cannot escape.

The acting is superb. The settings are beautiful. This is an excellent movie. Unfortunately, the writer has a romantic vision of individualism, as opposed to a Biblical understanding of personhood.

TITLE:	**THE LONELY PASSION OF JUDITH HEARNE**
QUALITY:	★★★
RECOMMENDATION:	Caution
RATING:	R
RELEASE:	1987
STARRING:	Maggie Smith and Bob Hoskins
DIRECTOR:	Jack Clayton
GENRE:	Drama/Romance
CONTENT:	Salty language and posterior male nudity
INTENDED AUDIENCE:	Adults
REVIEWER:	Doug Brewer

Judith, a middle-aged spinster, who was oppressed all her life by the unforgiving Aunt D'Arcy, places all her faith in her infatuation with Mr. Madden, mistaking his talk of "partnership" as a marriage proposal.

Although parts of the film are disturbing, there is a surprising parable-like quality to *The Lonely Passion of Judith Hearne* and her quest for spiritual fulfillment. This is a depressing look at the failure of faith and should be approached with that in mind. *The Lonely Passion of Judith Hearne* is recommended with caution for those who wish to see the price of giving up, as well as rebuilding a relationship with the Lord.

TITLE:	**MAC AND ME**
QUALITY:	★★★
RECOMMENDATION:	Acceptable
RATING:	PG
RELEASE:	1988
STARRING:	Jade Calegory, Jonathan Ward, Katrina Caspary, and Lauren Stanley
DIRECTOR:	Stewart Raffill
GENRE:	Science fiction
CONTENT:	Nothing objectionable
INTENDED AUDIENCE:	Families
REVIEWER:	David Outten

A U.S. space probe gathering rocks on a distant planet accidently sucks up a family of long-fingered creatures. Back in the lab, this family of aliens explodes out of the craft and escapes from the compound.

"Mac," the youngest of the creatures, is separated from his family and finds a young boy to befriend. "Mac" is pursued by the scientists anxious to give him a thorough examination while "Mac" is busy working to arrange a family reunion.

It used to be that films showed God performing miracles. However, in Hollywood today Jesus is disgraced and audiences must look to "Mac", ET, and Superman to overcome the laws of science.

For people who enjoy situation comedies, *Mac and Me* can be a lot of fun. For those who want surprises, *Mac and Me* could be a disappointment.

We recommend *Mac and Me* for those looking for light entertainment without nudity, vulgarity, or originality.

TITLE:	**MADAME SOUSATZKA**
QUALITY:	★ ★ ★ ★
RECOMMENDATION:	Caution
RATING:	PG-13
RELEASE:	1988
STARRING:	Shirley MacLaine, Peggy Ashcroft, Shabana Azmi, Twiggy, Leigh Lawson, Geoffrey Bayldon, and Navin Chowdhry
DIRECTOR:	John Schlesinger
GENRE:	Drama/Music
CONTENT:	Sex is implied, but not shown, and there is a vague hint of spiritualism
INTENDED AUDIENCE:	Adults
REVIEWER:	Glennis O'Neal

London: *Madame Sousatzka* teaches her students "The Sousatzka Method." Her latest discovery is Manek, the fifteen-year-old son of a New Delhi woman struggling to put food on their table. Madame Sousatzka lets nothing stand in the way of her ability to tap the boy's genius: "Oh, fiddle the money, I teach!" There the battle begins for the boy's control, the mother seeking an immediate concert and Madame Sousatzka holding a tight reign: "No. Not until he's ready!" She places her hands over his wooden fingers and brings the instrument "alive" as he never dreamed possible. His exposure includes: Jenny, the party-girl upstairs; Dr. Cordo, the lonely osteopath; and, Lady Emily, worried about being uprooted from the house she's lived in for so many years. Life-changing decisions force themselves upon each member of "the family," but not without exacting the price that each must pay.

Madame Sousatzka is truly *appassionata*. *Madame Sousatzka* could not be left behind, but got carried home by each viewer experiencing this masterpiece. *Madame Sousatzka* is a great movie, but we caution you that there is one coming-of-age adult scene where sex is implied, but not shown. Also, there is one profanity; and, there is a vague hint of spiritualism which is an anathema to God. On the other hand, there are many redeeming moral elements in this film.

TITLE:	**MADE IN HEAVEN**
QUALITY:	★★★
RECOMMENDATION:	Extreme Caution
RATING:	PG
RELEASE:	1987
STARRING:	Timothy Hutton and Kelly McGillis
DIRECTOR:	Alan Rudolph
GENRE:	Romance
CONTENT:	Gnostic world view
INTENDED AUDIENCE:	Teenagers and young adults
REVIEWER:	Doug Brewer

Mike dives into a river to rescue a family trapped in a rapidly sinking car. He gets stuck and drowns. Suddenly, he is standing in a white room. His Aunt Lisa explains that he is dead. She tells Mike that all he has to do is concentrate and he will transport himself. He ends up with Kelly McGillis. They fall in love.

Emmett, an androgynous redhead, appears to be "running things," which he denies, deferring to God, who seems quite distant, when Kelly is going away to be born on earth. Mike begs Emmett to let him go back to earth to find Kelly, and the adventure begins.

Unfortunately, this is a heaven without Jesus Christ. As a love story, *Made in Heaven* is a fresh treatment. As theology, it is awful. We are opposed to this worldview and warn Christians of the danger in this sort of gnostic propaganda.

TITLE:	**MAID TO ORDER**
QUALITY:	★★
RECOMMENDATION:	Extreme Caution
RATING:	PG
RELEASE:	1987
STARRING:	Ally Sheedy, Beverly D'Angelo, Michael Ontkean, Valerie Perrine, Dick Shawn, Tom Skerritt, Merry Clayton, Begona Plaza, and Rainbow Phoenix
DIRECTOR:	Amy Jones
GENRE:	Drama
CONTENT:	Some fairy tale elements and brief nudity

INTENDED AUDIENCE: Young adults

REVIEWER: Ted Baehr

Maid to Order could have been clean, good movie with a terrible title, but the filmmakers decided to throw in some unacceptable language and brief nudity in the very beginning of the film to capture a tough R-rating. Otherwise, *Maid to Order* tells the positive story of a rich girl, who matures from self-centeredness to caring, giving, and love. Why anyone would spoil this movie is beyond reason.

Ally plays the girl who has everything. Stopped for a speeding ticket, she is put in jail. Her father wishes he never had a daughter. His wish is granted; thus, the Cinderella story in the obverse. Her father forgets his daughter, and her Fairy Godmother has her released.

Now, she has no home, nor resources. She takes a job as a maid in the home of a wealthy music promoter. At first, she is unpleasant. However, the black cook, Audrey, has compassion on her and asks her to come for Sunday dinner. Ally is moved by their love. She finds out that Audrey was a famous Motown singer whose career collapsed. Ally begins to see each person as someone special. She decides to help her coworkers. Noting the change, Audrey asks if she has been born again. Ally falls in love with the young chauffeur/songwriter.

All of this culminates in a benefit for scholarships for poor children. The major music companies come to the party. The rock-and-roll singer gets hit on the head by a coconut and loses his memory. Audrey sings the chauffeur's song, and it is a hit. Miss Montgomery is reunited with her father, and everyone lives happily ever after.

Without the opening, this would have been an upbeat movie with no sexual immorality. The only potential problem is the Fairy Godmother. However, this is merely a device to move the plot along. In the final analysis, this film shows that love triumphs over selfishness. Unfortunately, it cannot be recommended.

TITLE:	**MAKING MR. RIGHT**
QUALITY:	★ ★ ★
RECOMMENDATION:	Extreme Caution
RATING:	PG-13
RELEASE:	1987
STARRING:	Ann Magnhuson and John Malkovich
DIRECTOR:	Susan Seidleman
GENRE:	Comedy
CONTENT:	Sexual Innuendo
INTENDED AUDIENCE:	Adults
REVIEWER:	Bret Senft

Making Mr. Right portrays the polarization between the sexes. Frankie Stone is the director of an image consulting firm in Miami. Her client is a would-be congressman who is also her philandering boyfriend. When the Chem-Tec approaches her to sell their android to the American public, Frankie discovers the android is more compassionate, more loving, and more human than any mortal man. The android, Ulysses, is the creation of the nerdy scientist Jeff Peters, who has trained Ulysses to avoid the "emotional muck" of friendship, love, and empathy which is destroying the human race.

The android is an idealized version of Peters himself. This allows a number of visual/ psychological gags. Jeff has avoided love, marriage and children, but has created his own child in the lab, thus achieving a perverse immortality through the android.

Ulysses, however, falls in love with Frankie. Slipping out of the lab one night, Ulysses follows Frankie home, stumbling into various misadventures. There is not one stable relationship in the entire film: someone, somewhere, is making someone else unhappy.

Viewers will find many humorous situations in *Making Mr. Right*. Nevertheless, the director's views on modern love, though keenly accurate, provide no real answers for the searching heart. In Seidleman's world, sadly, an android is a girl's best friend. Therefore, avoid *Making Mr. Right*. It is not a worldview anyone would want.

TITLE:	**A MAN AND A WOMAN—TWENTY YEARS LATER (Subtitles)**
QUALITY:	★★★
RECOMMENDATION:	Extreme Caution
RATING:	PG
RELEASE:	1987
STARRING:	Anouk Aimee and Jean-Louis Trintignant
DIRECTOR:	Claude Lelouch
GENRE:	Romance
CONTENT:	Extramarital affairs
INTENDED AUDIENCE:	Adults
REVIEWER:	Doug Brewer

Anne Gauthier was a beautiful, twenty-year-old script girl. She was in love with Jean-Louis Duroc, a dashing race car driver. Their story, filmed by Claude LeLouch, became the standard to which Americans compared other French films.

Lelouch has not merely made a sequel; he has created the illusion of a twenty-year intermission between the first and second acts. Anne is still beautiful, but she is no longer a script girl. She is now a producer. Searching for ideas, she turns to autobiography and calls Duroc to Paris to get his okay. Through flashbacks from the original film, as well as scenes from the movie they're shooting, Anne and Jean-Louis see their romance replayed in front of them.

A Man and a Woman—Twenty Years Later is touching, tender, extremely well-acted, and beautifully filmed. There is no profanity. However, there are two bedroom scenes. Although there is not an inch of nudity, I object to the assumption that sex is an extension of a loving relationship outside of marriage. This is wrong. Extreme caution is recommended because of the movie's cavalier attitude toward sex outside of marriage.

☆☆☆ MASTERPIECE ☆☆☆

TITLE:	**THE MANCHURIAN CANDIDATE**
QUALITY:	★ ★ ★ ★
RECOMMENDATION:	Acceptable
RATING:	PG-13
RELEASE:	1962
STARRING:	Frank Sinatra, Laurence Harvey, Janet Leigh, and Angela Lansbury
DIRECTOR:	John Frankenheimer
GENRE:	Spy/Detective
CONTENT:	Nothing objectionable, except an excessive use of alcoholic beverages
INTENDED AUDIENCE:	Adults
REVIEWER:	Ted Baehr

The Manchurian Candidate (based on a novel by Richard Condon) is back and should be seen by everyone. It speaks to the spiritual warfare being waged in our world today. It makes one think about the world, and then think again.

The Manchurian Candidate tells the story of a communist plot to send a brainwashed American Korean war hero back home to assassinate a presidential candidate. The suspenseful realization of the plot is enhanced by incisive humor. Most intriguing are the red herrings dragged across the trail of the mystery. For example, Shaw's McCarthyite parents turn out to be the Marxist agents, but even this disorienting twist proves the hideous nature of the evil men who have programmed the brainwashed Shaw.

See this masterpiece and ponder the dark conspiracies of the political world. *The Manchurian Candidate* is highly recommended.

TITLE:	**MAN FACING SOUTHEAST (Subtitles)**
QUALITY:	★ ★ ★
RECOMMENDATION:	Caution
RATING:	R
RELEASE:	1987
STARRING:	Lorenzo Quinteros, Hugo Soto, and Ines Vernengo
DIRECTOR:	Eliseo Sudiela
GENRE:	Science fiction/Religious

CONTENT:	Brief nudity
INTENDED AUDIENCE:	Adults
REVIEWER:	Diane Rich

How would our world react when confronted by a savior? Unfortunately, in this allegory, the messiah is an alien projection from outer space. However, this film could help the viewer to understand the dilemma a savior would face in our sinful world.

In an insane asylum in Argentina, Doctor Dennis tells a patient only God can help him. In the chapel, a new patient is brilliantly playing the organ. When Dr. Dennis interviews this patient, Rontez, he seems to be compelling and sincere. He tells the doctor he is on a mission from a world far away. The doctor thinks he is hiding from the law. The doctor asks why he chose the asylum. He says this is the only place where people listen.

Rontez stands for hours, looking East. Rontez says that he is a projection, not actually there. The mysterious box under Rontez' bed is found by cleaning people and brought to the doctor. It is filled with articles. Rontez said it contains information about humanity's worst enemy: stupidity (not sin!).

The authorities give Rontez shock treatments. He cries out, "Dr. Dennis, why have you forsaken me?" Rontez dies of a heart attack. The patients expect him to return in a space-ship.

Man Facing Southeast won the International Critics Award for good reason. It is an intelligent film which asks the right questions. Unfortunately, the mediocre savior demeans the true drama of the real Saviour: Jesus Christ. Because of brief frontal nudity and sexual immorality, this film cannot be recommended.

☆☆☆ MASTERPIECE ☆☆☆

TITLE:	**A MAN FOR ALL SEASONS**
QUALITY:	★ ★ ★ ★
RECOMMENDATION:	Acceptable
RATING:	None
RELEASE:	1966 (British)
STARRING:	Paul Scofield, Wendy Hiller, Leo McKern, Robert Shaw, Orson Welles, Susannah York, Nigel Davenport, and John Hurt
DIRECTOR:	Fred Zinneman
GENRE:	Biography
CONTENT:	Nothing objectionable
INTENDED AUDIENCE:	Adults and mature young people
REVIEWER:	Beth Humpert

A Man for All Seasons is a magnificent movie in which the hero is successfully portrayed as a man of faith, conviction, and courage. The film relates the events that led to the martyrdom of Thomas More (Paul Scofield), who was canonized as a saint in the Roman Catholic Church in 1935.

The main conflict of the story is King Henry VIII's decision to marry Anne Boleyn and the pressure he puts on his officials, including More, the Lord Chancellor, to accept and approve his divorce from the Queen and his remarriage to Anne. In good conscience, Thomas cannot and does not accept the King's plans, for those plans disagree with God's will: "'I hate divorce,' says the Lord God of Israel" (Malachi 2:16).

The Pope also refuses the king's request, so Henry makes himself the spiritual leader of England. More stands against Henry VIII's self-proclaimed status as the head of the Church of England.

The bishops of England soon acquiesce in the founding of the new church, and More hands in his resignation. The king then demands that More sign a writ of allegiance to him as head of church and state. More refuses and is quickly locked in the Tower of London.

More's faith affects his morals and guides his decisions, at the cost of his political career and, eventually, his life. In this respect, he follows in the footsteps of the apostles who did not rebel against authority, but accepted the human consequences (even unto death) of their decisions to obey God when God's Law conflicted with man's.

The screenwriter reveals More's incarnational character through his relationships as well as by his decisions. More is a lawyer and judge who is known for his fairness in the courts. He shows kindness and generosity to the boatmen who ferry him from the court to his country home. However, More has little sympathy for others, who forfeit personal integrity for advancement in government.

More is depicted as a man of faith. He prays with his wife and daughter before he leaves home to see the Chancellor. His prayer is unpretentious, simple, and even humorous. More displays Christ-like virtues in his personal and business relationships. His wife and daughter treat him with love and respect, and his friend Norfolk admires him, although he does not always understand More's personal convictions. The King regards More as a man who will tell the truth, but Henry refuses to be dissuaded from marrying Anne, and he does not let Sir Thomas stand in his way.

Though More is a strong character, he is also vulnerable. Through the persistence of his enemies in court, More is finally put in prison where, over a period of time he grows weaker physically. In the scene where More says goodbye to his family, he breaks down and weeps. In his time of fear and pain, More proves he is made of the same flesh as anyone else, but even though he knows death awaits him, Sir Thomas remains true to his faith.

He is tranquil and forgiving of the hooded man who takes his life, but he makes an impassioned speech against the actions of the king and his cronies, whom he feels are acting in the worst interests of God. More paid for his religious beliefs by having his head exhibited on London Bridge, though by that time he was with Christ, so:

> The perishable has been clothed with the imperishable, and the mortal with immortality, then the saying that is written will come true: 'Death has been swallowed up in victory.' (1 Corinthians 15:54)

☆☆☆ **MASTERPIECE** ☆☆☆

TITLE:	**MANON OF THE SPRING (Subtitles)**
QUALITY:	★★★★
RECOMMENDATION:	Caution
RATING:	PG
RELEASE:	1987
STARRING:	Emmanuelle Beart and Yves Montand
DIRECTOR:	Claude Berri
GENRE:	Drama/Historical
CONTENT:	Strong Biblical perspective, but some brief, distant nudity
INTENDED AUDIENCE:	Adults
REVIEWER:	Ted Baehr

Jean de Florette and its second part, *Manon of the Spring*, constitute one of the great Biblical epics of the decade, focusing on the moral and ethical values which govern the lives of everyday people living in a small French town. The depth of realism, the essence of the human personalities and the faithfulness to Biblical justice in these films is extraordinary.

Manon is the daughter of Jean de Florette, who died because his greedy neighbors, the Soubeyrans, cemented the spring on Jean's mother's farmland just before Jean claimed his inheritance. Cesar (nicknamed Papet) and his nephew Ugilon are the perpetrators of this travesty which forced her father to work himself to death trying to be a good steward of his inheritance.

Manon discovers their culpability and longs for revenge, serving as a shepherdess in the care of a local gypsy. Through a unique circumstance, she finds the source of the water for the town. She blocks the spring off, driving the town to its knees.

During a sermon which proclaims Jesus as Lord, the local priest chastises the residents for attending church only when it serves their self-interest, and accuses them of perpetrating injustices against their fellow man. This sermon brings out the truth. Ugilon, who has fallen in love with the beautiful Manon, commits suicide. Cezar learns from an old blind woman that Jean de Florette was more closely related to the town than anyone knew.

Although the miracles in this movie are not spontaneous Epiphanies, there are no accidents, or coincidences, either, for it is clear that God is the God of justice who acts through people to bring the unjust to judgment. The fact that the residents interpret Manon's revenge as an act of God seems to be a denial of miracles, but, on reflection, it becomes clear that God acts through Manon's revenge and repentance, as well as the intricate relationships in the town. There is a deeper theology here than the superficial magic which so often blinds people to the truth of God's mercy, grace, and justice.

It would be wonderful to recommend this powerful story of repentance and forgiveness without reservation. *Jean de Florette* and *Manon of the Spring* together offer one of the most

Biblical views of sin, judgment, and repentance ever seen in a film. However, *Manon of the Spring* must be recommended with caution because of a brief, innocent nude scene of the young Manon arising from a bath in a mountain spring, watched at a great distance by her nemesis. This non-erotic nudity demands that we not recommend this film.

☆☆☆ MASTERPIECE ☆☆☆

TITLE:	**THE MAN WHO SHOT LIBERTY VALANCE (Black and White)**
QUALITY:	★★★★
RECOMMENDATION:	Acceptable
RATING:	Not rated
RELEASE:	1962
STARRING:	James Stewart, John Wayne, Vera Miles, Lee Marvin, Edmond O'Brien, and Andy Devine
DIRECTOR:	John Ford
GENRE:	Western
CONTENT:	Nothing objectionable
INTENDED AUDIENCE:	All ages
REVIEWER:	Ted Baehr

This film has been called the last of the great black-and-white westerns. Like many of director John Ford's later efforts, it is a sentimental reunion. Much of the cast had appeared in earlier Ford films.

Stewart plays an lawyer who unwittingly rids a community of a monumentally evil man. It is John Wayne who actually pulls the strings.

This film is a masterful return to a noble genre by the man who practically invented it. You will love it.

TITLE:	**MARLENE**
QUALITY:	★★★
RECOMMENDATION:	Acceptable
RATING:	None
RELEASE:	1987
STARRING:	Marlene Dietrich and Maximilian Schell
DIRECTOR:	Maximilian Schell
GENRE:	Documentary
CONTENT:	Nothing objectionable
INTENDED AUDIENCE:	Adults
REVIEWER:	Ted Baehr

Marlene is a captivating film about the aging star, Marlene Dietrich. Throughout this documentary, which is partially in English and partially subtitled, Maximilian Schell has difficulty getting Marlene to reveal her true self.

There are some appealing aspects, such as Marlene's negative attitude toward psychology and her common sense attitude about feminism. There is also much which is disturbing, especially Marlene's rejection of God and her resignation to nihilism.

The clips from her old movies are splendid and show the beauty and seductive power of Marlene Dietrich. Marlene denies that she ever intended to be seductive; however, in her films, she is sexually appealing and captivating. She also denies her acting talent, yet it's clear from her scenes that she was a great actress.

For the most part, she is a person of positive, conservative drives. During WW II, she joined the American Army to fight against the Nazis. She believes in marriage. She doesn't believe in sexual promiscuity. She thinks most movies are rubbish.

This is an important film for anybody who wants to know about motion pictures. It is important to see how Hollywood manipulates people and how Marlene rose above Hollywood, and yet is trapped in her own nihilism and loneliness.

Often, Marlene lies about her past. These lies are easily discovered, such as her reducing the number of her silent films and denying the existence of her older sister. These lies amuse the secular critics, but should disturb Christians. Marlene has a strong moral worldview, but that worldview is not based on a renewed heart full of Truth. Marlene postures throughout the movie to try to command the most respect.

Marlene is highly recommended. See it if you have the opportunity and love movies.

TITLE:	**MARRIED TO THE MOB**
QUALITY:	★ ★ ★
RECOMMENDATION:	Extreme Caution
RATING:	R
RELEASE:	1988
STARRING:	Michelle Pfeiffer, Matthew Moudine, and Dean Stockwell
DIRECTOR:	Johnathan Demme
GENRE:	Comedy
CONTENT:	Nudity and profanity
INTENDED AUDIENCE:	Adults
REVIEWER:	Bret Senft

Angela is married to mobster Frank "The Cucumber" DeMarco. Frank dandles with "Tony-the-Tiger" Rousso's moll and snuffs it. Angela donates her worldly goods to charity and sets off for Lower Manhattan. She is trailed by FBI dog face, Mike Downey. Angela falls for him: they dance the night away at a local East Village dive and fall asleep in each other's arms. Downey spills all, and innocent Angela, trying to get clean of the mob and raise her ten-year-old son, agrees to bring Tony Rousso to justice in a contrived Sting Operation in swinging Miami Beach. Angela gets nerdy Mike; Rousso appears before the grand jury. It's happy ending time.

Director Demme lampoons Hollywood style mobster theatrics: the bad guys can't shoot straight, but get taken out with one shot from the lead characters. Winking at the audience, Demme leads Angela toward success against insurmountable odds.

We cannot recommend *Married to the Mob* because of some brief nudity and profanity. We suggest that you wait until it is edited for television.

TITLE:	**MATADOR (Subtitles)**
QUALITY:	★
RECOMMENDATION:	Evil
RATING:	Not rated
RELEASE:	1988
STARRING:	
DIRECTOR:	Pedro Almovodar
GENRE:	Drama
CONTENT:	Nudity, sex, violence, sexual perversion, and other evils
INTENDED AUDIENCE:	Adults
REVIEWER:	Nancy Hanger

This is the kind of film that produces Ted Bundys. Please stay away from *Matador*. Lots of secular reviewers are praising the films of Pedro Almovodar, but he is using graphic pornographic sex and violence to "entertain" the public, and the unwitting public is learning to accept this evil.

I was unable to sit through this film, but saw enough in the beginning to be able to state unequivocally that this film must be boycotted. The nudity and violence was shocking beyond anything I have ever reviewed. Take a stand against pornography: Boycott *Matador* and Almovodar.

TITLE:	**MATEWAN (132 Minutes)**
QUALITY:	★★★★
RECOMMENDATION:	Caution
RATING:	PG
RELEASE:	1987
STARRING:	Chris Cooper, Will Oldham, and James Earl Jones
DIRECTOR:	John Sayles
GENRE:	Historical
CONTENT:	Some violence and some off-color language
INTENDED AUDIENCE:	Adults
REVIEWER:	Loralee Lindley

Matewan is based on a true story of the coal mining town of Matewan, West Virginia. The Stone Mountain Coal Company decides to bring in immigrant Italians as cheap labor and cut the locals' pay. A group of black miners along with union organizer Joe Kenehan arrive to organize the miners to stand up to the coal company. The story is alive with the miners' struggle for a decent life.

Notable is the young preacher, Danny, who is one of the most positive Christian characters in a recent film. The dichotomy between evil and good is clearly depicted in this film.

We recommend *Matewan* to mature Christians with two warnings. The first is be ready for some bloody scenes. The other reservation of note is that Kenehan, who admits he is a communist, is painted as a savior of sorts. Like many contemporary movies Marxism is offered up as the solution to man's problems, when, in Truth, the only solution for man's problems is Jesus Christ.

Danny and the references to Christ may have been inserted to influence Christians with a form of heretical Marxist contextual theology in accordance with the communist drive to infiltrate the church. If you hold fast to the truth that only the blood of Jesus offers salvation, not unionizing, nor communism, nor the other philosophies of men, then *Matewan* has much to offer and will not deceive you with a false gospel.

TITLE:	**MAURICE**
QUALITY:	★ ★ ★
RECOMMENDATION:	Evil
RATING:	R
RELEASE:	1987
STARRING:	James Wilby, Hugh Grant, and Rupert Graves
DIRECTOR:	James Ivory
GENRE:	Drama
CONTENT:	Homosexual behavior
INTENDED AUDIENCE:	Adults
REVIEWER:	Laura Lindley

Maurice is a God-fearing young man at Cambridge confronted by a hedonistic student. Intrigued by the sinful bait, Maurice falls into the Devil's trap. He befriends the man's roommate, and the three become friends. Insidiously, the two tear down Maurice's Christian beliefs and ridicule them as fables. In their place, they offer vapid pseudo-superior idolatry, hedonism, and intellectual promises placing man at the center of the universe. Maurice falls under their sway, and Maurice is booted out of Cambridge as he becomes insubordinate and rebellious. Maurice becomes obsessed with homosexual ideals.

Tell your friends, Christian and non-Christian, to boycott *Maurice* because of its degenerate moral nature. This film is a tool of the Devil.

TITLE:	**MEMORIES OF ME**
QUALITY:	★★★
RECOMMENDATION:	Caution
RATING:	PG-13
RELEASE:	1988
STARRING:	Alan King and Billy Crystal
DIRECTOR:	Henry Winkler
GENRE:	Drama
CONTENT:	Profanity, obscenity, and sexual humor
INTENDED AUDIENCE:	Adults
REVIEWER:	John Evans, Preview's Movie Morality Guide.

Abe Polin is an aging comedian. He's a likable guy, but his son, Abbie, a young doctor, describes him as a "public embarrassment." Abbie decides to visit his dad more out of obligation than anything else. Abbie's girlfriend, Lisa, follows him to Los Angeles. The three have a fun, but rather turbulent, visit together. Their fun is muted, when Abbie discovers his dad has a serious brain disorder. This adds a touching note to this otherwise lighthearted, energetic comedy. Though Abe is facing death, it's sad that he has no spiritual base to sustain him during these times.

Being a comic, the older Abe takes great delight in quips and one liners. On occasion, they become off-color and sexually suggestive. Furthermore, crude and vulgar language are used a number of times. Also, Abbie and Lisa have a sexual relationship along with their romantic attachment. Sex is implied, but no nudity is shown.

Memories of Me portrays the loving relationship which develops between a father and his son, but is too flawed to merit our recommendation.

☆☆☆ CLASSIC ☆☆☆

TITLE:	**MERRILL'S MARAUDERS**
QUALITY:	★★★★
RECOMMENDATION:	Caution
RATING:	Not rated
RELEASE:	1962
STARRING:	Jeff Chandler, Ty Hardin, Peter Brown, and Andrew Dugan
DIRECTOR:	Samuel Fuller
GENRE:	War
CONTENT:	Battlefields with bloody and dead bodies

INTENDED AUDIENCE: Adult

REVIEWER: Protestant Motion Picture Council

This is an engrossing war drama about one of the most high-priced episodes of WW II in human lives. The exploits of the famous Merrill's Marauders in the Burma campaign are depicted with realism. The two-year effort to dislodge the Japanese from Burma is shown as the gruelling, decimating, heroic enterprise that it was.

In Burma in 1944, General Frank Merrill commands a 3,000 man regiment deep behind Japanese lines. Though exhausted by their long trek through the jungle, the men capture their objective like the well-trained, experienced fighting men they are.

As they sit resting, expecting to be relieved, Merrill receives orders to march them several more miles to capture a rail yard at Shadzup, and then on to Myitkina. He tells the men about Shadzup but doesn't tell them about the second objective.

By the time they reach their objective, the Myitkina airstrip, the unit was composed of 100 men estimated to be fit. Most of the few survivors were riddled with disease and wounds, but their feat of endurance, at a fearful price, is thought to be one of the turning points of the war.

This film is based on true facts and true people. It points up the heroism of ordinary mortals while being a shattering experience to watch.

A good many insertions of actual war shots increase the feeling of authenticity, even though it was filmed in the Philippines with the cooperation of the U.S. Army's Special forces and the Philippines armed forces.

This film is well directed and acted with superior Technicolor photography.

☆☆☆ MASTERPIECE ☆☆☆

TITLE:	**METROPOLIS (Black and White, Silent Feature)**
QUALITY:	★ ★ ★ ★
RECOMMENDATION:	Acceptable
RATING:	Not rated
RELEASE:	1927 (Germany)
STARRING:	Alfred Abel, Brigitte Helm, Gustav Frohlich, Rudolf Klein-Rogge, Theodore Loos, and Heinrich George
DIRECTOR:	Fritz Lang
GENRE:	Science fiction
CONTENT:	Nothing objectionable
INTENDED AUDIENCE:	Adult
REVIEWER:	Ted Baehr

Metropolis opens on a 1927 rendition of an futuristic, art-deco city of the year 2000. The sky is almost blotted out by the immense architecture. Quartered below are the workers.

Identically uniformed, they toil around the clock, cogs in the machines that power the city.

Metropolis is full of Biblical symbolism and allegory. The city represents heaven and earth, as well as the caste distinctions to be found in a mercantilist/socialist state. Maria preaches reconciliation and new life through the intervention of a mediator between the rulers and the people, between God and man. Rotwang, the priest/scientist, wants to be like God by creating creatures who will serve him. He is the Adversary who wants to make the world over in his image. Freder becomes the mediator, Christ-like and full of love, ready to sacrifice himself to save the children and Maria. Freder reconciles Jon to the workers, and the workers to Jon. The robot is the revolutionary leader who sows discord, not peace. Her lies incite the people to rebel.

As Adam Smith, the father of the free market, did in his *Wealth of Nations*, the filmmakers in *Metropolis* rebuke mercantilism wherein the bonds of privilege wed the rulers of the state and the rulers of the socialized business cartels. This film calls for reconciliation and freedom of opportunity so people work together in partnership. This movie rebukes the mercantilism which was rearing its ugly head as National Socialism in Germany, and its cousin International Socialism which was devouring Russia.

The film sternly condemns revolution and the revolutionary leader, the robot Maria, a counterfeit savior in the tradition of Barabbas, Hitler and Lenin, who leads the people to death and destruction. At the same time, it lifts up the Mediator and Reconciler, who comes not to sow discord, but to bring peace.

There are many levels of symbolism in this masterpiece, which are fun and enlightening to explore. However, in the final analysis all the elements have been woven together into a seamless fabric which is a delight to behold and a pleasure to watch. For this reason, *Metropolis* has stood the test of time and is as popular today as when it was made, even though it is a silent film.

☆☆☆ CLASSIC ☆☆☆

TITLE:	**MIDNIGHT LACE**
QUALITY:	★★★
RECOMMENDATION:	Caution
RATING:	Not rated
RELEASE:	1960
STARRING:	Doris Day, Rex Harrison, John Gavin, Myrna Loy, and Roddy McDowall
DIRECTOR:	David Miller
GENRE:	Suspense/Drama
CONTENT:	Adult situations
INTENDED AUDIENCE:	Adults and mature young people
REVIEWER:	Protestant Motion Picture Council

The American wife of a British financier hears a mysterious voice trailing her through thick London fog. It warns her of impending death. This occurrence is followed by accidents, telephone threats, and fear-inducing episodes. Eventually, it is intimated that these might be the imagined obsessions of an unbalanced mind if not outright lies.

This is the main theme of a mystery whose plot finally leads to the exposure of the least expected. It is a thriller produced in a refined way, with excellent acting, in authentic settings and with cumulative suspense.

TITLE:	**MIDNIGHT RUN**
QUALITY:	★★★
RECOMMENDATION:	Extreme Caution
RATING:	R
RELEASE:	1988
STARRING:	Robert DeNiro, Charles Grodin, Yaphet Kotto, and John Ashton
DIRECTOR:	Martin Brest
GENRE:	Action adventure/Detective
CONTENT:	No nudity, mild violence, but excessive profanity, vulgarity, and obscenity
INTENDED AUDIENCE:	Adults
REVIEWER:	Bruce Grimes

This is an entertaining blend of story, characters, and action fouled by excessive bad language. Jack Walsh is a bounty hunter, who is hired to bring in John "The Duke." John embezzled 15 million dollars from the mob, who wants him dead. The F.B.I. wants John for the information he has: John was the mob's accountant.

Jack tracks John, cuffs him, and off they go to the airport. For the next hour, Jack and John elude hundreds of pursuing mobsters, sheriffs, F.B.I. agents, even Jack's bounty hunter friends. Jack and John return to L.A., where the F.B.I. pins criminal charges on the leading mobster. In the confusion, Jack releases John, realizing he was trying to do something right, though trapped by his situation.

It is unfortunate that this film is so marred by filthy language. We cannot recommend it for anyone. Edited for television, it would be entertaining.

☆☆☆ CLASSIC ☆☆☆

TITLE:	**A MIDSUMMER NIGHT'S DREAM**
QUALITY:	★★★★
RECOMMENDATION:	Acceptable
RATING:	Not rated
RELEASE:	1961 (Czechoslovakia)

VOICES:	Richard Burton, Tom Criddle, Ann Bell, Michael Meachem, John Warner, Barbara Leigh-Hunt, Hugh Manning, and Alec McGowan
DIRECTOR:	Jiri Trnka and Howard Sackler
GENRE:	Children/Puppet film
CONTENT:	Supernatural fairies and magic
INTENDED AUDIENCE:	Children
REVIEWER:	Protestant Motion Picture Council

A fairy tale fantasy of the familiar Shakespeare play, this film is an ingenious and superlative animated puppet show. This is a beguiling way to enjoy Shakespeare, as this little masterpiece has a charm all its own.

In Cinemascope and Eastman color, the settings are imaginative, and the characters move sometimes by unearthly journeys through space, as puppets should. The story is told clearly and beautifully by Richard Burton, and the voices of the other characters are those of other Old Victorian players. Vaclav Trojan has composed a musical score with a modern touch.

A Midsummer Night's Dream, believed to have been performed at London's Globe theater circa 1565, involves creatures of the forest, chiefly fairies, and artisans who plan to put on a play to amuse the royal court.

Egeus demands that Hermia marry Demetrius, despite the fact that she is in love with Lysander. Unless she goes through with the nuptials, Theseus, the Duke of Athens, will severely punish her. Theseus himself is planning to marry Hippolyta, Queen of the Amazons. Hermia and Lysander elope, escaping to the forest, and Demetrius pursues them.

Meanwhile, the local artisans enter the forest to rehearse the play they intend to perform for Theseus' wedding. The rulers of the forest, the supernatural fairies, come to life. Their monarchs, Oberon and Titania, are quarreling. In a fit of pique during the lovers' squabble, Oberon orders the mischievous Puck to squeeze the juice of a passion flower into Titania's eyes so that she will fall madly in love with the first creature that she sees when awakening.

Puck, to complicate matters, playfully turns one of the local artisans, Bottom, into part animal, changing his head into that of an ass. This is the creature Titania first spots and instantly adores. Puck also uses the magic potion to alter the affections of the four lovers, so that Hermia and Lysander begin to hate each other.

Not until Oberon, Titania, Puck, and the scores of fairies in their netherworld kingdom depart the forest do things get back to normal. Bottom regains his head, and the lovers are reunited.

TITLE:	**THE MIGHTY QUINN**
QUALITY:	★ ★ ★
RECOMMENDATION:	Caution
RATING:	R
RELEASE:	1989

STARRING:	Denzel Washington, James Fox, Mimi Rogers, M. Emmet Walsh, and Robert Townsend
DIRECTOR:	Carl Schenkel
GENRE:	Detective
CONTENT:	Profanity and sexual references
INTENDED AUDIENCE:	Adults
REVIEWER:	Ted Baehr

Set in the Bahamas, *The Mighty Quinn* features a black police chief, Xaviar Quinn, fighting for truth and justice in a world of corruption. Quinn knows the difference between good and evil and persists in choosing the good. He stands out among his lawless peers.

He is investigating the murder of a white American billionaire, Donald Pater. Mr. Elgin, the manager of the resort where Mr. Pater was murdered, insists it is a simple case of the drifter, Maubee, killing Pater. Quinn realizes the case goes deeper than a simple island robbery/murder. The governor insists Quinn drop the case. Quinn persists. He is dedicated to justice. Although he is tempted often, he resists. In the end, good triumphs. In the processs, there is much good humor and enjoyable music.

This is a movie that we would like to recommend, since the movie demonstrates that justice is more important than compromise. There is no nudity, nor sex out of wedlock. However, there is profanity, so we can only caution you about this movie which is striving for morality. You will want to wait until *The Mighty Quinn* is edited for television.

TITLE:	**THE MILAGRO BEANFIELD WAR**
QUALITY:	★ ★
RECOMMENDATION:	Extreme Caution
RATING:	R
RELEASE:	1988
STARRING:	Ruben Blades, Christopher Walken, and Carlos Riquelme
DIRECTOR:	Robert Redford
GENRE:	Drama
CONTENT:	Profanity, idolatry, and confused supernatural socialism
INTENDED AUDIENCE:	Adults
REVIEWER:	Wendell B. Rhodes

The "good guys," a poor town and a leftover 60's activist, take on the "bad guys," a businessman in cahoots with politicians. The conflict begins when a poor peasant, Joe, kicks over a water canal sluice gate which proceeds to illegally irrigate his beanfield. The bad guys organize themselves to stop him from making a success of his farm so they can force him out and build a resort. When the conflict is finally resolved, you walk out of the theater with a resounding "Huh?"

The movie begins with a positive note, with old Aramante thanking God for another day of living. Unfortunately, Christianity is later equated with idolatry and spiritualism. Also, viewers should pay close attention to the film's view of authority and protest. I would like to recommend this film for its rich characters and culture. However, I caution Christians in regard to its clouding of the Christian worldview.

Another offense would be the unnecessary language. Robert Redford insisted on including profanity which the studio wanted removed to include families. Christians should take a stand to show that we will not pay to hear our Lord's Name taken in vain.

TITLE:	**MILLENIUM**
QUALITY:	★★
RECOMMENDATION:	Extreme Caution
RATING:	R
RELEASE:	1989
STARRING:	Kris Kristofferson, Cheryl Ladd, and Daniel J. Travanti
DIRECTOR:	Michael Anderson
GENRE:	Science fiction
CONTENT:	Profanity and nudity
INTENDED AUDIENCE:	Adults
REVIEWER:	Ted Baehr

Millenium is so high on concept it is very thin on story. The concept is: time travel into the past would change the present and the future.

Bill Smith is a top FAA official investigating a plane crash. The flight recorder and several digital watches running backwards suggest something is wrong. He questions a beautiful, mysterious stewardess who takes him to bed to get him off the investigation.

The stewardess, Louise Baltimore, came from the future where everyone is dying. It is her job to come back to our age to take people off planes that are about to crash, and ship them to the future to re-populate the world. Her sloppy workmanship left too many clues, and now she has to cover up.

There are several bungled travels through time, each one causing a paradox which ripples through the future-present bringing devastating changes. Louise and Bill fall in love. This destroys her future, so they're both sent to a new millenium where they can be together forever. Of course, no one cares about the thousands of extras who are left behind in the future she has destroyed.

We do not recommend *Millenium* because it's boring and there is profanity and nudity. We don't need *Millenium* II, III, IV and V.

TITLE:	**MILLION DOLLAR MYSTERY**
QUALITY:	★★
RECOMMENDATION:	Caution

RATING:	PG
RELEASE:	1987
STARRING:	Tom Bosley, Royce Appelgate, Pam Matteson, and Rick Overton
DIRECTOR:	Richard Fletcher
GENRE:	Comedy
CONTENT:	Some off-color language and crass commercialism
INTENDED AUDIENCE:	All ages
REVIEWER:	Ken Kistner

A nerdish, newlywed couple, a preppy couple and their son, and a would-be manager with three busty, blonde, backup singers stumble into a roadside cafe. A former White House aide, Sidney Preston, enters and orders a bowl of chili. He identifies the cook's secret ingredient—beer. The cook's sister warns him about heartburn, but he has a heart attack. For a kiss, he reveals a clue as to where four, separate, one-million-dollar stashes are hidden.

Greed seizes everyone in the cafe, and the predictable race for the money ensues. In the rush, each of our gold-seekers, except our newlyweds, looses his/her means of transportation and has to hitch rides with weird characters. Boring car chases and gags follow. Three of the four-million dollar stashes are found and lost to the wind, or a paper shredder. However, there are one million dollars still out there, and clues to its whereabouts are given in the movie. The audience is called to win the missing million dollars by solving the mystery.

Million Dollar Mystery is too predictable. In the final analysis, *Million Dollar Mystery* is not worth your time or money.

TITLE:	**MIO IN THE LAND OF FARAWAY**
QUALITY:	★ ★ ★ ★
RECOMMENDATION:	Acceptable
RATING:	G
RELEASE:	1988
STARRING:	Timothy Bottoms, Susannah York, Christopher Lee, and Nicholas Pickard
DIRECTOR:	Vladimir Grammatikov
GENRE:	Children/Animated
CONTENT:	Nothing Objectionable
INTENDED AUDIENCE:	All ages
REVIEWER:	Bruce Grimes

The King rules over a peaceful land, but tells his son, Mio, of the Evil King. Pure in heart, Mio knows that he must kill the Evil King, and sets out on a journey of unexpected adventures. With his best friend, he encounters such intrigues as "the most hungry man in the world" and the endless catacombs. They eventually reach the Evil castle, a brooding mass of stone set on an island. They are captured by the King's henchmen. With the aid of a sword made of perfected steel, Mio defeats the Evil King.

Not only is this movie well made, but it conveys numerous moral statements such as the value of the family, loyalty, courage, right over wrong, good over evil, and altruism versus greed. The story relies on fantasy to propel it, but not in a negative or demonic way. It is reminiscent of C.S. Lewis' fantasies *The Chronicles of Narnia*.

Mio in the Land of Faraway is exciting, creative family entertainment which is highly recommended.

TITLE:	**MISS FIRECRACKER**
QUALITY:	★★★
RECOMMENDATION:	Caution
RATING:	PG
RELEASE:	1989
STARRING:	Holly Hunter, Scott Glenn, Mary Steenburgen, and Tim Robbins
DIRECTOR:	Thomas Schlamme
GENRE:	Comedy/Drama
CONTENT:	Profanity
INTENDED AUDIENCE:	Adults
REVIEWER:	Ted Baehr

Miss Firecracker is a character study about the meaning of life, which concludes that our only hope is eternal grace. The movie opens with Molly, who was orphaned at a young age and has grown up with her cousins. She has no self-respect. She is desperate for love; however, she renounced sex as the answer and has just gone back to attending church.

She thinks her problems will be solved if she wins the Miss Firecracker beauty pageant. Everybody laughs at her. Her cousin Elaine, who won the pageant many years before, spends all her time preening and mocking Molly. Her other cousin, Delmont, puts down everyone he sees with an intense intellectual cynicism.

Surprisingly, Molly gets into the finals. She doesn't win, but she does find out that the answer is God's grace.

This movie has no sex, nudity, or violence. However, it does have some profanity and obscenity. This is unfortunate because it is clear that the writer was trying to draw people toward God with the story.

In fact, the movie leaves one in tears . . . joyous tears because Molly has discovered God's grace. Please pray that the next film by this team deletes the profanity so that we can recommend it.

TITLE:	**MISSION TO GLORY**
QUALITY:	★ ★ ★
RECOMMENDATION:	Acceptable
RATING:	PG
RELEASE:	1988
STARRING:	Ricardo Montalban, Cesar Romero, Rory Calhoun, Michael Ansara, Keenan Wynn, and Richard Egan
DIRECTOR:	Ken Kennedy
GENRE:	Historical
CONTENT:	Religious history of California
INTENDED AUDIENCE:	All ages, but especially youth who are learning about the early explorers
REVIEWER:	Betty Hill

Over 300 years ago, Padre Franciso Kin blazed a trail into unknown territory as a mapmaker, astronomer, and a man of God. Lower California became his mission. He proclaimed, "I want to bring them everlasting life."

In 1684, Padre Francisco Kin sails up the Pacific Coast trying to locate California. He brings trinkets for the Indians. He also brings Conquistadors. The Padre helps the Indians upgrade their lives. The Indians show the Padre how to irrigate crops. Scurvy breaks out, and the mission is abandoned. Padre returns to Mexico, where he writes a dictionary of the Indian language.

When the Padre returns, a chief requests that Kin stay with his people. This Christian chief is a gracious host, and a mission church is built.

A soldier with a cross around his neck impulsively attacks a Pima. The Pima's house is burned, and he is beaten. The Pima is angry and asks "How could a Christian have done this?" The Padre replies, "Some Christians aren't Christians."

When the same Indian is beaten again, he goes into a rage and burns the mission church. Another Padre is martyred. Padre Franciso proclaims, "Those responsible . . . must pay. . . . However, in our haste for justice, we must be sure only the guilty are punished. If we allow a slaughter for revenge, we will have lost . . . these people." The innocent Pimas listening to the Padre are massacred. The Pima respond by attacking the Conquistadors. The Padre is trusted by both, so he is sent to negotiate a peace.

Padre Francisco served in California for twenty-seven years. In his years of sacrifice, he gave of himself freely and generously. He came to a desert and spread the Word of God far and wide, bringing the promise of life everlasting.

TITLE:	**MISSISSIPPI BURNING**
QUALITY:	★ ★ ★ ★
RECOMMENDATION:	Extreme Caution

RATING:	R
RELEASE:	1988
STARRING:	Gene Hackman, Willem Dafoe, Brad Dourif, and Frances McDormand
DIRECTOR:	Alan Parker
GENRE:	Detective
CONTENT:	Obscenity, profanity, and violence
INTENDED AUDIENCE:	Adults
REVIEWER:	Troy Schmidt

The most frightening aspect of *Mississippi Burning* occurs in the opening moments; a date flashes "1964" across a black background . . . A little over twenty years ago. We've come a long way since then . . . we hope.

Mississippi Burning begins with the execution of two Jewish activists and their black friend after they try registering blacks to vote in a tiny Mississippi town. Gene Hackman and Willem Dafoe appear as two FBI agents sent to investigate the murders and find themselves up against an uncooperative town full of hate and suspicion. *Mississippi Burning* shows the pain of the victims when prejudice rules our lives.

Violence and profanity run free in this film. Also, the Bible is denigrated as the source of racism. On the contrary, bigotry flows from the sin which is inherent in every human being, and which is alleviated only by the shed blood of Jesus Christ. Neither law nor education will deliver us from our sinful natures. Only Jesus can reconcile us to God and others. The Bible is His Word written and testifies to this Truth.

The movie is based on a true story. However, the protagonists are an invention of the scriptwriter, and significant elements have been fictionalized.

☆☆☆ CLASSIC ☆☆☆

TITLE:	**MR. HOBBS TAKES A VACATION**
QUALITY:	★★★
RECOMMENDATION:	Acceptable
RATING:	Not rated
RELEASE:	1962
STARRING:	Jimmy Stewart, Maureen O'Hara, Fabian, Laurie Peters, Lili Gentle, John Saxon, and John McGiver
DIRECTOR:	Henry Koster
GENRE:	Comedy
CONTENT:	Drinking
INTENDED AUDIENCE:	Adults
REVIEWER:	Protestant Motion Picture Council

A St. Louis banker goes on a summer vacation with all the members of his family. His plan is to help renew the family ties, loyalties, and mutual acquaintances by taking a cottage on the West Coast seashore for thirty days of rest and relaxation, but it hardly turns out that way.

Jimmy Stewart shows himself to be a good, solid father in this satire on "togetherness" as he bumbles, comforts, connives, uses strong language, and partakes often from the contents of a well-stocked liquor cabinet. The relationship between these assorted characters is excellent. The philosophy of the paterfamilias is balanced between love, devotion and humility and a justifiable determination to confine his concern and activities to his good and loving wife, relinquishing responsibility over the growing-up agonies of his bewildering offspring.

There is humor, some of it very broad, and tenderness. The acting is good and amusement is plentiful. However, we object to the drinking and the some of the humor.

TITLE:	**MR. NORTH**
QUALITY:	★ ★
RECOMMENDATION:	Caution
RATING:	PG
RELEASE:	1988
STARRING:	Anthony Edwards, Robert Mitchum, Lauren Bacall, and Harry Dean Stanton
DIRECTOR:	Danny Huston
GENRE:	Drama
CONTENT:	Some off-color language
INTENDED AUDIENCE:	All ages
REVIEWER:	Bret Senft

Mr. North is a fairy tale set in Newport, RI in the 1920's. Theophilus North has a grand time: righting wrongs, healing the sick and exposing sham. A young girl suffers anxiety at the thought of being a debutante. A family patriarch is virtually imprisoned in his mansion by his scheming daughter, intent on securing her inheritance as quickly as possible. A young maid weeps over her true love, the heir to a family fortune in Boston. Mr. North sets them right. Mr. North holds no magical powers, he simply cuts through the sham of Newport society and provides enough fresh air to cure the entire town.

This film is a world of stagey performances. Dramatic action seems secondhand. This is a two-dimensional film. This film misses too many beats, muffles too many emotions and drops too many climatic moments to hold an audience. Danny Huston stifles the drama in his story and thus wastes an opportunity to give us a great film. *Mr. North* is far too staged to be of any worldly good.

☆☆☆ **MASTERPIECE** ☆☆☆

TITLE:	**MR. SMITH GOES TO WASHINGTON**
QUALITY:	★★★★
RECOMMENDATION:	Acceptable
RATING:	Not rated
RELEASE:	1939
STARRING:	Jimmy Stewart, Claude Rains, Jean Arthur, Harry Carey, Thomas Mitchell, and Beulah Bond
DIRECTOR:	Frank Capra
GENRE:	Drama
CONTENT:	Nothing objectionable
INTENDED AUDIENCE:	Adults
REVIEWER:	Bruce Grimes

Frank Capra, who later would direct Stewart and Mitchell in his finest achievement, *It's a Wonderful Life*, brings the corruption of Washington to the screen in this dramatic comedy.

Jefferson Smith (Jimmy Stewart) is chosen by the political machine to fill the shoes of an outgoing Senator, but only as a rubber stamp for the bigwigs. Smith, a young man of principle and dignity, refuses to compromise his position and tries to expose the corruption.

Aided by Jean Arthur, plus Capra's voice of wisdom (much like his use of the narrator in *It's a Wonderful Life*), Smith manages to survive, and salvage his democratic principles.

The film has one of the more memorable scenes ever filmed, when Smith, a hesitant, stammering figure filibusters his plan for a boys' camp for hours on end—only to eventually collapse. With Claude Rains' eloquent magnetism and speaking powers confronting Smith, it suggests Smith's innocence and frailty as he is assaulted by the power brokers.

When the film opened in Washington, D.C., Columbia Pictures was almost forced to withdraw it because of the negative reaction it received, including its assault on the "dignity" of government. However, *Mr. Smith Goes to Washington* went on to become a huge success. Jimmy Stewart received his first Oscar nomination for his performance. Also nominated were Capra for Best Director, the film for Best Picture, and two other nominations.

TITLE:	**A MONTH IN THE COUNTRY**
QUALITY:	★★★
RECOMMENDATION:	Caution
RATING:	Not rated
RELEASE:	1988

STARRING:	Colin Firth and Kenneth Branagh
DIRECTOR:	Pat O'Connor
GENRE:	Drama
CONTENT:	Nothing Objectionable
INTENDED AUDIENCE:	Adults
REVIEWER:	Bruce Grimes

Set in the English countryside after WW I, this story captures the pain that the "Great War" has left on two foot soldiers, one who has become a restorer of paintings, the other an amateur archaeologist. Birkin and Moon meet in a churchyard, where Moon has set up his field tent to excavate the grounds in order to locate an ancient grave. Birkin is restoring a lost fresco. His past haunts him as he stutters during conversations with the church rector, and nightmares awaken him in cold sweat.

This is a mournful, symbolic film, very hushed in its tone and tenor. The gray Yorkshire skies over the subtle green fields add to the subject it addresses: wounded men seeking redemption from a painful past. A few expletives dot this film, but nothing else is objectionable. The film does give "food for thought," and *A Month in the Country* is recommended as a portrait of the human condition.

TITLE:	**MOON OVER PARADOR**
QUALITY:	★★
RECOMMENDATION:	Extreme Caution
RATING:	PG-13
RELEASE:	1988
STARRING:	Richard Dreyfuss, Raul Julia, Sonia Braga, Jonathan Winters, and Fernando Rey
DIRECTOR:	Paul Mazursky
GENRE:	Comedy
CONTENT:	Sex, violence, and profanity
INTENDED AUDIENCE:	Adults only
REVIEWER:	Ted Baehr

An actor, Jack Noah, is forced to take over as dictator of a South American banana republic after the dictator, Alphonse Simms, has a heart attack. Jack does not want the part until he receives a rousing applause for his first speech. From then on, he's hooked on the part: so much so that he falls head-over-heels-in-love with Alphonse's mistress, Madonna. The country is really an oligarchy headed up by Roberto Straussman. Jack balks at this corporate-socialism and comes to the aid of the people of Parador so that the commie-revolutionaries can take over. Jack returns to New York where he watches the revolutionary inauguration on television.

Besides being filled with sex, violence, and profanity, *Moon Over Parador* is hopelessly confused with regard to politics and economics. The producers advocate revolutionary-socialism replacing corporate-socialism. Neither will work. Biblical economics alleviates poverty and solves the problems caused by statist socialism. Avoid *Moon Over Parador;* it's a waste of your time and money.

TITLE:	**MOONSTRUCK**
QUALITY:	★★★
RECOMMENDATION:	Extreme Caution
RATING:	PG
RELEASE:	1987
STARRING:	Cher and Nicholas Cage
DIRECTOR:	Norman Jewison
GENRE:	Romance
CONTENT:	Profanity, brief bedroom scene, and superstition
INTENDED AUDIENCE:	Young adults
REVIEWER:	Rebecca M. Robbins

Loretta Castorini lives in a very small world. One night Johnny Camarerri proposes to her. Johnny flies to the side of his dying mother in Sicily, asking only that Loretta invite his estranged brother Ronnie to the wedding. She meets a tormented man who blames Johnny for losing his hand in an accident five years earlier. They go abruptly from this trite conversation to Ronnie's bed. (Because he wants revenge on Johnny? We're not quite sure.)

Moonstruck is a comedy with a dark side that presents an unbiblical worldview. Superstition, references to death and immoral decisions detract from the funny moments. God is not seen as the sovereign ruler over the world. Instead, the moon and "luck" are controlling what happens to the characters. Although right is understood, the choice to do the right thing is not taken. Avoid *Moonstruck.*

☆☆☆ MASTERPIECE ☆☆☆

TITLE:	**MY DARLING CLEMENTINE (97 Minutes, Black and White)**
QUALITY:	★★★★
RECOMMENDATION:	Acceptable
RATING:	Not rated
RELEASE:	1946
STARRING:	Henry Fonda, Linda Darnell, Victor Mature, Walter Brennan, and Jane Darwell
DIRECTOR:	John Ford
GENRE:	Western

CONTENT:	Nothing objectionable
INTENDED AUDIENCE:	All ages
REVIEWER:	Ted Baehr

This classic western covers the familiar territory of the Earp brothers' stalking of the evil Clantons to the showdown at the O.K. Corral; however, it does so with such artistry that it stands above all the other variations.

Ford knew Wyatt Earp in the early silent days when Ford was an assistant prop boy. He used to give Earp a cup of coffee in exchange for details about Earp's legendary life:

"He would come up to visit pals, cowboys that he knew, a couple of times a year. A lot of them were in my company. So in *My Darling Clementine*, we did it exactly the way it had been. They didn't just walk up the street and start banging away at each other; it was a clever military maneuver."

The movie constantly maintains our interest in the relationship between Doc and Wyatt. Victor Mature had one of his rare good roles as Doc Holliday. He has a mysterious and intemperate aura that makes him unpredictable. He's one of Tombstone's more volatile characters, but his love for Wyatt is the inflexible center of this story.

TITLE:	**MY LITTLE GIRL**
QUALITY:	★ ★ ★
RECOMMENDATION:	Extreme Caution
RATING:	PG
RELEASE:	1987
STARRING:	James Earl Jones, Geraldine Page, Mary Stuart Masterson, Anne Meara, and Peter Gallagher
DIRECTOR:	Connie Kaiserman
GENRE:	Drama
CONTENT:	Profanity and obscenity
INTENDED AUDIENCE:	Adults
REVIEWER:	Ted Baehr

My Little Girl is the story of a sixteen-year-old girl, Franny Bettinger, from a very wealthy family who goes to work at a detention center for homeless children. Her grandmother, Molly, insists that she get involved with the "real" world. Fran tries to help the children and confronts Ike Bailey, the supervisor, and the social worker, who love the children but have fallen into the trap of accepting the process.

Illegally, Fran goes to a dismal children's home to rescue one of the children Joan, who has been moved from the detention center. Joan is picked up by the police and brought back to the detention center. Fran apologizes profusely to Mr. Bailey, and he fires her after she fulfills her task of having a talent show for the children. The kids love her, and the talent show helps them, but Mr. Bailey is worried about Fran's propensity to become too involved with the children and lets her go.

My Little Girl is a wonderful story about learning responsibility. It is a movie about love in action. The problem is the profuse obscenity and profanity, which destroys the movie for Christians. *My Little Girl* is an elegant, well-made movie, but we cannot recommend it for Christians.

TITLE:	**MY STEPMOTHER IS AN ALIEN**
QUALITY:	★ ★
RECOMMENDATION:	Bad
RATING:	PG-13
RELEASE:	1988
STARRING:	Dan Aykroyd, Kim Basinger, and John Lovitz
DIRECTOR:	Richard Benjamin
GENRE:	Comedy
CONTENT:	Nudity with seductive scenes and a few obscenities
INTENDED AUDIENCE:	Adults
REVIEWER:	Gene Burke

Physicist Steve Mills accidentally penetrates another galaxy with a radar beam, causing catastrophic results on the planet KOSIGN. Celeste is sent to earth to save her planet by having the process reversed. She quickly coerces physicist Steve Mills into marriage. After a series of tedious mayhem, Mills' daughter discovers that Celeste isn't human, and it's time to come clean. Then, the family works together to reverse the experiment and save KOSIGN. When this is accomplished, Celeste cannot bear to leave her "new earth family." Her Overlords ultimately approve, allowing Mills' brother to return in her place. He relishes the exchange when he learns that all the females on KOSIGN are as beautiful as Celeste.

This film has totally unnecessary offensive language since the film is aimed at youngsters and a family audience. Also, there is one of the most seductive bedroom scenes I've ever witnessed in a PG-13 film. *My Stepmother Is an Alien* will probably be described by the world as harmless fun, but I plead to differ. Disguised as a PG-13 movie, this film is a short-fuse to the sexual bomb that has already exploded throughout our country. For that reason, this film should be condemned.

TITLE:	**MY SWEET LITTLE VILLAGE (Subtitles)**
QUALITY:	★ ★ ★
RECOMMENDATION:	Caution
RATING:	Not rated
RELEASE:	1986
STARRING:	A Czechoslovakian cast
DIRECTOR:	Jiri Menzel

GENRE:	Drama
CONTENT:	Mild, off-color language and implied sexual situations
INTENDED AUDIENCE:	Adults
REVIEWER:	Susanne Steward

My Sweet Little Village is a pleasant movie about many, many characters in a small village, their attitudes, temptations, loyalties, practicalities, and tendernesses. The "center of the wheel" is the a retarded adult male who lives in a house which his parents willed him upon their deaths.

My Sweet Little Village is a small movie which was nominated for an Academy Award for Best Foreign Film. If you like character studies, *My Sweet Little Village* is for you. It is a very touching, human film. The atmosphere, acting and directing are superb. However, there are implied sexual situations, so caution is advised.

TITLE:	**MYSTIC PIZZA**
QUALITY:	★ ★ ★
RECOMMENDATION:	Extreme Caution
RATING:	R
RELEASE:	1988
STARRING:	Annabeth Gish (related to Lillian), Julia Roberts, and Lili Taylor
DIRECTOR:	Donald Petrie
GENRE:	Romance
CONTENT:	Foul language and implied sex with no nudity
INTENDED AUDIENCE:	Teenagers and young adults
REVIEWER:	Gene Burke

Regardless of how wonderfully delicious the everything-pizza is supposed to be, anchovies make it hard for me to swallow. In *Mystic Pizza*, the language is akin to putting anchovies in a very delicious pizza.

Mystic, Connecticut is the home of the Mystic Pizza Restaurant, where Leona sells her unforgettable, "secret recipe" pizza. The film centers on Leona's three female employees: Jo-Jo, who has cold feet in tying the knot with Bill; Daisy who is dedicated to landing a wealthy law student; and Kat, who has goals and hopes of entering Yale, which necessitates her working a second job as baby-sitter for a thirty-year-old father whose wife is on an overseas business trip.

Its weakness is the foul language and two scenes alluding to sex acts and adultery. As delicious as this small pizza film is, my taste buds still prefer to "hold the anchovy"—the distasteful language that prevents savoring an otherwise pleasant production and prohibits a recommendation for the film. Therefore, avoid this movie.

TITLE:	**THE NAKED GUN**
QUALITY:	★★
RECOMMENDATION:	Bad
RATING:	R
RELEASE:	1988
STARRING:	Leslie Neilsen, Priscilla Presley, Ricardo Montalban, O. J. Simpson, and George Kennedy
DIRECTOR:	David Zuker
GENRE:	Comedy
CONTENT:	Abundant off-color humor and offensive situations
INTENDED AUDIENCE:	Adult
REVIEWER:	Gene Burke

The action starts with wiping off Soviet Premier Gorbachev's forehead birthmark, exposing him as a fraud and using the Ayatollah Khomeini as a punching bag. No one is exempt from such idiocy. Sexuality, human body functions and bathroom humor constitute most of the so-called comedy. The movie is in very poor taste. An inept police detective is assigned to protect Queen Elizabeth on a visit to L.A. She is a buffoon. Baseball star Reggie Jackson is hypnotized and programmed to assassinate her.

From harmless to bawdy and distasteful, *everything* is done for laughs. These same folks created the irreverent and irritating film, *Ruthless People* as well as the *Airplane* series. *Naked Gun* is the same mindless, pointless, waste of time. It is not recommended.

TITLE:	**THE NEW ADVENTURES OF PIPPI LONGSTOCKING**
QUALITY:	★★★
RECOMMENDATION:	Acceptable
RATING:	G
RELEASE:	1988
STARRING:	Tami Erin, Eileen Brennan, and Dennis Dugan
DIRECTOR:	Ken Annakin
GENRE:	Children
CONTENT:	Nothing objectionable
INTENDED AUDIENCE:	Children
REVIEWER:	Lili and three little Baehrs

Pippi is separated from Captain Longstocking during a storm. Pippi makes her way to land and Villa Villekula, an old house in a great location that has attracted a developer who wants to build cluster homes. The plot revolves around Mr. Blackhart trying to get the house; Mrs. Bannister, the mistress of the orphanage who wants Pippi under her tutelage; and Pippi's neighbors, the Settigrens whose father sides with Mrs. Bannister, but whose mother accepts Pippi as she is.

When faced with life in the orphanage, Pippi runs away with the Settigren children in a homemade flying machine. They are rescued just as they is about to go over "Niagara Falls." Pippi goes to the orphanage, but escapes to send a message to her father via a bottle thrown to the ocean. The orphanage burns down, and Pippi risks her life to save some of the children. She is hailed as a heroine. At Christmas, the Captain returns to take Pippi away to become a princess.

Pippi was supposed to be a breath of fresh air, but she is not. Pippi is unrelentingly good-natured and always in control of all the adults. I kept wanting Pippi to become "real" at some point, but she never does. The movie is a comic strip. My young children liked it, but as Robby (three years old) said, "it was not the best."

TITLE:	**NEW YORK STORIES**
QUALITY:	★★★
RECOMMENDATION:	Extreme Caution
RATING:	PG
RELEASE:	1989
STARRING:	Woody Allen, Nick Nolte, Giancarlo Giannini, Rosanna Arquette, and Mia Farrow.
DIRECTOR:	Martin Scorsese, Woody Allen, Francis Ford Coppola
GENRE:	Drama
CONTENT:	Profanities, blasphemies, vulgarities, and sexual themes
INTENDED AUDIENCE:	Adults
REVIEWER:	Bruce Grimes

This trilogy takes three different looks at people in New York City. After it is over, we can only ask, "Why?"

Part I by Mr. Scorsese tells of a painter who lives in a loft with his girlfriend. They struggle with his success and her frustrations of living in his shadow. The girlfriend walks out, leaving him to find a replacement, which he does immediately.

Part II by Mr. Coppola examines the lives of a famous flutist, his wife and their daughter, Zoe. Mom and Dad are constantly traveling, leaving Zoe with the butler. Their marriage has been on the skids for some time, and Zoe tries to reconcile them. The three rendezvous in Athens, where "Pop" is playing with the Symphony. They live happily ever after.

Part III by Mr. Allen is the most enjoyable. Allen portrays a corporate attorney who is harangued by his Jewish mother. They go to a magic show, where his mother is picked to disappear in a large box. The magician performs the illusion, and mother disappears. The problem is, they can't get her back! Two weeks later, mother appears as an apparition floating over Manhattan and telling everyone about her son's problems!

Profanity, blasphemy, vulgarity, and sexual themes run rampant through the movie.

☆☆☆ **CLASSIC** ☆☆☆

TITLE:	**NIKKI, WILD DOG OF THE NORTH (74 Minutes)**
QUALITY:	★★★★
RECOMMENDATION:	Acceptable
RATING:	Not rated
RELEASE:	1961
STARRING:	Jean Coutu, Emile Genest, and Uriel Luft
DIRECTOR:	Jack Couffer, Donald Haldane
GENRE:	Nature/Animal adventure
CONTENT:	One animal fight-scene may be a little too brutal for the youngest in the family
INTENDED AUDIENCE:	Family
REVIEWER:	Protestant Motion Picture Council

Andre Dupas is a trapper in the Canadian woods whose Malemute dog Nikki runs into the forest and returns with a new-found friend, Neewa, a bear cub. He ties the two animals together, loads them into his canoe and heads downstream, but they are separated from him when the canoe overturns in the rapids. Most of the plot is concerned with these two animals as they roam the forest, seeking food and shelter. In their travels they encounter: wolves, muskrats, mice, marmot, wolverine, blue fox, elk, and many others.

Still leashed together, much humor results as Nikki and Neewa try to follow their own habits. Finally, the leash breaks and each goes his way, only to discover they need one another. They continue together on their adventures.

Jeopardy comes in the form of a man, Lebeau, who wants to exploit Nikki's ability to fight in the dog pit—thus bringing in some savage scenes. This results in Lebeau's destruction, with Nikki returning happily to Dupas.

There is an excellent combination of animals' antics and life, with an exciting plot, a fine script, and an unusually effective musical background. Nikki and Neewa are quite a team and surprisingly natural actors. Some of the sequences will make the viewer wonder how the producers ever got these animal thespians to behave with such realism. Filmed in and around Banff Park in the Rockies, adults will be charmed as well.

TITLE:	**1969**
QUALITY:	★★★
RECOMMENDATION:	Bad
RATING:	R
RELEASE:	1988

STARRING:	Robert Downey Jr., Kiefer Sutherland, Bruce Dern, Mariette Hartley, Winona Ryder, Joanna Cassidy, Christopher Wynne, Keller Kuhn, and Steve Foster
DIRECTOR:	Ernest Thompson
GENRE:	Drama
CONTENT:	Profanity, obscenity, and brief frontal nudity
INTENDED AUDIENCE:	Yuppies
REVIEWER:	Scott Dugan

Ralph and Scott's only goals appear to be hitchhiking and having pre-marital sex. Both are good at the first. Scott needs to catch up with Ralph on the second. With these two drifters as our protagonists, *1969* tries to explore the effects the war had on American families. Scott's dad is a decorated WW II vet who's all for America's effort, while stoic Mom is more ambivalent, and long-haired Scott is against it. Clean-cut Ralph is beginning to dabble in drugs as his pretty, younger sister delivers a naive anti-war speech to the local high school. Ralph's mom capitalizes on the rift between Scott's parents by having an affair with Scott's dad.

1969 seems to be just a bunch of things happening with '60's music and costuming outshining what could have been a better script. *1969* presents U.S. intervention in the war as "killing in the name of democracy," when it can be argued that it was a case defending in the name of freedom. Director Thompson suggests that peace is the answer to war. That's like saying that good health is the answer to bad health. The film is its most reprehensible in its unfair portrayal of Christianity as a carnival sideshow.

1969 has come and gone. Let *1969* do the same.

TITLE:	**NO MAN'S LAND**
QUALITY:	★★★
RECOMMENDATION:	Extreme Caution
RATING:	R
RELEASE:	1987
STARRING:	Charlie Sheen, D.B. Sweeney, Randy Quaid, and Lara Harris
DIRECTOR:	Peter Werner
GENRE:	Detective
CONTENT:	Some bad language and implied sex
INTENDED AUDIENCE:	Teenagers and young adults
REVIEWER:	Doug Brewer

No Man's Land is a morality play about the struggle between the soul and the flesh. Benjy is a rookie cop who tinkers with cars. A Lieutenant recruits Benjy to go undercover in a repair shop front for a stolen car ring. The shop's owner, Ted, shows Benjy the "good life." Benjy finds he likes stealing cars in return for vast sums of money. It is interesting to watch the changes in his attitude as he gets closer to Ted. The fine line between Ted and Benjy is drawn, blurs, and disappears as they plunge into friendship and eventual confrontation in a scene fraught with nervous energy.

Unfortunately, the writers portray love as sex. However, there is no nudity, and Benjy finds this relationship has no substance. *No Man's Land* is a well-conceived picture of the temptations of the world and the damage they can do; however, it is not for Christians.

TITLE:	**NO RETREAT, NO SURRENDER II**
QUALITY:	★
RECOMMENDATION:	Extreme Caution
RATING:	R
RELEASE:	1989
STARRING:	Lauren Avedon, Max Thayer, and Cynthia Rothrock
DIRECTOR:	Cory Yuen
GENRE:	Action adventure
CONTENT:	Violence and lewdness
INTENDED AUDIENCE:	Karate film fans
REVIEWER:	Phil W. Boatwright

Action/adventure about a Karate expert whose fiancee is kidnapped in Bangkok. After he partners up with a Hans Solo type and a perky blonde helicopter pilot, he goes into Cambodia to rescue his girl. Eighty-nine minutes later, after killing 200 bad guys via karate kicks, lots of explosives, and a futuristic cross bow, he gets the girl back.

There is no objectionable language or nudity, but some lewdness and a whole lot of chop suey violence. As for the acting and the script, ouch! I hope all involved kept their day jobs. How can a film with so many bombs be such a dud?

TITLE:	**NORTHSHORE**
QUALITY:	★ ★ ★
RECOMMENDATION:	Caution
RATING:	PG
RELEASE:	1987
STARRING:	Nia Peoples and Gregory Harrison
DIRECTOR:	William Phelps
GENRE:	Action adventure

CONTENT:	Some off-color language and sexual innuendo
INTENDED AUDIENCE:	Teenagers
REVIEWER:	Doug Brewer

Rick Kane, the surfing champion of Tempe, Arizona takes the $500 prize money and hops a jet to Hawaii where he hopes to spend time surfing the fabled Northshore. Along the way, his possessions are stolen. Left with only his surf board, he wanders around until he meets Chandler, the surfboard maker. Chandler teaches Rick the proper way to surf in exchange for an up-do-date logo for his company. The Bonsai Classic is coming up. Rick enters as an "unknown." The ending is a kind of Rocky Goes Surfing.

It is enjoyable. Surprisingly, there is no nudity and no profanity. The message of a small guy against the odds, as worn as it may be, is still heartwarming. *Northshore* appeared to be filmed with a handheld camera and a cassette player, but it is recommended. It is almost a documentary.

☆☆☆ CLASSIC ☆☆☆

TITLE:	**THE NOTORIOUS LANDLADY**
QUALITY:	★ ★ ★ ★
RECOMMENDATION:	Caution
RATING:	Not rated
RELEASE:	1962
STARRING:	Kim Novak, Jack Lemmon, Fred Astair, and Lionel Jeffries
DIRECTOR:	Richard Quine
GENRE:	Comedy/Mystery
CONTENT:	Some objectionable scenes for children (murder: premeditated, self-defense)
INTENDED AUDIENCE:	Adult
REVIEWER:	Protestant Motion Picture Council

Based on the story "The Notorious Tenant" by Margery Sharpe, this murder mystery-comedy has many witty lines, some hysterical slapstick and is intriguing in plot and action.

Jack Lemmon is an American Foreign Service employee who rents a flat in London. His landlady is under surveillance by Scotland Yard as a suspect in the case of her missing husband. Lemmon's boss and an inspector of the Yard asks him to snoop around, and he reluctantly agrees.

When the landlady's husband shows up, she kills him in self-defense after a battle over some jewels he'd stolen and can't find in the house. The cops tow her to jail, and she goes on trial. False testimony, blackmail, and a wild chase all rush toward a surprise ending.

TITLE:	**NUTS**
QUALITY:	★ ★ ★
RECOMMENDATION:	Extreme Caution
RATING:	R
RELEASE:	1987
STARRING:	Barbra Streisand and Richard Dreyfuss
DIRECTOR:	Martin Ritt
GENRE:	Drama
CONTENT:	Prostitution and insanity
INTENDED AUDIENCE:	Adults
REVIEWER:	Laura Lindley

Barbara Streisand plays a New York prostitute who is accused of murdering one of her clients. A hearing has to be set to determine if she is sane enough to stand trial. Her upper-class parents want her institutionalized, while her lawyer wants to prove she is competent. She was an abused child, and her stepfather's insistence on her mental illness is really only a cover for his own guilt. Searing stuff.

The problem is that the whole mess is so sordid and unhappy that I can scarcely recommend it to anyone except a few concerned Christians who are active in eliminating child abuse, otherwise save yourself the heartache. This is not a comedy, as some might think by the title and the stars. *Nuts* is a very intense film.

TITLE:	**OBSESSED**
QUALITY:	★ ★ ★ ★
RECOMMENDATION:	Caution
RATING:	PG
RELEASE:	1989
STARRING:	Kerrie Keane, Daniel Pilon, Saul Rubinek, and Alan Thicke
DIRECTOR:	Robin Spry
GENRE:	Drama
CONTENT:	Some violence and heartrending subject matter: a hit-and-run accident
INTENDED AUDIENCE:	Adults
REVIEWER:	Ted Baehr

Dinah Middleton witnesses her only child, Alex, dragged by the car of a hit-and-run driver. If the driver had stopped, the child would have survived. Alex dies, reuniting Dinah and her ex-husband, Max, who tries to help her locate the driver.

Dinah becomes obsessed with tracking down the driver. The police have more important things to do. She tracks down a wealthy American businessman, Owen Hughes, in New York. She cannot extradite him for prosecution in Canada because the extradition laws do not cover automobile accidents. Failing to lure Hughes to Canada, she kidnaps his son, David. While driving David to Canada, she recognizes the error of taking revenge into her own hands and returns David to his home. Hughes goes to Canada to find his son. When Dinah gets home, it is her forgiveness that drives Owen into despair and repentance. No longer defensive, Owen realizes the magnitude of his crime and is deeply shaken by guilt.

The theme of personal responsibility, forgiveness, and repentance is so strong that we commend the filmmakers. There is no profanity, blasphemy, or nudity in this film. We are encouraged that productions such as this are coming out of Canada.

TITLE:	**OLIVER AND COMPANY**
QUALITY:	★★★★
RECOMMENDATION:	Acceptable
RATING:	G
RELEASE:	1988
STARRING:	Voices of Joey Lawrence, Bette Midler, Billy Joel, Cheech Marin, Roscoe Lee Browne, Dom DeLuise, Richard Mulligan, Robert Loggia, and Sheryl Lee Ralph.
DIRECTOR:	George Scribner (Animator, Director, and Story)
GENRE:	Children/Animated
CONTENT:	Some tense moments in a few scenes; otherwise free of any offense
INTENDED AUDIENCE:	Children
REVIEWER:	Gene Burke

Oliver is an orphan kitten in present-day Manhattan. He is given refuge by the hobo Fagen, who leads a pack of bowery dogs. Fagen teaches Oliver the ways of "hoodlum-osity." While heisting a limousine radio, Oliver is found by Jenny. Oliver, content in his new surroundings, is unaware that Fagen's dog-family plans to rescue him. "Saved" by his friends, Oliver explains how happy he was with Jenny. Fagen realizes that Oliver may be loved so much by Jenny that her daddy will pay a ransom. When Jenny offers her small savings of coins, Fagen repents. Sykes, the villainous underworld kingpin, has other plans. He kit-naps Oliver to ransom Oliver himself. Fagen and company bravely band together to face their greatest adversary.

The folks from Disney have created a fresh, lovable character: the kitten Oliver. They have given us a brand new, music filled, heart-warming, full-length animated feature. Young children will understand and love *Oliver and Company*. Thank you Disney Studios for a good movie!

☆☆☆ CLASSIC ☆☆☆

TITLE:	**ONE HUNDRED AND ONE DALMATIANS (79 Minutes)**
QUALITY:	★ ★ ★ ★
RECOMMENDATION:	Acceptable
RATING:	G
RELEASE:	1961
STARRING:	Voices of Rod Taylor, Lisa Davis, Cate Bauer, Ben Wright, Frederick Worlock, Martha Wentworth, and Betty Lou Gerson
DIRECTOR:	Wolfgang Reitherman, Hamilton S. Luske, Clyde Geronimi
PRODUCER:	Walt Disney
GENRE:	Animation
CONTENT:	Nothing objectionable
INTENDED AUDIENCE:	Children and adults
REVIEWER:	Protestant Motion Picture Council

This is one of the best feature cartoons ever to come out of the Disney studios. Based on the book by Dodie Smith, the story is a nice blend of a romantic theme and an interesting detective twist, combined with exquisite caricatures of both humans and dogs.

Roles are reversed as Pongo, a Dalmatian, decides that his human master, Roger, a songwriter, needs a mate and chooses for him Anita. It seems design rather than accident that Anita owns a beautiful female Dalmatian dog named Perdita. Double marriage ensues.

In due time, Pongo and Perdita are parents of fifteen puppies. Enter Cruela De Vil, a villainess who covets the puppies for their fur. When Roger refuses, she is prompted to have them "dognapped" by a pair of Cockney crooks. Roger and Anita resort to all types of measures to locate the lost pups, but to no avail.

This makes Pongo resort to the "twilight bark," a system of barking signals which locates the puppies in a deserted mansion on the outskirts of London. Pongo, assisted by a dog named The Colonel, a horse, and a cat, then rescues the puppies from Cruela's clutches. In doing so, he also uncovers a total of 99 Dalmatians (plus Pongo and Perdita equal 101 Dalmatians), whom the wicked woman has gathered to make for herself a rare coat.

Throughout the story are subtle visual elements that give it an atmosphere that transcends a cartoon sense of reality. Additional depth is given to the caricatures through the voices used to compliment the personalities. Note the physical resemblance between many of the dogs and their masters.

This is a warm-hearted comedy, with excellent animation and appropriately catchy music. Its theme is a universal love of animals, more specifically dogs.

☆☆☆ MASTERPIECE ☆☆☆

TITLE:	**ONE, TWO, THREE**
QUALITY:	★★★★
RECOMMENDATION:	Acceptable
RATING:	Not rated
RELEASE:	1961
STARRING:	James Cagney, Horst Buchholtz, and Pamela Tiffin
DIRECTOR:	Billy Wilder
GENRE:	Comedy
CONTENT:	Nothing objectionable
INTENDED AUDIENCE:	Adults
REVIEWER:	Protestant Motion Picture Council

Everyone and every country involved, East and West Germany, the United States, and the Russian communists, come in for a full share of satire in this fast-moving comedy, surely one of the funniest in the 1960s.

Cagney is the fast-talking, hard-driving, self-made man who heads up Coca-Cola's bottling interests in Germany. His activities, his family and public life, what happens when the boss' daughter comes to visit, and the troubles she encounters and generates, all drive toward a humorous and sarcastic ending.

The various people and causes are pitted against each other. Heavy humor is piled upon the Germans. Americans abroad do not fare much better. Ideological differences are aired and are the recipients of bitter barbs.

The dialogue is crackling with "smart" repartee at a staccato tempo as it comes at the ears with Uzi-like speed. It may be very hilarious, but it also offers some serious consideration.

☆☆☆ CLASSIC ☆☆☆

TITLE:	**OPERATION AMSTERDAM**
QUALITY:	★★★
RECOMMENDATION:	Acceptable
RATING:	Not rated
RELEASE:	1960 (British)
STARRING:	Peter Finch, Eva Bartok, Tony Britton, and Alexander Knox
DIRECTOR:	Michael McCarthy
GENRE:	War

CONTENT:	Nothing objectionable
INTENDED AUDIENCE:	Adults
REVIEWER:	Protestant Motion Picture Council

This is a true story about $10 million worth of industrial diamonds being smuggled out of Holland during WW II by British secret agents for their safekeeping and possible use on the eve of the German occupation. This is a tense war drama.

The city of Amsterdam plays its own part, with some of its well-known locations as key factors in the story. A foursome has fourteen hours to accomplish the operation and catch a boat to England while avoiding local Nazi fifth columnists and beating the Germans.

The suspense is tremendous before a successful escape. It is well-balanced between heroics and intrigue, with good acting from a fine cast.

☆☆☆ CLASSIC ☆☆☆

TITLE:	**OPERATION PETTICOAT**
QUALITY:	★ ★ ★ ★
RECOMMENDATION:	Acceptable
RATING:	Not rated
RELEASE:	1959
STARRING:	Cary Grant, Tony Curtis, Joan O'Brien, Dina Merrill, Arthur O'Connell, Marion Ross, and Virginia Gregg
DIRECTOR:	Blake Edwards
GENRE:	Comedy
CONTENT:	Mild sexual innuendos
INTENDED AUDIENCE:	Adults
REVIEWER:	Protestant Motion Picture Council

It's after WW II in the Pacific, and the submarine *Sea Tiger* is about to be scrapped for a nuclear sub. The admiral, who was its captain, reminisces upon some of the events of the sub's life, and the picture unwinds in flashback . . .

It's December, 1941, and the tired sub can only function after the lieutenant supply officer secures supplies and gear in the most unorthodox manner. In one instance, he picks up five stranded nurses plus a couple of Filipino families and a goat to ferry out of harm's way. The minute these women come aboard, the usual complications caused by women aboard a ship arise, from the sub being painted pink to the busty nurses attempting to pass the sailors in the very narrow corridors of the sub.

Most of the jokes are sexist by today's standards. There's no thrust to the story other than one gag after another, most of which are bright and original.

By the time the picture ends, the lieutenant reforms and marries one of the nurses; the captain marries another.

There is good photography. The film is played for the farce it is.

☆☆☆ MASTERPIECE ☆☆☆

TITLE:	**OUR MAN IN HAVANA (Black and White)**
QUALITY:	★ ★ ★ ★
RECOMMENDATION:	Acceptable
RATING:	Not rated
RELEASE:	1960 (British)
STARRING:	Alec Guiness, Burl Ives, Maureen O'Hara, and Ernie Kovacs
DIRECTOR:	Carol Reed
GENRE:	Comedy
CONTENT:	Considerable amount of drinking, some of which is part of the plot
INTENDED AUDIENCE:	Adults and mature teenagers
REVIEWER:	Protestant Motion Picture Council

A tongue-in-cheek satire of the British secret service that is as hilarious as it is absurd. A man is needed to do undercover work in (pre-Castro) Cuba where threatening problems simmer under the surface. The most unlikely person is chosen, a mild-mannered vacuum cleaner salesman.

He realizes that he will make good money for every tidbit of information he passes along to headquarters in London. Knowing there is no real information to gather, he begins to invent information in order to provide the good things in life for his teenage daughter.

He is taken seriously, not only by the London Intelligence Bureau but also by enemy agents. The whole thing begins to crazily expand into a massive intrigue where no intrigue exists. Moreover, he has delivered preposterous drawings of giant weird-looking war machines in the mountains around Havana, but these are nothing more than huge fabrications based on what he knows: vacuum cleaners.

A rather surprising ending adds to the interest of an absorbing mystery in which acting and character development are paramount.

TITLE:	**OUTBACK**
QUALITY:	★ ★ ★ ★
RECOMMENDATION:	Acceptable
RATING:	PG
RELEASE:	1989
STARRING:	Jeff Fahey, Tushka Bergen, and Steven Vidler
DIRECTOR:	Ian Barry

GENRE:	Drama/Western/Action adventure
CONTENT:	Nothing objectionable
INTENDED AUDIENCE:	Adults
REVIEWER:	Ted Baehr

What a great joy it is to see a movie that holds your attention, uplifts you and doesn't have profanity, sex, nudity, or obscenity. *Outback* is a beautifully crafted movie, reminiscent of the great American epics. The Australians seem to be inheriting the wholesome movie-making mantle. This is good family fare where good triumphs over evil, and marriage and family are uplifted.

Outback tells the story of the Richards family, who were one of the first families in the Outback of Australia. They have bred an extraordinary line of horses. Their problem, however, is that Mr. Richards is deeply in debt, and his neighbor, Mr. Allenby, will do anything to get Richard's land and horses.

Mr. Richard's headstrong daughter, Alice, at first rebels against the restrictions of polite society. However, with the death of her father, she realizes who her real friends are, and she saves the plantation with the help of the handsome Ben Creed.

This is a very entertaining movie full of Biblical values, which is highly recommended. The photography is beautiful, reminiscent of John Ford's great Westerns. The acting is superb. The story holds you in rapt attention without giving itself away too soon, or exposing its punches.

This is high drama. *Outback* is what movies should be.

TITLE:	**OUT COLD**
QUALITY:	★★★
RECOMMENDATION:	Bad
RATING:	R
RELEASE:	1989
STARRING:	John Lithgow, Teri Garr, Randi Quaid, and Bruce McGill
DIRECTOR:	Malcom Mowbray
GENRE:	Comedy
CONTENT:	Profanity, obscenity, and nudity
INTENDED AUDIENCE:	Adults
REVIEWER:	Rebecca Wayt and Billy Tyler

Out Cold is a black comedy/murder mystery with numerous plot twists. A couple of high school chums start a butcher shop. Ten years later, they feel dissatisfied with their lot in life. When greed and duplicity finally getting the best of him, Ernie, a womanizing lout, seeks to get rid of his partner Dave. His amoral, sleazy wife, Sunny, hires a seedy private detective to blackmail her husband. Dave, a hard-working misanthrope, mistakenly believes he has killed his partner, so he locks him in the freezer. The plot becomes more and more tenderized with each cheap cut of cube steak.

While we were impressed by the good performances, we cannot recommend *Out Cold* to Christian audiences due to the unredeeming qualities of this movie. There are three profanities and thirteen obscenities, plus frontal male and female nudity. This is not wholesome entertainment, but the worst in film noir.

TITLE:	**THE OUTSIDE CHANCE OF MAXIMILLIAN GLICK**
QUALITY:	★ ★ ★ ★
RECOMMENDATION:	Caution
RATING:	Probably PG
RELEASE:	1989
STARRING:	Saul Rubinek, Jan Rubes, Aaron Schwartz, and Noam Zylberman
DIRECTOR:	Allan Goldstein
GENRE:	Comedy/Drama
CONTENT:	Some lewdness
INTENDED AUDIENCE:	Families
REVIEWER:	Ted Baehr

What a blessing it is to see an entertaining movie which teaches Biblical values. *The Outside Chance of Maximillian Glick* is a story of a young Jewish boy, Max, who lives in a tiny Canadian town and is about to be bar mitzvahed. However, he would prefer to play in a piano concert with his Ukrainian girlfriend.

Enter Rabbi Calvin Tittleman who teaches Max the importance of faith in God, respecting your father and mother, and the necessity of being truthful, especially to oneself. Rabbi Tittleman does this with great love and humor.

He also challenges all of the Pharisees, both Jewish and Christian, in the town to love one another. On Brotherhood Day, the rabbi tells the joke of the rabbi who complains to God that his son has gone to Jerusalem and turned into a Christian. God responds that He faced the same problem Himself.

This movie does not denigrate the differences between the faiths; rather, it lifts up faith in God as being the most important aspect of life. This is a movie that children and adults should see; it is also a film which will entertain and amuse you. Everyone involved in this film is to be commended.

TITLE:	**OVERBOARD**
QUALITY:	★ ★ ★
RECOMMENDATION:	Extreme Caution
RATING:	PG
RELEASE:	1987
STARRING:	Goldie Hawn and Kurt Russell

DIRECTOR:	Garry Marshall
GENRE:	Comedy
CONTENT:	Profanity and adult situations
INTENDED AUDIENCE:	Teenagers and young adults
REVIEWER:	ACM

Joanna Slayton is a spoiled woman. When she decides the closet on her yacht is too small, a local carpenter, Dean Proffitt, is hired to do the work. After enduring numerous insults, Proffitt decides the torture is not worth the money. That night, Joanna falls off the boat. When she washes ashore, she has amnesia. Grant, Joanna's husband, discovers Joanna is missing. This is his opportunity to rid himself of this shrew. When Dean discovers Grant has abandoned Joanna, his desire for revenge mushrooms into a cunning scheme. He identifies Joanna as his wife and takes her home to his hovel filled with four filthy boys whose mother has been dead for over a year. Joanna and Dean fall in love. The boys accept her as their mother.

Profanity makes it impossible for us to recommend this movie. *Overboard* promotes the idea that there is no consequence for sin, whether it be adultery or deception. Joanna's psychologist states the underlying message of this film: "Nothing is ever wrong." Avoid this humanistic travesty.

TITLE:	**PADRE NUESTRO (Subtitles)**
QUALITY:	★ ★ ★
RECOMMENDATION:	Extreme Caution
RATING:	Not rated
RELEASE:	1987
STARRING:	Fernando Rey and Francisco Rabal
DIRECTOR:	Francisco Regueiro
GENRE:	Religious
CONTENT:	Some nudity
INTENDED AUDIENCE:	Adults
REVIEWER:	Ted Baehr

Padre Nuestro is a beautiful Spanish film which is a dialogue between two brothers, the priest Fernando, and his atheist, brother Abel. Moreover, it is a story of the redemption of Fernando as he realizes how much evil he has caused in his life, and the fact that only God can save him. *Padre Nuestro* shows that the wages of sin are death. It shows that Fernando's sin has caused the town to die, the vineyards to die, his brother to shrivel up, and his daughter to destroy herself. It shows that the church cannot give absolution. Fernando's only salvation is in Christ, not in the church, nor in indulgences, nor in acts of penance.

Padre Nuestro is an intriguing movie, but caution is recommended because of its earthiness. *Padre Nuestro* is the type of movie pagans should see. Although it shows the weakness of the clergy, it also shows that the only place we can turn for salvation is Jesus Christ, since all of us are sinners. *Padre Nuestro* is a portrait of weakness of institutional religion and our need for God.

TITLE:	**PAPA WAS A PREACHER**
QUALITY:	★ ★ ★
RECOMMENDATION:	Acceptable
RATING:	G
RELEASE:	1986
STARRING:	Robert Pine, Georgia Engel, Dean Stockwell, and Imogene Coca
DIRECTOR:	Steve Feke
GENRE:	Drama
CONTENT:	Nothing objectionable
INTENDED AUDIENCE:	All ages
REVIEWER:	Ted Baehr

Papa Was a Preacher is a gem—a well-crafted movie about a preacher and his family. This is a movie which Christians should see.

Papa Was a Preacher tells the story of a Methodist preacher, Paul Candler, who has a loving wife and seven children and who is called to revive a Texas church which has fallen on hard times. He realizes that only God can revive a dying church, and he gives Him all the glory. Through the grace of God acting in his life, the church is saved from the bank, and we are treated to the beautiful story of how a Christian family works together under the Headship of Jesus Christ to overcome adversity.

The script, direction, and acting in this movie are commendable. I did not expect this to be such a well-produced movie. There are some minor flaws, and it is apparent that the budget was tight, but, in all, this is a beautiful movie worthy of acclaim as a Christian movie.

Papa Was a Preacher never errs from Biblical theology and is entertaining and touching.

TITLE:	**PAPERHOUSE**
QUALITY:	★ ★ ★ ★
RECOMMENDATION:	Caution
RATING:	PG-13
RELEASE:	1989
STARRING:	Ben Cross, Glenne Headly, and Elliott Spiers
DIRECTOR:	Bernard Rose
GENRE:	Drama

CONTENT:	Nothing objectionable, but some scenes may be too intense for young children
INTENDED AUDIENCE:	Teenagers and adults
REVIEWER:	Bruce Grimes

Anna Madden, a beautiful English girl, has had a few fainting spells. Her father travels extensively with his job. Anna likes to draw. One particular drawing is a stone house with an upper window with a boy in it. Once, when she faints, her drawing becomes the setting for her dream. She tries to get into the house, but the boy in the upper window, Mark, says she cannot come up. There are no stairs. Anna revives.

Before she goes to sleep, she draws the steps to the upper room. That night, Anna is successful in walking upstairs to Mark. Mark has legs, but they are useless. This interplay between her dreams and her drawing continues. Suddenly, Anna turns quite sick with glandular fever, and her dreams become hallucinations.

Paperhouse is a brilliantly crafted film that deserves the highest accolades. This film works on many emotional and intellectual levels and never cheapens itself with foul language, nudity or violence. It's a film that grabs you visually and emotionally. We highly recommend this movie.

TITLE:	**PARENTS**
QUALITY:	★
RECOMMENDATION:	Bad
RATING:	R
RELEASE:	1989
STARRING:	Randy Quaid and Mary Beth Hurt
DIRECTOR:	Bob Balaban
GENRE:	Comedy
CONTENT:	Mature theme, violence, and cannibalism
INTENDED AUDIENCE:	Adults
REVIEWER:	Philip Boatright

A young boy discovers his parents are cannibals in this black comedy/horror film. The performances by Quaid and Hurt are very good, but that is not reason enough to see this film. Personally, this reviewer was nauseated by the spoken and visual references to cannibalism. It is downright gross. *Parents* is almost a fulfillment of God's righteous word against those who disobey Him:

> If in spite of this you still do not listen to me but continue to be hostile toward me, then . . . I myself will punish you for your sins seven times over. You will eat the flesh of your sons and the flesh of your daughters . . . and I will abhor you. (Leviticus 26:27–30)

This movie is bad. Extreme caution is certainly suggested due to the violence and abusive treatment by the parents toward their young son, and anyone else who happens to mess with their culinary habits. Hollywood just keeps pushing the boundaries of "taste." Perhaps if a few filmmakers pushed the other way, they might discover that a return to "basic value" is what offers real "taste."

☆☆☆ CLASSIC ☆☆☆

TITLE:	**THE PARENT TRAP**
QUALITY:	★★★★
RECOMMENDATION:	Caution
RATING:	Not rated
RELEASE:	1961
STARRING:	Hayley Mills, Maureen O'Hara, Brian Keith, and Charlie Ruggles
DIRECTOR:	David Swift
GENRE:	Comedy
CONTENT:	Protestant minister and counselors are the objects of caricature
INTENDED AUDIENCE:	Teenagers
REVIEWER:	Protestant Motion Picture Council

This movie is based on the novel *Das Doppelte Lottchen* by Erich Kastner and centers around two twins separated at birth. One goes off with the father, and the other with the mother after the parents divorce. They are reunited at a summer camp where they discover their relationship despite their glaring personality differences. Made to share accommodations, they heartily dislike one another at first but soon become friends.

The girls scheme to bring their parents back together and reunite the family by switching places when camp is over. This leads to some rather incredible adventures, some farcically contrived, to achieve their goal. Plotting to bring about the desired reunion with all kinds of tricks and schemes, the twins succeed when the parents decide to make a second trip to the altar.

The amazing performance of Hayley Mills playing a double part, and the handsome looks of Maureen O'Hara are notable. The lady camp counselors and a Protestant minister, however, are the objects of caricature which is regrettable.

TITLE:	**PASCALI'S ISLAND**
QUALITY:	★★★
RECOMMENDATION:	Caution
RATING:	PG-13
RELEASE:	1988

STARRING:	Ben Kingsley, Charles Dance, and Helen Mirren
DIRECTOR:	James Dearden
GENRE:	Spy
CONTENT:	Non-erotic nudity and some obscenity
INTENDED AUDIENCE:	Adults
REVIEWER:	Ken Kistner

Pascali's Island, based on the book by Barry Unsworth, is a beautiful film set on Nisi island in the declining days of the Ottoman Empire, which tells the story of a Turkish spy, a British adventurer, and a beautiful Viennese aristocrat. Inhabited by Greeks, Turks, and wealthy vacationers, Nisi has become a breeding ground for conspiracy.

Pascali, the spy, has obediently reported to Constantinople for twenty years. Constantinople never replies, but continues to send his meager fee. The elegant Bowles schemes to swindle the Pasha (Turkish ruler). Pascali loves Lydia, but Lydia falls for Bowles. Bowles discovers archaeological treasure, but Pascali finds Bowles has been seeding the sight with false relics. Bowles offers to set Pascali up for life. Pascali panics, and Bowles and Lydia are gunned down. Returning home, Pascali finds out that he was wrong.

There is very little off-color language in *Pascali's Island*. Unfortunately, there is skinny-dipping about which we caution you. Without that misguided realism, this would be an excellent film dealing with trust, faith, and honesty.

☆☆☆ CLASSIC ☆☆☆

TITLE:	**PAY OR DIE (Black and White)**
QUALITY:	★ ★ ★ ★
RECOMMENDATION:	Caution
RATING:	Not rated
RELEASE:	1960
STARRING:	Ernest Borgnine, Zohra Lampert, and Alan Austin
DIRECTOR:	Richard Wilson
GENRE:	Detective
CONTENT:	Violence, graphic murders
INTENDED AUDIENCE:	Adults, mature young people
REVIEWER:	Protestant Motion Picture Council

A New York City policeman of Italian extraction is dedicated to his work far above and beyond the call of duty. Leading a squad of loyal officers in the days of the "Pay or Die" terror inflicted by the Mafia (1906-1909), he attempts to get the neighborhood out of their grip.

In the name of "protection", there is extortion, beatings, bombings, and murder. He pursues his quest until he too is a victim of the dreaded criminals. He was able to prove that the gangsters were ruled from Sicily, even though his assassins were never found, nor the documents carried at the time of his death, yet the back of the organization was broken.

There is much violence (even to putting a bound man in his own baking oven), but the story could not have been told without it. The portrayal of background and people involved in New York's Little Italy of that day is quite well realized, and the drama is convincing.

This is an authentic, well-documented gangster story in which the hero is a policeman—a welcome change.

TITLE:	**PEGGY SUE GOT MARRIED**
QUALITY:	★ ★ ★
RECOMMENDATION:	Bad
RATING:	PG-13
RELEASE:	1986
STARRING:	Kathleen Turner, Nicholas Cage, Barry Miller, and Catherine Hicks
DIRECTOR:	Francis Ford Coppola
GENRE:	Romance/Comedy
CONTENT:	Obscenity, occultism, and sexual immorality
INTENDED AUDIENCE:	Adults
REVIEWER:	Ted Baehr

Peggy Sue Got Married almost makes it, but takes an absurd turn at the end which destroys the picture. Peggy Sue passes out at a high school reunion and goes back to her senior year. She tries to change her life by avoiding her sweetheart/husband-to-be who left her in the future for another woman just before the reunion.

Peggy Sue brings to the fifties the knowledge she has from the eighties and influences history, but she still has a night of love-making with her sweetheart, which gets her pregnant and forces their marriage. When she comes back, it appears she will be reconciled with her husband.

The story is acceptable until Peggy Sue starts coming on to her husband-to-be with disgusting language and has an affair with a high school poet. The worst part is when her grandfather takes her to an absurd Masonic Lodge, where they try some cosmic magic to return her to the future.

In the final analysis, avoid *Peggy Sue Got Married*.

TITLE:	**PELLE THE CONQUEROR (Subtitles)**
QUALITY:	★ ★ ★ ★
RECOMMENDATION:	Extreme Caution

RATING:	Not rated
RELEASE:	1989
STARRING:	Max Von Sydow and Pelle Hvenegaard
DIRECTOR:	Billie August
GENRE:	Historical
CONTENT:	The hardships of farm life in the 1800's with two brief scenes of rustic nudity
INTENDED AUDIENCE:	Adults
REVIEWER:	Ted Baehr

Pelle and his father, Lasse Karlsson, are huddled on a ship headed to Denmark. Lasse says Denmark is a wealthy land where everyone eats roasts with raisins. Survival in Sweden is impossible, so thousands have migrated to Denmark.

When they arrive, Lasse is not hired because he is too old and Pelle is too young. Finally, a farm manager, who arrives late, hires Lasse and Pelle. The manager is a cruel task master. Lasse is assigned to the barn, and Pelle herds the cows. They sleep in the barn. Lasse cries out to Jesus to help him. Mr. Kongstrup, the owner, married his wife for her money. When she couldn't have children, he became a philanderer, siring many bastards. Fed up, Mrs Kongstrup castrates him. Pelle wants to leave. Lasse is too old to venture forth again.

All of the vagaries of mankind are manifest in those who live in and around the farm. *Pelle the Conqueror* is typically Nordic in its melancholic view of life. Even the prayers to Jesus seem unanswerable. This is such a faithful portrait of 19th century agrarian life. *Pelle the Conqueror*, based on the book by Martin Anderson Nexo, is a great movie. It is well worth seeing and quite captivating. Caution is advised because of brief rustic nudity and violence.

TITLE:	**PERSONAL CHOICE (96 Minutes)**
QUALITY:	★ ★ ★
RECOMMENDATION:	Extreme Caution
RATING:	PG
RELEASE:	1989
STARRING:	Martin Sheen, Christian Slater, Sharon Stone, and Robert Foxworth
DIRECTOR:	David Saperstein
GENRE:	Drama
CONTENT:	Profanities
INTENDED AUDIENCE:	Adults
REVIEWER:	Ted Baehr

How delightful to find a movie seeking a relationship with God. Unfortunately, the film-maker was not sensitive to profanity, even though Jesus' Name was used here as an expletive and not a curse.

Eric wants to be an astronaut. His father has been with NASA, and Eric spends every waking hour building rockets and dreaming about space. When he accidentally fires a rocket through his high school's window, his mother sends him away for a month to his father in Oregon. There he meets Colonel Paul Andrews, an astronaut who was saturated with radiation during his brief time on the moon's surface. Paul is dying and angry. However, Eric's love and respect turns Paul away from his hate toward a reaffirmation of life.

In the end, Paul makes it clear to Eric that God is all that matters and we must care for God's creation. When Paul looks like he is about to die, he prays.

"Christ" is used several times as an expletive and an appeal. We would like to recommend this beautifully made film, with its profound character studies, but cannot because of the profanity.

TITLE:	**PHANTASM II**
QUALITY:	★
RECOMMENDATION:	Evil
RATING:	R
RELEASE:	1988
STARRING:	Angus Scrimm, James Le Gros, Reggie Bannister, Paula Irvine, Samantha Phillips, and Kenneth Tiger
DIRECTOR:	Don Coscarelli
GENRE:	Horror
CONTENT:	Nudity, extremely gory violence, obscenities, vulgarities, blasphemies, and a mockery of Christianity
INTENDED AUDIENCE:	Not recommended for any audience
REVIEWER:	Bruce Grimes

The Tall Man, an evil mortician, exhumes dead bodies to make them into his legion of helpers. Mike, Reggie, and Liz track down The Tall Man to revenge the killing of their friends with his lethal silver spheres. They encounter an alcoholic priest, a buffoon who succumbs to The Tall Man. Mike hurls one of the spheres at The Tall Man, which slows him down. Reggie, Mike, and Liz escape to the hearse and are murdered by The Tall Man.

Phantasm II gives evil supremacy over good. This upside-down worldview can only harm the people who see this film. The film is grotesquely violent and cannot be recommended. Christians must stop this type of satanic attack which mocks God. God is sovereign and will judge everyone.

☆☆☆ MASTERPIECE ☆☆☆

TITLE:	**THE PINK PANTHER**
QUALITY:	★ ★ ★ ★
RECOMMENDATION:	Acceptable
RATING:	Not rated
RELEASE:	1964 Color
STARRING:	Peter Sellers, David Niven, Robert Wagner, Claudia Cardinale, Capucine, and Fran Jeffries
DIRECTOR:	Blake Edwards
GENRE:	Comedy
CONTENT:	Nothing objectionable
INTENDED AUDIENCE:	All ages
REVIEWER:	Ted Baehr

Few movie characters are as memorable as the bumbling inspector Jacques Clouseau. The inspired lunacy of the mercurial Peter Sellers turned a simple caper flick into a side-splitting classic.

The first film spun a criminal and romantic imbroglio around the efforts of a master jewel thief to snatch the priceless Pink Panther diamond from an Indian princess on holiday in the Alps. The genius of Peter Sellers turned this film into one of the screen's most profitable series.

David Niven is the film's nominal star as the international arch thief and Robert Wagner is his rascally nephew. However, it is Sellers, in his in-and-out role as the zealous, but incompetent police inspector who commits grand screen larceny.

Clouseau is the kind of person incapable of crossing a room without leaving virtually every stick of furniture in splinters. The accident-prone inspector not only discovers that his icy, ravishing wife (Capucine) is cheating on him with the very criminal he's trying to catch, but also manages to get himself framed for the robbery and tossed into jail, only to emerge in several more popular movies.

In addition to Sellers' incomparable Clouseau, Henry Mancini's dynamic score and its now-standard title theme is exceptional. Also, the animated credits began a new trend in movies, and gave birth to two cartoon series.

☆☆☆ CLASSIC ☆☆☆

TITLE:	**THE PIT AND THE PENDULUM**
QUALITY:	★ ★ ★ ★
RECOMMENDATION:	Caution
RATING:	Not rated

RELEASE:	1961
STARRING:	Vincent Price, John Kerr, Barbara Steele, and Luana Anders
DIRECTOR:	Roger Corman
GENRE:	Horror
CONTENT:	Implications of torture and death
INTENDED AUDIENCE:	Adults
REVIEWER:	Protestant Motion Picture Council

This mystery-drama period piece is based on Edgar Allen Poe's classic tale. All the maca-bre scenes stand out against a background of misty blues and blurring colors to bring forth horror. This is a story of retribution presented in a very melodramatic manner with excellent acting, weird settings, and maintained suspense. It has become a classic.

Nicholas Medina is the owner of a large, spooky, and remote castle which houses an elaborate torture chamber built by his father during the Spanish Inquisition. Stricken with grief after the death of his wife, Elisabeth, Medina becomes obsessed with the no-tion that he accidentally buried her alive. Elisabeth's brother, Francis, suspects foul play and travels to the castle looking for answers.

What he finds however, is that Medina is slowly going mad and claims he can hear Eliza-beth's voice calling to him from throughout the house. Eventually it is revealed that Elisabeth is not dead at all, but had conspired with her lover, the family doctor, to drive her husband insane. To put the seal of doom on her husband, she calls to him and he follows her voice to the crypt where she rises from the grave. His mind snaps, much to their delight (they now can inherit his fortune), but suddenly Medina assumes the iden-tity of his father and becomes a lord high torturer of the Inquisition.

In a fight with Medina, the doctor falls into the pit to his death. Elisabeth is locked in an iron box. The innocent Francis is strapped under the swinging and ever-descending pen-dulum which has a massive steel blade attached to the end.

Just as the blade is about to slice him in two, Francis is rescued by Medina's sister and the butler. While attempting to stop them, Medina falls into the pit and his sister declares that she will seal up the torture chamber forever, not realizing that Elisabeth is still alive in the iron box.

The message is clear that the wages of sin is death. In a genre (horror) that is usually abhorrent, *The Pit and the Pendulum* is one of the better movies.

TITLE:	**PLANES, TRAINS AND AUTOMOBILES**
QUALITY:	★ ★ ★
RECOMMENDATION:	Extreme Caution
RATING:	R
RELEASE:	1987
STARRING:	Steve Martin and John Candy
DIRECTOR:	John Hughes

GENRE:	Comedy
CONTENT:	One scene in which profanity is used unceasingly
INTENDED AUDIENCE:	Adults
REVIEWER:	Doug Brewer

Stolen taxis, snooty flight attendants and re-routed planes are only the beginning. Neal is trying to get to Chicago to celebrate Thanksgiving with his family. His flight is delayed. While he's waiting, he recognizes the man who stole his cab, Del Griffith. Del insists he knows Neal from somewhere. Neal snarls "you stole my cab," but Del apologizes and explains he never forgets a face. What follows is an hilarious trek through Del's world: the motel in the boondocks where the manager knows Del; the folks he gave shower curtain rings at bargain prices; and distant relations who owe him favors.

It is a shame that this funny film should be marred by the quest for the R-rating. There is one scene in which Neal blows off steam at a rental car clerk by using the same four-letter word over and over again. I liked this movie as a whole, but upon mention of the title, my mind jumped to that awful scene. This one scene was far too strong for me to recommend *Planes, Trains and Automobiles*. Wait until it is edited for television.

TITLE:	**POLICE ACADEMY 5: ASSIGNMENT MIAMI BEACH**
QUALITY:	★★
RECOMMENDATION:	Extreme Caution
RATING:	PG
RELEASE:	1988
STARRING:	Bubba Smith, David Graf, Michael Winslow, Leslie Easterbrook, Marion Ramsey, Janet Jones, and Lance Kinsey
DIRECTOR:	Alan Myerson
GENRE:	Comedy
CONTENT:	Crude language and lewdness
INTENDED AUDIENCE:	Teens
REVIEWER:	John Evans, Movie Morality Ministries

This episode takes the motley, bumbling *Police Academy* crew to Miami Beach. The Commandant of the academy is to be honored at a police convention. However, his ranking officer, Captain Harris, goes along to discredit him. The action starts when the Commandant accidentally picks up a bag of stolen jewels at the airport. The inept jewel thieves who lost the bag are on the Commandant's trail. Slapstick mix-ups, kidnappings, battles, and wild chases continue unabated throughout the film.

Dumb and crude pretty well sum up this latest addition to the *Police Academy* series. The comedy is developed around women's brassieres, an attempted girl pickup, and passing gas. Vulgar and profane language are thrown in with the usual bikini-clad girls and low-cut dresses. If you or your kids like fast-moving, slapstick comedies, you can find much more acceptable movies on videotape. This stupidity does not deserve your time or money.

TITLE:	**POLICE ACADEMY 6**
QUALITY:	★
RECOMMENDATION:	Caution
RATING:	Not available
RELEASE:	1989
STARRING:	Bubba Smith, Michael Winslow, and Leslie Easterbrook
DIRECTOR:	Peter Bonerz
GENRE:	Comedy
CONTENT:	Disrespect for authority, vulgarity, and obscenity
INTENDED AUDIENCE:	Teenagers
REVIEWER:	Glennis O'Neal

A crime wave explodes all over the city, masterminded by a mysterious figure who brags that he knows what the cops are gonna do before they do. Police Commissioner Hurst stations his men "undercover." They wash windows, so they can listen at suspect office operations. Such are the antics throughout the film. Nothing comes of those efforts until they set a trap for the "Princess' Jewels." They wait for the thieves to strike. However, the thieves are in a manhole with a Brinks truck covering them, while they use lasers to cut around the jewel-display, which is hauled into the truck. Scenes build to a chase and suspicions about the "leak" narrow to the department.

From beginning to end, this is definitely "slapstick," intended for teenagers. However, it is so ridiculous that teenagers will have a hard time swallowing it. Furthermore, isn't it shameful that filmmakers stoop to depicting our public service agencies as inept imbeciles rather than reliable, capable and protective bodies of government. Nothing can be recommended about this movie—except *stay away!*

☆☆☆ MASTERPIECE ☆☆☆

TITLE:	**POLLYANNA**
QUALITY:	★★★★
RECOMMENDATION:	Acceptable/Must for children
RATING:	Not rated
RELEASE:	1960
STARRING:	Hayley Mills, Jane Wyman, Richard Egan, Kevin Corcoran, Nancy Olson, Donald Crisp, Agnes Moorehead, and Karl Malden
DIRECTOR:	David Swift
GENRE:	Comedy
CONTENT:	Nothing objectionable

INTENDED AUDIENCE: Family

REVIEWER: Protestant Motion Picture Council

This is a superior family film about a girl whose name "Pollyanna" has become a part of the English vernacular to mean someone who is an inveterate optimist.

Upon the death of her parents, Pollyanna comes to live with her Aunt Polly. Aunt Polly, a wealthy woman in a small 1912 town, is severe, domineering and busy in community affairs which she expects to rule. The village is filled with naysayers and depressing townsfolk, but Pollyanna plays the "glad game" imparted by her late missionary father.

She shows that one can be glad about something. Her bright outlook becomes contagious, and she is soon changing matters by always managing to find something good to say in even the blackest occurrence.

As Pollyanna plays her "game," she makes friends in many circles—the town's misanthrope, a mischievous boy escaping from the orphanage, an embittered old hypochondriac invalid who revels in the attention others pay her, and the town's roaring preacher who has little tolerance for anyone and is apparently losing his congregation. When Pollyanna visits him one afternoon, he reads an amulet around her neck with a quote which reads "If you search for the evil in man expecting to find it, you certainly will." The pastor is transformed by the quote, learning that love and gentleness can reach more people and serve them better.

Through Pollyanna's pleading, the cooperation of the preacher and her new friends, the building of a new orphanage takes place and is a huge success. (This is one of the highlights of the film and an ambitious production, full of interest and entertainment.) It brings the townspeople together in a happy bond. When Pollyanna, however, meets with an accident, she nearly loses the "game," but her philosophy shared by many brings its own reward, and the story ends on a touchingly happy note.

The selection of the cast is a wise one, all entering heartily into their parts. Young Hayley Mills is a remarkable Pollyanna, giving a shining performance. She has a fine companion in Kevin Corcoran, the orphan boy. The flavor of the time (1912) is captured successfully in the settings, the costumes, the manners and behaviors of the people.

Based on the novel by Eleanor H. Porter, this is one film which can be enjoyed without reservation by the whole family.

TITLE: **POLTERGEIST III**

QUALITY: ★ ★

RECOMMENDATION: Evil

RATING: PG-13

RELEASE: 1988

STARRING: Tom Skerritt, Nancy Allen, and Heather O'Rourke

DIRECTOR: Gary Sherman

GENRE: Horror

CONTENT: Obscenity, violence, occultism, and spiritual deception

| INTENDED AUDIENCE: | Teenagers and young adults |
| REVIEWER: | Rick Hight |

"[The devil] was a murderer from the beginning, not holding to the truth, for there is no truth in him. When he lies, he speaks his native language, for he is a liar and the father of lies." (John 8:44)

Poltergeist III is one of the most evil and dangerous movies I have ever seen. Moreover, the plot is full of holes and the acting is amateurish.

Carol Anne is living in a Chicago high-rise building with her aunt and uncle because of evil spirits. The spirits, led by Preacher Cain, are stuck in limbo since her father built his house on their grave site. The spirits invade her high-rise to get Carol Anne. A psychic from the previous two films, the most annoying actress in the history of American cinema, comes to save Carol Anne. In the end, magic triumphs over evil, and peace returns.

Witchcraft is an anathema to God. Magic is evil. The name of God is only used as a curse word in this movie. Avoid *Poltergeist III*. If you come across someone who saw this film but who is not mature in Christ, we encourage you to educate them concerning the lies of the devil and the truth of God's Word.

TITLE:	**A PRAYER FOR THE DYING**
QUALITY:	★ ★ ★
RECOMMENDATION:	Extreme Caution
RATING:	R
RELEASE:	1987
STARRING:	Mickey Rourke, Bob Hoskins, Sammi Davis, and Alan Bates
DIRECTOR:	Mike Hodges
GENRE:	War
CONTENT:	Violence and obscenity
INTENDED AUDIENCE:	Adults
REVIEWER:	Doug Brewer

Martin Fallon is a killer for the Irish Republican Army. When he sees a bus full of children destroyed by a bomb meant for a British convoy, he decides it's time to quit. He strikes a deal with a gangster for safe passage to America; however, he must commit one more murder. Unfortunately, he fulfills the deal in front of a priest. The gangster refuses to pay until the priest is silenced.

The movie suffers from Rourke's inconsistent accent and his swaggering. However, in an era of heroes who win by killing everyone else, a man who chooses the right way in the end is surprising. We recommend that Christians avoid *A Prayer for the Dying* because of the violence and rough language.

TITLE:	**PREDATOR**
QUALITY:	★ ★ ★
RECOMMENDATION:	Extreme Caution
RATING:	R
RELEASE:	1987
STARRING:	Arnold Schwarzenegger and Carl Weathers
DIRECTOR:	John McTiernan
GENRE:	Science fiction
CONTENT:	Obscenity, vulgarity, and violence with mild gore
INTENDED AUDIENCE:	Adults
REVIEWER:	Bruce Grimes

Schwarzenegger is hired by the CIA to drop into a hostile Latin American country and rescue an American diplomat. He assembles a team, and they parachute into the jungle to carry out their mission. The story was a ruse to get the rescue squad to eliminate a base camp for a Communist push into a neighboring country.

Then, their troubles begin. Also in the jungle is an unseen alien. One by one, the evil creature begins to kill them. Each of the men are killed by the "thing" that attacks from the treetops. Arnold is the sole survivor. His cunning and strength pits him against the alien.

The film offers plenty of action and heart-pounding suspense. If a dozen obscene words, two unfunny jokes and maybe ten seconds of footage had been removed from this movie, it would have been excellent entertainment. However, nothing will be removed, so *Predator* is not recommended for Christians.

TITLE:	**THE PRESIDIO**
QUALITY:	★ ★
RECOMMENDATION:	Extreme Caution
RATING:	R
RELEASE:	1988
STARRING:	Mark Harmon, Sean Connery, and Meg Ryan
DIRECTOR:	Peter Hyams
GENRE:	Detective
CONTENT:	Profanity, premarital sex, and violence
INTENDED AUDIENCE:	Adults
REVIEWER:	Nancy Hanger

The Presidio reminded me of a generic television police show with unsuitable language. Sean Connery is a Army colonel stationed in the Presidio base in San Francisco. Harmon was an "MP" there, but is now a police detective. He has a bone to pick with Connery, who backed an officer years ago during a run-in between Harmon and that officer. Harmon and Connery must work together to solve a murder. The murdered woman used to be Harmon's duty partner when he was in the Army. The murder weapon matches one owned by the officer with whom Harmon had trouble. He can't wait to get even. He does—in a gruesome chase scene through Chinatown.

Connery's daughter seduces Harmon the first day they meet; they fall in love during the movie. Connery and his daughter have communication problems which they work through in the story. The movie deals with relationships more than the cops-and-robbers plot.

The movie's profanity and loose morals are unacceptable. It won't be remembered as an epic film, if it is remembered at all.

TITLE:	**THE PRINCE OF PENNSYLVANIA**
QUALITY:	★ ★ ★
RECOMMENDATION:	Extreme Caution
RATING:	R
RELEASE:	1988
STARRING:	Keanu Reeves, Fred Ward, Bonnie Bedelia, and Amy Madigan
DIRECTOR:	Ron Nyswaner
GENRE:	Drama
CONTENT:	Bad language, sex, drugs, and rebellion
INTENDED AUDIENCE:	Teenagers and adults
REVIEWER:	Troy Schmidt

Rupert, a lackadaisical high school drop out, is living at home. Due to wild ambition and a radical hippie lifestyle, he and his father do not get along. As a means of escaping their Pennsylvania mining town, he and a love-interest plan to kidnap the father so they can steal the ransom from his property. Even a crazy premise can sometimes be convincingly performed and made to work. Keanu Reeves' portrayal of Rupert, a lost and misunderstood youth, mirrors a painful character as impressive as in previous roles. He's a complex individual: a sort of intelligent rebel or lazy genius.

The Prince of Pennsylvania suffers from a "theme of hopelessness," demonstrated by the pessimism that led to the 1960's social rebellion. It captures the frustration of youth, the anger of hypocrisy, yet offers no glimpse of love or encouragement to adolescents watching the film. Answers such as running away, rebelling, or dropping out are not what our children need to hear.

You will find depression behind the humor. Christians may want to pass on this one.

TITLE:	**THE PRINCESS BRIDE**
QUALITY:	★ ★ ★
RECOMMENDATION:	Caution
RATING:	PG
RELEASE:	1987
STARRING:	Cary Elwes, Mandy Patinkin, and Peter Falk
DIRECTOR:	Bob Reiner
GENRE:	Fantasy/Romance/Action adventure
CONTENT:	An exclamatory profanity and one obscenity
INTENDED AUDIENCE:	Teenagers and adults
REVIEWER:	Lili Baehr

A young boy is home in bed sick. His grandfather comes to read him a story. The story "comes to life" as he reads it . . .

The story is about "true" love and is full of adventure, comic ruffians, sword fights, and mean villains. Our hero, Wesley, is a farm hand, our heroine, Buttercup, is the owner's daughter. They are in love. Wesley goes off to seek his fortune. Buttercup hears that he has been killed by pirates. She knows she will never love again. The mean Prince is looking for a bride and chooses her. She tells him that she can never love him. That does not upset him, he announces their engagement. That night she is abducted by three ruffians and the adventure begins . . . eventually to reach a classic fairy tale ending.

The movie is fun and funny. The negatives are two dirty words, an exclamatory profanity and the fact that our hero has spent some time being a pirate.

Also, this movie is produced by Norman Lear of the People for the American Way. Christians may not want to put money into his pocket to be used against us.

TITLE:	**THE PRODIGAL**
QUALITY:	★ ★ ★ ★
RECOMMENDATION:	Acceptable
RATING:	PG
RELEASE:	1984
STARRING:	John Hammond, Hope Lange, John Cullum, and Morgan Brittany
DIRECTOR:	James F. Collier
GENRE:	Drama
CONTENT:	Nothing objectionable

| INTENDED AUDIENCE: | Adults and young adults |
| REVIEWER: | F.L. Lindberg |

This is top quality production. The pace is measured, so your pulse is not racing as you try to guess what they will do. Total chaos is kept at bay—barely.

The Stuarts are an American family in trouble. Father is successful; Mother is charming; one son is in seminary; and the other son is a "drop-out" who turns tennis pro. The seminarian has the least problems, but all of them suffer deep soul-searching and hardships. Drugs, alcohol, "the fast track," extramarital temptations, and other crises of modern life are ever ready to trip them up.

Dramatic situations are handled delicately, but always with an air of realism. The prodigal son wanders in and out of an affair with a rich, female photographer. Remarkably, this is done with no nudity or objectionable language. How this family copes with life is an inspiring tale.

Billy Graham helps to resolve their torments. When his crusade comes to town, each of the four family members is ready to take a stand for Jesus. Stand they do, together, in triumph over problems and heartaches. Backs turned on false friends and false goals, they find the strength to make a new start.

The Prodigal is sensitive, subtle family drama. Top-notch acting, a well-matched musical score, and beautiful cinematography have been blended masterfully.

TITLE:	**PROJECT X**
QUALITY:	★ ★ ★
RECOMMENDATION:	Caution
RATING:	PG
RELEASE:	1987
STARRING:	Matthew Broderick
DIRECTOR:	Jonathan Kaplan
GENRE:	Science fiction/Action adventure
CONTENT:	Mild off-color language and some anti-authoritarian elements combined with a Darwinian worldview
INTENDED AUDIENCE:	Teenagers
REVIEWER:	John Raines

Virgil the chimpanzee is brought from the jungle to Dr. Terry McDonald for her research. She teaches Virgil sign language; however, her grant is not renewed. Virgil is shipped off to the Air Force Weapons Research facility in Florida. Jimmy Garrett, who recently lost his wings, is demoted to testing chimpanzees. He teaches the chimps to fly in a flight-simulator. One day, he is told to evacuate the chamber and leave the chimp. He doesn't notices a radiation device is irradiating the cockpit to see if a human pilot can make it to Russia through heavy radiation after a nuclear attack. Jimmy tells the Review Board that people will act differently because they fear death.

The chimps break into the chamber where they destroy the simulator. Everyone fears a meltdown, but Virgil unjams the reactor. Jimmy and Terry take Virgil and his girlfriend to a plane which they steal to escape. Virgil and a few chimps take off without Jimmy and Terry. They crash in the Everglades. Because the project is so top-secret, the Air Force decides to abandon the plane rather than make a fuss. Everyone lives happily ever after.

The problem with *Project X* is that it presumes an evolutionary worldview and treats the chimpanzees as human beings. However, it is a entertaining movie, which will not harm anyone who has a strong Biblical worldview.

TITLE:	**PUNCHLINE**
QUALITY:	★ ★ ★ ★
RECOMMENDATION:	Extreme Caution
RATING:	R
RELEASE:	Fall, 1988
STARRING:	Tom Hanks and Sally Field
DIRECTOR:	David Seltzer
GENRE:	Comedy
CONTENT:	Rough language, bawdy humor, and obscenity
INTENDED AUDIENCE:	Adults
REVIEWER:	Gene Burke

A successful career as a stand-up comic is determined by the delivery of the punchline. *Punchline* very successfully does that, with heart and much more. It depicts friendship, love, and the importance of family.

Punchline presents two distinctly different individuals. Both desire to make others laugh. A student moonlights as a comedian at a nightclub to get through medical school. He is considered the most likely to be discovered. A wife and mother of two girls with a dedicated husband performs at the same club. The strain on each of them is incredible. The pressure on the student causes a near-breakdown, while her marriage is being threatened. They encourage each other through friendship. When the typical script would have depicted an affair, this film describes true friendship, love and commitment to family values.

This is a powerful and wonderful story that affirms the commitment to avoid temptation, whatever the cost—to protect "that which God has joined together." However, we must caution you that there are two scenes where very vulgar jokes are told, one by a little girl.

TITLE:	**PURPLE PEOPLE EATER**
QUALITY:	★ ★ ★
RECOMMENDATION:	Caution
RATING:	PG

RELEASE:	1988
STARRING:	Ned Beatty and Shelley Winters
DIRECTOR:	Linda Shayne
GENRE:	Children/Drama
CONTENT:	Kidnapping, rough treatment, and one exclamatory profanity
INTENDED AUDIENCE:	Children
REVIEWER:	Charlotte Knox

Grandfather Sam stays with Billy for the summer while his parents are on vacation. While working, they discover some old records and Billy starts playing them. When the *Purple People Eater* record plays, Billy sees a flash of light and goes to see what it was. He finds a purple people eater sitting in a tree.

Billy discovers "Purple" can play jazz. They form a band. The band soon decides to hold a benefit concert to save the apartments where Sam lives. Purple gets "thingnapped" by the owner of the apartments to stop the concert. Purple escapes and tells Billy that he must return and leaves in a puff of smoke. Billy goes on with the concert and makes an appeal to the City Council to save the apartments. The council decides the apartments will not be destroyed.

Caution is advised because there is one exclamatory profanity, but there is no obscenity, sex, violence, or nudity. All of the characters are enjoyable except the greedy landlord. Of course, it is necessary to have a villain, but it is sad that property rights are once more lambasted, while government intervention is lauded. Unfortunately, this film condones the city stealing the landlord's property rights.

TITLE:	**RACHEL RIVER**
QUALITY:	★★★
RECOMMENDATION:	Caution
RATING:	PG-13
RELEASE:	1989
STARRING:	Craig T. Nelson, James Olson, and Pamela Reed
DIRECTOR:	Sandy Smolman
GENRE:	Drama
CONTENT:	Vulgarity, obscenity, minor expletives, and one suggestive sexual encounter
INTENDED AUDIENCE:	Adults
REVIEWER:	Bruce Grimes

Mary Graving, a gifted writer and divorced mother, lives in Rachel, Minnesota. In her forties and attractive, she cares for her children and works part time at a radio station. Her former husband takes the children camping, leaving Mary alone. Momo, the "town idiot," discovers the body of a reclusive widow. The sheriff determines she died in her sleep. The undertaker consoles the family. The two men are attracted to Mary. The mortician, who has an intellectual bond with Mary, is too self-conscious to be an effective suitor. The good ol' boy deputy sheriff is obnoxious, but confidently sexy and not as stupid as the mortician insists. The importance of loving others and having meaning in one's life is explored. The story unfolds the pain many people suffer in life: growing old; no sense of direction; and no sense of worth. The film is sensitive and insightful, never blatant or obvious.

The film is a well-crafted work with excellent performances, a good script, beautiful cinematography, and strong direction. Unfortunately, the film is sprinkled with obscene words. We urge caution.

TITLE:	**RAIN MAN**
QUALITY:	★★★★
RECOMMENDATION:	Extreme Caution
RATING:	R
RELEASE:	1988
STARRING:	Tom Cruise and Dustin Hoffman
DIRECTOR:	Barry Levinson
GENRE:	Drama
CONTENT:	Some extremely rough language and one quick-flash breast scene
INTENDED AUDIENCE:	Adults
REVIEWER:	Gene Burke

Fast-talking Charlie Babbit is about to close another deal when his father dies, leaving him to handle the aftermath. He discovers he has an older autistic brother, Raymond, living in a special home. When this brother inherits his father's $3 million, Charlie sets out to trick Raymond out of the inheritance. Charlie, as a youngster, had an imaginary friend who sang to him. He discovers "Rain Man" was not imaginary; rather, he was Raymond. While attempting to weasel his brother out of the money, Charlie is taught life's lessons by Raymond, who is incapable of understanding these lessons. When Charlie "uses" Raymond in Los Vegas to raise money for a debt and Raymond accomplishes Charlie's request, Charlie is stopped cold in his estimation of Raymond's abilities.

Through Dustin Hoffman's brilliant performance, God's love for the "weak among us" is evident. As the film unfolds, Charlie turns from being a selfish, conniving young man to a giving, understanding human being. Extreme caution should be exercised as the language in this film is rough. Also, there is an unacceptable flash of nudity. However, the overall impact of *Rain Man* is powerful and uplifting.

TITLE:	**RAMBO III**
QUALITY:	★★★
RECOMMENDATION:	Bad

RATING:	R
RELEASE:	1988
STARRING:	Sylvester Stallone, Richard Crenna, and Marc de Jonge
DIRECTOR:	Peter MacDonald
GENRE:	Action adventure
CONTENT:	Violence
INTENDED AUDIENCE:	Adults
REVIEWER:	Doug Brewer

Rambo is living in a Buddhist monastery, hoping to find peace (which can only be found in Jesus Christ, not Buddhism). At night, he goes into a warehouse in Bangkok and has little Thais bet on him as he stick-fights with a burly opponent. When John Rambo's old commanding officer and mentor, Colonel Trautman gets captured by the Russians, Rambo rides into Afghanistan, shows the Rebels how a real man fights a war, and rescues Trautman by single-handedly destroying the Red Army.

Laced with an overly melodramatic score, *Rambo III* is about: explosions, Sylvester Stallone with no shirt, blood, and killing. It's cheesecake, covered with red-tinted Karo syrup, trying to pass itself off as a cause.

All in all, *Rambo III* is a violent fantasy that will probably make a pot of money and spawn another sequel or two. The only question left is, "How many more?" As for this one, we say, "That's three, Sly. You're outta here."

TITLE:	**RAISING ARIZONA**
QUALITY:	★★★
RECOMMENDATION:	Extreme Caution
RATING:	PG-13
RELEASE:	1987
STARRING:	Nicolas Cage, Holly Hunter, Trey Wilson, John Goodman, and Bill Forsythe
DIRECTOR:	Joel Coen
GENRE:	Comedy
CONTENT:	Violence and profanity
INTENDED AUDIENCE:	Adolescents and adults
REVIEWER:	Brandy Egan

Herbert I. McDonough, "Hi," is repeatedly arrested for robbing convenience stores. He falls in love with Edwina, "Ed," the police officer who fingerprints him each time. They get married.

They want a family, but she fails to get pregnant. The doctor suggests they adopt. Nathan and Florence Arizona have quintuplets. Ed and Hi decide they will take one of the Arizona babies because "they have more than they can handle." Hi's boss realizes that the baby is one of the Arizona quintuplets. Offering a $25,000 reward, Mr. Arizona has the police department and FBI tracking his kidnapped son. Two brothers, who have just escaped from prison, show up at Hi's trailer, and they take the baby for the reward money.

There follows a series of comic episodes. In the end, Hi and Ed take the baby back to the rightful parents. Mr. Arizona tells them not to give up on having their own children.

Raising Arizona implies that murder, kidnapping, and robbery are okay; whereas, all are sins! Therefore, extreme caution is recommended.

☆☆☆ CLASSIC ☆☆☆

TITLE:	**RAYMIE**
QUALITY:	★★★
RECOMMENDATION:	Acceptable
RATING:	Not rated
RELEASE:	1960
STARRING:	David Ladd, Julie Adams, John Agar, and Charles Winninger
DIRECTOR:	Frank McDonald
GENRE:	Drama
CONTENT:	Nothing objectionable
INTENDED AUDIENCE:	Family

On a California fishing pier with a number of seasoned veterans, a young boy sets his heart on catching a legendary giant barracuda, "Old Moe," who is responsible, according to the fishermen, for all the "ones that got away." When he eventually hooks the fish, he finds that the effort and the desire counted more than the realization. He lets the majestic barracuda go, considering him an old friend.

An easy-going, natural, calmly told story, with some homely philosophy well-expressed and which has good effect on those involved. This, with a simple plot and some pertinent observations on friendship, make for good entertainment. It has some mild excitement, but no violence.

TITLE:	**RED HEAT**
QUALITY:	★★★
RECOMMENDATION:	Bad
RATING:	R
RELEASE:	1988

STARRING:	Arnold Schwarzenegger and James Belushi
DIRECTOR:	Walter Hill
GENRE:	Action adventure
CONTENT:	Profanity, nudity, violence, and obscenity
INTENDED AUDIENCE:	Adults
REVIEWER:	Ted Baehr

Red Heat is a hard driving action film with a Stalinist tempo. Except for the KGB pacing, humor, and action, this is a grotesque mockery of everything decent. *Red Heat* idolizes Gestapo tactics, lionizes violence, and undermines morality.

Red Heat tells the story of a Soviet cop, Ivan Danko, who chases a Russian drug pusher, Viktor, to Chicago where Danko teams up with the foul-mouthed Detective Art Ritsig. After much blood and guts, nudity and profanity, rebellion and destruction of property, Danko and Art get Viktor.

This lightweight plot sells several deceptive messages which are clearly stated in the dialogue. *Red Heat* starts off with excessive nudity and ends with excessive violence. Avoid this grotesque Hollywood cop film. You will be glad you did.

TITLE:	**RED SORGHUM (Subtitles)**
QUALITY:	★★★★
RECOMMENDATION:	Caution
RATING:	Not rated
RELEASE:	1988
STARRING:	Gong Li, Jiang Wen, and Liu Ji
DIRECTOR:	Zhang Yimou
GENRE:	Drama
CONTENT:	Three vulgarities in the subtitles since the dialogue is spoken in Chinese Mandarin; also, child nudity
INTENDED AUDIENCE:	Adults
REVIEWER:	Bruce Grimes

Set in the 1920's in southern China, the story revolves around a young woman who is "sold" to the owner of a vineyard. The owner dies, and she inherits his estate. It is a difficult life with no luxuries and few necessities, but with her faithful helpers, the woman is able to harvest the red sorghum and turn it into wine. The woman falls in love with a worker, and they marry. Nine years later, their nine year old son frolics in the wine barrels as they work. The Japanese invade China. The troop trucks arrive at the winery, and the Chinese from surrounding villages are gathered. The Japanese force the Chinese to destroy the red sorghum crops, and the brutal occupation begins as the Japanese torture the Chinese leaders. The woman, her husband, and the workers seek revenge, and justice is served on the Japanese.

Red Sorghum is a breathtaking film of stunning proportion. It is a small gem that is visually and contextually rewarding. Winner of the Golden Bear Award at the 1988 Berlin Film Festival, *Red Sorghum* is the best film to emerge from China in many years.

☆☆☆ MASTERPIECE ☆☆☆

TITLE:	**REPENTANCE (Subtitles)**
QUALITY:	★★★★
RECOMMENDATION:	Caution
RATING:	PG
RELEASE:	1987
STARRING:	Avtandil Makharadze, Ia Ninidze, and Merab Ninidze
DIRECTOR:	Tengiz Abuladze
GENRE:	Drama
CONTENT:	A scathing expose of the evils of communism
INTENDED AUDIENCE:	Adults (Most children will fail to grasp the story)
REVIEWER:	Ted Baehr

Repentance was banned in its homeland, Russia, because it exposes the evils of communism, statism, and totalitarianism while lifting up the suffering Church and triumphant, eternal Christianity. Christians should see and support *Repentance*.

Repentance is an allegory about Russia under Stalin. It tells about Varlam, the communist mayor of a small town who tries to destroy all individuality and Christianity, but ends up destroying himself and his family.

Repentance opens with Keti baking cakes in the shape of churches. Then, it cuts to Mayor Varlam's funeral. After his burial, someone exhumes his body to everyone's horror. This grisly activity continues until we discover that Keti has been exhuming him because he persecuted unto death both her father, Sandor, an artist who loved Jesus, and her beautiful mother, Nina. Sandor is a Christ-figure, who suffers with quiet strength the avaricious machinations of the state.

Varlam is proud of himself. He is full of banal wit and pretends to deal with every situation with aplomb. He is the devil incarnate, as we see when his son confesses to a priest only to find that the priest is Varlam the Devil. In the end, Varlam's grandson takes his own life because of the atrocious sins of his father and his grandfather. The boy's father repents, exhumes Varlam and throws him off a cliff. Likewise, *Repentance* calls the people of the world to repent of the sin of communism by throwing it into the dustbin of history.

God is the center of this film. The Spirit He gives us cannot be defeated by the Devil, or petty Marxist tyrants. The last dialogue in this heartrending film captures its essence:

Old Woman: "Does this road lead to a church?"

Keti: "This is Varlam street. It will not take you to a church."

Old Woman: "What good is a road, if it doesn't lead to a church?"

This is a beautiful film. There are moments of great suspense and moments of laughter. We recommend *Repentance* very highly, but with caution. There is a brief scene of shadow nudity; an unfortunate blemish in one of the most Christian films to come along in years.

Also, some parts of *Repentance* may fail for some Americans because it has references that only Russians will understand, but it is well worth seeing, even with these obscure moments. For others, *Repentance* may require work and persistence, but if you apply the effort to get into it, it is very, very rewarding.

If you have friends who are drifting into humanism, socialism, communism, or any other statist evil, convince them to see *Repentance* so they can understand that the truth is to be found in Jesus Christ, not in the state.

☆☆☆ CLASSIC ☆☆☆

TITLE:	**REPRIEVE (AKA: CONVICTS FOUR)**
QUALITY:	★★★
RECOMMENDATION:	Acceptable
RATING:	Not rated
RELEASE:	1962
STARRING:	Ben Gazzara, Stuart Whitman, Vincent Price, Rod Steiger, Broderick Crawford, and Sammy Davis, Jr.
DIRECTOR:	Millard Kaufman
GENRE:	Prison Drama
CONTENT:	Nothing objectionable
INTENDED AUDIENCE:	Adults
REVIEWER:	Protestant Motion Picture Council

With John Resko as advisor, his autobiography as source material, his paintings featured, and with the cooperation of Folsome prison officials, this unusual prison drama is graphically told. Beginning with the preparations for Resko's electrocution in Sing Sing for the slaying of a storekeeper two years before, to the commutation of his sentence twenty minutes before his execution, the story unfolds, carefully detailed to all aspects of prison life.

He is transferred to Dannemora where he attempts an escape. With the coming of a new Principal Keeper with modern theories on rehabilitation, Resko's life suddenly changes when his artistic abilities are discovered. He helps others to reach their potentialities, gets a reprieve in 1949 and finds a place in the art world through his own contributions and the interest of others.

All of this makes an absorbing film, even if it ignores the basic sinfulness of man.

☆☆☆ MASTERPIECE ☆☆☆

TITLE:	**REQUIEM FOR A HEAVYWEIGHT**
QUALITY:	★★★★
RECOMMENDATION:	Caution
RATING:	Not rated
RELEASE:	1962
STARRING:	Anthony Quinn, Jackie Gleason, Mickey Rooney, Julie Harris, Jack Dempsey, and Cassius Clay
DIRECTOR:	Ralph Nelson
GENRE:	Drama
CONTENT:	One drunk scene
INTENDED AUDIENCE:	Adult
REVIEWER:	Protestant Motion Picture Council

After taking a brutal pounding in what proves to be his last fight, a heavyweight who had nearly been a champion, learns that he is "finished." A doctor tells him that if he fights again he will probably be blinded. He finds through bitter experience that he is good for nothing else. He has been the victim of his manager and of a gambling syndicate who count on the profits he can accrue.

An encounter with a state employment counselor who's interested in his welfare might have made a difference, but his manager gets him drunk, and he loses his chance. The man's misery builds to a climax of near servitude, when, broken in heart and spirit, he becomes a caricature wrestler under the management of the man he once trusted. Any vestige of humanity is destroyed, and complete deterioration is envisaged.

This drama, which had been a television presentation, acquires stature on the screen where it moves inexorably among the low characters in theme, settings and situations, with appropriate dialogue. Directed with sensitivity, it is well-acted with realism. Anthony Quinn is truly outstanding as a man whose whole life has been boxing and who now must leave it behind, along with what dignity he had acquired through his noble suffering. In the end, he debases himself for the benefit of a friend who really isn't.

TITLE:	**THE RESCUE**
QUALITY:	★★★
RECOMMENDATION:	Caution
RATING:	PG
RELEASE:	1988
STARRING:	Kevin Dillon, Christina Harnos, Marc Price, Ned Vaughn, Ian Giatti, Charles Haid, Edward Albert, Timothy Carhart, Michael Gates Phenicie, Mel Wong, and James Cromwell

DIRECTOR:	Ferdinand Fairfax
GENRE:	Action adventure
CONTENT:	Some profanity
INTENDED AUDIENCE:	Family
REVIEWER:	Glennis O'Neal

At the U. S. Naval Base in South Korea, Admiral Rothman sends in the SEAL SQUAD to blow up an inoperable U.S. submarine that has been testing the latest equipment. Action must be taken before the North Koreans seize the new equipment. The SEALs parachute into the ocean, locate the sub, and blow it up. As they surface, a Korean patrol captures them. "Roth" overhears his father, Admiral Rothman, schedule a meeting for rescue plans. Later, he, Shawn and Adrian listen to the details of the rescue operation, coded as "The Phoenix." When the Admiral announces that the rescue will be cancelled, J.J. insists on going through with the rescue. Pursued over land and sea by no-nonsense North Koreans, this adventuresome pack of teenagers keep charging in hopes of rescuing their fathers.

It's worth every minute to join these courageous young people as they venture out to free the fathers they love. This would have been a perfect family adventure were it not for the light profanity. Therefore, we recommend that you exercise caution.

TITLE:	**THE RESCUERS**
QUALITY:	★★★★
RECOMMENDATION:	Acceptable
RATING:	G
RELEASE:	1977
STARRING:	Voices of Bob Newhart, Eva Gabor, Geraldine Page, and Joe Flynn
DIRECTOR:	Wolfgang Reitherman, John Lundsbery, and Art Stevens
GENRE:	Animation/Fantasy
CONTENT:	Nothing objectionable
INTENDED AUDIENCE:	Children
REVIEWER:	Troy Schmidt

The Rescuers is another Walt Disney movie which will entertain the children.

A corked bottle with an urgent note inside from a kidnapped orphan girl floats from the sea into New York harbor. Two beachcomber mice take it to the basement of the United Nations building, where a delegation of mice from the International Rescue Aid Society are meeting. The note reads: "To Morningside Orphanage. I'm in terrible trouble. Help!—Penny."

Miss Bianca, the ambassador from Hungary, and Bernard, a shy little janitor, set out to rescue Penny. The girl is being held captive in a swamp by the villainous Madame Medusa. Comic relief is provided by a bird named Orville, who transports the mice as they search for the girl.

Eva Gabor's unmistakable voice brings sweetness and innocence to a very classy cartoon character. Bob Newhart's Bernard is exceptionally gratifying, as his hard luck, worrisome stutter is the perfect contrast to Bianca's confident nature. The voices are all well-suited to the characters.

This film is visual, colorful and slapstick. Children will love it; adults might be slightly bored.

A tiny cautionary note: one character, a hillbilly mouse, gulps down a liquid at times that makes his eyes water and his mouth catch fire. Unquestionably this is moonshine, though no name is given it. On the other hand, little Penny prays for help before she goes to bed and gets it—a tremendous lesson in God working in our lives.

TITLE:	**THE RETURN OF THE SWAMP THING**
QUALITY:	★ ★
RECOMMENDATION:	Caution
RATING:	PG
RELEASE:	1989
STARRING:	Louis Jordan, Heather Locklear, Sarah Douglas, and Dick Durock as "Swamp Thing"
DIRECTOR:	Jim Wynorski
GENRE:	Comedy/Horror
CONTENT:	Limited profanity and some sexual references
INTENDED AUDIENCE:	Teenagers and young adults
REVIEWER:	Troy Schmidt

The Return of the Swamp Thing is based on a D.C. comic book scientist who has mutated into part man, part plant-creature. He's the good guy who saves others from the bad guys. Enter sinister Dr. Arcane, who tests his anti-aging formula on unsuspecting humans. When his beautiful step-daughter comes to ask questions about the death of her mother, Dr. Arcane realizes that he needs her blood type to make him young again. It's Swamp Thing to the rescue!

A major problem with *The Return of the Swamp Thing* is that it's not campy enough. Also, the action could have been a little more exciting. The cast knows it's a bad film, so they try to act bad and that's okay. The language was mild with one exception and no nudity except for a few sexual references. Compared to network television, this was Romper Room.

However, we do not recommend that you pay the price of admission to see *The Return of the Swamp Thing*. This is boring.

TITLE:	**RETURN TO SNOWY RIVER**
QUALITY:	★ ★ ★
RECOMMENDATION:	Caution
RATING:	PG
RELEASE:	1988
STARRING:	Tom Burlinson, Sigrid Thornton, and Nicholas Eadie
DIRECTOR:	Geoff Burrowes
GENRE:	Action adventure
CONTENT:	Profanity and loose morality
INTENDED AUDIENCE:	Families
REVIEWER:	Christian Jackson with Hannah Jackson

An Australian mountaineer, Jim, has been rounding up wild horses to gain the wealth he needs to win Jessica's hand. When Jim returns to Snowy River, he finds that Jessica is being courted by Alistair Patton, the local banker's son. Through many twists in the plot, Jessica decides for Jim. Alistair steals Jim's herd as revenge, and the movie takes off. Not a moment passes without a thrill. The film gives an exceptional view of the beauty of the horses, making you feel as if you are on horseback at full gallop.

The Lord's Holy Name is used profanely once. It is very disturbing that Jessica decides to go to live with Jim without benefit of marriage. However, there are no sex scenes. Please write Disney Productions (500 South Buena Vista Street, Burbank, CA 91521) and ask why they undermined this beautiful family film with one profanity and an endorsement of living together outside of marriage. Disney should be encouraged to be inclusive of Christians, not exclusive.

TITLE:	**REVENGE OF THE NERDS II: NERDS IN PARADISE**
QUALITY:	★
RECOMMENDATION:	Bad
RATING:	PG-13
RELEASE:	1987
STARRING:	Robert Carradine and Anthony Edwards
DIRECTOR:	Joe Roth
GENRE:	Comedy
CONTENT:	Profanity and coarse sexual humor
INTENDED AUDIENCE:	Teens
REVIEWER:	Christopher Farrell

In their battle against discrimination, Lamda Lamda Lamda sets out for Fort Lauderdale,

the site of the National Greek Council Meeting. Vicious Alpha Beta fraternity boys pro-
pose a physical requirements rule designed to exclude nerds. The nerds of "Tri-Lam"
defeat the bill. The Alpha Betas then set the poor computer geeks up for a conduct violation, which is thwarted just in time.

Drawing upon such creative wellsprings as Love Boat and Gilligan's Island, this film will
attract the same audience, but will disappoint even this crowd as the gags are most often
lewd and rarely funny. I also find it disturbing that both nerd films show the protagonists
smoking dope, as if it were in character for such "squares" and acceptable for everyone.

Nerds in Paradise is a feature-length argument against sequels. My sentiments are best
expressed in Proverbs 26:11 which says: "As a dog returns to his own vomit so a fool
repeats his folly."

TITLE:	**RIVER'S EDGE**
QUALITY:	★ ★ ★
RECOMMENDATION:	Evil
RATING:	R
RELEASE:	1987
STARRING:	Crispin Glover, Keanu Reeves, Ione Skye, Roxana Zal, Daniel Roebuck, Joshua Miller, and Dennis Hopper
DIRECTOR:	Tim Hunter
GENRE:	Drama
CONTENT:	Nudity, violence, profanity, drugs, and evil
INTENDED AUDIENCE:	Teenagers
REVIEWER:	Ted Baehr

River's Edge is a portrait of the evil nature of the youth of today. *River's Edge* opens up with
Samson, otherwise known as John, having just strangled a young girl, Jamie, to death
for no reason at all. He is seen by a twelve-year-old, Tim, who tells several friends. They
come out, look at the body and go back to school. One of the teenagers, Len, makes a big
deal of protecting John.

After a while, one of them, Matt, calls the police, thinking that other people are doing
the same. None of the teenagers cares. They just act out of vague memories of what they
should do. Eventually, the local dope addict, Feck, who killed his girlfriend twenty years
earlier, becomes John's friend and then kills him. At the end, there is a funeral for Jamie.
Everybody is cleaned up, sitting in the church.

No one in the movie has any sense of right or wrong. *River's Edge* is a statement against
the decadence of our society. None of the other characters has any hint of human decency. Christians should avoid *River's Edge*. It is full of nudity, cruelty, and nihilism. We
need to look upon the true, the good, and the beautiful; not on the world as it is presented in *River's Edge*.

TITLE:	**ROBOCOP**
QUALITY:	★★
RECOMMENDATION:	Evil
RATING:	R
RELEASE:	1987
STARRING:	Peter Weller, Nancy Allen, Daniel O'Herlihy, Ronnie Cox, Kurtwood Smith, and Miguel Ferrer
DIRECTOR:	Paul Verhoeven
GENRE:	Science fiction
CONTENT:	Extreme violence and profanity
INTENDED AUDIENCE:	Adults
REVIEWER:	Chris Farrell

Robocop is a futuristic thriller. The scene is Detroit in the 21st Century. Alex Murphy is assigned a precinct where an officer was just killed. He is blown apart by a gang his first time out.

Meanwhile, in the conference room of the corporation in charge of police, CCP (a reference to the Soviet Union), new law enforcement ideas are being presented. Cut to Murphy's body in the emergency room. We see through his eyes the transition out of his old life into his new one as Robocop. Murphy is to be erased from the cyborg memory of Robocop, but soon familiar faces and places trigger the biological memory inside this mechanical superman. As Robocop tracks down the gang, the paths of justice and revenge lead straight to the upper offices of CCP . . . his inventors, his owners.

This film is full of violence, profanity, and gloom. Nothing redeems the film conceptually or technically. Spare yourself from the worldly confusion, depravity, and seductive horror of *Robocop*.

TITLE:	**ROCKET GIBRALTAR**
QUALITY:	★★★
RECOMMENDATION:	Caution
RATING:	PG
RELEASE:	1988
STARRING:	Burt Lancaster
DIRECTOR:	Daniel Petrie
GENRE:	Drama
CONTENT:	Profanity, mildly crude language, implied sex, and social drinking

322 REVIEWS OF SELECTED MOVIES

INTENDED AUDIENCE:	All ages
REVIEWER:	John Evans of Movie Morality Guide

Seventy-seven-year-old Levi Rockwell is comfortably retired at a large home near the Atlantic seashore. To celebrate his birthday, his children arrive with their families for a festive party. The mood is subdued, since Levi has a heart condition. All share a deep love for Levi, including the children. One night when Levi and the kids are strolling along the beach, Levi tells them he'd like to have a Vikings' funeral. The Vikings didn't bury their dead, but set them afloat in a boat and ignited the boat with flaming arrows. The kids secretly start preparing such a funeral for Levi.

The families are concerned about young, single "Aunt Agnes" who brings her boyfriend. Some of the dialogue concerning her affair gets rather explicit. Levi recites some comical poetry which is also suggestive, as are some remarks of the younger set.

It's sad that Levi has no spiritual base or hope for eternity. *Rocket Gibraltar* can be recommended with caution.

TITLE:	**THE ROSARY MURDERS**
QUALITY:	★ ★ ★
RECOMMENDATION:	Extreme Caution
RATING:	R
RELEASE:	1987
STARRING:	Donald Sutherland and Charles Durning
DIRECTOR:	Fred Walton
GENRE:	Mystery
CONTENT:	Some blood, some profanity, and adult subject matter
INTENDED AUDIENCE:	Adults
REVIEWER:	Marlys M. Moxley

Should a priest break the seal of the confessional and give police information that would help solve the murders of several priests and nuns in the Detroit area? Another priest observes, "We are in the business of saving souls, not saving lives." Thus, the audience is not only given a mystery to solve, but a moral lesson to consider.

The movie received an R-rating because of adult subject matter and some rather coarse language. Keeping this in mind, it is encouraging to see a man of the cloth portrayed as an upright, honest, and reverent individual. However, the subject matter is definitely not for Christian moviegoers, so be forewarned.

TITLE:	**R.O.T.O.R.**
QUALITY:	★ ★
RECOMMENDATION:	Acceptable
RATING:	PG

RELEASE:	1988
STARRING:	Richard Gesswein, Margaret Trigg, and Jane Smith
DIRECTOR:	Cullen Blaine
GENRE:	Science fiction
CONTENT:	Violence, but not excessive
INTENDED AUDIENCE:	Teenagers and adults
REVIEWER:	Ted Baehr

R.O.T.O.R. tells the story of a scientist with the Dallas Police Department, Dr. Coldyron, who has designed a robotic policeman to cure the crime problems of the world. The mayor thinks that Dr. Coldyron needs to be removed from the artificial policeman project, so the mayor can use R.O.T.O.R. for his political advantage. When Coldyron walks out, the robot escapes and goes wild. Dr. Coldyron tracks down his runaway robot and brings it under control.

This standard action fare is devoid of the profanity, excessive violence, and sex. *R.O.T.O.R.* is acceptable viewing for anyone who likes action adventure. In spite of its low budget, it is beautifully filmed, exhibiting the promise of the new creative team.

TITLE:	**ROXANNE**
QUALITY:	★★★★
RECOMMENDATION:	Extreme Caution
RATING:	PG
RELEASE:	1987
STARRING:	Steve Martin and Dayrl Hannah
DIRECTOR:	Fred Schepisi
GENRE:	Comedy
CONTENT:	Profanity, drug/alcohol, nudity, violence, and sexual innuendos
INTENDED AUDIENCE:	All ages
REVIEWER:	John Evans

Charlie is a fire department chief in a small town, liked by all the townspeople. He has an unusually long, comical nose. A young woman, Roxanne, arrives in town to study astronomy and soon calls on Charlie for help when she gets locked out of her house. Roxanne is attracted to one of Charlie's firemen, Chris, but Chris is too bashful to pursue her. Although Charlie secretly loves Roxanne himself, he helps Chris write letters to Roxanne when she is away for a few days. Eventually, Roxanne realizes she loves Charlie instead of Chris when she discovers that Charlie wrote the letters.

This comical story is polluted with continuous crude, vulgar language and profanity. Sexual intercourse is discussed and implied. When Roxanne is locked out of her house without any clothes on, her nudity is shown in an obscured manner. Unfortunately, the offensive language in *Roxanne*, along with the film's sexually suggestive content, make it unacceptable viewing for discriminating moviegoers. Avoid *Roxanne*.

TITLE:	**RUMPELSTILTSKIN**
QUALITY:	★★★
RECOMMENDATION:	Acceptable
RATING:	G
RELEASE:	1987
STARRING:	Amy Irving, Robert Symonds, Clive Revill, Priscilla Pointer, John Moulder Brown, Billy Barty, and Yael Uziely
DIRECTOR:	David Irving
GENRE:	Children
CONTENT:	Magical thinking
INTENDED AUDIENCE:	Families
REVIEWER:	Bruce Grimes

Rumpelstiltskin is one of Cannon's Movie Tales. This series aimed at families with young children is surprisingly well-produced. Christians should warn their children about the fact that these tales are pure fantasy and the magic in them is not real or commendable, rather God and His Truth are to be commended. However, each movie has a moral, and they do not promote magical thinking, so they are recommended for families where the parents have educated their children about the Biblical worldview.

A long time ago in a small kingdom, the beautiful Katie and her father Victor, a poor miller, live in a small cottage. Victor boasts Katie can spin straw into gold. This information finds its way to the King Mezzer and Queen Grizelda.

Katie is summoned to the palace and ordered to turn a bale of hay into gold. Katie despairs, but a dwarf named Rumpelstiltskin appears. He offers to help Katie in exchange for her mother's necklace. They spin the hay into gold.

The King orders Katie to produce more gold. Katie tries, but fails. Rumpelstiltskin appears and accepts Katie's payment of a ring.

The King demands a third pile of gold, declaring Katie will marry the Prince if she succeeds. If she fails, the Queen notes, "She dies!" Katie cries to Rumpelstiltskin that she has nothing left. The dwarf says he'll turn the straw into gold in exchange for her firstborn child. Reluctantly, Katie agrees.

The King keeps his promise and allows Katie and the Prince to be married. When their first baby is born, Rumpelstiltskin comes to collect. Katie begs him not to take her child. He gives Katie one chance: if she can guess his name within three days, he will give up his claim. Katie fails to guess his name on the first and second day. The night before the final day, the dwarf's raven flies into the bedroom of the King's spy and whispers the name. The next morning, the spy tells Katie what she's heard. Katie guesses the dwarf's name and he is swallowed up by a chasm. Katie, the Prince and their child live happily ever after.

Evil is thwarted by knowing its name and rebuking it. The dwarf is a type of devil, a Mephistopheles, who wants Katie and her child in hell. The moral is, "Do not sell your soul for gold." Another moral is, "Do not bargain with the devil." Unfortunately, victory is not achieved through Jesus, but through human cleverness and the double cross of the dwarf's raven. Evil always betrays itself.

Even if this is not a Biblical tale, parents can make Biblical analogies. *Rumpelstiltskin* is a movie which your children can enjoy if you give them the proper Biblical worldview.

TITLE:	**RUNNING ON EMPTY**
QUALITY:	★ ★ ★
RECOMMENDATION:	Caution
RATING:	PG-13
RELEASE:	1988
STARRING:	Christine Lahti, River Phoenix, Judd Hirsch, Jonas Abry, Martha Plimpton, and Ed Crowley
DIRECTOR:	Sidney Lumet
GENRE:	Drama
CONTENT:	Profanity and other off-color language
INTENDED AUDIENCE:	Adults
REVIEWER:	Ed Bez

Running on Empty is an intelligent insight into the consequences of actions undertaken without counting the cost.

Seventeen-year-old Richard Pope is riding his bike down a deserted street. A car drives slowly past. The scene is tense. Richard ditches the bike and runs through a field to a dilapidated house.

We find that the Pope family has been traveling all over the country for the past fifteen years. Arthur and Annie were anti-Vietnam protestors in the 1960's, who were responsible for blowing up a military installation. Unfortunately, a man was severely maimed and blinded in the attack. Consequently, the FBI and the military secret police have been trying to catch them ever since. Every few months, they change their names, hair color and facial appearances and start all over again; only to be uprooted when the authorities get too close.

Running on Empty is a sensitive human drama of suffering which reminds us that the sins of the fathers are visited upon their children. However, because of unnecessary language, we recommend extreme caution.

TITLE:	**RUSKIES**
QUALITY:	★ ★
RECOMMENDATION:	Caution

RATING:	PG
RELEASE:	1987
STARRING:	Whip Hubley and Leaf Phoenix
DIRECTOR:	Rick Rosenthal
GENRE:	Action adventure
CONTENT:	Mild obscenity
INTENDED AUDIENCE:	Teenagers
REVIEWER:	Ken Kistner

Ruskies centers on three boys obsessed with the exploits of their comic book hero, Sergeant Slaughter. They discover evidence of a Russian beach landing and capture a Russian sailor. They find that he has a family he loves and there are just as many misconceptions about Americans in Russia as there are about Russians in America. The boys take on the challenge of getting their Russian friend home.

This is pretty strong propaganda. On one hand, every person everywhere deserves love, but that does not deny the fact that every person is a sinner who needs Jesus the Christ. *Ruskies* betrays a naive accommodation of the Soviet system. There is no peace apart from that which is to be found in Christ Jesus. Any counterfeit peace only plays into the hands of the Devil. As long as there is sin, there will not be peace in the world. Jesus is the only Peace.

☆☆☆ CLASSIC ☆☆☆

TITLE:	**SAFE AT HOME (84 Minutes, Black and White)**
QUALITY:	★ ★
RECOMMENDATION:	Acceptable for children
RATING:	Not rated
RELEASE:	1962
STARRING:	Mickey Mantle, Roger Maris, William Frawley
DIRECTOR:	Walter Doniger
GENRE:	Drama
CONTENT:	Nothing objectionable
INTENDED AUDIENCE:	Young boys
REVIEWER:	Protestant Motion Picture Council

Young boys will enjoy this simple and entertaining story, since it is mainly concerned with Hutch, a ten-year-old Little Leaguer, who tells his teammates that his father is best buddies with Mickey Mantle and Roger Maris. When he has to prove his story, the lie catches up with him, and he makes brave efforts to extricate himself. He converts to an honesty that is eventually rewarded.

Friendship, loyalty, and family solidarity are shown as desirable. Being taken behind the scenes at the Yankee camp in Florida will delight the young. Good direction and acting produce this wholesome family fun. Times certainly have changed.

TITLE:	**SALAAM BOMBAY! (Subtitles)**
QUALITY:	★ ★ ★ ★
RECOMMENDATION:	Caution
RATING:	Not rated
RELEASE:	1988
STARRING:	Shafiq Syed, Hansa Vithal, Aneeta Kanwar, and Nana Patekar
DIRECTOR:	Mira Nair
GENRE:	Drama
CONTENT:	The subjects of drugs and prostitution, but there is no nudity; some vulgarities (in the sub-titles); dialogue spoken in Hindi
INTENDED AUDIENCE:	Adults
REVIEWER:	Bruce Grimes

This is an absorbing portrayal of the slums of Bombay, India. Krishna is a ten-year-old boy who is kicked out of his house by his mother after he ruins his brother's bicycle. She tells him not to return until he has 500 rupees to pay for the damages. He quickly looses his naivete and wakes up to the harsh realities of a world of beggars, prostitutes, pimps, and drug dealers. Krishna's life typifies the existence of millions like him.

Salaam Bombay! paints a true picture that is grim, yet captivating. It is not a documentary about street children, but a drama with characters who are multi-dimensional, not just poor. The director used non-professionals to act in this film, and the performances are overwhelmingly excellent. Beautifully photographed and with a tight script, the film deserves the accolades it is receiving. *Salaam Bombay!* is an extraordinary film worthy of viewing. However, viewers should be aware that it deals candidly with prostitution and drug abuse, though there is no nudity and no graphic scenes of IV use.

TITLE:	**SALSA**
QUALITY:	★ ★
RECOMMENDATION:	Extreme Caution
RATING:	PG
RELEASE:	1988
STARRING:	Bobby Rosa and Rodney Harvey
DIRECTOR:	Boaz Davidson
GENRE:	Dance/Musical

CONTENT:	Erotic dancing
INTENDED AUDIENCE:	Teenagers
REVIEWER:	Nancy Hanger

The only way you can enjoy *Salsa* is if you really like the Latin dance. It is beautiful, although this version contains erotic variations. Rico dances at La Luna club and dreams of going to Puerto Rico. Other characters are Rico's family, his girlfriend, women who want him, and his best male friend, who falls in love with Rico's younger sister. Rico tries to dominate his sister's life, and his excessive repression of her development is unsympathetic.

There are scenes meant to appeal to a teenager's fantasies, such as close-ups of skimpy dance costumes. A sexual relationship is implied, but there is no nudity and no sex. There is no profanity and only two or three expletives. However, for edifying entertainment and value for your money, *Salsa* cannot be recommended.

☆☆☆ CLASSIC ☆☆☆

TITLE:	**THE SAND CASTLE**
QUALITY:	★ ★ ★ ★
RECOMMENDATION:	Acceptable
RATING:	Not rated
RELEASE:	1961
STARRING:	Barry Cardwell, Laurie Cardwell, and George Dunham
DIRECTOR:	Jerome Hill
GENRE:	Fantasy/Children
CONTENT:	Nothing objectionable
INTENDED AUDIENCE:	Adults and families
REVIEWER:	Protestant Motion Picture Council

One may call this a "film poem" or a musical fantasy, for it is both. A boy and his sister are left by their mother to spend an afternoon on the beach.

After being snubbed by a group of older boys who don't need their help in building a sand fort, the pair wanders to the water's edge where the boy finds a seashell. He pretends to hear in the seashell a voice that tells him to build his own sand castle. His work is a marvelous edifice and attracts a horde of visitors: a fat woman, a drunk, a bikini-draped sun goddess, some muscle men, a skin-diver, and some softball-playing nuns.

A rainstorm begins and the two children seek the shelter of a beach umbrella. Falling asleep, the boy dreams of the people who visited his sand castle. In the dream, they take the form of paper cutouts, stop-motion animated, against a real model of the castle. They move in colorful settings of exploding hues, and the music adopts several descriptive styles which help to make the dream more alive than reality. The boy meets, as it were, the "genius" of the seashell and learns that the castle is within him, even when the tide washes it away. It remains his own, the product of his creative art.

This highly imaginative piece is a neat exercise in filmmaking. The live-action sequences are shot in black-and-white with the dream portrayed in wonderful, contrasting color. The paper cutouts are well-animated, inspired by the paper cutout theater for children presented in the 19th century. The director handles the material nicely, wisely underplaying the story with moments of great subtlety.

While this may be considered for family entertainment, the two main characters being children, it is, in many ways, an adult picture.

TITLE:	**THE SCARLET AND THE BLACK**
QUALITY:	★ ★ ★ ★
RECOMMENDATION:	Acceptable
RATING:	Television movie—no rating
RELEASE:	1983
STARRING:	Gregory Peck, Christopher Plummer, and John Gielgud
DIRECTOR:	Jerry London
GENRE:	Drama/War
CONTENT:	Nothing objectionable
INTENDED AUDIENCE:	Youth and adults
REVIEWER:	Betty Hill

This is the true story of Monsignor Hugh O'Flaherty who was in the Vatican while the German commander Colonel Herbert Kappler occupied Rome. It was a constant battle between these two men.

O'Flaherty secretly hides 4,000 Jews and prisoners-of-war throughout Rome, and Kappler secretly tries to find and destroy them. Both men are aware of the actions of the other, while their image to the public represents only their formal positions.

Colonel Kappler lives with his wife and two children. He is seen telling his family that, "Rome is ours!" He's a loving family man that takes them to visit tourist sites.

At Christmas, his wife is shocked when their son unwraps a toy gun. How could he give such a violent present? Later the young boy sneaks up on his dad with the gun. Kappler yells, and his comment reveals that there isn't time for them to get out of Rome. The Allies are coming.

Kappler requests Monsignor O'Flaherty to meet him secretly at the Coliseum, where the Christians in the past were persecuted. Monsignor O'Flaherty observes that conquerors may come and go, but the Holy Church must remain the same. Kappler has been watching O'Flaherty closely for years. He observes, "I know about you . . . your Church. They say you can't pass a beggar, or a lame dog, but you help anyone in danger. It's a part of your faith. I have three more for your mercy wagon: my wife and two children."

Monsignor O'Flaherty refuses to help him. Doesn't a man that tortured priests deserve his punishment. How could Kappler ask such a question? The end of this story is surprising.

The movie, based on the novel *The Scarlet Pimpernel of the Vatican* by J. P. Gallagher, is tastefully presented without any violence being shown on screen. The film isn't preachy, but to fully get the subtle message it's necessary to read the words that appear on the screen after the film is over. It should be shown to non-Christian friends.

TITLE:	**SCROOGED**
QUALITY:	★★
RECOMMENDATION:	Bad
RATING:	PG-13
RELEASE:	1988
STARRING:	Bill Murray, Karen Allen, and Bob Goldthwait
DIRECTOR:	Richard Donner
GENRE:	Comedy
CONTENT:	Profanity, obscenity, and violence
INTENDED AUDIENCE:	Family
REVIEWER:	Gene Burke

This is another cheap shot out at a traditional Christmas. As an ultra-expensive attempt to update a simple moral lesson, the result is more vile than a cheap "slasher" film. There is nothing good about this film.

Scrooge, a television executive in this version, is brought to his senses by the final spirit. The screenwriter's view of what initiates that change, however, is not his visit to Hades, but what he assumes is a more frightening death, having his body cremated in his coffin. This worldly view of what punishment awaits those exemplifying unkind behavior towards their fellowman typifies the belief that what happens to the physical body is all that matters in this film. The spiritual part of man is given no account. This Scrooge's desire to change is for himself only, like many who seek the Lord on their terms.

Aside from warning the "true believers" to avoid this film, we hasten to add that everyone connected with this production of *Scrooged* should offer an apology to Charles Dickens.

TITLE:	**SEE NO EVIL, HEAR NO EVIL (95 Minutes)**
QUALITY:	★★★★
RECOMMENDATION:	Evil
RATING:	R
RELEASE:	1989
STARRING:	Richard Pryor and Gene Wilder
DIRECTOR:	Arthur Hiller
GENRE:	Comedy

CONTENT:	Much, much profanity, obscenities, blasphemies, and nudity
INTENDED AUDIENCE:	Adults and mature young people
REVIEWER:	Gene Burke

See No Evil, Hear No Evil is a very funny comedy about a deaf newsstand operator, Dave, and his blind assistant, Wally, who are mistakenly accused of murdering one of their customers. Neither are to blame, but are framed to look like they did it. At the time of the victim's death, they take into their possession a computer chip made to look like a rare coin. The real murderer is after this coin, deducing that Wally and Dave must have it. Chased by the police and the real murderer, Wally and Dave evade capture and ultimately expose the real culprit.

The premise for the film is great, and it has tender and honest moments of two friends helping each other. The film is sadly ruined by the most offensive onslaught of obscene language I've ever heard in a comedy. It is non-stop use of four letter words. It shamed and angered me that good comedy had to be littered with such foul adjectives. It overshadows any quality this film has.

It is a shame that this film is aimed at a young and impressionable audience and contains so much illicit sexual references, female nudity, and revolting bathroom language. Regretfully, this film must be avoided for its content.

TITLE:	**SEE YOU IN THE MORNING**
QUALITY:	★★★
RECOMMENDATION:	Bad
RATING:	PG-13
RELEASE:	1988
STARRING:	Jeff Bridges, Farrah Fawcett, and Drew Barrymore
DIRECTOR:	Alan J. Pakula
GENRE:	Drama/Romance
CONTENT:	Vulgarities and profanities, as well as several graphic sexual encounters
INTENDED AUDIENCE:	Adults
REVIEWER:	Stephanie L. Ray

This painful psychological drama opens with a family gathering. Through a series of confusing sequences, we see Larry Livingstone in bed with and then giving a wedding gift to his future bride, Beth Goodwin. Peter Goodwin has died, and Larry Livingstone is divorced.

The plot centers around the difficulties involved in making a second marriage successful. The Goodwin children are at odds with their own grief over their father's death. One ends up shoplifting a pair of earrings; while the other plays a tape of his cello performance to his father's tombstone. Larry is constantly bombarded by television commercials of his first wife. He is living in a dead man's house. He is a psychiatrist in need of a psychiatrist by the world's standards, but really in need of Jesus Christ.

The film is boring and very slow-paced due to stiff dialogue. Seeing this film would, in this viewer's opinion, be submitting yourself to actually living through the pain and torments of two fictitious families in turmoil. Why spend the money when we know that Jesus is the Answer, not a change of mates?

TITLE:	**SEPTEMBER**
QUALITY:	★★
RECOMMENDATION:	Caution
RATING:	PG
RELEASE:	1987
STARRING:	Mia Farrow, Dianne Wiest, and Sam Waterston
DIRECTOR:	Woody Allen
GENRE:	Drama
CONTENT:	Mild vulgar language
INTENDED AUDIENCE:	Adults
REVIEWER:	Bret Senft

September is an extension of Woody Allen's existentialist worldview. Six characters interact within the confines of a summer home in Vermont owned by Lane. Lane's mother Dianne and her new husband Lloyd, a physicist, come to visit. Lloyd, studies a universe that is, "haphazard, morally neutral and unimaginably violent . . . and they pay me to prove it." Here is a polite, rational man who only wants what is best for the people he loves. Such a genteel man must be telling the truth. Precisely for that reason, Mr. Allen presents Lloyd as a loving husband and stepfather, a very sympathetic character—if only to make such an otherwise horrifying, worldview so palatable to a mass audience.

September, despite its short running time, seems interminable. This might be explained by the staginess of the setting and the speed of the dialogue. Everyone speaks calmly, even when raging against an "unimaginably violent universe." Although the viewer appreciates Mr. Allen's courage in producing a somber theater piece for the screen, the film may do well only at future film festivals, where it can be viewed in the context of the film maker's more accessible work.

☆☆☆ MASTERPIECE ☆☆☆

TITLE:	**SERGEANT YORK (Black and White)**
QUALITY:	★★★★
RECOMMENDATION:	Acceptable for all ages
RATING:	Not rated
RELEASE:	1941

STARRING:	Gary Cooper, Walter Brennan, Joan Leslie, George Tobias, Stanley Ridges, and Margaret Wycherly
DIRECTOR:	Howard Hawks
GENRE:	Biography
CONTENT:	Nothing objectionable
INTENDED AUDIENCE:	Adults
REVIEWER:	Benson Poy

Sergeant York is a true story about one of the most incredible feats in military history by one of America's most famous war heroes. The movie takes you through Alvin York's life in the backwoods of Tennessee, where he grows up as a rowdy, rebellious young-un, to the WW I front line in France and back home as a hero. The beauty of this movie is in the transformation of a person from ornery, devil-may-care to respectful, humble, caring, and loving.

On the battlefield in France, Alvin performs an incredible act of courage: singlehandedly capturing 132 German soldiers, the largest bagging of prisoners by a single soldier in history. He astounds his major by telling him that "I'm as much agin killin' as ever but when I heard them machine guns . . . well, them guns was killin' hundreds, maybe thousands, and there weren't nothin' anybody could do but to stop them guns. That's what I've done." The major stares at him and says, "You mean to tell me you did it to *save* lives?"

Alvin returns to the States to raise money for war bonds. The state of Tennessee gives him a beautiful home and land. Yet, Alvin York does not get a swelled head or a bellyful of pride. All he can say is, "They gave me this for killing people? The Lord sure do move in mysterious ways."

TITLE:	**THE SEVENTH SIGN**
QUALITY:	★ ★ ★
RECOMMENDATION:	Extreme Caution
RATING:	R
RELEASE:	1988
STARRING:	Demi Moore, Michael Biehn, and Jurgen Prochnow
DIRECTOR:	Carl Schultz
GENRE:	Science fiction/Religious
CONTENT:	Some rough language and brief nudity
INTENDED AUDIENCE:	Adults
REVIEWER:	Doug Brewer

Considering Hollywood's inclination to promote the Adversary, we entered this screening with wariness. *The Seventh Sign* is not what we expected. Abby's first child was stillborn. This time, she hopes for a healthy delivery. However, everywhere in the world a strange man appears, something bizarre happens. The mysterious man, David Banner, rents Abby and Russell's apartment. She finds that the key to her problems is her willingness to believe David when he says that she must give in order to receive. However, this is not blind obedience; they have a confrontation scene that is both suspenseful and sensitive.

The Seventh Sign is a well-made thriller that will probably have armchair theologians arguing for a while, but its message that "greater love hath no man than this, that a man lay down his life for his friends," is refreshing. It's great to see Abby turn to the only One who believes in her.

The message of *The Seventh Sign*, that "there is something to Christianity," should be applauded. However, because of rough language, innocuous nudity, and weak Biblical underpinning, we cannot recommend *The Seventh Sign*.

☆☆☆ MASTERPIECE ☆☆☆

TITLE:	**SHAME**
QUALITY:	★★★★
RECOMMENDATION:	Caution
RATING:	R
RELEASE:	1968
STARRING:	Liv Ullmann, Max von Sydow, and Gunnar Bjornstrand
DIRECTOR:	Ingmar Bergman
GENRE:	Drama
CONTENT:	Adultery and graphic carnage
INTENDED AUDIENCE:	Adult
REVIEWER:	Ted Baehr

Shame is a stark, chilling film by Ingmar Bergman which exposes the sinfulness of the human heart. The film takes place in an unnamed country during a civil war.

Eva and Jan Rosenberg are husband and wife concert musicians who flee to an tiny, isolated island to avoid the atrocities that have gripped their country. Their peace is short-lived, as the island becomes a battleground. They are forced to face the horrors they tried so hard to escape.

As the fighting intensifies, their marriage disintegrates. They have never before had to fend for themselves to stay alive. The strains placed on them radically alter their perspective.

Eva sleeps with a friend of Jan's to get out of jail. Jealous, Jan refuses to help the friend after he's arrested. He even allows the man to be killed.

This is just the beginning of the depths to which Jan sinks. He goes as far as to kill an innocent soldier just for his boots.

Eva becomes distraught. Upon leaving the island on a small boat, the two travel through a sea filled with floating dead bodies. This dreamlike scene is stark and vivid.

The key line in the movie is expressed by Jan, "Did you ever think we were in someone's dream, and they were ashamed?" This is the dark side of Bergman's evangelical upbringing, for here he captures the essence of sin. We are God's creation, and we have shamed Him by rebelling against Him and our fellow man.

Shame effectively illustrates the evil which lurks just under the thin veneer of every civilized human being. It is this evil which produced the Holocaust in Germany and the pogroms in Russia. For those who have forgotten man's sin nature, this film will bring the human condition home to them in a way that no other film can.

Both Ullmann and von Sydow do an excellent job of portraying personalities exposed to the harshness of reality. *September* should be seen with its obverse, *The Tree of Wooden Clogs*, which shows God's grace present in the simplest aspects of our lives.

TITLE:	**SHE'S HAVING A BABY**
QUALITY:	★ ★ ★
RECOMMENDATION:	Extreme Caution
RATING:	PG-13
RELEASE:	1988
STARRING:	Kevin Bacon and Elizabeth McGovern
DIRECTOR:	John Hughes
GENRE:	Comedy
CONTENT:	Some vulgar language and adult situations
INTENDED AUDIENCE:	Adults
REVIEWER:	Robbie and Lisa Padgett

We've seen the story a hundred times, but this time it's fresh, creative and funny. The film revolves around a newlywed couple and their first years together. It starts with a humorous marriage ceremony, plows through the dark school years, tightropes into the first job, and collides with the first attempts at home and family. Many scenes are not only funny, but full of insight. They contain all the temptations of life, but the characters' reactions are surprisingly moral for a change. The clear message is that the institution of marriage, along with fidelity and commitment, can survive in today's world.

We would like to recommend *She's Having a Baby*; however, discretion must be advised, as there are instances of strong language and some adult situations. Therefore, we suggest that you write Paramount Pictures, 9440 Santa Monica Blvd, Beverly Hills, CA 90210, to tell them they need not use off-color language and adult situations to make a good point.

TITLE:	**SHOOT TO KILL**
QUALITY:	★ ★ ★
RECOMMENDATION:	Extreme Caution
RATING:	R

RELEASE:	1988
STARRING:	Sidney Poitier, Tom Berenger, Kirstie Alley, and Clancy Brown
DIRECTOR:	Roger Spottiswoode
GENRE:	Detective
CONTENT:	Violence and profanity
INTENDED AUDIENCE:	Adults
REVIEWER:	Doug Brewer

Special agent Warren Stanton is tracking a killer on the loose. When the killer shoots a fisherman and assumes his identity on a fishing trip, Warren must get Jonathan to guide him through the mountains to find the killer, before the party reaches the Canadian border. The adventure is exciting and dangerous, punctuated with comical scenes, as they move from antagonism to grudging respect. Sidney Poitier is superb as a man who upholds the law, no matter what cost. It is refreshing to see a hero who is respected for his competence without resorting to Dirty Harry tactics.

Unfortunately, because of the violence and mild language, we can only recommend *Shoot to Kill* with extreme caution.

TITLE:	**SHORT CIRCUIT 2**
QUALITY:	★ ★ ★
RECOMMENDATION:	Caution
RATING:	PG
RELEASE:	1988
STARRING:	Fisher Stevens, Cynthia Gibb, Michael McKean, Jack Weston, and Tim Blaney
DIRECTOR:	Kenneth Johnson
GENRE:	Comedy/Science fiction
CONTENT:	Offensive language and a brief scene in a bar
INTENDED AUDIENCE:	Adults
REVIEWER:	Glennis O'Neal

Ben, a native of India, displays his miniature robots on a busy city street. He has no sales until one robot tours a department store. Cindy, a buyer for the store, sees the robot as the novelty that will boost sales and insure her job. She orders 1,000 robots; to be delivered within thirty days. Robot #5 arrives from Montana to produce the robots in a warehouse adjoining a bank. "He" disrupts bankrobbers who are digging a tunnel to the vault. #5 leaves the workshop to explore the city. "He" goes to confession to find out why "he" is not accepted by people. "He" craves acceptance. A long line of bad humans try to deceive, destroy, and capture the robot worth sixteen million dollars.

The audience accepts #5 as the star of the show. This second film succeeds on the formula of the first: clear, clever imagination. Unfortunately, there is some offensive language and a brief scene in a bar. Caution is recommended.

TITLE:	**SING**
QUALITY:	★ ★ ★
RECOMMENDATION:	Extreme caution
RATING:	PG-13
RELEASE:	1989
STARRING:	Lorraine Bracco, Peter Dobson, Patty LaBelle, and Jessica Steen
DIRECTOR:	Richard Baskin
GENRE:	Musical/Dance
CONTENT:	Vulgarities
INTENDED AUDIENCE:	Young audience
REVIEWER:	Gene Burke

Sing involves an attractive teacher, committed to "giving back" to her students what she was given as a student. She is assigned directorial duties for the annual theatrical competition among New York high schools. When interest wanes, she questions the attitude of the present-day students.

She is mugged by a masked assailant, but escapes by biting him on the hand. The next day she notices a bandaged hand on her most unruly student, Dominick. Threatening to turn him into the principal, she forces him to enter the Sing competition.

Dominick annoys the other participants. They challenge him to perform better than any of them. When he exhibits that he is the most talented dancer, self-esteem replaces his rebelliousness. A bond of trust and loyalty is formed with the others, and the teacher's tactic to rehabilite Dominick proves successful.

The School Board has elected to close Brooklyn High, eliminating them from the competition. On their own, they raise money to fund their show, and it's a doozy. Dominick becomes the Sing hero.

This film is relatively free of offensive content. However, the language is very rough, so be cautioned. The dance numbers and songs are good. I would love to recommend this film. However, because of the foul language, I cannot give my recommendation.

☆☆☆ MASTERPIECE ☆☆☆

TITLE:	**SINK THE BISMARCK! (97 Minutes, Black and White)**
QUALITY:	★ ★ ★ ★
RECOMMENDATION:	Acceptable

RATING:	Not rated
RELEASE:	1960 (British)
STARRING:	Kenneth More, Dana Wynter, Carl Mohner, and Laurence Naismith
DIRECTOR:	Lewis Gilbert
GENRE:	War
CONTENT:	Nothing objectionable
INTENDED AUDIENCE:	Adults
REVIEWER:	Protestant Motion Picture Council

This tense, war-time saga is based on the real story of how the German's most powerful naval fighting machine was destroyed by the British. It starts with actual newsreel footage as the Bismarck is launched to the cheers of Nazi chiefs in 1938. Flash forward to 1941 and the War Room of the British Admiralty where a campaign begins to blow the battleship out of the water.

The story follows the intricate plotting and strategy that led to the destruction of the mighty ship after Winston Churchill gave order to "Sink the Bismarck! This is a battle we cannot afford to lose."

The personalities of the men in command of the opposing forces are brought into strong focus as well as the reasons behind their actions, both personal and official. There is the Feuhrer-adoring German, as well as the icy cold Britisher with a score to settle.

The actual sea warfare seems repetitous, although the film is a marvel of intercutting as it goes from the War Room, to action aboard the German battleship and then to all the other British ships as they begin to tighten the noose.

TITLE:	**SKIN DEEP**
QUALITY:	★ ★
RECOMMENDATION:	Evil
RATING:	R
RELEASE:	1989
STARRING:	John Ritter and Vincent Gardenia
DIRECTOR:	Blake Edwards
GENRE:	Comedy
CONTENT:	Nudity, profanity, sex, vulgarity, grotesqueness, lust, alcoholism, and other immorality
INTENDED AUDIENCE:	Adults
REVIEWER:	Ted Baehr

What happens to an immoral pagan when he realizes that he can die? In *Skin Deep* Blake

Edwards suggests that he drowns himself in alcohol and sex. However, Blake doesn't tell us that this is wrong, only that a person can't change his character.

Zachary Hutton is a writer with inexhaustible wealth who is afraid of death and therefore sleeps with every woman he meets. His wife, Alex, kicks him out, aggravating his addictions. By the end of the movie, he has blasphemed God, walked around with a fluorescent condom on his private parts and thoroughly disgusted this reviewer. However, his wife takes him back and all the women in his life think he's cute. This promotion of adultery and alcoholism without any moral qualm, is abhorrent.

This movie is sleazy beyond belief and the sight gag of two fluorescent condoms fighting in the night is grotesque. The fact that the audience was amused by this deviant adolescent behavior is depressing. Why God postpones judging us when our society produces works such as this is beyond me.

☆☆☆ CLASSIC ☆☆☆

TITLE:	**THE SNOW QUEEN**
QUALITY:	★ ★ ★
RECOMMENDATION:	Acceptable for children
RATING:	Not rated
RELEASE:	1959 (USSR)
STARRING:	Voices of Sandra Dee, Tommy Kirk, Patty McCormack, and Louise Arthur
DIRECTOR:	Phil Patton
GENRE:	Animated/Children
CONTENT:	Nothing objectionable
INTENDED AUDIENCE:	Family (especially children)
REVIEWER:	Protestant Motion Picture Council

An excellent animated Soviet version of Hans Christian Anderson's fairy tale. A homey prologue introduces the story and brings it within the circle of the American audience.

Art Linkletter is surrounded by a group of the children he loves and understands. From the gifts under the tree, he selects a book, *The Snow Queen*, presenting it to a little girl. It is promptly turned into screen animation.

This is the story of two children playmates, Kay, the boy, and Gerta, the girl. In good weather, they enjoy the flowers on the porch and the stories they are told.

When the cold of winter heavily frosts the windows, they are surprised by the Snow Queen whose wicked magic entices Kay to her far northern kingdom. This begins extraordinary adventures for the two children when Gerta leaves to look for Kay.

Distance is of no concern as a magic boat, animals, or the wind provide transportation. People helpful, or hindering, are met on the way until Gerta reaches the evil Snow Queen's palace far, far away in the frozen north. Kay, who has fallen under the magic spell, has all but forgotten the simple pleasures of the rose-bedecked porch.

As in all good fairy tales, however, all ends well with the children returning home and the bad magic broken. Since imagination is the best guide to such a plot, it must have free reign for enjoyment of this beautiful production.

TITLE:	**SOME KIND OF WONDERFUL**
QUALITY:	★ ★ ★
RECOMMENDATION:	Extreme Caution
RATING:	PG-13
RELEASE:	1987
STARRING:	Craig Sheffer and Lea Thompson
DIRECTOR:	Howie Deutch
GENRE:	Romance
CONTENT:	Profanity and some risque scenes
INTENDED AUDIENCE:	Teenagers
REVIEWER:	Ted Baehr

This could have been a good movie, but someone decided to allow profanity into the dialogue.

A decent young man falls in love with the prettiest girl in his high school, Amanda Jones. Unfortunately, Amanda is the property of the school snob, and our hero is from a poor family. Our hero, the consummate artist, fails to notice the musician, Watt, who is in love with him. Amanda has a falling out with her snob and our hero asks her for a date. She accepts. He spends his college savings to give Amanda an evening she will never forget. At one point in the evening, they both confess they have been using each other, and they apologize.

They confront the snob with the fact that he has been manipulating people and his time is up. Amanda shows our hero that he really loves Watt. Amanda realizes that she does not need to pander to wealth to be somebody.

This is a positive, decent story, except for the profanity, which is inexcusable. Furthermore, the movie is slow in parts and does not hit the high note at the end which would take the audience's breathe away. Christians should avoid *Some Kind of Wonderful*.

TITLE:	**SOMEONE TO LOVE**
QUALITY:	★ ★
RECOMMENDATION:	Extreme Caution
RATING:	R
RELEASE:	1988
STARRING:	Orson Welles, Henry Jaglom, Michael Emil, Andrea Marcovicci, and Sally Kellerman
DIRECTOR:	Henry Jaglom

GENRE:	Biography/Drama/Documentary
CONTENT:	Profanity and obscenity
INTENDED AUDIENCE:	Adults
REVIEWER:	Ted Baehr

Henry Jaglom has cast his family and friends in this cinematic group-encounter session which looks at the despair facing baby boomers who have not been able to break free of the humanistic deceptions of our age.

After Henry and his girlfriend argue about their relationship, Henry decides to throw a Valentine's Day party for his single show business friends to find out how they feel about being alone. He tells them that just as hunger tells us to feed our bodies, so loneliness tells us we need a spouse. Sally Kellerman and other personalities concur that they have been unable to sustain relationships. Orson Welles notes that the sexual revolution has destroyed the family and that families survive best in societies where there is a faith in something beyond oneself.

This is not an entertaining movie. Profanity and obscenity make it unacceptable for Christians. However, for those who are still in the world, it is a stirring condemnation of humanism.

☆☆☆ CLASSIC ☆☆☆

TITLE:	**SONG WITHOUT END**
QUALITY:	★ ★ ★ ★
RECOMMENDATION:	Acceptable
RATING:	Not rated
RELEASE:	1960
STARRING:	Dirk Bogarde, Capucine, Genevieve Page, and Patricia Morison
DIRECTOR:	Charles Vidor and George Cukor
GENRE:	Musical/Biography/Romance
CONTENT:	Illicit love affairs
INTENDED AUDIENCE:	Adults
REVIEWER:	Protestant Motion Picture Council

Franz Liszt was a sensational success as a pianist in his 20's. He was a genius who attracted love and gave it lightly, enjoying its adulation. When he found enduring affection only to encounter opposition in its fulfillment, he came to Christ and entered orders in the Roman Catholic Church where his composing turned to organ music.

His successive love affairs are an admitted fact and a dramatic setting to the musical career which they greatly influenced. The main value of the drama is in the music, which is excellent.

With settings of ornate palaces, concert halls and opera houses, with elaborate costumes and princely patrons of the arts, this is a production of quality and elegance. Infinite care has been bestowed on musical presentations with pianist Jorge Bolet's playing flawlessly synchronized in sound and action.

The Los Angeles Philharmonic orchestra and Robert Wagner Chorale are also featured. Acting is outstanding by all principals and a large cast.

TITLE:	**SPACEBALLS**
QUALITY:	★
RECOMMENDATION:	Bad
RATING:	PG
RELEASE:	1987
STARRING:	Joan Rivers, Mel Brooks, and John Candy
DIRECTOR:	Mel Brooks
GENRE:	Comedy
CONTENT:	Crudeness, profanity, sexual perversion, and scatological stupidity
INTENDED AUDIENCE:	Adults
REVIEWER:	Doug Brewer

There is no reason that this movie should have been made. It is not funny. Brooks has used comic devices common to high schools the world over, such as double entendres and references the body parts. Profanity for the sake of profanity is abundant.

There is no plot. The acting is deplorable. The language intolerable. The motivations of the characters is so blatantly hedonistic as to be sad. Do not go see *Spaceballs*. Mel Brooks should write a little note to the proper authorities saying, "Stop me before I do it again."

TITLE:	**THE SQUEEZE**
QUALITY:	★ ★
RECOMMENDATION:	Extreme Caution
RATING:	PG-13
RELEASE:	1987
STARRING:	Michael Keaton, Rae Dawn Chong, and Ronald Guttman
DIRECTOR:	Roger Young
PRODUCER:	Rupert Hitzig and Michael Tannen
GENRE:	Comedy
CONTENT:	Obscenity, gambling, and lax morals
INTENDED AUDIENCE:	Adults
REVIEWER:	Ted Baehr

The Squeeze is one of those Hollywood movies which looks like they threw money at it to solve the script problems. It is a movie that never gets off the ground. At several points, the writer seems to be speaking through the dialogue saying, "Where do we go from here?" The story just stops dead at points. The excellent premise that love triumphs over greed is obviated by the totally uninteresting characters. *The Squeeze* tells the story of Harry, an aspiring artist in New York City, who makes gigantic lizards and rhinoceroses out of hundreds of old television sets. He gets caught up in a ridiculous scam to fix lotto games. The connection between the lotto game and the scam is very tenuous.

The Squeeze is a film that you can miss. Save your money. It is embarrassingly dull. The distributor will move it quickly into the video stores, and I suggest you save your money there, too.

TITLE:	**STACKING**
QUALITY:	★ ★ ★
RECOMMENDATION:	Caution
RATING:	PG
RELEASE:	1987
STARRING:	Christine Lahti, Megan Follows, and Frederic Forrest
DIRECTOR:	Martin Rosen
GENRE:	Drama
CONTENT:	Occasional swearing and one fistfight
INTENDED AUDIENCE:	Adults
REVIEWER:	Doug Brewer

Stacking is a well-acted movie for people who appreciate a good story without all the Hollywood tinsel. It is a quiet film that says a lot.

Anna Mae is fourteen. Her father is in the hospital. Her mother is a terminal dreamer with a bad case of wanderlust. Anna Mae has her hands full. It's time to cut the hay, and there's no one to do it. She recruits Buster, a part-time handyman and admirer of Anna Mae's mother. The neighbors, who own most of the land Anna Mae's daddy used to own, make sly comments about the time that Buster's spending with Anna Mae. This erupts into a fistfight between Buster and Gary, who feels that Buster is moving in on Anna Mae, which is absurd. In the end, it becomes clear that the work Anna Mae and Buster contract to do on the neighboring farms must be done.

☆☆☆ MASTERPIECE ☆☆☆

TITLE:	**STAND AND DELIVER**
QUALITY:	★ ★ ★ ★
RECOMMENDATION:	Caution
RATING:	PG

RELEASE:	1988
STARRING:	Edward James Olmos and Lou Diamond Phillips
DIRECTOR:	Ramon Menendez
GENRE:	Drama/Biography
CONTENT:	Excellent triumph of compassion, but there is some rough language and iconography, although there is no sex, violence, or profanity
INTENDED AUDIENCE:	Adults and teenagers
REVIEWER:	Ted Baehr

Stand and Deliver tells the powerful true story of compassion triumphing over alienation. Jaime Escalante gives up his lucrative computer design job to teach at an Hispanic high school. Jaime tells his class he doesn't care what their problems are: they are going to learn. The department head gives the socialist response that these students can't learn because of their socio-economic background. Jaime notes that it is not a matter of environment, nor politics, but of the individual's decision to excel. The movie is a triumph which must be seen to be appreciated.

Never has a movie so motivated an audience to achieve excellence. However, we must urge caution because this accurate portrayal contains obscenities and a few rebellious attitudes. Also, icons common to the tradition of these Hispanic teenagers may annoy some individuals. This is not blasphemy, because they believe in forgiveness and Jesus Christ.

We hope that you will see *Stand and Deliver* and see beyond the ghetto setting, noting that caring is the only daring. We need movies like this with no sex, no violence and a positive portrayal of man created in the image of God.

TITLE:	**STEALING HOME**
QUALITY:	★ ★
RECOMMENDATION:	Bad
RATING:	PG-13
RELEASE:	1988
STARRING:	Mark Harmon, Jodie Foster, Blair Brown, and John Shea
DIRECTOR:	Steven Kampmann and Will Aldis
GENRE:	Drama
CONTENT:	Profanity, obscenity, nudity, and lust
INTENDED AUDIENCE:	Adults
REVIEWER:	Ted Baehr

Billy was going nowhere when his mother called to tell him that his childhood baby-sitter, tutor, and lover had committed suicide, leaving her ashes to him. Cut to a ten-year-old Billy with Katie, the baby-sitter who broke the rules. Next, cut to Billy stealing home to win the high school baseball game which leads to an offer to play in the minors.

Coming home, Billy looses his virginity and wakes up to find his father died in a car accident. Katie spends the summer trying to console him. Cut to Billy with Katie's ashes. He gets drunk, throws her ashes into the sea and goes back to baseball. The last scene shows him stealing home to win the game.

This is a pitiful plot. One cannot steal home in real life. Jesus is the only Answer, but His presence in this movie is no more than a curse word. This perverse movie has excessive voyeurism, sex, profanity, and suicide. Avoid this depressing film.

☆☆☆ CLASSIC ☆☆☆

TITLE:	**STOWAWAY IN THE SKY**
QUALITY:	★★
RECOMMENDATION:	Acceptable/Good for children
RATING:	Not rated
RELEASE:	1962 (French)
STARRING:	Pascal Lamorisse, Andre Gille, and Jack Lemmon (Narrator)
DIRECTOR:	Albert Lamorisse
GENRE:	Children
CONTENT:	Nothing objectionable
INTENDED AUDIENCE:	Children
REVIEWER:	Protestant Motion Picture Council

A visually stunning adventure filled with aerial photography, this picture offers some awe-inspiring views of the Eiffel Tower, the Arc de Triumph, and numerous other Parisian sights. What undermines the poetic nature of the film is a voice-over added by Jack Lemmon for English-speaking audiences.

A small boy stows away in his grandfather's sixty-foot balloon. They skim over the French rooftops, are followed by a flight of migrating flamingos, nearly touch the ice-covered Alps, and land for a moment in the midst of a country wedding celebration. Then, they're off again, as they follow a fleeing stag with red-coated hunters and their dogs in pursuit.

When they draw too near a forest fire the balloon explodes, bringing on a crash landing. However, once again they take off in a pattern of beauty and color.

The light humor, with whimsical comments, slight buffoonery, and the artistic quality of the production create enchantment.

TITLE:	**STRANGERS ON A TRAIN (Black and White)**
QUALITY:	★★★
RECOMMENDATION:	Acceptable
RATING:	Not rated

RELEASE:	1951
STARRING:	Farley Granger, Ruth Roman, Robert Walker, Leo G. Carroll, and Patricia Hitchcock
DIRECTOR:	Alfred Hitchcock
GENRE:	Mystery
CONTENT:	Nothing Objectionable
INTENDED AUDIENCE:	Adults
REVIEWER:	Betty Hill

A chance meeting on a train allows Bruno Anthony to explain his theory of the perfect murder to tennis star Guy Haines: if two people would each like to get rid of someone, simply have them trade victims. Haines dismisses it all as a macabre joke, until Anthony kills Haines' wife and wants Haines to honor his half of the bargain. Appalled and terrified, Haines does his best to elude the demonical Anthony, swearing he never made the diabolic bargain. Anthony ignores the pleas, and by blackmail and cunning he inexorably pushses Haines ever closer to committing murder.

Alfred Hitchcock can be seen carrying a double bass as he boards a train. Hitchcock's brilliance shines throughout: from the opening where he shows only the feet of those arriving at a train station to the unforgettable finale on an out-of-control merry-go-round.

TITLE:	**SUMMER (Subtitles)**
QUALITY:	★ ★ ★
RECOMMENDATION:	Extreme Caution
RATING:	R
RELEASE:	1985
STARRING:	Marie Riviere
DIRECTOR:	Eric Rohmer
GENRE:	Drama
CONTENT:	Beach nudity and some language
INTENDED AUDIENCE:	Adults
REVIEWER:	Ted Baehr

A young secretary, Delphine, is jilted by her boyfriend two weeks before summer vacation. She heads off on several vacations, but is defeated in enjoying them by her inability to give of herself. While tearing herself to shreds, she poses as morally superior. Delphine needs Jesus Christ, but there is no mention of the Lord in this movie. Finally, Delphine meets an attractive young man to whom she opens up. At last, she sees the flash of green, the last ray of the setting sun, which suggests her life is turning around.

Summer has many good messages; such as: love is a decision; giving triumphs over loneliness; and, maturity recognizes the uniqueness of others. However, these messages are muted by abundant superstition.

Delphine is not egocentric, but solipsistic—she can not imagine that other people do not think the way she does. Eric Rohmer has done a remarkable job of portraying the problem of a grown adult who is solipsistic, but has failed to realize that the last stage of maturity is passed when the individual recognizes the existence of God.

If one can look beyond the Biarritz beach nudity, then *Summer* is an instructive look at the solipsistic nature of our civilization. However, because of the brief nudity and the absence of God, *Summer* can not be recommended for Christians.

TITLE:	**A SUMMER STORY**
QUALITY:	★ ★ ★ ★
RECOMMENDATION:	Caution
RATING:	Not rated
RELEASE:	1988
STARRING:	James Wilby, Sophie Ward, and Susannah York
DIRECTOR:	Piers Haggard
GENRE:	Romance
CONTENT:	A powerful portrait of the wages of sin, some profanity, and some shadow nudity
INTENDED AUDIENCE:	Adults
REVIEWER:	Ted Baehr

In 1922, two British gentlemen are hiking across the moors when one, Mr. Frank Ashton, sprains his ankle. They take a room at a farm, and Frank falls in love with Megan. Infatuated, he says he will take Megan to London with him. However, when he travels to the nearest town to cash a check, circumstances delay his return. He meets an old acquaintance and his friend's sister. He decides to stay within his class. Megan goes searching for him. Ashamed, he avoids her, hiding from his sin. She has a child and dies in childbirth. Years later, he visits the farm and is confronted by the farmhand who tells him about Megan and points out that everyone thought Mr. Ashton was a gentleman, but he wasn't.

The film comes down hard against indulging oneself at the expense of others. The film is marred by a sex scene in the hayloft with shadow nudity. Also, profanity, though condemned in the story, is used. On the other hand, positive references to God also salt the dialogue. *A Summer Story* is a profound story with a Biblical message condeming sin. Extreme caution is recommended.

☆☆☆ MASTERPIECE ☆☆☆

TITLE:	**THE SUNDOWNERS**
QUALITY:	★ ★ ★ ★
RECOMMENDATION:	Caution
RATING:	Not rated

RELEASE:	1960
STARRING:	Deborah Kerr, Robert Mitchum, Peter Ustinov, and Glynis Johns
DIRECTOR:	Fred Zinnemann
GENRE:	Drama
CONTENT:	Some gambling, drinking, and fighting
INTENDED AUDIENCE:	Family
REVIEWER:	Protestant Motion Picture Council

This Australian Western tells the full story of the life and hardships facing a single family in the outback the 1920s. Based on the novel by John Cleary, it vividly portrays how they interact with the pioneers around them, how they extract a living from the land, and how they live, love and cope.

Paddy Carmody, his wife and teenage son have no money and no assets; just a great love between the three and a continuing hope that things will get better. They roam the land and live wherever they stop when the sun goes down (to which the title refers).

The wife and son long for a home, a place they can call their own, but the man is a rover. He takes on a job herding more than a thousand sheep on a long trek.

They run into a forest fire from which they and their sheep barely escape. After the fire, they all settle down for awhile, take jobs and try to save money to buy a farm. When the money has been saved, Paddy gambles it all away. With the money gone, their chance to buy a home is lost, so they start off for another job with the promise that some day they will have a place of their own.

Portrayed is a rough, crude life in the Australian outback. Drinking, gambling, and fighting are as much a part of it as in our Westerns. The photography of the beautiful country, its native birds and animals, and the close-up pictures of the forest fire, so close that the trees can be seen slowly bending in their red-hot cloak, is superb.

The acting is good. The story is dotted with wit, sly philosophy, and solid motivated action.

☆☆☆ MASTERPIECE ☆☆☆

TITLE:	**SUNRISE AT CAMPOBELLO**
QUALITY:	★★★★
RECOMMENDATION:	Acceptable
RATING:	Not rated
RELEASE:	1960
STARRING:	Ralph Bellamy, Greer Garson, Hume Cronyn, and Jean Hagen
DIRECTOR:	Vincent J. Donehue
GENRE:	Biography/Drama

CONTENT: Some drinking

INTENDED AUDIENCE: Family

REVIEWER: Protestant Motion Picture Council

Dore Schary has given personal attention and direction to the transfer of his play to the screen. It seems to have acquired exuberance and size in the process.

It's 1921 and the Roosevelt family is vacationing on the small island of Campobello, off New Brunswick. Franklin Delano takes to bed to get over a "chill." When his legs suddenly become paralyzed, he's whisked to the hospital where he learns he's the victim of polio and will never walk again. His life is changed, and in overcoming his physical limitations with his persistent will and indomitable courage, he attains what he had planned: the political career which eventually leads him to the presidency of the United States.

The film covers three years, from the time FDR succumbed to the dreaded illness to the day when, at the 1924 Democratic Convention, he nominated Alfred E. Smith for President. This gives an insight into what might be called an "American success story" in the realm of politics.

Actual settings include an island summer home, the New York City residence and the Roosevelt estate at Hyde Park, N.Y. It is regrettable that alcoholic beverages are shown as being served in an American home during Prohibition years.

TITLE: **SUPERMAN IV: THE SEARCH FOR PEACE**

QUALITY: ★ ★

RECOMMENDATION: Caution

RATING: PG

STARRING: Christopher Reeve, Margot Kidder, Jackie Cooper, Gene Hackman, Sam Wanamaker, and Muriel Hemingway

DIRECTOR: Sidney J. Furie

GENRE: Science fiction

CONTENT: Nothing objectionable except political naivety

INTENDED AUDIENCE: All ages

REVIEWER: Bruce Grimes

The Man of Steel comes back in this third sequel to the original, 1978 Superman. Although he has vowed never to alter earth's history, Superman decides to confront the threat of nuclear war by removing all the nuclear weaponry from earth, hurtling them into the sun where they explode. A parallel plot also develops. As Lex Luther, Superman's nemesis, escapes from a prison work detail and sets about creating an evil counterpart to Superman, Nuclear Man. Superman confronts Nuclear Man, and in a fight from one end of the earth to the other and into outer space, the two supermen battle. Superman is hurt and retreats to gain back his strength. Superman figures out Nuclear Man's weaknesses, and in a battle on the moon, Superman destroys this evil foe.

Superman IV is an entertaining production. Much commentary could be written about the nuclear issue, but the film doesn't propagandize. The only distraction is the lack of quality special effects. Beyond these budget limitations, *Superman IV* is an enjoyable film for all ages.

TITLE:	**SUSPECT**
QUALITY:	★★
RECOMMENDATION:	Extreme Caution
RATING:	R
RELEASE:	1987
STARRING:	Cher, Dennis Quaid, and Liam Neeson
DIRECTOR:	Peter Yates
GENRE:	Detective
CONTENT:	Some violence and obscenity
INTENDED AUDIENCE:	Adults
REVIEWER:	Doug Brewer

A public defender (Cher) is assigned an open-and-shut murder case: a deaf and dumb indigent was seen breaking into a car to get warm and the owner of the car had her throat cut. A congressional advisor (Quaid), called for jury duty, decides to help her. Together they uncover coincidences surrounding the victim: she worked at the Justice Department and was linked to a judge who recently committed suicide. Using a fire alarm to cover his escape from jury quarters, Quaid rescues Cher from the real culprit.

Suspect is a likeable movie. However, the plot appears to have been thrown together at the last minute, and the film is spliced together haphazardly. Finally, the fact that the heroes went outside the law to uphold it is not justified. We recommend against *Suspect* because of its message and lack of coherence.

TITLE:	**SWITCHING CHANNELS**
QUALITY:	★★★
RECOMMENDATION:	Extreme Caution
RATING:	PG
RELEASE:	1988
STARRING:	Kathleen Turner, Christopher Reeve, and Burt Reynolds
DIRECTOR:	Ted Kotcheff
GENRE:	Comedy
CONTENT:	Profanity and sexual innuendoes
INTENDED AUDIENCE:	Adults
REVIEWER:	Ted Baehr

This lightweight comedy, though funny, misses the mark established by its progenitor, *The Front Page*, and careens into the trash can of unacceptable films because of a preoccupation with profanity.

Cable anchor woman Christy is driven by her ex-husband news director, Sully, through the fast-paced world of television news to the point of exhaustion. She takes a vacation and meets millionaire Blaine, who sweeps her off her feet. Sully wants her back so he convinces Christy that her timely report can save the convicted Ike Roscoe, a meek father who killed the drug pusher who killed his son, from the electric chair. Blaine can't understand her preoccupation with the news and tells Christy they are not suited for each other. Christy goes back to her ex-husband and the news.

Switching Channels has a positive message in the re-union of Christy and Sully, who are married for a second time at the end of the story. However, the compensating values are not strong enough to support the profane language and sexual innuendoes. We cannot recommend *Switching Channels*.

TITLE:	**TAI-PAN**
QUALITY:	★
RECOMMENDATION:	Extreme Caution
RATING:	R
RELEASE:	1986
STARRING:	Bryan Brown and John Stanton
DIRECTOR:	Daryl Duke
GENRE:	Action adventure
CONTENT:	Nudity, violence (some graphic), and adulterous situations
INTENDED AUDIENCE:	Adults
REVIEWER:	Bruce Grimes

Based on the epic novel by James Clavell, *Tai-Pan* is another costly, handsomely produced, boring film from the DeLaurentiis family. *Tai-Pan* is set in the late 1830's in the Canton region of China.

Strewan, who is the Tai-pan or head man, is a British trader, whose livelihood skirts both sides of the law. The story follows Strewan as he gains a foothold on the island of Hong Kong. We watch the unfolding of how this island colony developed, with the intrigue, bawdiness and ruthlessness necessary for its inclusion into the British Empire. Strewan's main antagonist is Tyler Brock, who also wants to be the Tai-pan, taking the title from Strewan. Brock fails, and Strewan remains Tai-pan until his death in a typhoon. The film ends with a wide shot of modern day Hong Kong, which may be an indication of who financed this multi-million dollar picture.

Eliminating the nudity and graphic violence, cutting some of the love scenes and tightening the editing, would make this two hour and five minute film an acceptable ninety minute television movie. As it is, avoid *Tai-Pan*.

☆☆☆ MASTERPIECE ☆☆☆

TITLE:	**A TALE OF TWO CITIES (Black and White)**
QUALITY:	★ ★ ★ ★
RECOMMENDATION:	Acceptable
RATING:	Not rated
RELEASE:	1935
STARRING:	Ronald Colman, Elizabeth Allan, Edna May Oliver, Blanche Yurka, Reginald Owen, and Basil Rathbone
DIRECTOR:	Jack Conway
GENRE:	Historical
CONTENT:	Nothing Objectionable
INTENDED AUDIENCE:	Family
REVIEWER:	Gary DeMar

The causes and effects of the French Revolution come alive through this cinematic rendering of the Charles Dickens' classic *A Tale of Two Cities* published in 1859. As the viewer will see, there's more to *A Tale of Two Cities* than the bloodstained blade of the guillotine.

A Tale of Two Cities could also be called "A Tale of Two Worldviews." France's revolution of bloodshed and the deification of man, the "citizen" and "the people," were in stark contrast to the American Revolution that perpetuated a Christian moral order.

This is a movie that will challenge you intellectually and please you artistically.

☆☆☆ MASTERPIECE ☆☆☆

TITLE:	**THE TALK OF THE TOWN (Black and White)**
QUALITY:	★ ★ ★
RECOMMENDATION:	Acceptable
RATING:	Not rated
RELEASE:	1942
STARRING:	Ronald Colman, Cary Grant, Jean Arthur, Edgar Buchanan, Glenda Farrell, and Rex Ingram
DIRECTOR:	George Stevens
GENRE:	Comedy
CONTENT:	Nothing objectionable
INTENDED AUDIENCE:	Adults
REVIEWER:	Betty Hill

Nominated for five Academy Awards, *The Talk of the Town* is an unusual film even for the Golden Age of light comedy. Screenwriters Irwin Shaw and Sidney Buchman have tried to incorporate a drama of ideas within a light comedy. More thoughful and less sentimental than Capra's films, a little coldness creeps in, but the quality of the writing, performances, and George Stevens' direction pulls it through with honors.

Leopold Dilg, a principled hell-raiser in a New England town, escapes from jail where he has been framed for arson. Hiding out in the house rented by a distinguished professor of law, he is discovered by the young girl who is preparing the house for rental. Masquerading as the gardener, Dilg spars with the professor philosophically on legal theory vs. direct action. At the climax, Dilg is threatened with lynching unless the professor intervenes.

The Talk of the Town provides so much charm and wit that it escapes being perceived as a message picture. Such it certainly is and years ahead of its time too. Fortunately, Christians can reject part of this message, but still enjoy the movie.

TITLE:	**TALK RADIO**
QUALITY:	★ ★ ★
RECOMMENDATION:	Extreme Caution
RATING:	R
RELEASE:	1988
STARRING:	Eric Bogosian, Alec Baldwin, and Ellen Greene
DIRECTOR:	Oliver Stone
GENRE:	Drama
CONTENT:	Infrequent rough language and sexual innuendoes
INTENDED AUDIENCE:	Adult
REVIEWER:	Gene Burke

Barry Champlain is the talk show host people love to hate. Controversy, notoriety and ratings, the formula for success has been proven. A syndicator offers to air the show nationally.

This pulls the pin on his grenade-like hostility. He mercilessly attacks all races, colors and creeds. Callers begin to make threats on his life in retaliation. A different breed of caller has been ignited by his attacks, bent on teaching this "Jew Boy" a lesson.

In an attempt to help him, his wife calls. Posing as a "caller," she shares with him her deep desire to return to her husband. He rips her apart emotionally. He chooses to be the author and finisher of his fate with no reference to any help in any higher power other than himself. He wears his religion as one would wear a "one-of-a-kind" designer jewelry.

This film is not recommended. It left me with too many questions, no answers, and saddened me. Pray that those that do see this film choose to "knock" and sincerely "ask" for they will receive the Answer. *Talk Radio* will only describe one person who did not.

TITLE:	**TAP**
QUALITY:	★ ★ ★ ★
RECOMMENDATION:	Caution
RATING:	PG-13
RELEASE:	1989
STARRING:	Gregory Hines, Sammy Davis, Jr., Suzanne Douglas, Savion Glover, and Terrence McNally
DIRECTOR:	Nick Castle.
GENRE:	Dance/Musical
CONTENT:	Profanity, obscenity, and vulgarity
INTENDED AUDIENCE:	Teenagers and adults
REVIEWER:	Glennis O'Neal

TAP is a 1989 streetwise, atomic toe-tapping musical. Imprisoned Maxi hears his father, Sonny, a great tap-dancer, instructing him how to dance as a child. Maxi decides to work within society's system to gain his freedom.

Paroled, he is forced to work as a dishwasher. It takes a while to return to Times Square where his father's dance school is operated by Moe. Moe lives for the moment when "Sonny's boy" will mix tap with rock 'n' roll. Amy arranges a Broadway audition for Maxi, but the director feels threatened by such overpowering talent. At his lowest point, who should knock at his door but the devil's old gang who want to lure Maxi back to "easy money," silk suits and stretch limousines.

The storyline is perfect for recording a bit of tap-dancing history. Cinematography, choreography and special effects are a unique blend to focus on New York as dance-kingdom of its day. Gregory Hines is to *TAP* what Baryshnikov is to ballet.

Unfortunately, there are a few elements in this fine film which should be offensive to Christians and which are unnecessary to telling the story. Three profanities and the suggestion of sex out of wedlock could have easily been avoided and could easily be edited out of the movie. If *TAP* is edited for television, it will be a great movie. As it is, we urge caution.

TITLE:	**TEEN WOLF TOO**
QUALITY:	★ ★ ★
RECOMMENDATION:	Caution
RATING:	PG
RELEASE:	1987
STARRING:	Jason Bateman and James Hampton
DIRECTOR:	Christopher Leitch
GENRE:	Comedy

CONTENT: Implied sexual relations

INTENDED AUDIENCE: Teenagers

REVIEWER: Christopher Farrel

The plot is identical to the first *Teen Wolf*; only the setting and some of the characters have changed. However, there are significant differences in the tone of this film. Unlike the first film, there is no foul language, the party scene does not involve drinking, drugs, or sexually oriented games. The characters are more innocent. The dialogue, plot and acting are very simple, and the special effects are less than spectacular. This film will be considered silly and corny by anyone over twelve.

Teen Wolf Too is not uplifting, or artistic, but neither is it blasphemous, or destructive. The removal of the offensive material from Michael Fox's *Teen Wolf* is the film's only contribution to the series. For anyone seeking a hard and fast recommendation, *Teen Wolf Too* is not worth a trip to the theater, but it probably won't hurt anyone either.

TITLE:	**TEQUILA SUNRISE**
QUALITY:	★ ★ ★
RECOMMENDATION:	Bad
RATING:	R
RELEASE:	1988
STARRING:	Mel Gibson, Michelle Pfeiffer, Kurt Russell, and Raul Julia
DIRECTOR:	Robert Towne
GENRE:	Detective/Action adventure
CONTENT:	Filthy obscene language and concentrated graphic sex
INTENDED AUDIENCE:	Adults
REVIEWER:	Glennis O'Neal

Tequila Sunrise opens with two male voices filling the empty darkness. Never mentally out of the dark, it travels physically into the light via the motel bathroom where McKusik stuffs a bag of cocaine into the commode. Hal, Federal Investigator, upbraids the Lieutenant for not capturing McKusik. The Police Lieutenant says he will not be a party to "manufactured" evidence. The Lieutenant and McKusik were best buddies at high school. Finally, the Lieutenant faces the fact that friends are not always for life. Hal operates on the hunch that Jo Ann, the restaurant hostess, and the restaurant are staffing questionable Mexican labor. It is also where they hope to catch a tie-in with Carlos, the king cocaine operator that no one else has seen, except McKusik.

We said this film starts in the dark and gets darker and darker and darker. Creating dirty dialogue and sexlogues for the sake of raking in the money at the box office should give the filmmakers just what they deserve, a good case of indigestion. For all those connected with this attempt at entertainment, we suggest they stop contriving "quick-buck movies." Avoid *Tequila Sunrise*.

TITLE:	**TERROR WITHIN**
QUALITY:	★
RECOMMENDATION:	Bad
RATING:	R
RELEASE:	1989
STARRING:	Andrew Stevens and Starr Andreeff
DIRECTOR:	Thierry Notz
GENRE:	Science fiction
CONTENT:	Profanity, obscenities, explicit love scene, and violence
INTENDED AUDIENCE:	Teenagers and up
REVIEWER:	Glennis O'Neal

In the desert, a land lab is established which discovers the remains of inhabitants wiped out by aliens. David and Sue capture Karen, a survivor whom they take back to the lab for study. Examination reveals she's three months pregnant. Her "abnormal" cell count means she's been exposed. Next morning, the medical crew reexamines her. "Last night she was three months, this morning she's seven months."

The "baby" births itself, splattering the mother's blood and escaping through the duct system. Each crew member takes turns at going after the monstrosity, with each paying a painful price for running into it. The women are spared for the purpose of conceiving and reproducing. Survival is the thrust of this film; survival for the lab crew and survival for the invading sub-humans.

Profanity, obscenities, and an explicit love scene are most objectionable. Action, of course, takes the place of high caliber acting, just as "layers" of blood add anything but authenticity to scenes. Avoid this "D" movie. The *Terror Within* is the thought that anyone would pay hard earned money to see this banal film.

TITLE:	**THAT'S LIFE**
QUALITY:	★
RECOMMENDATION:	Evil
RATING:	PG-13
RELEASE:	1986
STARRING:	Jack Lemmon, Julie Andrews, and Sally Kellerman
DIRECTOR:	Blake Edwards
GENRE:	Comedy
CONTENT:	Profanity, blasphemy, immorality, and sorcery
INTENDED AUDIENCE:	Adults
REVIEWER:	Ted Baehr

That's Life tells the story of Harvey Fairchild, a millionaire architect who is turning sixty and is petrified by the thought of growing old. Harve's wife, played by Julie Andrews, is having a biopsy to see if she has cancer of the throat. She keeps her torment to herself. However, Harve, who is told by all the doctors that he has absolutely nothing wrong with him, is convinced that he is dying of some disease or another.

Harve is ready to go back to the Roman Catholic Church, but stops on the way to see a fortune teller who gives him crabs when they make love. Harve continues to church, squirming because of the crabs, and is asked to read the Bible (which is on adultery) by the alcoholic priest who was Harve's roommate at college.

The fortune teller is present at his birthday party, and Harve tells a friend to have his palm read, knowing what will happen. Harve's next door neighbor, a nymphomaniac, goes after the priest. The movie ends with the wife finding out that she didn't have cancer.

That's Life is totally blasphemous. It has no semblance to real life at all. Jesus is cursed, and the clergy is mocked. Profanity, obscenity, and adultery are promoted. Boycott *That's Life* and tell your friends.

TITLE:	**THE THIN BLUE LINE**
QUALITY:	★ ★
RECOMMENDATION:	Extreme Caution
RATING:	Not rated
RELEASE:	1988
STARRING:	Documentary
DIRECTOR:	Errol Morris
GENRE:	Documentary
CONTENT:	Some profanity, mild sexual scenes, recreational drug and alcohol use, and some violence; uses documentary footage
INTENDED AUDIENCE:	Adults
REVIEWER:	Troy Schmidt

Errol Morris' documentary, *The Thin Blue Line,* searches for the truth in the 1976 slaying of a Dallas police officer. One night in 1976, the police stopped a car. As an officer approached, five shots were fired, killing the policeman. Dave Harris a sixteen-year-old was driving. He had picked up Randall Adams hitchhiking. Harris is apprehended for stealing the car he drove that night. Harris is accused of the murder, but he points the finger at Randall Adams. After Randall's arrest, in exchange for naming Randall as the killer, the judicial system gave Dave Harris immunity. Years later, Randall Adams sits on Death Row for murdering a man during a kidnapping attempt.

The Thin Blue Line probes into the investigation like a fine-tuned Columbo, but the film becomes overloaded with facts and repetitious re-creations of the murder. *The Thin Blue Line* is for documentary buffs only. Because of some profanity, mild sexual scenes, recreational drug and alcohol use, and some violence (although none of these elements are glorified), you will probably want to pass on this one. However, it should be noted that this film prompted the state to release Adams.

TITLE:	**THINGS CHANGE**
QUALITY:	★★★
RECOMMENDATION:	Caution
RATING:	PG
RELEASE:	1988
STARRING:	Don Ameche, Joe Mantegna, and Robert Prosky
DIRECTOR:	David Mamet
GENRE:	Comedy
CONTENT:	Obscenity and rear nudity
INTENDED AUDIENCE:	Adults
REVIEWER:	Ted Baehr

Things Change is a mistaken-identity comedy. Gino is shining shoes in Chicago when found by thugs who drag him to the local mob boss. The boss shows him a picture of a man who looks "exactly" like him. The man in the picture is being charged with murder. The boss wants Gino to take the rap so the Don can be freed. They offer Gino money for each year he serves in jail. Gino accepts.

He is then handed over to Jerry, who's supposed to watch him for the weekend before Gino goes to court to confess the murder. Jerry decides to give Gino a weekend he'll remember. He takes Gino to Lake Tahoe, where he's treated like the mafia Don he will be impersonating. Just as they begin to enjoy the luxurious lifestyle, the boss from Chicago comes to Tahoe for a "family" meeting. Thus, Gino's escape begins.

The movie has very little obscene language and no profanity but does have some retreating nudity. For a mob picture, it is surprisingly clean and well-intentioned, besides being funny. We caution you about some of the casino gambling scenes. Overall, *Things Change* is not a malicious film, but it is probably not worth your time.

TITLE:	**THREE MEN AND A BABY**
QUALITY:	★★★
RECOMMENDATION:	Extreme Caution
RATING:	PG
RELEASE:	1987
STARRING:	Tom Selleck, Steve Guttenberg, and Ted Danson
DIRECTOR:	Leonard Nimoy
GENRE:	Comedy
CONTENT:	Profanity, obscenity, and implied immorality

INTENDED AUDIENCE: Adults

REVIEWER: Ted Baehr

Three Men and a Baby is an American remake of the successful French film, *Three Men and a Cradle.* The story is the same, but the French film's light, moral humor has been replaced by scatological humor. The French film introduced morality and responsibility into a hedonistic culture. The American film indicates you can have your cake and eat it too.

The story tells about three bachelors. Peter and Michael receive two packages one Sunday. One is Jack's baby, from his former lover, Sylvia. The other is heroin. Jack is acting in a film in Turkey. At first overwhelmed, Peter and Michael come to love the baby, Mary. The police and the pushers wreak havoc trying to find the heroin. Jack returns. The bachelors catch the pushers. Sylvia moves in with them.

Forget this American rip-off and look for the French original which will delight you with its moral conclusions.

TITLE:	**THREE FUGITIVES**
QUALITY:	★ ★ ★
RECOMMENDATION:	Extreme Caution
RATING:	PG-13
RELEASE:	1989
STARRING:	Nick Nolte and Martin Short
DIRECTOR:	Francis Verber
GENRE:	Comedy
CONTENT:	Profanity and obscenity
INTENDED AUDIENCE:	Adults
REVIEWER:	Gene Burke

Daniel Lucas, released from prison, is opening a bank account and beginning a new life free of crime. Just at that time, a novice bank robber, Ned Perry stages a robbery and takes Lucas hostage. Lucas is thought to be an accomplice. Ned is robbing the bank to pay for his emotionally disturbed five-year-old daughter Meg's medical bill. Lucas is shot in the leg and forced to run all because of this idiot. Ned needs Lucas' expertise to allude the cops.

Slowly, Lucas' gruff attitude becomes that of a concerned guardian. Ned, Lucas, and Meg head for Canada to find a new life. The film ends with Meg and Lucas waiting in a car for Ned to open a bank account. Suddenly, police cars surround the bank and Ned is dragged out of the bank by a robber who is taking him hostage.

As unbelievable as all this is, there are sensitive moments. Meg's acquired love for this mean brawler Lucas, is the incentive that allows her to again talk, and it changes his nature, too. This film offers very funny laughs free of the habitual innuendos.

Unfortunately, there is profanity and obscenity that needs to be cautioned. Taking the Name of God in vain is never acceptable.

TITLE:	**THROW MOMMA FROM THE TRAIN**
QUALITY:	★ ★ ★
RECOMMENDATION:	Bad
RATING:	R
RELEASE:	1987
STARRING:	Danny DeVito and Billy Crystal
DIRECTOR:	Danny DeVito
GENRE:	Comedy
CONTENT:	Profanity, obscenity, and heinous cruelty
INTENDED AUDIENCE:	Adults
REVIEWER:	Doug Brewer

Throw Momma from the Train is Danny DeVito's misguided rendition of Hitchcock's *Strangers on a Train*. Owen is taking a creative writing course taught by Larry. Larry's ex-wife has stolen his last book and published it under her name. Owen's mother abuses Owen at every chance. He has fantasies of murdering her. Owen doesn't understand why Larry pans his murder story. When they sit down to talk about story construction, Larry mentions the switch that takes place in *Strangers on a Train*. Owen thinks Larry is telling him to kill Larry's ex-wife. So, he heads off to Mexico to kill her. Owen insists that Larry ice Momma in exchange.

There are some funny scenes in *Throw Momma from the Train*, but there is nothing funny about matricide. The language is offensive, and there is constant violence. *Throw Momma from the Train* is a dark, brooding idea trying to disguise itself as a comedy. Avoid *Throw Momma from the Train*.

TITLE:	**THY KINGDOM COME, THY WILL BE DONE**
QUALITY:	★ ★ ★
RECOMMENDATION:	Evil
RATING:	Not rated
RELEASE:	1988
DIRECTOR:	Antony Thomas
GENRE:	Documentary
CONTENT:	Mocking Christianity and God
INTENDED AUDIENCE:	Adults
REVIEWER:	Ralph Barker and Joe Moorecraft

This biased documentary frames church leaders as right-wing extremists and Christians as airheads. What this film really boils down to is religious bigotry.

The first message in this film is that it is wrong for Christians to be involved in politics. Anyone who falls for this has not read the Bible.

The second message declares that the monies the mega-churches and TV evangelists raise are misspent and that the money collected was more important than the people it was supposed to help. This message idolizes money to the same degree that one possessed by greed worships money.

The film footage of Christian leaders was usually old and of substandard quality, implying that the Christian mentality is out of step with the world. In fact, we are not of this world, but born of His Spirit.

The first twenty-five minutes contained enough Gospel to be effective in sharing the love of Christ. So we pray that the many members of the secular world who see it will be exposed to the Gospel of our Lord. Wouldn't it be great if a film meant to deride Christianity ended up leading members of its audience to share in the joys of eternal salvation?

☆☆☆ CLASSIC ☆☆☆

TITLE:	**TIGER BAY (Black and White)**
QUALITY:	★★★★
RECOMMENDATION:	Caution
RATING:	Not rated
RELEASE:	1959 (British)
STARRING:	John Mills, Hayley Mills, and Horst Buchholtz
DIRECTOR:	J. Lee Thompson
GENRE:	Action adventure
CONTENT:	Nothing objectionable
INTENDED AUDIENCE:	Adults and mature young people
REVIEWER:	Protestant Motion Picture Council

A Polish sailor, on leave from his ship, is outraged to find that his one-time mistress is living with another man, so he kills her. Unseen by the murderer, a lonely tomboy is the only witness to his crime. She gets hold of the murder weapon, convinced that having a gun will make her popular with her peers when they play cowboys and Indians. When the police catch up to her, the precocious youngster is confronted by a detective, but she only frustrates him by telling him a convincing string of lies.

Eventually, the seaman catches up with her and kidnaps her, taking her on his long run to join a foreign ship on which he hopes to escape. A surprisingly close relationship and mutual dependence builds between these two. The confidence and the protective affection of the child is reciprocated by the seaman's instinct for saving her from danger which thwarts his own safety, thus providing a fascinating plot in addition to mounting suspense.

The crime is not condoned. The whole drama holds one absorbed. The performances are outstanding, especially that by Hayley Mills, the small orphan child, which is remarkable. Her face registers a gamut of emotions, never once letting an unnatural feeling show. The direction is also exacting, drawing out the human qualities of the story while never forgetting that this is also a crime film. J. Lee Thompson's ability to combine the thriller elements with the story of a young girl's lonely search for attention and love is a highly accomplished effort.

☆☆☆ CLASSIC ☆☆☆

TITLE:	**TOBY TYLER**
QUALITY:	★ ★ ★
RECOMMENDATION:	Acceptable for children
RATING:	Not rated
RELEASE:	1960
STARRING:	Kevin Corcoran, Henry Calvin, Gene Sheldon, and Bob Sweeney
DIRECTOR:	Charles Barton
GENRE:	Children/Action adventure
CONTENT:	Nothing objectionable
INTENDED AUDIENCE:	Children
REVIEWER:	Protestant Motion Picture Council

This is another one of those Disney pictures that is beyond the limitations of time, having as much relevance today as it did when it was first released.

Having disagreed with his aunt and uncle, young Toby runs away from home to join a traveling circus. He gets a job as an assistant to a somewhat dishonest concession stand operator, is befriended by the strong man and adopts a chimpanzee as his companion.

He is brought into the exotic world of the circus, with all its eccentric characters, its excitement and wild animals. After a few mishaps, he becomes an attraction in his own right, and so does the monkey, Mr. Stubbs.

By the end, the tot discovers that his family really does care about him, and has, in fact, been trying to contact him. He returns to the farm, having grown through his experiences with the circus. A little wiser, he has learned that it takes all types of people to make up the world—a world he has encountered in microcosm in the circus.

This story is what it purports to be, "Ten weeks with a circus," and the audience is carried along with the people and the animals as they make their way into the hearts of the town and country folk.

Special emphasis is placed on friendship, love of an animal pet, diligence, obedience, faithfulness, "on with the show" tradition, and the desirability of truthfulness. All of these are on the credit side, as are the production values, the blare of the circus music and the scenic backgrounds.

Young Kevin Corcoran is a fine Toby, and he meets keen competition from Mr. Stubbs who is a scene stealer from the start.

☆☆☆ CLASSIC ☆☆☆

TITLE:	**TOPPER (97 Minutes, Black and White)**
QUALITY:	★ ★ ★ ★
RECOMMENDATION:	Caution
RATING:	Not rated
RELEASE:	1937
STARRING:	Constance Bennett, Cary Grant, Roland Young, and Billie Burke
DIRECTOR:	Norman Z. McLeod
GENRE:	Comedy
CONTENT:	Ghosts
INTENDED AUDIENCE:	Family
REVIEWER:	Betty Hill

The insouciant wackiness of this top-budgeted 1937 screwball fantasy altered the course of producer Hal Roach's career, and those of its stars. The movie's delightful screenplay initiated a new trend in '30s film farce with its "supernatural" trick photography that special-effects cameraman Roy Seawright worked out with *Topper's* nominal cinematographer Norbert Brodine. Veteran comedy director Norman Z. McLeod maintains an appropriately light touch as he guides his skilled farceurs through this whimsy about a devil-may-care couple, George and Marion Kerby, who are killed in an auto crash and return as spirits dedicated to improving the lot of their henpecked pal Cosmo Topper.

Most of the fun in this souffle is in Topper's gradual metamorphosis, under the Kerbys' tutelage, from milquetoast to man-about-town. Young, in particular, delivers a performance of such charm that it won him an Oscar nomination as 1937's best supporting actor. Topper's success inspired a pair of sporadically amusing sequels, *Topper Takes a Trip* (1939) and *Topper Returns* (1941), as well as a popular '50s television series and a lackluster 1979 TV-movie. The original 1937 film remains the classic.

Christians should object to spirits and spiritism, but this is pure fluff and can be corrected with a few well-chosen words on God's perspective toward the supernatural. Caution is recommended if you don't have the time to discuss this fine film with your family.

TITLE:	**TORCH SONG TRILOGY**
QUALITY:	★ ★ ★
RECOMMENDATION:	Evil
RATING:	R
RELEASE:	1988
STARRING:	Harvey Fierstein, Anne Bancroft, Matthew Broderick, and Brian Kerwyn

DIRECTOR:	Paul Bogart
GENRE:	Drama
CONTENT:	Rough language, references to homosexual activities, and male kissing instances
INTENDED AUDIENCE:	Confused adults
REVIEWER:	Gene Burke

There is no doubt that *Torch Song Trilogy* perfectly fulfills Romans 1:22–32:

> Although they claimed to be wise, they became fools and exchanged the glory of the immortal God for . . . a lie, and worshiped and served created things rather than the Creator. . . . Because of this, God gave them over to shameful lusts.

> Men committed indecent acts with other men, and received in themselves the due penalty for their perversion. Furthermore, since they did not think it worthwhile to retain the knowledge of God, he gave them over to a depraved mind, to do what ought not to be done. They have become filled with every kind of wickedness, evil, greed and depravity.

> They are gossips, slanderers, God-haters, insolent, arrogant and boastful; they invent ways of doing evil; they disobey their parents; they are senseless, faithless, heartless, ruthless. Although they know God's righteous decree that those who do such things deserve death, they not only continue to do these very things but also approve of those who practice them.

Five-year-old Arnold gets caught "in the closet dressing like a woman." In his next scene as an adult, he is a female impersonator. Alan comes along. They fall "in love" and after three years, Arnold wants to adopt a child. Alan is killed by a gang. The adoption takes place, and David, a fifteen-year-old abused by his parents, arrives, as does Ed, his previous "true love," who returns to live with them. This "happy family" of homosexuals is now complete.

Arnold's mother is visibly shocked to find the evidence of Arnold's chosen lifestyle. Mom is outraged and lights into him: "How can you compare your illicit affair to a thirty-five-year relationship I had with your father that resulted in bringing two children into this world?" She leaves without saying good-bye.

What makes this film so reprehensible is its intent to legitimize Arnold's chosen lifestyle—a lifestyle which only leads to eternal damnation. Regardless of how the pagans may honor this deceiving film, we must condemn it as another *Last Temptation of Christ*. We pray that those who see this film and are bound by this lifestyle will truly "come out of the closet" and turn their life around by accepting Christ. Avoid this abominable film.

TITLE:	**TOUGH GUYS**
QUALITY:	★
RECOMMENDATION:	Extreme Caution
RATING:	R

RELEASE:	1986
STARRING:	Burt Lancaster, Kirk Douglas, Charles Durning, and Eli Wallach
DIRECTOR:	Jeff Kanew
GENRE:	Comedy
CONTENT:	Vulgarity, profanity, obscenity, off-color jokes, and some violence, though not graphic
INTENDED AUDIENCE:	Adults
REVIEWER:	Bruce Grimes

Tough Guys reunites two of the most prominent veterans of the silver screen, Burt Lancaster and Kirk Douglas, in a script that doesn't do their acting abilities justice.

In 1956, two men attempted to rob the California Flyer, the train that goes between Los Angeles and San Francisco. They were caught and spent thirty years in jail. They are released from prison to find a different world from the one they left: homosexual bars, punk rockers, spiked hairdos, and banks with cameras. They have trouble adjusting; therefore, they decide to highjack the Southern Flyer one last time.

The majority of the film has a superficial tone. There is an excessive amount of obscene language in the movie, as well as Mr. Douglas exposing his naked buttocks as a final goodbye to Charles Durning, who plays the cop chasing them. Come on writers, give us a break! Stop writing! The best advice we can give is for you to avoid *Tough Guys*. It is a sad commentary on the decay of the movie industry.

☆☆☆ MASTERPIECE ☆☆☆

TITLE:	**THE TREE OF THE WOODEN CLOGS (185 Minutes, Subtitles)**
QUALITY:	★ ★ ★ ★
RECOMMENDATION:	Acceptable
RATING:	Not rated
RELEASE:	1979 (Italian)
STARRING:	Luigi Ornaghi, Francesca Moriggi, and Omar Brignoli
DIRECTOR:	Ermanno Olmi
GENRE:	Drama
CONTENT:	Nothing objectionable
INTENDED AUDIENCE:	Adults
REVIEWER:	Ted Baehr

A sacramental portrayal of Italian peasants which looks with great realism at the hand of God in their lives. Although they live a very hard life and barely eke out a living from the land, in almost all that they do, they see God and give thanks to Him.

When a young boy is sitting next to a cow, the milk maid talks about God's grace as it is manifest in the cow. When a baby is born, God is there.

The movie concentrates on three peasant families and their daily experiences for the period of about one year. They live on an estate governed by a practically nonexistent landlord and work his land with the greatest of care and devotion. This is a living parable of how we are called to serve God.

The movie neither glorifies the peasants, nor looks down on them. It merely presents them in a truthful and beautiful manner, with all their hopes and failings. The movie concentrates on the bond between people, as well as their relationship to the land.

However, it is made perfectly clear that they do believe. They love the land. They are close to God.

This exquisite film won the Golden Palm at the 1978 Cannes Film Festival. Director Olmi, who directed, scripted, photographed, and edited the film is a committed Christian, whose work testifies to God's glory.

This film is the obverse of Ingmar Bergman's *Shame*. Parallel scenes emphasize that the people in this film are created by God and He delights in them. Whereas in *Shame* the key line said that the characters were in God's dream, but He was ashamed of their sinfulness.

The Tree of the Wooden Clogs may be the most beautiful, most reverent, most sacramental movie ever made.

TITLE:	**TROOP BEVERLY HILLS**
QUALITY:	★ ★
RECOMMENDATION:	Extreme Caution
RATING:	PG 13
RELEASE:	1989
STARRING:	Shelly Long and Craig T. Nelson
DIRECTOR:	Jeff Kanew
GENRE:	Comedy
CONTENT:	Many sexual innuendos and some obscenity
INTENDED AUDIENCE:	Adolescents
REVIEWER:	Gene Burke

A spoiled, about-to-be-divorced mom is bored with shopping and volunteers to lead her daughter's scout troop. No previous leader of Troop Beverly Hills lasted more than a month. Wilderness activities are not the highest priority of this Gucci group. She must prove to her skeptics, led by her husband, that she will not quit. Committed, she incorporates her own novel ideas for "roughing it" with designer uniforms, designer accessories and room service from a hotel. With her unorthodox innovation, she instills excitement into her group. Money is no object and excesses abound, in contrast to other "less fortunate" troops. Troop Beverly Hills ultimately competes victoriously against the perennially favored troops. Her success brings her husband back, and they are reunited and live happily ever after.

This is nothing more than spoiled, rich kids getting their way and demeaning the work ethic. Aimed at a younger audience, it is annoying to see wealth squandered in foolishness and blatantly exhibited as humorous. Nothing in this film is funny, though attempts are made over and over again. *Troop Beverly Hills* is not recommended for any audience.

TITLE:	**TRUE BELIEVER**
QUALITY:	★ ★
RECOMMENDATION:	Bad
RATING:	R
RELEASE:	1989
STARRING:	James Woods, Robert Downey, Jr., and Margaret Colin
DIRECTOR:	Joseph Ruben
GENRE:	Drama
CONTENT:	Profane and obscene language throughout
INTENDED AUDIENCE:	Adults
REVIEWER:	Ken Kistner

Roger, an optimistic law graduate, seeks out the brilliant lawyer he has read so much about in legal case studies at school—Edward Dodd. Our story opens with the youngster showing up for a trial in which Mr. Dodd is defending a cocaine pusher and proceeds to extend accolades to the distinctive-looking gentlemen sitting behind the defense desk. Roger has to catch his breath as the man he assumed was the drug dealer starts screaming about Constitutional rights. Specializing in drug cases, Mr. Dodd has become a prisoner of this last lost cause of the '60's. An avid drug user himself, he takes drug cases to subsidize his habit.

This whole idea makes the film unsavory. To insinuate there is some crusader who will fight for the right to use "controlled substances" is irresponsible. Vulgar language is used extensively throughout the film. Avoid *True Believer* not only because of its attitude toward drugs, but more especially because it's boring. The few interesting twists in the story are lost in a poorly written script.

☆☆☆ CLASSIC ☆☆☆

TITLE:	**THE TRUTH ABOUT SPRING**
QUALITY:	★ ★ ★ ★
RECOMMENDATION:	Acceptable
RATING:	Not rated
RELEASE:	1965

STARRING:	Hayley Mills, John Mills, James MacArthur, Lionel Jeffries, Harry Andrews, and Niall MacGinnis
DIRECTOR:	Richard Thorpe
GENRE:	Romance/Comedy/Adventure
CONTENT:	Nothing objectionable
INTENDED AUDIENCE:	Family
REVIEWER:	Protestant Motion Picture Council

A widowed, seafaring man and his teenaged daughter (played by real life father and daughter John and Hayley Mills) are two Americans who live by their wits, ingenuity, and resourcefulness in the Caribbean. Having built a houseboat on which they live, he is dedicated to giving his daughter the kind of life he believes every human being should have. As an unshaven old codger who applies his knowledge of human nature, for good and evil, to his daily adventures, he amply provides for their needs by scrounging, begging and outsmarting a couple of unscrupulous fortune hunters.

The daughter, who has never known any other life, but that planned by her father, awakens to love and femininity in a charming manner. This comes when she meets a young man who's bored with his life on his uncle's yacht and stays with the pair on their houseboat for a couple weeks of the simple life.

Adventures abound, including search for a supposed treasure coveted by some rough characters who are defeated by our cruising seaman. He uses a collection of old maps as bait as it is certain that the buried gold is only in his imagination and serves as a pretext for getting some quick cash.

The young man finds it difficult to leave the girl behind, and she loves him enough to want to go, in spite of the heartbreak of parting from her father, the sea and the old boat. He asks her father for permission to marry her, and of course he gets it. Dad leaves the young people on the yacht and takes his houseboat off to new scenery.

Though the characters and plot are simplistic, this is played with good feeling. The cast is quite amiable and makes the modest comedy work nicely. The youthful love affair is natural and consistent, scenes of sea and rocky passages are impressive.

Based on the story, "Satan: A Romance of the Bahamas," this movie contains genuine suspense, humor, and some wisdom. The direction is fine for the film, with good light pacing.

TITLE:	**TUCKER: THE MAN AND HIS DREAM**
QUALITY:	★ ★ ★ ★
RECOMMENDATION:	Caution
RATING:	PG
RELEASE:	1988
STARRING:	Jeff Bridges, Joan Allen, Martin Landau, and Frederic Forest
DIRECTOR:	Francis Ford Coppola

GENRE:	Drama/Biography/Historical
CONTENT:	Some obscenity and expletives
INTENDED AUDIENCE:	Adults and teenagers
REVIEWER:	Ted Baehr

Tucker: The Man and His Dream comes close to being the Great American Movie. Set in the late 1940's, *Tucker* tells the true story of a visionary who wants to build the best car ever. Tucker's car has disc brakes, fuel injection, seat belts, and other innovations which the Big Three won't incorporate into their cars for many years because of the cost of retooling. Detroit feels threatened and enlists a senator to destroy Tucker and his dream. Tucker is brought to court on trumped-up charges. His family and friends support him. In his closing speech, he argues for free enterprise and against the corporate socialism which is destroying the American dream.

The light technical grace with which this movie was made is extraordinary. There is no sex, violence, nor excessively foul language. We do caution you about a few expletives, but there hasn't been a movie in years so entertaining and so free from offensiveness.

This is the American Dream. Everyone who wants to experience that dream should see *Tucker: The Man and His Dream*.

TITLE:	**TWINS**
QUALITY:	★★★
RECOMMENDATION:	Caution
RATING:	PG
RELEASE:	1988
STARRING:	Arnold Schwarzenegger and Danny DeVito
DIRECTOR:	Ivan Reitman
GENRE:	Comedy
CONTENT:	Profanity and obscenity
INTENDED AUDIENCE:	Youth and family
REVIEWER:	Gene Burke

In a genetic experiment, twins are produced, but everyone is led to believe that the "baby" died at birth. One is raised in an urban orphanage. The other on a remote island.

Thirty-five years later, Julius, the twin raised under perfect conditions, sets out to find his brother. Vincent is a small-time car thief. Vincent wants to con Julius, and he does. Vincent accidentally falls into a five-million-dollar scheme for delivering stolen cars to Houston. They discover that Mom lives on the way. Though madcap experiences occur, all concludes happily. Julius convinces Vincent to return the stolen property and money. Seemingly, Julius has taught Vincent a lesson in honesty, but we learn that he returned only four million dollars of the five million mob payoff.

Arnold Schwarzenegger and Danny DeVito give the best performances of their careers.

The chemistry between them is enjoyable. This cute little film has unnecessary profanity and obscenity, as well as one scene that insinuates sexual intercourse outside of marriage. Therefore, it is not recommended.

☆☆☆ CLASSIC ☆☆☆

TITLE:	**UNDER TEN FLAGS**
QUALITY:	★★★★
RECOMMENDATION:	Caution
RATING:	Not rated
RELEASE:	1960
STARRING:	Van Heflin, Charles Laughton, and Mylene Demongeot
DIRECTOR:	Duilio Coletti
GENRE:	War
CONTENT:	Some salty language
INTENDED AUDIENCE:	Adults
REVIEWER:	Protestant Motion Picture Council

Based on the autobiography of Admiral Bernhard Rogge during WW II, this suspense-filled war drama chronicles the exploits of the commander of a German merchant surface raider, *The Atlantis*. The vessel adopted a bewildering array of disguises such as repainting the ship, flying neutral flags, erecting false smokestacks, and even having crewmen dress as women passengers promenading up and down the deck, all in order to lure ships close enough to drop the disguise, hoist the Nazi ensign and blow the ship out of the water with its concealed guns. Despite the trickery, the officer is a compassionate man, picking up survivors out of the water from the twenty-two British and Allied craft he sank.

Meanwhile, British Admiral Russell is assigned to investigate the mysterious sinkings. Although the two men never meet, the film concerns the battle of wits between them.

This is an absorbing tale, with excellent direction, action and production, technical precision, and fascinating details. Even if the old navy captains use salty language, it seems in character.

TITLE:	**UNDER THE SUN OF SATAN (Subtitles)**
QUALITY:	★★
RECOMMENDATION:	Extreme Caution
RATING:	Not rated
RELEASE:	1989
STARRING:	Gerard Depardieu, Maurice Pialat, and Sandrine Bonnaire
DIRECTOR:	Maurice Pialat

GENRE:	Religious
CONTENT:	Some violence and sexual references
INTENDED AUDIENCE:	Adults
REVIEWER:	Troy Schmidt

In France around the 1920's, a priest, struggling with his devotion to God, sets out on a journey to help another parish when he comes across a stranger in the night who is none other than Satan himself. Father Donissan also encounters Mouchette, a beautiful sixteen-year-old girl who is pregnant with the baby of a man she just killed. Father Donissan finds himself with the ability to see into her soul and begins to wonder where his allegiance lies—for good or evil.

Admittedly, this description is a bit confusing because the theme and story are not clearly presented. The director, Maurice Pialat, tackles the issues of faith, good and evil, devotion and love, with scrambled egg theology. The favorable points, good acting and writing, with short, crisp dialogue, are cancelled by incongruent scenes.

This movie missed an excellent opportunity to offer a theological debate that would ask profound questions. One wonders whether this production is the filmmaker's ultimate joke on today's eclectic art film audience—a movie so deep that nobody can understand it. As it is, *Under the Sun of Satan* is about nothing.

TITLE:	**THE UNTOUCHABLES**
QUALITY:	★★★
RECOMMENDATION:	Extreme Caution
RATING:	R
RELEASE:	1987
STARRING:	Robert DeNiro, Kevin Costner, and Sean Connery
DIRECTOR:	Brian DePalma
GENRE:	Detective
CONTENT:	Profanity, obscenity, and violence
INTENDED AUDIENCE:	Adults
REVIEWER:	Ted Baehr

The Untouchables is Brian DePalme's film remake of the television series. *The Untouchables* tells the story of the United States Treasury Agent, Elliot Ness, who successfully challenged Al Capone and put him behind bars.

The movie opens when the eager, naive, special prosecutor Elliot Ness comes into the Chicago Police force on a special assignment for the Treasury to stop Al Capone, the leader of the Mafia in Chicago. Elliot quickly learns that Al Capone is a brutal man who has the police in his pocket. Ness finds a few good men who are willing to stand against Capone. Slowly, Ness chips away at Capone's empire. In the end, Ness gets Capone sent up the river for eleven years.

The Untouchables is not for Christians. There are some compensating scenes of prayers and faith in God, but the violence is gruesome and the profanity is inexcusable. DePalme takes the heroic theme of a principled man, who defeats an evil empire, and turns it into an ironic theme where an ordinary man succeeds in spite of his limitations. Ness and his men are not motivated by faith, nor by a calling to do justice; rather, they are just prideful men spoiling for a fight. *The Untouchables* boils down to a gang war between Elliot Ness and Al Capone's gang. *The Untouchables* is mediocre entertainment.

TITLE:	**U-2 RATTLE AND HUMM**
QUALITY:	★★
RECOMMENDATION:	Extreme Caution
RATING:	PG-13
RELEASE:	1988
STARRING:	The Band U-2: Larry Mullen, Jr. (drums); Adam Clayton (bass); The Edge (piano, guitar and vocals); and Bono (vocals and guitar).
DIRECTOR:	Phil Joanow
GENRE:	Musical/Documentary
CONTENT:	Rock Music
INTENDED AUDIENCE:	Teenagers
REVIEWER:	Gene Burke

Concert films are not my favorite; however, U-2 is billed as a "Christian" group and the most popular rock group since the Beetles. *U–2 Rattle and Humm* is about music "with a message." The lyrics are full of radical political and spiritual questions and statements. One problem is an inability to hear the lyrics over the instruments. From apartheid to worldwide injustices, they call on the audience to join them in defiance, with love. A frequently heard message which sounds vaguely like the calls for Barabbas when the citizens of Jerusalem voted for a political, rather than a spiritual solution.

I left the theater not knowing who the U–2 rock group is. If they are Christian, there should be more evidence than a few lyrics and a necklace with a cross worn by the lead singer. There are two verbal expletives and verbal obscenities. This film is not recommended for Christians. It's message is too confused. However, to a non-believer, it is certainly a message to heed and a small step in a seemingly right direction.

TITLE:	**VICE VERSA**
QUALITY:	★★
RECOMMENDATION:	Extreme Caution
RATING:	PG
RELEASE:	1988
STARRING:	Judge Rheinhold and Fred Savage
DIRECTOR:	Brian Gilbert

GENRE:	Comedy
CONTENT:	Profanity and occultism
INTENDED AUDIENCE:	Teenagers
REVIEWER:	Scott Dugan

Marshall and Charlie wish they could be each other, and an Oriental skull grants the wish. Charlie fills in for Dad at the office and Marshall goes to school as Charlie. Fred Savage is interesting as the pint-sized father, but there is something demented about a child drinking martinis and muttering profanities. The skull was slipped into Marshall's luggage to bypass customs in Hong Kong by a pair of fiendish art collectors. When the art collectors locate the skull, our father and son team intercepts them as they are about to escape to New York. By making a wish while both are touching the skull, they reverse the spell, becoming themselves again after having gained a greater appreciation for one another.

Vice Versa has enough of the same elements of *Like Father, Like Son* to make you wonder why any studio would release so similar a film six months after the original. Minus the profanity and a sexual allusion, this film would be okay, if you haven't already been bored by *Like Father, Like Son*. As it is, we cannot recommend *Vice Versa*.

TITLE:	**VINCENT**
QUALITY:	★ ★ ★
RECOMMENDATION:	Caution
RATING:	Not rated
RELEASE:	1988
NARRATOR:	John Hurt (narrated)
DIRECTOR:	Paul Cox
GENRE:	Documentary/Biography
CONTENT:	A documentary on the life of Vincent van Gogh
INTENDED AUDIENCE:	Adults
REVIEWER:	Ted Baehr

Vincent, a beautifully crafted documentary, focuses on the inner life of Vincent van Gogh. It opens with the spoken words from Vincent's letters to his brother Theo.

In the beginning, Vincent is an ardent Christian who wants to become an evangelist. Somehow his theological studies, which he pursued with zeal, did not pan out. About the same time, he becomes infatuated with his cousin Kay. Kay rejects him, but he promises to pursue her until she changes her mind.

Eventually, in frustration, he ends up with a woman of the streets. From that point, he "turns from God toward art." He becomes a compulsive painter. During his life, his brother, Theo, sells only one of Vincent's paintings. He feels the world has rejected him. He ends up in the South of France in a lunatic asylum, trying to communicate to the world through his paintings. He dies at age thirty-seven, in 1890.

It is clear that Vincent condemned himself by turning from God. This beautiful documentary is recommended with caution because of the harsh reality of Vincent's life. However, the moral is clear and worth hearing.

TITLE:	**WALL STREET**
QUALITY:	★★
RECOMMENDATION:	Bad
RATING:	R
RELEASE:	1987
STARRING:	Charlie Sheen, Michael Douglas,and Darryl Hannah
DIRECTOR:	Oliver Stone
GENRE:	Drama
CONTENT:	Brief nudity, profanity, and obscenity
INTENDED AUDIENCE:	Adults
REVIEWER:	Bret Senft

Wall Street is hampered by embarrassing writing and poor direction. Gordon Gekko consumes corporations via hostile takeovers. This means ruined lives for thousands of workers, but so be it. Gekko puts Bud to work spying on a rival raiders. Visiting Gordon's beach house, Bud meets decorator Darian Taylor. After rolling in the sheets with Darian, Bud crawls to the balcony of his apartment, surveys Manhattan and gasps "Who am I?" The audience laughed.

Wall Street is riddled with such exclamations. When Bud is being sent to prison, his dad says, "Well Son, in a way, maybe it's the best thing that could ever happen to you." Now, spending a night in jail is one thing; three to five years in Attica is something else. "You're right, Dad. Thanks," says Bud, admiringly. The audience wept with laughter.

Mr. Stone, the director, exchanges sincere emotional response for cinematic cliches. Mr. Stone's intentions, to present the consequences of greed and immoral actions, are undercut by his inability to address the subject. *Wall Street* is an adolescent film in a Brooks Brothers suit which reveals Mr. Stone's immaturity. Avoid this film.

☆☆☆ MASTERPIECE ☆☆☆

TITLE:	**THE WAR OF THE WORLDS**
QUALITY:	★★★★
RECOMMENDATION:	Acceptable
RATING:	Not rated
RELEASE:	1953
STARRING:	Gene Berry and Ann Robinson
DIRECTOR:	Byron Haskin

GENRE:	Science fiction
CONTENT:	Nothing objectionable
INTENDED AUDIENCE:	All ages
REVIEWER:	Ted Baehr

The War of the Worlds, adapted from H.G. Wells' graphic novel, presents an external, rather than internal, view of the problems facing humanity—in this case, an alien invasion, which can be understood as an allegorical treatment of a demonic attack. In dealing with this attack, *The War of the Worlds* has a very clear, Biblical perspective.

The minister and the Christian faith is portrayed in a very positive light throughout the movie. In the middle of the movie, one of the leading characters says the world was created in six days and wonders if it will be destroyed in the same amount of time. At the end, as the Martians are conducting their final assault on the earth, people are gathered for prayer in various different churches.

It is clear that the victory over the alien invaders comes only as a result of God's grace. In fact, the last line tells us, " . . . it is the littlest things that God in His wisdom had put upon the Earth that save mankind."

The movie opens with the explanation that Mars is a dying planet. The Martians are looking for somewhere to resettle and decide on Earth. When they land in California, the first reaction of mankind is to welcome the aliens, but it is clear that they do not come in peace when they disintegrate the first three greeters. Still, a minister tries to approach the Martians with a message of peace in the Name of God, but they vaporize him.

The war starts and it seems that the Martians are invincible. Dr. Clayton Forrester, from Pacific Laboratories, works with the army to discover a vulnerable chink in the Martian's armour.

In the process, he falls in love with a self-sacrificing minister's niece, Sylvia Van Buren. She leads him back to church and faith in God.

At the end, Los Angeles is being destroyed. Having been separated by the invasion, Clayton searches frantically for Sylvia. They are reunited in a church and pray for salvation. God gives it, and all ends well.

The War of the Worlds is just as exciting as any of the science fiction films being released today, and it is Biblical. It is a movie well worth seeing—several times. Rather than rent *ET* at your video store, you may want to consider renting *The War of the Worlds*, which is a much better movie.

TITLE:	**WATERWALKER**
QUALITY:	★★★
RECOMMENDATION:	Acceptable
RATING:	None
RELEASE:	1988
STARRING:	Bill Mason
DIRECTOR:	Bill Mason

GENRE:	Nature/Religious/Biography
CONTENT:	Entirely acceptable
INTENDED AUDIENCE:	All audiences
REVIEWER:	Christopher Farrell

This film involves Canada's Lake Superior region with its water and woodlands, Bruce Cockburn's music, and Bill Mason's perspective on life. This is not a linear film, but a still-life in motion—a good look at the indescribable beauty of Canada's outdoors. Bruce Cockburn's music never overpowers the natural sounds, but often draws us closer to the perpetual motion of the waters. The narration is warm and friendly, embracing gratefully the wonder of God's creation, acknowledging the Father and gleaning wisdom from Scripture.

Bill Mason's concluding statements formulate the philosophy for this film from Peter's experience on the water: we've forgotten how to walk on water, having taken our eyes off of God, who is right in front of us. How true to this ideal does Mason seem, who enjoyed the peace and trusted the provision of God in a way few Christians do. For Bill Mason, this message is a reality, a reverence, an act of worship, and, through this film, a ministry.

TITLE:	**WE OF THE NEVER NEVER**
QUALITY:	★ ★ ★
RECOMMENDATION:	Caution
RATING:	G
RELEASE:	1983
STARRING:	Angela Punch McGregor, Arthur Dignam, and Tony Barry
DIRECTOR:	Igor Auzins
GENRE:	Historical/Western
CONTENT:	The word "damn" is used several times and there is native aborigine "nudity"
INTENDED AUDIENCE:	Adults
REVIEWER:	Betty Hill

This is the true story of a Christian woman who married and moved to the Australian Outback. The "Never Never" is said to be so beautiful that once it hooks you, you'll never, never leave it. Getting Jeanie to her new home is an ordeal. After a train trip from Melbourne, she meets her husband, Arias, in the pouring rain. Cowboys join them for a mud-splattering wagon ride. When Jeanie endures without complaint, the men accept her.

The farm house is filled with cobwebs. The back door falls off at her touch. The aborigines exist in horrid huts nearby. Jeanie accepts Arias' invitation to join their four-week cattle drive. An aborigine tells a fable about the creation of the moon and stars. At the campfire, he asks, "Boss, where white feller star come from?" Jeanie answers, "God made the stars . . . the stars, the moon, everything!" The aborigine satirically asks, "If white feller's God made everything, why didn't he make white feller some bush (land) of their own?"

She walks with the natives and learns the names of birds. Refusing to believe the blacks are inferior, she visits their camp and invites an orphan to eat in her house. This shocks the cowboys and her husband.

This movie contains no sex or violence. It is a beautiful demonstration of lifestyle evangelism.

TITLE:	**WE THE LIVING (Approximately 180 minutes, Subtitles)**
QUALITY:	★ ★ ★
RECOMMENDATION:	Caution
RATING:	Not rated
RELEASE:	1942
STARRING:	Rossano Brazzi, Alida Valli, and Fosco Giachetti
DIRECTOR:	Goffredo Allessandirni
GENRE:	Historical
CONTENT:	Relationships outside of marriage
INTENDED AUDIENCE:	Adults
REVIEWER:	Glennis O'Neal

Dressed in patched clothing, the once wealthy Argounova family returns to Petrograd after fleeing the Russian Revolution five years before. They consider it a miracle to find three shabby rooms. Kira, fleeing an amorous cousin one evening, walks into the Red-light District, where she's propositioned by Leo. He senses Kira is not a prostitute. She tells her family she's moving in with Leo, which causes them to denounce her. She discovers Leo will die of tuberculosis unless he goes to Crimea for treatment. Kira takes advantage of a Russian officer's admiration. The officer, Andrei, gives her money with which she finances Leo's sanitarium treatment. Cured, Leo returns and makes enough blackmail money to give himself the finer things of life. He begins looking at a wealthy woman. Andrei insists on marriage, which forces Kira to confess that she used him in order to save Leo.

Ayn Rand, the writer of this novel, is as powerful today as the day she wrote of life in a totalitarian state. She hated communism and warred constantly against an individual's freedom being owned and controlled by the State. However, she showed a total lack of responsibility when her characters defiantly broke Biblical moral codes. What difference is there in being enslaved by the State or enslaved by an individual for self-gratification? If only she had made "soul over State" a priority, she and her readers might have known the true value of freedom—through the Lordship of Christ.

TITLE:	**WE THINK THE WORLD OF YOU**
QUALITY:	★ ★
RECOMMENDATION:	Caution
RATING:	PG
RELEASE:	1989
STARRING:	Alan Bates, Gary Oldham, and Betsy
DIRECTOR:	Colin Gregg
GENRE:	Drama
CONTENT:	Some obscenity
INTENDED AUDIENCE:	Teenagers and up
REVIEWER:	Troy Schmidt

Johnny goes to jail for stealing, leaving behind his wife, children and dog, Evie. Frank turns down Johnny's request to watch his dog, but when he sees Johnny's parents mistreat the dog, he gains custody of it. This leads to problems with his other relationships.

Dog-lovers will appreciate the love for animals this film nurtures, and some "dogless" viewers might be tempted to get a pooch for their very own. Alan Bates delivers a heartwarming, easy performance as the man turned dog-lover. The relationship between Bates and Betsy is one of true love, and that's the plot behind the film—a love triangle. It's an unusual, unique way to present this age old theme. We see love not of the sexual kind, but of the eternal, heartfelt kind.

Unfortunately, the negatives outweigh the positives. The accents are difficult to understand. There are no explanations for certain character motivations, nor why the plot twisted so radically. As for the love triangle, it was treated too subtly. Since the filmmakers delivered a bone with so little meat on it, we are unable to give We Think the World of You a favorable wag. However, this movie won't hurt anyone.

TITLE:	**WHALES OF AUGUST**
QUALITY:	★ ★
RECOMMENDATION:	Extreme Caution
RATING:	Not rated
RELEASE:	1987
STARRING:	Bette Davis, Lillian Gish, and Vincent Price
DIRECTOR:	Lindsay Anderson
GENRE:	Drama
CONTENT:	Profanity and obscenity
INTENDED AUDIENCE:	Adults
REVIEWER:	Ted Baehr

The *Whales of August* has glimmers of hope and some good acting, but the direction is too staid, too stilted, and too slow. It looks like a scene study acting class. The elderly are not so measured and controlled.

The movie studies two sisters aging in Maine. Sarah takes care of Libby who is losing her sight. At first, Libby is recalcitrant and negative. By the end, Sarah has given up hope and Libby is hopeful. This role reversal is meaningless in terms of eternity. In fact, *Whales of August* is more humanist nostalgia than an insight into the process of aging.

Whales of August is not recommended. Sad to say, God is merely a profane reference. The whales are more important for they bring in the seasons. It is a movie that does not find its center because whoever wrote it did not know that the center is God. God created these women, and there is something more in life than aging. This humanist vision of the elderly is pathetic.

TITLE:	**THE WHISTLE BLOWER**
QUALITY:	★★★
RECOMMENDATION:	Caution
RATING:	PG
RELEASE:	1987
STARRING:	Michael Caine, Nigel Havers, James Fox, and Sir John Gielgud
DIRECTOR:	Simon Langton
GENRE:	Spy/War
CONTENT:	Mild violence
INTENDED AUDIENCE:	Adults
REVIEWER:	Byron Cherry

The Whistle Blower is a dramatic spy thriller with the customary cloak-and-dagger events. Set in London, the story's events revolve around Frank Jones, a patriotic Korean War vet, and his son, Bob Jones, a Russian language specialist in British intelligence. Bob becomes a victim in a series of mysterious suicides that befall his section when it is learned a coworker is a Soviet double agent. Frank attempts to solve the mystery of his son's death, disturbed by his son's statement about the "invisible government."

The Whistle Blower examines the erosion of Frank's respect for England's political system as he learns of the questionable practices used to keep the country's face clean. Conversely, Bob, before his death, was disturbed by Russia's sinister undercurrent of evil. Sin undermines both systems, although British face-saving pales in comparison with Soviet treachery.

The Whistle Blower will entertain spy thriller lovers, but those who prefer other types of movies may be impatient with this film. Furthermore, the political naivete of the scriptwriter undermines the effectiveness of the story. Caution is recommended.

TITLE:	**WHO FRAMED ROGER RABBIT?**
QUALITY:	★ ★ ★
RECOMMENDATION:	Caution
RATING:	PG
RELEASE:	1988
STARRING:	Bob Hoskins and Christopher Lloyd
DIRECTOR:	Robert Zemeckis
GENRE:	Comedy/Animated
CONTENT:	Some rough language and bawdy humor
INTENDED AUDIENCE:	All ages
REVIEWER:	Ted Baehr

Who Framed Roger Rabbit is an imaginative mystery set in a world where humans and cartoon characters coexist. Sadly, after a funny opening, the humor dies. The funny moments thereafter are too few in a movie whose premise says that humor overcomes evil.

Set in 1947, *Who Framed Roger Rabbit* tells the story of a cartoon rabbit who is set up by a mean villain to unwittingly give the villain control over Toon Town so that he can replace the cartoon neighborhood with gas stations and shopping strips to serve a future freeway exit. A detective, Eddie Valient, is set up to set up Roger Rabbit by taking compromising pictures of Roger's curvacious wife Jessica with Mr. Acme. When he realizes he was duped, Eddie comes to Roger's rescue and, after many adventures, solves the mystery.

Who Framed Roger Rabbit is a bonanza for cartoon character fans. Unfortunately, some rough language and bawdy humor blemish this technically brilliant feature film.

TITLE:	**WHO'S HARRY CRUMB?**
QUALITY:	★
RECOMMENDATION:	Bad
RATING:	PG-13
RELEASE:	1989
STARRING:	John Candy and Jeffrey Jones
DIRECTOR:	Paul Flaherty
GENRE:	Comedy
CONTENT:	Lewdness, lust, rough language, and greed; one pornographic scene; jokes about adultery, premarital sex, and infidelity

INTENDED AUDIENCE:	Teenagers and adults
REVIEWER:	Clint Manning

Harry Crumb is the descendant of a famous detective who's empire, Crumb and Crumb, is headquartered in Los Angeles. No Crumbs are running it, since Harry inherited none of his progenitor's savvy. Crumb receives a call from L.A., and is told that he will be investigating the kidnapping of a millionaire's daughter. To call someone as inept as Harry arouses suspicion that corruption must be involved. In fact, the president of Crumb and Crumb, played by Jeffrey Jones, arranged to have the girl kidnapped. Jeffrey lusts after the girl's stepmother who is lusting after her husband's money. After over-blown and unimaginative antics, Harry solves the case.

Harry's pomposity is annoying. There is quite a bit of lewdness in this movie. There is one pornographic sight gag that takes place in a mud-bath. There are numerous jokes about "private parts." This film condemns greed and theft, but treats sexual immorality flippantly. *Who's Harry Crumb?* is too vulgar for most people. Avoid this film and tell your friends to avoid it. They should thank you for saving them from this travesty.

TITLE:	**WILLOW**
QUALITY:	★★
RECOMMENDATION:	Evil
RATING:	PG
RELEASE:	1988
STARRING:	Val Kilmer, Joanne Whalley, Warwick Davis, Billy Barty, and Jean Marsh
DIRECTOR:	Ron Howard
STORY BY:	George Lucas
GENRE:	Sword and sorcery/Action adventure
CONTENT:	Occultism, witchcraft, and evil
INTENDED AUDIENCE:	All ages
REVIEWER:	Ted Baehr

If George Lucas hadn't produced *Willow*, it would have quickly ended up on independent television. Most people will be bored. Cliche after cliche is thrown at the audience. If there had been more humor, this might have been bearable. However, a movie which promotes magic should be shunned as an evil influence on a decadent society.

Willow tells the story of a baby prophesied as the one to overthrow the evil sorceress Queen Bavmorda. The Queen commands her army to kill all babies. The baby Elora is saved by a midwife who deposits her in the river. She washes ashore at the farm of the nelwyn named Willow. Willow must protect the baby and teams up with the warrior, Madmartigan, two fairies and the witch Rissel. Willow ends up defeating the Queen by tricking her. Deception triumphs over evil.

Willow is not a Biblical allegory. It is occultism which God abhors. This combined with the boring script is enough to recommend that you avoid *Willow*.

★★★ CLASSIC ★★★

TITLE:	**THE WIND CANNOT READ**
QUALITY:	★ ★ ★
RECOMMENDATION:	Acceptable
RATING:	Not rated
RELEASE:	1958 (British)
STARRING:	Dirk Bogarde, Yoko Tani, Ronald Lewis, and John Fraser
DIRECTOR:	Ralph Thomas
GENRE:	War/Romance/Drama
CONTENT:	Nothing objectionable
INTENDED AUDIENCE:	Adults
REVIEWER:	Protestant Motion Picture Council

This film, based on the novel by Richard Mason, tells of an East and West romance in India during World War II. It is effectively told, splendidly acted, and well directed.

After action in Burma jungle warfare, a Royal Air Force officer is sent to India to recuperate and attend a Japanese language school so he can interrogate prisoners of war. He falls in love with his instructor, Suzuki San, a charming Japanese girl.

The pair do a lot of sightseeing, and a love story develops with great delicacy against the backdrop of war in exotic surroundings: Delhi, with its bazaars and crowded places; the pink city of Jaipur, with its amber palace and caparisoned elephants; the Taj Mahal; and the lush jungle and arid places.

Shortly after their secret marriage, the husband is sent back to Burma, where he's captured by the Japanese, tortured, and humiliated. Suzuki San meanwhile, has joined All India Radio and is beaming British propaganda to the enemy.

He learns that she is suffering from an incurable brain disease, and with the help of a fellow Britisher, stages a daring escape through dense jungles back to their own lines in Delhi. They have a touching reunion and the assurance that even death will not separate them.

The general impression is one of beauty, the accent is on the love story, with war complications and a few service men rivalries to set the scene. It is a production of merit, with good use of Indian music in the background.

TITLE:	**WINGS OF DESIRE**
QUALITY:	★ ★ ★
RECOMMENDATION:	Caution
RATING:	PG-13
RELEASE:	1987

STARRING:	Bruno Ganz, Otto Sanders, Solveig Dommartin, Peter Falk, and Curt Bois
DIRECTOR:	Wim Wenders
GENRE:	Romance/Religious
CONTENT:	Sexual innuendo and a flash of non-frontal nudity
INTENDED AUDIENCE:	Adult
REVIEWER:	Wendell P. Rhodes

Timeless questions are asked, but not answered in *Wings of Desire*, the story of an Angel, named Damiel, who desires to become human. The angels "observe, collect, testify, preserve" and are invisible comforters to those in trouble. In Damiel, we hear the message: life should be relished and appreciated, whether good or bad. To risk, to love, to feel—these should be sought after more than "knowing the answers." To the filmmakers, the ultimate experience is the relationship between a woman and a man. This is the best life has to offer.

You and I know this is not all there is! Immortality is not boring, and mortality not the end of it all. To know God, to have His presence in our lives and to live with Him in eternity is better than anything we can experience here.

This movie requires you to think. If you can explore (without being offended) the thought processes of a fallen world, perhaps you will walk away as I did, wanting to shout the Name of Jesus from the rooftops.

TITLE:	**WINTER PEOPLE**
QUALITY:	★★★★
RECOMMENDATION:	Extreme Caution
RATING:	PG-13
RELEASE:	1989
STARRING:	Kurt Russell, Kelly McGillis, and Lloyd Bridges
DIRECTOR:	Ted Kotcheff
GENRE:	Drama
CONTENT:	Few incidences of profanity; one tense scene of violence
INTENDED AUDIENCE:	Adults
REVIEWER:	Gene Burke

Waylon Jackson and his ten-year-old daughter are in prayer over his recently deceased wife. This touching scene sets the tone for the rest of the film. While crossing a river in the Appalachian mountain range, their car becomes stuck. Going for help, they are at first turned away by Cauley Wright and her infant, who leaves them in the freezing cold. When she sees his daughter, she realizes she must help and offers them lodging for the night in the barn.

The next morning, Waylon's car is ransacked by the Campbell family, arch enemy of the Wrights. Unable to do anything, Waylon helplessly watches.

Cauley and Waylon begin to help one another. The town hires Waylon to build a clock tower in the center of town. A new spirit of hope and joy is ushered in as the townspeople work together on a common goal. Family values are shared, prayer is exercised and a Godly respect for each other is exhibited. The only mystery is the secret Cauley keeps, which is the identity of the father of her child.

A deal is eventually struck between the two families, and on the day of Waylon's and Cauley's wedding, in the most moving scene of the film, the hard-hearted Campbell patriarch forgives Waylon and Cauley. The film ends in a glowing and warm tribute to forgiveness, restitution, and the value and importance of an infant and family.

The pro-family, pro-life, pro-godly message is thoroughly enlightening, entertaining and most encouraging. The film, based on the novel by John Ehle, is PG-13 and too intense for younger audiences. We do not condone the use of profanity, but the positive messages embedded in this film merit commendation with extreme caution.

TITLE:	**WITCHES OF EASTWYCK**
QUALITY:	★ ★ ★
RECOMMENDATION:	Evil
RATING:	R
RELEASE:	1987
STARRING:	Jack Nicholson, Cher, Susan Sarandon, and Michele Pfeiffer
DIRECTOR:	George Miller
GENRE:	Horror
CONTENT:	Blasphemy, evil, profanity, and sex
INTENDED AUDIENCE:	Adults
REVIEWER:	Glennis O'Neal

This film, based on the book by John Updike, is unquestionably the Devil's masterpiece, presenting every perverted, evil thought imaginable to the human mind. It tells the story of three modern women who inadvertently fall in with the Devil. The moral, if one can be found, is that playing the Devil's game is not only dangerous, but also death to the players.

A lot of money has been wasted to pass off this evil creation as entertainment. The author brings 1640 themes out of history's graveyard and turns Jack Nicholson loose to portray his naturally devilish character. Unfortunately, none of this effort has any redeeming value.

Avoid *Witches of Eastwyck*. It is evil, insane propaganda which no one should bother to see.

TITLE:	**WITHOUT A CLUE**
QUALITY:	★ ★ ★
RECOMMENDATION:	Caution
RATING:	PG
RELEASE:	1988
STARRING:	Michael Caine, Ben Kingsley, and Jeffrey Jones
DIRECTOR:	Thom Eberhardt
GENRE:	Comedy
CONTENT:	Subtle sexual references, mild violence, and some obscenity
INTENDED AUDIENCE:	Adults
REVIEWER:	Troy Schmidt

Without a Clue exposes the truth behind the legend: Dr. Watson was the brains and Sherlock was nothing but a drunken ex-actor named Reginald Kincaid whom Watson hired to play the character. Tired of living in the shadow of his creation, Watson kicks Sherlock out of their Baker Street abode. A case involving arch enemy Doctor Moriarty and two stolen printing plates from the Treasury comes up; however, no one allows Watson to work without Sherlock. After wooing Sherlock back, they take the case and follow the clues in their elementary manner. Watson has his hands full feeding Sherlock the proper information, tracking down the culprits, and keeping Holmes out of trouble.

Without a Clue is basically a one-joke movie. Removing any references to drinking, gambling, and womanizing, *Without a Clue* would have a G-Rating. As it is, caution is recommended. Unfortunately, it's not a particularly hilarious one, but an easy, relaxing, and quirky film. The biggest thing going for *Without a Clue* is its welcomed attempt at providing low key comedy to the PG segment of our population.

TITLE:	**THE WIZARD OF LONELINESS**
QUALITY:	★ ★ ★ ★
RECOMMENDATION:	Caution
RATING:	PG-13
RELEASE:	1988
STARRING:	Lukas Haas, Lea Thompson, and John Randolph
DIRECTOR:	Jenny Bowen
GENRE:	Drama
CONTENT:	Some profanity and sexual violence, which is not graphic
INTENDED AUDIENCE:	Teenagers and adults
REVIEWER:	Bret Senft

In Los Angeles in 1944, Wendall Oler, age twelve, sees his father, Fred, off to war. Wendall is on a first name basis with Fred, part of the tough-guy stance he adopted in the face of his mother's death. Wendall is transferred to Stebbensville, Vermont where he inspects the troops: old Doc Oler and Grandma Cornelia, as well as Fred's brother and sister, John T. and Sybil, and Sybil's boy, Tom, who badgers Wendall into big brotherhood. The Oler family extends enough tenderness to quench the grief in Wendall's heart.

Duffy, the high school hero who was almost killed in the war, turns up on the train that carries Wendall into town. Duffy terrorizes Wendall, rapes Sybil, and snatches Tom from his bedroom. In a shootout with MP's in the town square, Duffy bites the dust for real, as the family closes ranks around Wendall.

The Wizard of Loneliness touches on sentimentality, but never overreaches itself. As the family gathers around the piano to sing "Silent Night," they appear as a Norman Rockwell painting come-to-life. Good triumphs over evil, and the family is uplifted, but some of the elements in this film deserve caution.

TITLE:	**WOLVES OF WILLOUGHBY CHASE**
QUALITY:	★ ★ ★ ★
RECOMMENDATION:	Acceptable
RATING:	G
RELEASE:	1989
STARRING:	Stephanie Beacham, Mel Smith, Jonathan Coy, Eleanor David, Emily Hudson, Aleks Darowska, and Geraldine James
DIRECTOR:	Stuart Orme
GENRE:	Fantasy/Adventure/Children
CONTENT:	Nothing objectionable
INTENDED AUDIENCE:	All ages
REVIEWER:	Ted Baehr

The *Wolves of Willoughby Chase* is an elegant period piece set in the imaginary reign of King James III. Ravenous wolves surround Willoughby Chase, home of young Bonnie. When her parents, Lord and Lady Willoughby sail overseas, Bonnie and her cousin Sylvia are left in the care of Miss Slighcarp, the new governess.

With the help of Grimshaw, her greedy accomplice, Slighcarp hatches an evil plot to make the Willoughby wealth her own. As her reign of terror takes hold, the comfortable home becomes a cold prison for Bonnie and Sylvia.

Slighcarp arranges for the ship on which the Willoughbys sail to be lost at sea. She fires all but two servants and sends Bonnie and Sylvia to the orphanage, where children toil night and day at the mercy of Mrs. Brisket.

As Bonnie learns to care for others besides herself, she acquires strength to face Miss Slighcarp. The last third of the movie, which shows how good triumphs over evil, is masterfully constructed. Armed only with courage, the girls risk their lives in a breathtaking escape. Through marauding wolves, Slighcarp pursues them until the girls reach the safety of Willoughby Chase. However, Slighcarp and the evil wolves are not finished yet . . .

This story has no sex, violence, or profanity. It is a children's story which will keep adults on the edge of their seats. Costuming, camera work, and settings are beautiful.

The entire movie is a Christian parable. It is assumed that living life as a Christian is the highest goal. The *Wolves of Willoughby Chase* is recommended without reservation.

TITLE:	**A WORLD APART**
QUALITY:	★ ★
RECOMMENDATION:	Evil
RATING:	PG
RELEASE:	1988
STARRING:	Barbara Hershey and Jodhi May
DIRECTOR:	Chris Menges
GENRE:	Biography/Drama
CONTENT:	Profanity and communist propaganda
INTENDED AUDIENCE:	Adults
REVIEWER:	Bret Senft

The story of the "Roths" dramatizes Shawn Slovo's family's life in South Africa in 1963. In the film, her name has been changed to Molly Roth. Her father left the country rather than face imprisonment for treason as the head of the South African Communist Party. Diane, her mother, struggles against the government. Our sympathies are divided between this woman willing to risk all for a cause, and what we sense about Diane politically. During interrogation, she is branded a communist and shown a photograph of mutilated body killed during a communist attack. She does not deny the charges. Molly (Shawn) visits a township. A Mandela-like activist calls for armed insurrection. As troops arrive, the "congregation" reverts to hymn singing ("Amazing Grace" no less). It is difficult to root for such "heroes" when their religious beliefs are portrayed as an outright sham.

The film skirts Roth's true political identity. *A World Apart* is a film divided against itself, undercut by an ambiguous political agenda. Slovo (Roth) has been responsible for the gruesome death of thousands of innocent blacks. This film is ambiguous, because one of the four promises of communism is the abolition of the family, yet to attract an audience, the filmmakers had to focus the drama on the family. We recommend that you avoid this deception and thereby forego giving money to the cause of communism.

☆☆☆ MASTERPIECE ☆☆☆

TITLE:	**THE WRECK OF THE MARY DEARE**
QUALITY:	★ ★ ★ ★
RECOMMENDATION:	Acceptable

RATING:	Not rated
RELEASE:	1959
STARRING:	Gary Cooper, Charlton Heston, and Michael Redgrave
DIRECTOR:	Michael Anderson
GENRE:	Adventure/Drama
CONTENT:	Nothing objectionable
INTENDED AUDIENCE:	Adult
REVIEWER:	Protestant Motion Picture Council

In this unusual, yet heroic sea drama, based on the novel by Hammond Innes, mystery and suspense abound. The acting is excellent.

A ship salvager comes upon a seemingly derelict freighter, the *Mary Deare,* in the English Channel. He boards the smoldering ship, which apparently had been set afire before being abandoned. While exploring the ship, it is not found to be completely abandoned as one man is on board, who opposes her salvaging.

The men, antagonists at first, join forces and bring the ship to rest on a shoal. Eventually, they uncover a plot which nearly leads to their death.

The mystery emerges bit by bit, after a board of inquiry has conducted an investigation. Thus, a good part of the story is given over to a fascinating court session which adds a great deal of interest to the whole movie.

☆☆☆ MASTERPIECE ☆☆☆

TITLE:	**YOU CAN'T TAKE IT WITH YOU**
QUALITY:	★★★★
RECOMMENDATION:	Acceptable
RATING:	Not rated
RELEASE:	1938
STARRING:	Jean Arthur, Lionel Barrymore, Jimmy Stewart, Edward Arnold, Mischa Auer, Ann Miller, and Spring Byington
DIRECTOR:	Frank Capra
GENRE:	Comedy
CONTENT:	Nothing objectionable
INTENDED AUDIENCE:	Adult
REVIEWER:	Ted Baehr

You Can't Take It with You is a hilarious, entertaining movie. It is bursting with so much wacky activity that there is precisely a laugh-a-minute. Director Capra assembled a superior cast, and each scores solidly in their roles.

Martin Vanderhof is an eccentric patriarch of a family of frustrated artists. He retired from the rat-race thirty years before and uses his wealth to encourage his family and friends to pursue the vocations that really interest them.

He has taken up painting, which he does badly, but he enjoys himself. His daughter, Penny writes mystery novels, because a typewriter was left on the doorstep one day. Her husband, Paul, tinkers with explosives in the basement. Their daughter, Essie, wants to be a ballet dancer while her contemptuous Russian teacher follows her around barking instructions. Essie's husband practices the xylophone.

The huge house is a frenzy of activity. In the middle of it all is Vanderhof's other granddaughter, Alice, who is pursuing a normal life working as a receptionist in the offices of a powerful businessman. The businessman has been known to make unsavory deals and wants the Vanderhof mansion torn down so he can build on the property. Alice is in love with the businessman's son, Tony. While Tony is amused at her family's idiosyncrasies, he fears that his father will never approve of a girl from such a family.

Eventually, Tony's parents meet Alice's family at a dinner, but are shocked by the strange activities. A flurry of fireworks is accidentally set off in the basement and the whole neighborhood enjoys the show. Tony's parents force him to break up with Alice.

Concerned that she will never have a normal life if she stays in the house, Alice decides to leave. She is dissuaded by Vanderhof who tells her he's selling the mansion and moving the clan to the country.

Tony is angry with his father because of the situation with Alice and the fact that he has discovered his father's shady business dealings. He lets loose with a outburst of invectives, concluding that his father is a heartless monster. He then leaves to join Alice as her family moves out of the mansion.

As Vanderhof sits on a box and surveys his empty home, Tony's father arrives for a heartfelt chat with his nemesis. His son's harangue struck a cord in him. He has decided to give up the pursuit of money and live again. He gives the house back to Vanderhof and the former enemies celebrate by staging a delightful harmonica duel that attracts the whole family.

The film ends joyously as they all share a laugh together.

PART THREE

CONCLUSION

6

IN CONCLUSION: REJOICE!

Rejoice always, pray without ceasing, in everything give thanks; for this is the will of God in Christ Jesus for you.
—*1 Thessalonians 5:16–18*

I t is our hope and prayer that you have enjoyed Volume II of *The Christian Family's Guide to Movies and Video* and found that it was helpful for you, your family, and your friends. As you have discovered, there are good movies to enjoy, there are movies to avoid, and there are movies that we *should* see since they teach Biblical principles.

We must exercise discretion in our entertainment choices, which will come through the study of God's Word written, prayer, and a sincere desire to walk in His Will under the guidance of His Holy Spirit. The key is to be careful, especially where your children are concerned. Remember: "As He who called you is holy, you also be holy in all your conduct, because it is written, 'Be holy, for I am holy'" (1 Peter 1:15-16).

Our intention is to publish another volume of *The Christian Family's Guide to Movies and Video* to include reviews of the most recent movies, as well as other classic movies. This series will be your most complete reference to movies from a Biblical perspective. Each volume will include new material to equip you to take every thought captive in your own life and in the mass media for Jesus Christ.

Please remember that *The Christian Family's Guide to Movies and Video* appears first as "MovieGuide: A Biblical Guide to Movies and Entertainment," a two-minute radio program on many Christian radio stations around the country, and as a column in selected newspapers and magazines. For a complete listing of stations, newspapers, and magazines, please contact us.

If you would like "MovieGuide" to air on your local radio station, please send us the name, address, and telephone number of that station. In addition to writing us, it will help if you call or write your local station and ask them if they want to carry "MovieGuide."

Also, "MovieGuide" is available for publication in newspapers and magazines. Please write us and send us the name, address, and telephone number of the publication in which you want "MovieGuide" to appear. If you write that publication, it will help them to decide to carry "MovieGuide: A Biblical Guide to Movies and Entertainment."

Please remember, you can make a difference. If Christians would stop supporting immoral, anti-Christian entertainment, producers would change their approach to regain our viewership and our dollars. In the case of movies, our economic support is easy to see: we spend money at the box office for a ticket. In the case of television, we pay when we wash, not when we watch. In other words, with TV we support immoral programs when we support advertisers who sponsor immoral programs.

The solution is simple. Support moral programs and movies aimed at the mass audience, not just those programs aimed at Christians, so producers will make more of them.

Boycott immoral movies and the advertisers who sponsor immoral television programs, letting the producer, advertiser, or other key person know of your action and why.

Witness to those involved in communications whether that person is a video store owner, a ticket taker, a writer for the local paper, or a big-time producer.

Encourage Christians to produce quality movies and television programs for the general public.

Live exemplary, holy lives through the power of His Spirit so that the mass media will be at a loss to find fault with us and will be convicted by the quality of our lives.

If you would like more information on what you can do, please call or write us.

Also, please join with us in praying that Christians will occupy the mass media for Jesus Christ and that the day will come when you will be able to take your family or friends to any theater and see an uplifting, wholesome movie. Until that day comes we hope that *The Christian Family's Guide to Movies and Video* will help you to choose the best in motion picture entertainment.

"Submit to God. Resist the devil and he will flee from you. Draw near to God and He will draw near to you. Humble yourselves in the sight of the Lord, and He will lift you up" (James 4:7-8, 10).

May God Bless you in all that you do.

END NOTES

CHAPTER 1: THE STUFF OF WHICH DREAMS ARE MADE

1. Gary Smalley and John Trent, *The Language of Love* (Pomona, CA: Focus on the Family, 1988), 20.

2. Videotape interview between Dr. James Dobson and Ted Bundy. Taped January 23, 1989. Presented by Focus on the Family, Pomona, CA 91799.

3. David Scott, "Pornography and Its Effects on Family, Community and Culture," Family Policy Insights, Vol. 11, No. 2, March 1985, 6.

4. Victor B. Cline, Ph.D., "Aggression Against Women: The Facilitating Effects of Media Violence and Erotica" (Salt Lake City, Utah: University of Utah, 1986).

5. Victor B. Cline, Ph.D., "The Effects of Pornography on Human Behavior: Data and Observations," presentation to National Pornography Comm. (Houston, TX: Sept. 11, 1985).

6. *Attorney General's Commission on Pornography: Final Report*, Washington, D.C., 1986.

7. "The Impact of Televised Movies About Suicide," *New England Journal of Medicine*, Issue 317, Sept. 24, 1987, 809.

8. Interview between Bill Moyers and David Puttnam, "A World of Ideas," broadcasted nationally, September 1988 on PBS.

9. Richard Halverson, Chaplain to the U.S. Senate, *Perspective*, Vol. XL, No. 18, August 31, 1988.

10. "The Motion Picture Code of Self-Regulation," The Motion Picture Association of America (Sherman Oaks, CA: 1956), 5–6.

11. *Wall Street Journal*, April 8, 1988, Vol. 211, Issue 69, 1.

12. Don Kowlet, *American Family Association Journal*, April 1988, Tupelo, MS, 4. Reprinted from an article appearing in *The Washington Times*.

CHAPTER 2: THE SLIPPERY SLOPE

1. Edward E. Ericson, Jr., "Solzhenitsyn—Voice From the Gulag," *Eternity*, (Oct. 1985), 23–24.

2. Most major book stores have a film/cinema/television section. Also, libraries today offer much of this popular literature. Further information on

the history and chronological events of the entertainment industry can be provided by these two sources.

3. Arthur Knight, *The Liveliest Art* (New York: New American Library, 1979), 111.

4. The studios were forced to divest themselves of their monopoly from script to screen in the late 1940s. Many theaters were owned by the studios, and were used to showcase their own productions.

5. Ann Lloyd, *Movies of the Fifties* (London: Orbis Books, 1982), 167.

6. Billy Graham, *Answers to Life's Problems* (Dallas: Word Publishing, 1988), 9.

7. The average studio picture can take from a few weeks to several months to shoot. Most television episodic programs take about six days to shoot, but cost over one million dollars.

8. The nudist film is the precursor to the "nudie" film. These were also cheap, exploitive "documentaries" about people living at nudist camps. This approach offered independent producers a way around the censor, as the film was a look at nudist camp activities, rather than a dramatic presentation. Some of these nudist films were even given the seal of approval of the American Sunbathing Association.

9. A burlesque movie is the filming of a burlesque show, usually with the camera in a "locked down" position, which means the camera is static and records everything that happens on stage from a wide angle.

10. "Roughies" were films that mixed sex with violence. Depending on the ratio of sex to violence, a film could also fit into the category of "kinkies" or "ghoulies." Films such as *Satan's Sadists, Lorna,* and *Orgy of the Golden Nudes* are examples of roughies. A kinkie would be *Love Camp Seven,* about Nazis and their prison camp perversions with the female inmates.

11. Excerpt from a videotape interview of David Friedman.

12. Vale and Juno, *Research Report #10: Incredibly Strange Films* (San Francisco: Re/Search Publications, 1986), 27 [Hereinafter referred to as *Strange Films*].

13. William H. Mooring, *Mooring's Film and TV Feature Service,* newsletter, September 23, 1966, 1.

14. Arthur Knight and Richard Alpert, *Sex in Cinema* (San Francisco: Playboy Press, 1970), 157.

15. *Newsweek Magazine,* Vol. LXXVI, Issue #25, (New York: December 21, 1970), 26.

16. *Strange Films,* 108.

17. Kenneth Turan and Stephen F. Zito, *Sinema* (New York: Praeger Publishers, 1974), 143.

18. *Final Report of the Attorney General's Commission on Pornography,* edited by Michael J. McManus (Nashville: Rutledge Hill Press, 1986), 352. [Hereinafter referred to as *Commission*].

19. Jay Nash and Stanley Ross, *The Motion Picture Guide* (Chicago: 1988), 2763 [hereinafter referred to as *Motion Picture Guide*].

20. Two examples of this practice include the films *Angel Heart* and *Hellbound: Hellraiser II*. The first added additional sex scenes, while the second added approximately five minutes of utter gore.

21. Delivery systems are the means by which a video signal is transmitted or delivered to the viewer. This includes cable, broadcast transmission, and video cassette.

22. Phil Kloer, "'Live-In' Aimed at Teens, but It Sinks with a Thud," *The Atlanta Journal*, March 15, 1989.

23. Cable channels now provide total nudity with certain movies. These are usually the "R" rated films, but nudity that is not as graphic or explicit is present in "PG-13" and "PG" films.

24. This could include the videotaping of live events, such as "female mud and oil wrestling," and sex acts as described in the movie *Sex 69*, produced by Alex DeRenzy. Given the recent history of film and television, we can almost be assured that what is the bizarre and fringe today will be the mainstream ten to twenty years from now, if not sooner.

25. *Midnight Blue*, broadcast on a local access cable channel in Manhattan, is a prototype of this type of programming. It regularly features totally nude individuals and simulated sex scenes.

26. Lock-boxes (or lock-out systems) are devices placed on VCRs or cable system decoders to prevent the indiscriminate use of the equipment. They are used by parents who want to control the use of video in the home. However, what this simple little device will do is divert attention away from the producers and to the parents. It will insist that censorship and restriction is the responsibility of the parent, not the producer. This will allow producers and delivery systems to do just about anything in the way of programming.

CHAPTER 3: DEVELOPING DISCERNMENT: ASKING THE RIGHT QUESTIONS

1. God's Word is Jesus Christ (John 1). God's Word written is the Bible. God's Word written was used often by the reformers to emphasize the relation between God the Father, God the Son, and His holy Scripture.

2. Lajos Egri, *The Art of Dramatic Writing* (New York: Simon & Schuster, 1946, 1960), 6.

3. Note that moviemaker is being used here to refer to all those people who are responsible for authoring a movie, including the screenwriter, the director, the producer, and the executive producer.

4. Stewart M. Hoover, "Television and Viewer Attitudes About Work," The Annenberg School of Communications (April 10, 1981).

5. Telephone interview with Horton Foote on June 23, 1986, at 5:18 P.M.

6. Submitted to: *The Christian Family's Guide to Movies and Videos* by Dr. Rick Clifton Moore, December 8, 1988

INDEX BY TITLE

SUBJECT INDEX

CLASSIC MOVIES INDEX

MASTERPIECE MOVIES INDEX

ABOUT THE AUTHOR

Dr. Theodore Baehr, CEO of Good News Communications, has been actively involved in Christian oriented television, radio, and other media programming for over fifteen years. He is the host of the weekly radio program, "Religionwise: A Weekly Look at the News through the Eyes of Religion," and the host/producer of "MovieGuide: A Biblical Guide to Movies and Entertainment," syndicated on radio stations and published in newspapers and magazines throughout the country.

Dr. Baehr has authored many books, including *The Christian Family Guide to Movies and Video*, Volume 1 (Wolgemuth and Hyatt); and *Getting the Word Out* (Harper and Row). He has also written numerous articles for Christian periodicals.

A member of the Society of Motion Picture and Television Engineers, the National Academy of Television Arts and Science, and a board member of the National Religious Broadcasters, Dr. Baehr continues to be an active Christian influence in the movie and television industries.

Ted Baehr lives in Atlanta, Georgia, with his wife, Liliana, and their four children, Peirce, James, Robert, and Evelyn.

PLEASE CALL OR WRITE . . .

After reading this book, if you would like to subscribe to *Movie-Guide: A Biblical Guide to Movies and Entertainment*, a bi-weekly publication of Good News Communications that keeps you updated on current movies, please write or call us.

Also, if you would like to purchase any of the movies listed in this book on videotape, or you would like any other help, please contact us.

You can reach us at:

MovieGuide
P.O. Box 9952
Atlanta, GA 30319
(404)237-0326